Cargo Security:

A Nuts and Bolts Approach

Cargo Security:

A Nuts and Bolts Approach

Lawrence S. Jones, R.I.C.

BUTTERWORTH PUBLISHERS
Boston • London
Sydney • Wellington • Durban • Toronto

The cover illustration was taken from a compilation of early American art produced by Dick Sutphen Studios, Inc., Minneapolis, Minnesota, 1962.

All references in this book to personnel of male gender are used for convenience only and shall be regarded as including both males and females.

Library of Congress Cataloging in Publication Data
Jones, Lawrence S., 1929-
    Cargo security.

    Includes bibliographical references and index.
    1. Cargo theft—Prevention. I. Title.
HV6652.J66   380.5'24   83-6072
ISBN 0-409-95095-5

Published by Butterworth Publishers
10 Tower Office Park
Woburn, MA 01801

10 9 8 7 6 5 4 3 2

Printed in the United States of America.

This is my contribution to an industry that is my life

Lawrence S. Jones, 1982

Contents

Preface

The major objective of this book is to indicate the steps that business executives, security directors, security consultants, and law enforcement personnel can take to combat cargo thefts. These steps are management and procedure oriented.

Business executives and security people must cope with many problems other than cargo theft, but theft is a primary concern with far reaching effects on business and on every consumer in this country. A principal objective of this book is to provide some insight into the extent of involvement of nonprofessional and of organized criminal activity in the theft and subsequent disposition of cargo. Such involvement includes criminal groups referred to collectively as organized crime.

This book represents the distillation of over 25 years of experience, hundreds of coast-to-coast interviews, and of thousands of pages of hearings, white papers, reports, articles, and other printed matter pertaining to various aspects of cargo theft. Those interviewed were affiliated with federal, state, county, and local agencies or commissions, national and local associations of shippers and carriers, various shippers and consignees, private security groups and consultants, insurers, and management and industrial security associations. Many of these sources requested anonymity; their contributions are greatly appreciated.

The principal conclusion derived from the interviews is that the responsibility for combatting cargo theft must be evenly divided among the affected parties and done so on a coordinated basis. Acting alone, no single group can make a significant dent in the problem, not law enforcement, not carriers, not shippers. Each group must implement appropriate counter-measures and dovetail them with those initiated by others. The transportation chain should be just that—a series of equally strong links. If one of those links breaks, the opposition is sufficiently organized to exploit the weakness.

Accordingly, an effort has been made to condense in these chapters material that could comprise several books. Although little has been written on the subjects of trucking, rail, air, and marine cargo thefts, I hope to impart a basic understanding of approaches and recommendations that will effect sound and reliable security practices. The chapter on motor cargo is intentionally brief since this material is scattered throughout the rest of the book as intermodal transportation.

It should be clear at the onset that *cargo* refers to anything that enters, and is moved by, the nation's transportation systems, beginning at the shippers' loading platform and terminating at the consignees' receiving dock. *Cargo theft* refers both to acts of theft (stealing the entire carton or container) and of pilferage (stealing only some of the carton contents).

Unfortunately, the solutions to cargo theft are quite complex. One company's answer may be another's disaster. Many of the ingredients to solutions are presented herein, but these ingredients must be selected, combined, and enriched in ways conforming to the unique conditions facing each situation or firm. Thus, to get the most benefit from this book, one must do more than read it—one must follow through and build upon it.

It is important to understand the nature of organized crime in relation to cargo theft. Organized crime can be said to be involved in a great deal of cargo theft because much of what is stolen is taken to a third party for resale and/or entry into an illicit distribution system. Thus, the existence of "fences," although perhaps themselves unorganized, constitutes a type of organized crime that contributes greatly to increased cargo theft.

At the other end of the organized crime scales are those groups, or "families," dominated by well-known racketeers belonging to organizations. When this type of organized crime enters the picture, it may in fact control and direct cargo theft.

Both of these types of organized crime require effective law enforcement actions, leading to apprehension and prosecution. Neither type, however, leaves management hopelessly unequipped to meet the problem. On the contrary, tailored and effective application of the type of management control procedures that are described in this book can reduce the vulnerability of attractive cargo and prevent theft losses in the first instances.

Although defined in greater detail at a more appropriate point in the book, the term *organized crime* refers to the unlawful activities of those who are members, in fact or in effect, of any of the criminal associations—including, but not restricted to, the underworld group comprised of crime families that possess a variety of illegal goods and services (basically, this corresponds to the skeletal definition found in the Omnibus Crime Control and Safe Streets Act).

Much has been written about the magnitude of the cargo theft losses. Analysis by the Office of Transportation Security, working with industry, shows that for all transportation modes, EXCEPT rail, 85% of cargo theft losses occur at terminal locations during normal operating hours in less than carload quantities and involve persons and vehicles authorized by management to be on facility premises. It also revealed that 13 commodity categories account for 90% of the total theft losses. These are items with instant marketability such as clothing, electric appliances, auto accessories, hardware, electronic games, alcoholic beverages, and tobacco and food products.

If the reader finds this book interesting, informative, and a learning tool, then a primary objective has been achieved. It is hoped that readers will use these pages as a working document, that is, as the framework on which to build an informed response to cargo theft, a problem that even when considered from the most charitable point of view, has reached totally unacceptable proportions.

Lawrence S. Jones, R.I.C.

Acknowledgements

I owe sincere thanks and appreciation to Richard Stevens of the Department of Transportation for his never-ending assistance in the writing of this book. My friend, I thank you for providing me with the material and contacts that helped to make this book possible.

I would also like to acknowledge the contributions of:

- J. Patrick Carter, Superintendent of Police, Santa Fe Railroad, Los Angeles, California.
- Harry W. Goodwin, Manager of Transportation, F.J. Brooks, Newark, New Jersey.
- Jerald L. Jansen, Special Agent, Union Pacific Railroad, Salt Lake City, Utah.
- John D. Lorraine, Special Agent, Union Pacific Railroad, Los Angeles, California.
- Edward J. McGowan, Executive Director, Airport Security Council, Forest Hills, New York.
- John Murphy, Darras Murphy, Inc., Los Angeles, California.
- C.W. Shaffer, Jr., General Director, Union Pacific Railroad, Salt Lake City, Utah.
- Leonard A. Sipes, Jr., National Criminal Justice Reference Service, Rockville, Maryland.
- Richard Stevens, Department of Transportation, Washington, D.C.

To all my other friends in the industry, my heartfelt thanks for your contributions. To my typist Virginia Armstrong, many, many thanks for all the late nights and weekends you gave up to prepare the manuscript. I can never repay your help and support.

Introduction:
What Is At Stake?

Managers face many pitfalls during the course of fulfilling their responsibilities, and one of the most dangerous is to reach a decision based on an inaccurate assessment of the problem at hand. Unfortunately, this occurs too often when the problem requiring attention is cargo theft.

To bring into sharp focus just what is at stake when executives confront the cargo theft issue is one of the primary goals of this book. Despite protests that the issue has already been more then adequately defined, the evidence is ample, as documented later, that the cargo theft problem is still poorly perceived by many of those directly or indirectly involved in the transportation industry—carriers, consignees, shippers, insurers, warehouse and terminal operators, unions, law enforcement and other governmental units, the consuming public, and others. Because each of these groups must shoulder part of the responsibility for combatting cargo theft if it is to be controlled adequately, each link in the chain of responsibility must possess considerably more than tunnel vision. Only if all concerned will place cargo theft in full perspective can the private sector fulfill two prerequisites for an effective counterattack relatively free from governmental mandates: the will to act and coordinated action based on understanding.

The Less Visible Impact of Cargo Theft

Whether stolen cargo consists of securities, salami, shavers, shoes, or steel, what usually attracts the most attention is the value of the goods—the direct financial loss. But, as the president of a trade

This chapter is adapted from U.S. Department of Transportation *Cargo Theft and Organized Crime*, P 5200.6. Washington, D.C.: U.S. Government Printing Office, October, 1972.

association noted, "The direct financial losses are only the most obvious consequence." A waterfront commission spokesman went one step further: "The actual dollar value of lost cargo, though large, is of least importance." This appears to be true in the vast majority of cargo thefts.

Although the initial, direct financial loss may be least important, it is by no means unimportant. The dollar value of goods stolen while in the transportation system is substantial. Nonetheless, in the overall picture, the value of these goods represents the relatively small exposed tip of an iceberg whose true dimensions can be estimated only by looking beneath the waterline. Submerged are those cargo theft losses that are the consequences of the initial, direct financial loss represented by the value of the stolen goods. Some of these subsequent losses are outlined below. Many pose legitimate public interest issues and warrant close attention by government at all levels in the absence of effective private-sector action.

Insurance. The president of a trucking firm specializing in transporting cigarettes used to have his insurance premium paid by the shipper. After hijackings, this arrangement ceased and he began paying a $17,500 annual premium for a policy with a $2500 deductible and a maximum coverage of $35,000 per incident. After another hijacking, the premium increased to $28,000. The deductible was hiked to $5000. Maximum coverage per incident dropped to $20,000 (the value of half a load), and he was covered only to the extent that his cumulative losses did not exceed $50,000 per year. As a result, the trucker decided to go out of business.

A spokesman for a clothing manufacturers association cited these statistics: 33 of 89 manufacturers indicated that, as the result of cargo thefts, premiums increased an average of 67%; 31 of 83 reported that insurers added deductible clauses to policies; 10 of 38 whose policies were cancelled had difficulty in obtaining new insurance, while 5 could not secure coverage at all.

Administration of Cargo Theft Claims.   Estimates indicate that the claimant and the party against which the claim is filed each frequently spend from two to seven times the amount of the settlement in order to cover processing and litigation costs.

Delayed Sales. Statement of the traffic director of an apparel manufacturer: "Until fairly recently all apparel manufacturers sold their goods f.o.b. their shipping point. This is rapidly becoming unrealistic as a result of the high incidence of lost merchandise owing to theft and pilferage as well as the refusal of carriers to pay claims. The retailer has been forced to take the position that he does not pay for goods he does not receive. Therefore, the situation is rapidly getting to the point where the manufacturer does not make a sale until the goods are in the retailer's store." Additionally, extra claims personnel must be hired and disrupted manufacturing and delivery schedules revised.

Lost Sales. An insurance investigator relates that a hijacked truckload of imported woolens valued at $50,000 resulted in a net loss to a men's wear manufacturer of $250,000 because the goods were seasonal and irreplaceable.

Counsel to a retailer association has observed that even if a retailer were paid for the full value of goods stolen en route, he is not made whole. "He has the possible loss of sale; he has lost his customer's goodwill if the merchandise is not available at the time of the sale; he has had his money tied up over a period of time in merchandise which he has not been able to turn over."

An executive of a large apparel manufacturing firm explained what happens when custom-made clothing is stolen in transit: "The manufacturer does not have anything with which to duplicate his order, and the retailer is in a position where he cannot duplicate the order from any other source."

Commenting on a situation where "the greatest problem is the systematic pilferage and theft of comparatively small quantities from almost every shipment," a spokesman for an importers association emphasized that "while the actual loss may be small in terms of dollars and cents, the main headache is not having available a complete line of styles and sizes to fill their orders."

On the behalf of several watch manufacturers, an executive stated that because of cargo thefts, "Promotions scheduled by customers had to be cancelled. There have been instances in which catalogs have been circulated featuring merchandise which failed to arrive and which was essentially irreplaceable."

Lost Business by Carriers. Not surprisingly, consignees and shippers frequently switch carriers in order to minimize cargo theft losses. An insurance director of a manufacturer of a theft-prone product asserts, "We have changed airlines a number of times based on loss experience, and based upon information supplied to us by our trade association and by our customs broker. In fact, at this point our insurance carrier requires that all shipments from Western Europe be shipped by only one air carrier because of . . . the feeling that their security . . . is better than others. . . ."

Not only are more and more carriers concluding that adequate countermeasures against cargo theft represent a cost of keeping business, but many are also realizing that outlays for such countermeasures are a cost of staying in business. According to a past president of an association of security officers, "Theft of individual shipments, theft of complete trailers, and hijack of complete trailers have become such a complete problem that to eliminate them or not eliminate them meant the difference between staying in business and bankruptcy."

Embargoes and Interference with the Flow of Commerce. Some carriers are quite frank in admitting that one way to minimize theft and pilferage is to refuse to haul theft-prone items. States a carrier association executive: "...I didn't mention what we do when we find a commodity that is high theft, high loss. We just drop it; we are forced to embargo it. .... That's how we get around a lot of our cargo problems."

The results of a 1980 survey of several manufacturer associations regarding their claims-associated problems indicated that 96 carriers refused to pick up theft-prone goods at more than 70 of the 89 manufacturers responding to the questionnaire. Ten of the 96 carriers refused to service more than 5 different manufacturers. Said a manufacturers' association spokesman, "This refusal takes various forms from outright refusal to just not showing up or lack of equipment, not enough drivers, too many losses, value too high. . . ."

Representing a national shippers' association, a transportation executive in his address to a cargo theft conference concluded that theft "is the most rapidly increasing cause of economic loss in the transportation of cargo by the nation's common carriers." Increasing at "an alarming rate," cargo theft "is restricting the free flow of commerce from and to some areas of the nation," maintains the executive. In 1971, the president of the Air Transport Association of America voiced his concern by noting that "the incidence of cargo theft has now reached the point of interfering with the delivery intact of too much of our mail."

As is the case with many other types of crime, small business is particularly hard hit. The small-business executive usually has no alternative except to use common carriers, and his shipments are frequently highly susceptible to theft or pilferage since they are transported in small quantities and require above-average handling. Also, the management of the smaller business is unable to exert the economic leverage that larger competitors can apply to balky carriers. Thus, when carriers decide in effect to boycott theft-prone products, the small enterprise is, as one traffic manager put it, "virtually without transport service." Finally, small businesses usually are not in a position to recoup their losses through price increases.

Threat of Violence, Injury, and Damage. During a recent interview, the security director of a large rail carrier commented on the ressurection from the steam-locomotive era of methods by which trains are stopped or derailed for the express purpose of "boxcar burglary." His 1971 testimony before the Senate's Select Committee on Small Business also alluded to this: "Although the number of obstructions on rails, the tampering with switches and signals, and stonings may appear insignificant in relation to the geographical size of the railroad, I would like to point out that they sometimes result in derailments causing serious personal injuries, catastrophic freight loss and damage. . . ."

Attempts to control theft on the waterfront have frequently resulted in personal injury through "accidents" or direct assaults. A 1970 report by the Waterfront Commission of New York Harbor referred to the plight of port watchmen, who are hired by terminal operators. An agent of the commission testified that watchmen have "either been frightened away from an area or frightened into neutrality." One pier guard told him, "I would never turn one of these men in because I have to come back here tomorrow. What would I do? This is where I earn my bread and butter. Accidents happen every day and I don't need an accident." A pier guard who admitted he had not made one apprehension during his 40 years on the piers remarked that he tried to live up to his responsibilities once but was assaulted.

One of the most extreme examples of the effects of the fear and violence stemming from cargo theft was described by an official of a tobacco distributors' association. Testifying in early 1972 before the New York State Commission of Investigation, he drew attention to an alarming situation:

> Where are we today? . . . . About 12 of the major firms who carry a lot of cigarettes ride shotgun . . . . They either ride shotguns in the cab . . . . or they have another car behind it.
>
> And it is so bad that when motor carriers stop at a jobber's place of business, two or three men get out with guns, and they stand there all around; they scare the living daylights out of jobbers, and everybody around, but that is what this business is doing right now.
>
> We are having difficulty with our drivers because they say, "We are the pigeons, and the men riding shotgun are getting paid more."
> It has increased the costs tremendously . . . . if you talk to some of the old line people who have been in this business for years, they are starting to move out; they are afraid. They don't want to stay in the business any more.

Diversion of Cargo, Relocation of Business, and Image Problems. When cargo is diverted and businesses are relocated to other cities because of a high incidence of cargo theft in a given locality, the adverse impact on the economic climate and health of the afflicted, gateway center, city, or region is obvious. The answers supplied by importers to a 1970 questionnaire pertaining to waterfront theft in a major city are illuminating:

1. "Had to move to other ports since increase in prices to cover losses reduced number of customers."
2. "Lost too many customers because of short deliveries—now use other ports."
3. "Using other ports since . . . losses caused tripling in insurance premiums in three years."

In all, 14 of the 49 importers replying to the questionnaire had moved at least part of their operations to other ports of entry.

The director of merchandising for a large department store in the Midwest was quoted as saying his company diverted the bulk of its $13-million yearly import business from the nearby inland port to an Atlantic port. Trucks brought the goods inland. A Swedish candy company made a similar decision because not one direct shipment to the inland port arrived intact during a six-year period.

A similar situation was rapidly developing on the West Coast, according to an official of a cargo council there: "The fact was that these ports were getting so bad a reputation among shippers and vessel operators throughout the world that many were considering bypassing the area."

According to a government official, the impetus behind a recent study in Canada on how to lure more air freight traffic to a large city there was the adverse history of cargo theft at a competing United States international airport.

Once shippers begin to bypass a port of entry, cargo facility, or even a given mode of transport because of an unacceptable cargo theft record, such a tarnished image tends to persist—as do the attendant economic losses—long after conditions have improved. For example, the abysmally poor public image that JFK International Airport generated for itself during the latter half of the 1960s as a result of a high incidence of theft and pilferage still hangs over the facility, even though its more recent on-premises theft record, as attested to by many of those interviewed for this book, has improved markedly with the advent of the Airport Security Council.

Under some conditions, cargo theft may threaten the reputation of an industry. For instance, at the early 1972 hearings of the New York

State Commission of Investigation, this exchange occurred between a tobacco industry witness and the Commission:

Witness   . . . no one wants anyone in an illegitimate, unsavory type business being connected with even the very fringes of an industry. And we are getting to the point today that it is coming home closer because the ICC trucks and the vans and things coming from the manufacturer now are starting to be hijacked.

Commission   In other words, the legitimate cigarette industry is concerned, is it not, with the growth of organized crime or the influence of organized crime upon its operations?

Witness   And rightly so, sir.

That motor carriers are acutely aware of the significance of maintaining a good reputation is attested to by the minutes of a trucking industry meeting in 1969 on theft and hijacking: "Affirmative and positive action without delay is needed to offset and forestall current publicity unfavorable to the industry as a whole. Public information that the trucking industry recognizes the problem, and is taking tangible steps to overcome it has a very high positive value to the industry."

Prices and Freight Rates Increase. Says an industry association spokesman: "Since the importer must recover his losses sustained through cargo theft, in almost every case reported to the association the losses have been either partially or wholly recovered through increased prices to the consumer." According to a large shipper, "While cargo claims can be made, they never fully recover the losses suffered by the shipper and whatever reimbursement we do receive is eventually reflected in higher cargo rates." And a major freight forwarder declares, "Meeting the challenge to keep cargo secure is a big task and is one of the most costly expenses absorbed by our industry today. Thus, this expense in turn must be passed on to the consumer in the form of rates and charges for getting his goods to market."

Loss of Government Revenue. A Treasury official sums up the situation at the federal level: "The Treasury also loses because customs may not be able to collect duty on cargo which has been stolen and because lower taxes are paid by importers who (1) fail to receive . . . merchandise which they would otherwise sell at a profit, and (2) claim a deduction on their income tax returns for uninsured theft losses. The loss of export cargo also has an obvious effect on our critical balance of payments situation." Similarly, collection of various state and local taxes also suffers.

Unfair Competition and Erosion of the Competitive Process. Grossly underestimated by many is the extent to which stolen cargo reenters commercial channels and thereby constitutes a highly unfair and illegal competitive weapon. The extent and process by which this occurs will be discussed later. For now, suffice it to say that this byproduct of cargo theft is one of the most serious. When instances come to light where a wholesaler's prices cannot compete with those at the retail level, when law enforcement and other sources report that more and more heretofore ethical businessmen are beginning to succumb to competitive pressures by also purchasing stolen cargo at cut-rate prices, and when criminal interests and enterprises are enriched and strengthened in the process—when this and more is occurring, the time has long since arrived for the many facets of the private sector that have a stake in the outcome of the cargo theft problem to pull together and implement coordinated countermeasures.

The foregoing litany of losses inflicted after, and as a consequence of, the actual theft of cargo could be considerably expanded and embellished. But enough has been indicated to establish that, in the long run at least, these follow-on impacts constitute the most significant loss category, considerably outweighing the financial distress represented by the dollar value of stolen cargo.

DIRECT DOLLAR IMPACT OF CARGO THEFT

Although the tip of the iceberg, the dollar value of goods stolen while in transit usually receives the greatest emphasis in the press and frequently represents a bone of contention between carriers and shippers/consignees, as well as between carriers and government officials. At times, the debate is over the completeness or validity of cargo loss statistics in the first place.

This is not to say that statistics reflecting the direct dollar loss from cargo theft are unimportant. Although reflecting a relatively small part of the cargo theft problem, direct-loss statistics are the least difficult to compile and provide at least a rough indicator by which to put into perspective the costs associated with preventive measures and to gauge the effectiveness of those measures. Indeed, without reasonably accurate direct-loss statistics—and much remains to be done in this area—arguments for or against spending a given sum to implement proposed remedial steps lose considerable credibility.

According to the information available to the Senate's Select Committee on Small Business, which has held extensive hearings on cargo theft, in 1970 approximately $1.5 billion worth of goods were stolen while in the nation's transportation system (motor carriers, $900 million; railroads, $250 million; marine carriers, $210 million; air carriers $110 million). Based on an estimated average annual increase of 20%, cargo theft would now amount to over $2 billion annually. This loss, states the committee, represents only the wholesale or released liability values of the goods.

Depending on which group of carriers one talks with, the committee's figures are said to be on the high side by a factor ranging from 1.4 to 45. A common reaction by carriers to the committee's cargo theft estimate is the comment of an official of the Association of American Railroads: ". . . we are not aware of the basis for this figure or sources of data from which the total is compiled. . . . While the railroads recognize full well that theft and pilferage are increasing at a rapid rate, the information currently available to us indicates that the economic loss from (theft and pilferage) does not even remotely approach $250 million."

However, the Transportation Cargo Security Council, an independent organization whose members include carriers, shippers, consignees, insurers, and labor, assessed the situation at the end of 1971 this way: "One of the more serious problems confronting the transportation industry is the theft of cargo. The magnitude of losses is not known; however, best available estimates place the direct dollar loss at $1.7 billion annually."

The weight of current evidence strongly suggests that if a statistically valid cargo theft figure were available it would be closer to the estimate of Select Committee on Small Business than to the total of the amounts reported by the carriers.

A major reason for this rests with a factor over which the carriers have little or no control; that is, many losses are either not reported by shippers and consignees or are underreported to carriers and insurers. This may occur for a variety of reasons:

1. Spokesman for an importers association: "Many losses are not reported by importers for two reasons. The first is the fear of retaliation against their cargo, trucks, or personnel, and the second is the further escalation of their ever-increasing insurance premiums and, perhaps, even the fear of being dropped by their insurance underwriter as a severe risk."
2. Chamber of Commerce executive: ". . . all losses are not recorded; they are not declared. We have the losses of the

man who insures his own cargo. And we have importers that
establish a fund aside to parry their own losses. We have the
man that has no recourse."

3. Replies to a questionnaire sent to wholesalers: "We never
file claims under $25 as it is too costly." "Shortages and
damages are costly to be sure; the thing that costs the most
is the expenses and time spent trying to collect from the
freight companies."

In some instances, even when carriers were aware of thefts, resultant complaints have been covered up or ignored because of the fear
of bad publicity. A common cover-up used by some terminal operators
on the waterfront is to record stolen goods as short-landed, which
indicates that the goods never came off the ship (and also indicates
that no duty has to be paid). In one city, a waterfront commission
established two stores to fence stolen cargo. Stolen cargo with a retail
value of $277,000 was recovered. Only $2000 has been recorded as
stolen; pier records described the balance as short-landed.

Another reason why the cargo theft estimates of some carriers
are understated is described by the security officer of a trucker:
"Carriers keep records of claims paid for missing freight in two
columns: one identified as shortages, and the other as thefts. Since
the average carrier has not grown sophisticated enough to have a theft
reporting system, the money ends up in the column simply entitled
'shortage.'" Similarly, a spokesman for a carrier association candidly
acknowledged that "when we speak of 'lost' shipments, we are actually
speaking, for the most part, of stolen shipments."

On the other side of the coin, carriers correctly point out that in
numerous instances, goods that shippers or consignees initially claimed
as stolen had never left the shipper's loading dock, were misrouted
because of confusing labels affixed by the shipper, or were actually
received by the consignee but not recorded as such. According to an
official of the American Trucking Association, during a one-month
period, a major carrier had 14,000 claims filed against it, but within
a few days 5000 were disposed of on the basis of clear delivery receipts
signed by consignees.

Thus, the statistical confusion over the extent of direct dollar
losses attributable to cargo theft is caused by the users as well as by
the suppliers of transportation services. But the net effect has been
an understatement of cargo theft losses by most carriers.

To help clear the air of mutual suspicion and recrimination
generated by shippers/consignees, carriers, and government sources over
each other's cargo theft estimates, the basis for such figures should be

clearly explained. First, the means by which value is assigned to stolen cargo should be clear—wholesale price, manufacturer's or foreign invoice value, retail price, or whatever seems appropriate. Second, the degree to which reported cargo theft losses are adjusted upward to compensate for the nonreporting factor should be made explicit. Third, the extent to which indirect losses are included in theft statistics should be revealed. Fourth, uniform and meaningful criteria are needed for attributing losses to such causes as theft, pilferage, shortage, short-landed, lost shipment, etc. Finally, cargo theft statistics should be capable of being broken down by products or commodity groups, at least with respect to particularly theft-prone goods. A single gross figure is of limited value and accomplishes little more than to bury problem areas.

Direct Losses—Trend and Response

Although an overall cargo theft figure that can legitimately bear the label "statistic" has yet to make an appearance, there is an overwhelming consensus among all concerned that, despite a few emerging bright spots, the cargo theft trend is continuing its upward swing.

Testifying before the Senate's Committee on Commerce, a spokesman for the Freight Forwarders Institute echoed the experience of many other transportation executives: "As we enter the decade of the 1980s, the situation continues to deteriorate. I have been advised that current figures of some members of our industry indicate shortages to represent as much as 70% of their claim losses." Continuing, he reported, "Our industry has experienced an alarming increase in costs arising out of the theft of cargo. This crime cost has outpaced any corresponding increase in tonnage or revenue."

A representative of the railroad industry noted in 1980 that "despite our best efforts, our experience is worsening." "Speaking on behalf of the American Institute of Marine Underwriters, an insurance executive declared in 1980 that "until recent years, the principal causes of loss to these goods in transit were represented by (incidents) that produced destruction of a largely fortuitous nature . . . Today, crime losses rank number one in dollar value of all causes of losses suffered by goods in transit, outranking such traditional causes as ship sinking, storms, vehicle collisions, fire, and the various type of handling damages."

This trend has been apparent for years. And so has been the response of users and suppliers of transportation services. With some exceptions and with increasing indications that a more enlightened approach is being taken, the traditional response has been one of general apathy, buck-passing, and a type of negative competition where most everyone tries to keep the cargo theft problem "trade neutral" by pursuing the policy of doing as little as possible about it. In this regard, the carriers have received more than their fair share of the blame. Shippers, receivers, warehousemen, manufacturers, law enforcement, the courts, insurers, unions, and others must also shoulder responsibility for the momentum cargo theft has achieved.

The following responses to cargo theft are cited not to assess blame but to highlight the reasoning behind the opinion that unless there is a swift rejection of such traditional reactions to cargo theft, the private sector stands an excellent chance of becoming considerably less private as government involvement accelerates and expands.

Characteristic of the rationale behind many policies dealing with cargo theft is this description of the reaction of a stevedore's representative when asked why he had not stationed a guard to watch a high-theft location: ". . . the representative took a pencil out of his pocket, computed the value of the radios stolen against the guard's salary and said it was cheaper to suffer the loss. When asked what would happen if the goods had a higher value, he replied: 'Well, insurance takes care of that.' "

And, until recently, insurance was an easily accessible crutch. Now, as noted previously, premiums and deductibles are higher and policies are more difficult to obtain and retain. Also, as one insurer put it, what is required "goes far beyond anything that the 'muscle of insurance' can or should be responsible to restrain. . . . An insurance policy is not a deterrent to crime. . . ." In the same vein, another insurance executive noted that the millions of dollars insurers pay annually for the reimbursement of crime losses "automatically enriches the nonproductive and predatory criminal element of society. . . .there is a difference between reimbursing industry for goods damaged or lost in specie due to fortuitous happenings as opposed to reimbursement for goods that have been diverted into illegal channels."

Unfortunately, some insurers have not always acted according to such an enlightened view. An interviewed law enforcement source noted with disapproval that occasionally some insurers will buy back stolen merchandise when the price is right, thus in effect creating a market for stolen cargo. Similarly, according to the findings of a study, "We have encountered a good deal of feeling among police departments and central stations, confirmed by observers within the insurance industry, that insurance personnel in the past have encouraged a laxity in precautions against crime because of the availability of insurance compensation."

Nor has law enforcement always been up to the task of combatting cargo theft. In 1971, a ranking Justice Department official remarked, "Because of a lack of coordination and cooperation between (federal, state, and local law enforcement agencies) in many instances, a great deal of valuable time may be lost in commencing an investigation or possibly no investigation may be undertaken at all." However, this problem is being attacked through informal agreements between United States attorneys and their state and local counterparts concerning the investigation and prosecution of cargo thefts.

The attitude of some labor organizations has not always been constructive, as typified by the statement in 1971 of a large union's assistant research director that he had not even read the widely publicized 1968 hearings of a state's investigation unit into the extent of organized crime's control over a powerful local comprised of cargo handlers and truck drivers. And wildcat strikes protesting legitimate measures to enforce security have cost management thousands of dollars.

Illustrating the "we are not hurt so why worry?" attitude exhibited by some businessmen, an interviewed insurance investigator mentioned the lack of response to circulars sent to the relatively few firms that were capable of processing certain stolen goods which could be easily identified because of unique inherent characteristics.

When an airline at a large international airport on the West Coast took the intelligent step of tightening cargo accountability by requiring piece counts when accepting cargo from forwarders, the latter threatened to tender their business to competing airlines that did not require such "red tape." Piece counts were finally implemented when all airlines jointly agreed to the procedure.

Despite rising losses, consignees have unduly exposed their goods to theft by failing to take prompt delivery. Shippers have encouraged theft through poor packaging and by a failure to remove old address labels from reused cartons, thereby increasing the likelihood of misrouted shipments, which are prime candidates for theft.

The head of a carrier-supported security organization at a major cargo complex told a congressional committee about conditions when he first assumed his position: "It was evident to me . . . that security had neither responsible management concern or there had been an appreciable lack of awareness at top management concerning these conditions. I found that indifferent attitudes prevailed . . ."

A carrier-sponsored report sums up the situation this way: "A widespread general apathy toward the problems and challenges of security has been found at all levels among shippers, receivers, manufacturers, carriers . . . and warehousemen."

The upshot has been that because so many have failed to make prevention of cargo theft part of their business, the tendency has developed for all concerned to deny or evade responsibility when a loss does occur. Too frequently, therefore, policies are oriented not toward tackling the problem head on but toward skirting it by embargoing (in fact or in effect) theft-prone goods, by pressing for more stringent released valuation policies, by raising prices and rates, by appealing for higher carrier liability limits, by relying on insurance, etc. In the meantime, however, the cargo theft problem has grown to the point where there is very little room left for such evasive action.

1. The Basic Approach

Cargo theft and pilferage losses in today's multimodal transportation system result in higher operating costs, increased insurance rates, and lower net profits. Time, at high rates per hour, is lost performing many unproductive activities. The adjustment of claims diverts managerial talent from normal tasks. Customers, unhappy over non-delivery, seek other means of moving their cargo. What was once a minor annoyance to the industry has become a chronic threat.

There is no universal one-time solution to the problem of cargo security. Each mode of transportation, each terminal, each transfer point is unique. Each has particular strengths and weaknesses to be considered in the preparation of a security plan. There are, however, certain basic principles of cargo security that are discussed in this book. They can be adapted by management to accommodate any mode of transportation or any facility, large or small.

FUNDAMENTAL CONSIDERATIONS

Certain general considerations dictate how the transportation manager should proceed:

1. Management may exercise its obligation directly through a security officer. If a security officer is employed, management cannot simply delegate authority but must provide adequate guidelines and resources to security personnel.

This chapter is adapted from U.S. Department of Transportation, "Guidelines for the Physical Security of Cargo," P5200.2. Washington, D.C.: U.S. Government Printing Office, May, 1972.

2. Each shipment, regardless of type or size, must be identified and accounted for continually. Such accountability is difficult because cargo is in motion, exists in large quantities that defy piece-by-piece tallying, undergoes frequent changes of accountability, and is transferred rapidly by modern mechanical handling devices.
3. Absolute security is attainable; however, costs usually dictate the degree of protection that will discourage intruders and guard against loss or damage.
4. It is not necessary to provide the same degree of security for all facilities. The protection warranted for any particular facility is determined by two factors: critical value and vulnerability. Cargo is critical if it has high strategic value or if it has high value and can be easily handled and sold. A facility is vulnerable if it can be easily penetrated or if it is confused by the constant movement of large volumes of cargo. If a facility is both highly critical and highly vulnerable, an extensive physical security program is necessary.
5. The degree or type of physical security needed for a facility is affected by its size and complexity, as well as by the volume and value of the cargo handled in it. Other factors to be taken into account are the economic and geographic situation of the facility, the availability of local law enforcement agencies, and the crime statistics of the area.
6. When a number of firms use the same facility, such as a large metropolitan airport, all of the firms must coordinate their activities. Close cooperation with the facility management is necessary also.

Consideration of these factors will allow development of a plan that will provide neither more nor less security than is warranted by the situation. Development of the plan however, does not end management's responsibility. The criticality or vulnerability of a facility may change from time to time, necessitating periodic review and modification to accommodate changing circumstances.

The costs of implementing a cargo security system normally will be more than justified when compared to the costs incurred in the past in cargo loss, theft, or damage. The development of an effective cargo security system should be based on future loss potential as well as past experience.

Building and maintaining an effective security program challenges the skill and leadership of those who administer it. They must instill interest in the success of the program in employees at all levels within the organization, impressing each employee with his or her personal stake in the success of the security plan.

THE PLAN

The cargo security plan is the foundation upon which the success or failure of the entire program depends. It must be stated simply, yet in sufficient detail to cover all contingencies. Above all, it must be flexible and dynamic, adjusting to new problems as they arise. The first step is to identify the hazards, natural and man-made, that threaten cargo within the transportation system of the facility to be protected. It is the purpose of the plan to circumvent those hazards.

Storm, flood, and fire are the most frequently experienced natural hazards. They cannot be totally prevented by physical security means; however, their consequences can be minimized by implementation of a good disaster plan. Any one of them can reduce the effectiveness of existing security measures. Perimeter fences may be down, lights and alarms systems may be inoperative, vehicles may be out of service, and cargo that is scattered over a wide area may be in danger of loss, theft, or pilferage. These eventualities demand preplanning for immediate reinforcement of the general force and implementing action of disaster procedures to protect the facility and cargo that has been made vulnerable.

Man-made hazards are more diverse. To protect the system against them requires a correspondingly great amount of management attention. Every security plan must be based on the assumption that the transportation system is vulnerable to the risks of pilferage and theft.

PILFERAGE

Pilferage is difficult to detect, evidence of it is hard to obtain, and its consequence is too costly to ignore. Thus, the prevention of pilferage becomes one of the primary concerns of the security program and the security force.

A pilferer usually acts alone, frequently on impulse. He will remove a small amount of merchandise when the opportunity presents itself and when there is little risk of detection. Although unsystematic, his depredations may attain a high cumulative effect if permitted to continue unchecked.

Pilferage most commonly occurs in a terminal while cargo is awaiting transshipment from one vehicle or mode of transportation to another. Here cargo is apt to be left unprotected on hand carts, dollies, or other intraterminal vehicles. During this time, it is most susceptible to pilferage.

Small items capable of being concealed on the person or in an automobile are the customary pilferage targets. A pilferer usually does not intend to sell the property he steals, and the items taken may be of either high or low value.

Specific measures for the prevention of pilferage can be based only on an analysis of existing conditions at a particular facility. Among the deterrents to be considered are:

1. Personnel movements controls.
2. Parcel check systems, requiring that all parcels be declared to a facility and inspected upon departure.
3. Exclusion of privately owned vehicles from the area inside the parcel check point or immediately adjacent to a terminal building or exposed cargo.
4. A continuing security education program, stressing the moral wrong of pilferage and encouraging employees to be alert and to report thefts.
5. Cargo accountability controls to provide rapid, accurate information of losses.
6. Sustained high employee morale and the development of mutual respect between security personnel and other employees.

THEFT

At present, planned theft has become so widespread that it constitutes the most serious threat to the flow of commerce and the transportation system. It is management's first responsibility, working with law enforcement agencies, to identify occurrences of theft and report them.

It is not easy to determine the amount of loss experienced at any one point in the transportation system. Consequently, many losses are not discovered until a shipment is received by the consignee. He may be a long distance from the scene of the crime and the company accountable for the delivery may be different from the company responsible at the time of the theft.

Since a thief steals for profit, usually he does not act on impulse but plans his crimes and frequently works with accomplices, often employees of the companies to be victimized. Most frequently, their function is to provide information to the thief concerning the movement of high-value cargo. This is the thief's first task—to be selective according to the available market.

Obtaining possession of the cargo is the thief's second problem. If physical safeguards are effective, he may attempt to bribe a member of the guard force, falsify shipping documents, or commit an act of vandalism to create a diversion while the actual theft is taking place. When employees are involved, obtaining possession of the cargo presents few problems, especially where management accountability procedures are weak or nonexistent.

The thief must remove the stolen cargo from the facility, and this is most often accomplished by authorized vehicles present at the terminal for legitimate pickups or deliveries. In some instances of inadequate gate control, the thief will steal an entire truck or trailer.

Finally, the thief must profitably dispose of the stolen goods. Usually, he will sell the stolen cargo to a fence. For maximum personal profit, he seeks out items that currently fence for the highest prices and enjoy a ready market.

Certain elements of the transportation system are more vulnerable to theft than others. Terminal operations are extremely vulnerable. Facility personnel and truck drivers have direct contact with each other and a ready opportunity for collusion. A receiving clerk can certify receipt of property the driver has actually disposed of prior to his arrival. Conversely, a facility employee can provide a driver with cargo and removal from the terminal. An employee can also execute a false invoice that will appear to be legitimate when inspected by security personnel.

Railway employees assigned to switching duty at a terminal can operate in a similar manner by diverting a railway car to a siding outside the terminal so that it is accessible to a thief's confederates. Transferring the cargo from the car to another means of transportation demands more people, however, and as the size of the gang increases, so does the possibility of discovery and apprehension.

Trash disposal and salvage activities provide excellent opportunities for theft. Items of value can be concealed in waste material to be removed by a confederate employed to remove trash from the facility.

It is not necessary for a thief to be an employee or to be in collusion with employees. Forged credentials will often allow representation as an employee of a real or nonexistent company. This is particularly true in the overcrowded terminal facilities in large metropolitan areas.

Unlike a casual pilferer, a professional thief will not be deterred by psychological measures. Only active physical security measures will effectively eliminate losses from this source. Some of these measures are:

1. Establish guard surveillance at entrances and exists to the facility or to certain controlled areas.

2. Establish an effective personnel and cargo movement control system.
3. Locate vehicle parking areas for employees and transients outside the fence at the perimeter of the cargo handling area.
4. Employ a careful screening procedure during the hiring procedure.
5. Investigate all cargo losses quickly and efficiently.
6. Establish an effective key control system.
7. Provide adequate security patrols to inspect all perimeter fencing, buildings, yards, and docks for suspicious or unauthorized movements.
8. Install mechanical, electrical, and electronic intrusion detection devices.
9. Install appropriate fencing and lighting.
10. Store all cargo in enclosed, controlled security areas.
11. Maintain close liaison with law enforcement agencies.
12. Require strict adherence to existing procedures and maintain continual management supervision and presence to ensure that procedures are followed, especially in the warehouse and loading areas.

In addition to the above, information concerning the movement of high-value cargo must be safeguarded. Without information a thief cannot act.

PHYSICAL SECURITY

Planning the physical security measures necessary to circumvent the hazards discussed is the responsibility of management and its appointed security officer. These measures cannot interfere with the operating requirements of the facility. The receipt, sorting, processing, and moving of cargo must proceed unimpeded by the security measures. To determine the type and extent of physical protection required, the following factors should be considered:

1. The volume of cargo moved through the facility.
2. The value of cargo in the facility at normal peak periods.
3. The amount of time required for cargo to move through the facility.

4. The area to be protected, the kind of activity within it, and the number of personnel working there.
5. The vulnerability of the type of cargo to loss, damage, or theft.
6. Maintenance and custodial services needed in the facility.
7. Environmental factors affecting the operation of the facility.
8. Current labor-management relations.
9. Cost to purchase, operate, and maintain physical protection for critical areas and activities.
10. The possible expansion, relocation, or retrenchment of the facility.
11. Alternate methods of providing protection.

The plan must provide that all security measures employed complement and supplement each other. In large facilities, where a number of companies operate, individual security plans must be integrated. Failure to do this can waste resources and jeopardize the security of all.

OUTLINE PLAN

A security plan will provide for proper and economical use of personnel, be flexible to allow changes to meet emergencies, and should contain the following:

1. Purpose of the plan.
2. Definition of the areas considered critical and priorities for their protection.
3. Restrictions on access into security areas, including personnel, cargo, vehicle, and key control.
4. Mechanical aids to security, including perimeter barriers, protective lighting, alarm systems, and communications.
5. Guard force organization with general instructions for all guards; detailed instructions for special areas, added restrictions, and standard operating procedures should be appended.
6. General instructions for emergency actions; detailed plans, such as for fire or flood, should be appended.
7. Instructions to assure coordination with shift management, other security forces, and law enforcement agencies.

When the security plan has been completed and implemented, it should not be considered inflexible. It should be a dynamic document, readily modified to reflect changing conditions or requirements. To assure that this is the case, management should conduct frequent critical physical security surveys to identify deficiencies in the system. Security personnel are able to make specific recommendations for the elimination or minimization of any weaknesses found. Circulation of the overall security plan within the organization should be controlled, and the physical security surveys should show that it is properly implemented and up-to-date. Such procedures should result in improvement of the loss and theft record of the facility.

CONTROLLED AREAS

A controlled area is any area whose access is governed by special restrictions and controls. In establishing controlled areas, consideration must be given to preserving the facility and to the cargo—its moving capability as well as its past loss and theft record.

All high-value cargo, unless it is locked or sealed in the vehicle that transports it, should be under surveillance or in a controlled area. Carrier vehicles, particularly trucks, trailers, and railway cars, containing high-value cargo must be guarded or protected by a controlled area until they are released to authorized personnel for movement. To be fully effective, a controlled area should be under surveillance by physical or electronic methods and movement within the area controlled. A barricade providing limited access does not, in itself, constitute a controlled area.

The transportation industry provides a public service. As a result, some of its operations must be open to the general public. The general offices, personnel office, and freight receiving offices may need to be outside the controlled area. Where practical, consideration should be given to the installation of convex mirrors or rotating TV cameras in the storage areas, so that supervisory and guard personnel can have additional surveillance capability.

A controlled area can extend over many acres and include vehicle marshalling yards, docks, warehouses, and service or supply buildings. Such an area is a first line of defense for the protection of cargo in the transportation system.

Limited Area

Within the controlled area, a limited area can be established. This will provide a higher degree of security. A different pass, issued to fewer people, should be necessary for entry to a limited area. Sorting, recoopering of crates, and storage may be accomplished here.

Exclusion Area

An exclusion area can be located inside the limited area. Again, a different pass should be required and the number of people granted access strictly limited. The exclusion area is used only for handling high-value, low-volume cargo. The crib, vault, or cage that comprises the exclusion area should be kept locked or under surveillance at all times.

Access points to any controlled area, regardless of the degree of security involved, should be locked whenever they are not under physical or electronic surveillance. Strict control of the keys or combinations to locks is essential. In addition to checks by security representatives, management should make periodic checks to determine the integrity of controlled areas.

Vehicle Control

Only bona fide cargo-carrying or handling vehicles should be allowed inside a controlled area. It is especially important that employees and visitor parking lots be located outside the controlled area. If a controlled area is not fenced then private vehicles should be required to park behind a clearly defined line well removed from cargo or storage buildings.

Generally, there are three types of vehicles that operate within a controlled area: (1) the facility work vehicles, primarily small trucks, cargo-handling vehicles and cargo-loading vehicles; (2) the freight pickup and delivery and freight-forwarded vehicles; and (3) the cargo-carrier vehicles.

Facility vehicles usually remain in a controlled area, but if it is necessary for them to leave, their departure should be recorded. The freight pickup and delivery vehicles and the freight forwarder vehicles should be checked in and checked out, with records maintained to assure that they are the authorized vehicles for particular cargo. Cargo carrier vehicles should be inspected and manifested upon arrival at or departure from the facility.

All vehicles entering or departing a controlled area should pass through a service gate controlled by physical or electronic means. The size of the facility will determine the complexity of the gate procedures used. Where guards are considered necessary the inbound procedures should include, but are not limited to:

1. Truck register on which should be noted driver's name (obtain from driver's license), truck or tractor license (obtain from

registration), trailer or container number, company name, number of waybill, delivery notice, prelodge, or other document being used to authorize pickups and deliveries at time of entry.

Note: A Regiscope or similar camera could be used to record all the above data and that record could be a substitute for, or used in conjunction with, a truck register.

2. A seal check on inbound loaded trailers.
3. A pass or time check card, identifying the vehicle and driver, to be time stamped on entering and leaving the facility. The pass should also indicate the building or door designated for the pickup or delivery.

The procedures for outbound vehicles should include, but not be limited to, the following:

1. Pick up gate pass or time check card and verify for discrepancies.
2. Open doors and check vehicles if not sealed. Interline vehicles should not be locked until checked by gate control (partial loads, especially those containing numerous marks, are effectively checked only by returning vehicles to dock and restripping cargo under security supervision. This should be done on a periodic, random basis as a deterrent to use of these vehicles for removing stolen cargo).
4. Inspect cabs of vehicles for possible stolen items.

Loading and unloading operations should be carefully supervised and under periodic unobserved surveillance to prevent unauthorized material from leaving the facility in the vehicles. It is widely accepted that the majority of the cargo loss occurs at the dock during the operating hours. Continuing and efficient supervision and security at this point is essential if losses are to be reduced.

SECURITY OF SHIPPING AND RECEIVING AREAS AND PERSONNEL

Control of shipping and receiving areas and personnel at a plant, warehouse, or distribution center can do much to prevent cargo theft. A number of practical measures are available to shippers and receivers for improving security or cargo-handling areas and controlling personnel to minimize opportunities for theft. To provide better physical security, shippers and receivers may find it to their advantage to adopt the following precautions in areas where cargo is moved to or from carrier equipment.

1. Maintain perimeter controls. Mark off a perimeter area a suitable distance, at least 20 feet, from dock edge and from the wall of the office where carrier personnel report. Place signs reading "Restricted Area—Authorized Personnel Only" along the perimeter line facing the dock and office. Make sure that shipping and receiving areas are well lighted. Use lighting with a foot candlepower level of 59–60 if possible. Include floodlights to light the interior of railcars and truck vans.
2. Keep all cargo doors closed when not loading or unloading.
3. Do not allow cargo being loaded or unloaded to remain in the operating area between dock front and perimeter line or, generally, in close proximity to railcars or trucks.
4. Provide a secure room in the shipping and receiving area for control of sensitive or high-risk cargo during the shipping or receiving process. Limit access to this room and exercise tight control over movement of such cargo to the carrier or from the carrier to storage.
5. Maintain strict control and accountability for all keys to locked areas, security rooms, and containers.
6. Store seals securely within the office area. Limit issuance of seals to a few select employees. Maintain accurate records of all seals issued.

Strong measures of physical security are essential, and shippers and receivers run serious risk of cargo theft if they are neglected. Close personnel control and supervision are even more important. They provide the key to high-level security for shipping and receiving operations. Good personnel control begins with preemployment screening. Employers should make the screening process as thorough as possible and should include a check with previous employers and other available sources. After hiring, employers may find it advisable to take the following precautions:

1. Require identification badges with photographs for every employee.
2. Maintain an up-to-date signature file or other verification system for all employees authorized to sign receipts and other shipping documents.
3. Require employees to enter and leave the premises through a single personnel door or gate. Prohibit access of employee vehicles to the cargo area.

4. Maintain controls such as special passes for employees who leave the facility during duty hours.
5. Limit to a select few the employees authorized to process shipments of sensitive and high-value items and receipts for cargo generally.
6. Require identification badges for all persons visiting the facility.
7. Instruct all personnel to challenge persons moving about the facility who are not accompanied by an employee.
8. Periodically remind all employees of the penalties for theft, including loss of jobs, and the possible impact of serious theft on the company.

Good supervision will do much to improve cargo security at the shippers' and receivers' premises. The shipper and receiver may find it useful to instruct the supervisors to observe the following practices:

1. Make their presence conspicuous in the shipping and receiving areas, continually overseeing cargo-handling operations.
2. Make frequent checks of the quantities of inbound and outboard cargo being handled. Make occasional unannounced spot audits, especially of loading operations.
3. Rotate cargo-handling personnel among different carriers when feasible.
4. Rotate cargo checkers and handlers on different work cycles when possible.
5. Prevent nonemployees from assisting in shipping and receiving operations.
6. Report any suspicious activity to the security office.

2. The Employee

EMPLOYEE

A basic management responsibility is the screening and evaluation of job applicants and employees. In addition to their ability to perform the duties required, related factors such as honesty, integrity, and reliability are most important considerations.

The basis of any good security program is proper selection of employees. For any program to be viable, it must be recognized that it is the employees who take things or pass information along to thieves.

It's one thing to hire a person because of immediate need and a strong back and another to properly screen an application and an applicant's background. On most occasions, it is the former rather than the latter situation that prevails. Will this person be influenced by the temptations afforded? The shipper who wants to thwart theft and pilferage must make sure his employees are not likely to be tempted by the chance to steal. Background checks on candidates can be done by a number of firms specializing in security. These checks examine a person's past for information on arrests and convictions, work experience, and credit history. It must be remembered that the person who is heavily in debt is more likely to steal than the person who is not.

Not all thieves are caught in the preemployment screen, so additional precautions are needed. The most important of these is the creation of "an atmosphere of security." There must be a program that highlights security, and an atmosphere of security is created when

This chapter is adapted from U.S. Department of Transportation *Guidelines for the Physical Security of Cargo*, P5200.2. Washington, D.C.: U.S. Government Printing Office, May, 1972.

a company recognizes the need for security, then demonstrates to its employees that it sees that need and shows a willingness to prosecute. To strengthen that atmosphere, the company must make supervisors aware that security is part of their responsibility and that they will be held responsible for a lack of security.

There are two aspects of a foundation of good security: a good program of security screening and a tough stance that lets employees know the company is serious about security. With these two sections in place, a shipping company can add a variety of security devices and practices. Without these two building blocks, all the fancy equipment in the world will not deter theft.

PERSONNEL SECURITY CHECKLIST

This check list has been prepared as an action guide for transportation industry management to use in upgrading personnel security measures.

The *DOs* and *DON'Ts* contained herein should not be considered to be all-inclusive, but should be viewed as steps from which to build a more effective personnel security program.

DO

- Recognize that employees are participants in a substantial majority of theft and pilferage losses.
- Promulgate company policy regarding personnel security measures by

1. Assigning authority and responsibility for execution of the personnel security program to officials within the organization.
2. Involving personnel security considerations in the decision making process of the organization.
3. Providing support and cooperation at all levels of management for the personnel security program.

- Integrate personnel security measures into the existing employment system, including a firm commitment by management to elements of the program, by

1. Identification of weaknesses inherent in the present employment process that might allow employment of applicants with questionable backgrounds.

2. Examination of procedures being used by security-conscious employees for screening and investigating their applicants.
3. Implementation of procedures designed to upgrade employment practices regarding personnel security.
4. Adopting measures to assure periodic review of the personnel security program.

DON'T

- Evade the problem of employee theft and pilferage.
- Respond to the problem with "Lip Service" policy and ineffective procedures.
- Ignore the economic advantages of incorporating effective, but relatively inexpensive, personnel security measures into existing employment process through the exercise of certain management prerogatives.

Employment Application Forms

DO

- Require submission of a detailed employment application by all prospective employees, including applicants for clerical and maintenance positions as well as applicants for cargo handling positions.
- Design the application form to include information that will be helpful in judging the applicant in terms of honesty, integrity, and reliability. The following information should be required on the application forms:

1. Gaps in employment continuity.
2. Frequent job shifts.
3. Complete employment history, including
   A. Reasons for leaving.
   B. Sufficient data with which to make contact with former employers and supervisors.
   C. Salary information.
   D. Brief statement of duties and responsibilities.
4. Educational background, including specific information regarding schools attended, dates, etc.
5. All names used by the applicant.
6. Type of military discharge.
7. Citizenship.

8. Present residence and residence information for the past 10 years.
9. Affiliations and organizations.
10. Selective service classification.
11. Personal references.
12. Bonding history.
13. Criminal history: indictment, arrest, and conviction data should be obtained when permitted by law.
14. Conditions to which applicant agrees by signing the application form include
    a. Misrepresentations on the form shall be considered acts of dishonesty.
    b. Permission is granted to the employer or his agent to investigate the applicant's background, including a credit check.
    c. The application for employment in no way obligates the employer to hire the applicant.
    d. Permission is granted to the employer to require the applicant to submit to a lie detector examination in the event there is a theft or loss of any kind.

• Carefully review the employment application form for accuracy and completeness prior to consideration for processing.
• Consider the use of a separate form for obtaining security-related information, such as fingerprints, driving record, criminal history, etc. Such a procedure makes the applicant aware of the organization's interest in employing personnel with a high degree of honesty, integrity, and reliability.

DON'T

• Employ applicants prior to submission of a detailed employment form.
• Use a standard type of application form that makes little or no provision for obtaining security related information.
• Accept applications that are inaccurate or incomplete.

Fingerprinting and/or Photographing Applicants

DO

• Include the fingerprinting of applicants and the taking of identification photographs in the preemployment process.

• Make arrangements with the local police department for finger-printing and a local photographer for taking ID photos if in-house facilities for such procedures are not feasible.

DON'T

• Fail to recognize the discouragement to undesirables and the deterrence to thieves or wanted persons provided by fingerprinting and photographing requirements.

Interviews

DO

• Make provisions for a personal interview of all applicants to be conducted by trained interviewers.
• Design the interview session to assure that the following security-related elements are completed:

1. Verification of information submitted on the employment application form.
2. Clarification of details regarding questionable or derogatory information detailed on the application form or during the initial preemployment background investigation.
3. Obtaining additional information not contained in the application.
4. Obtaining information from the applicant that will help to appraise personality, character, motivation, honesty, integrity, and reliability, and to judge appearance and personal characteristics face-to-face.
5. Informing the applicant about the company, including security policies and procedures.

DON'T

• Allow interviews to be conducted solely by department managers or line supervisors.
• Expose the applicant to a brief, noncomprehensive type of interview that does not include security considerations.

CONFIRMATION OF PERSONNEL DATA

DO

• Confirm significant data contained on the application form and contact references.

• Conduct a thorough background investigation; go beyond the basic confirmation of factual data. Include searches for information regarding the applicant's character, integrity, honesty, and reliability. Such information should include, but not be limited to

1. Any deliberate misrepresentation, falsifications, or omission of material facts.
2. Any criminal, infamous, dishonest, immoral, or notoriously disgraceful conduct, habitual use of intoxicants to excess, or drug addiction.
3. Conviction of crimes of violence, including assault with a deadly weapon.
4. Any facts that furnish reasons to believe that the individual has been subjected to coercion, influence, or pressure that may cause him to act contrary to the best interests of the company.
5. Any previous dismissal from employment for delinquency or misconduct, theft, or embezzlement.

• Select the most effective method of conducting background investigation within the existing capabilities of the organization. Methods available include

1. Mail verification.
2. Telephone interviews.
3. Contacts with outside firms, ranging in cost from $10.00 to $70.00 each, depending upon the service required.

• Search applications being processed against local security and/or trade association indices to ascertain whether any derogatory information is on file regarding

1. The applicant.
2. The name of applicant's spouse.
3. The identity of applicant's friends or relatives working in the industry.

- Organize local trade indices to minimize the chances of hiring applicants already determined to possess undesirable characteristics by another member of the transportation industry.
- Consider the inclusion of a credit check in the preemployment process. Credit checks provide information that may be indicative of financial pressures exceeding salary, wages, or other income at the applicant's disposal.
- Establish the relevancy of credit check data to determining the applicant's suitability for employment.

DON'T

- Adopt procedures that allow the employment of applicants without completion of a thorough background investigation.
- Let the cost or the time required to conduct a background investigation be the sole factor in rejecting such procedures.
- Restrict background investigations to mere verification of fact and data.
- Limit the scope of background investigations by subscribing to only one method. Tailor procedures to the need and to the resources available locally.
- Fail to conform to the applicable provisions of the Consumer Credit Protection Act in the conducting of credit checks and consideration of the results.

EMPLOYEE EDUCATION PROGRAMS

DO

- Design a well organized, continuing security education program to develop and perpetrate security consciousness and attitudes among all employees of the organization.
- Conduct a security orientation for all present employees and arrange for such orientation of all future new employees. Such orientation should include

1. Objective of the security program
2. Relationship of the security element to other components or the organizational structure
3. Employee responsibility for the safekeeping of company and customer property
4. Specific security procedures

5. Review of the criminal laws that could be violated in a particular job and penalties for violation thereof
6. Statement of company policy when laws or company rules are violated

• Take advantage of in-house mode of presentation to employees, including

1. Bulletin boards
2. Entrance/exit displays
3. Lunchroom posters
4. Orientation conferences
5. Organization newsletter
6. Employee handouts

DON'T

• Conduct employee security education in a haphazard, non-goal-directed manner.
• Fail to communicate security to all employees, taking advantage of the many resources available to contribute to the effectiveness of the security education program in changing attitudes and behavior.

IDENTIFICATION AND CONTROLS

Many people employed in every mode of the transportation system are involved in handling cargo or its documentation. To ensure that unscrupulous persons are not permitted to hide within the large body of law abiding workers, a positive identification and control system should be established. This will permit necessary compartmentalization of activities and preclude unauthorized entry to restricted areas. Simple, easily understood identification and control measures should be used. At the same time, care should be exercised to prevent these measures from interfering with the primary function of the facility: the expeditious and efficient movement of cargo.

Personnel control is achieved by determining those who have a valid need to be in a specified area, then allowing only those persons to enter the area. Access lists, personnel identification, identification cards and badges, badge exchange procedures, and personnel escorts contribute to the effectiveness of identification and control systems. Unauthorized personnel will not easily be able to penetrate a properly administered control system.

By the frequent monitoring of areas where losses occur and proper use of paperwork such as correct signatures on forms and accurate counts of shipments, losses could be minimized without the use of full-time guards or expensive equipment.

Identification Systems

A system should be established at each facility, both to identify all employees and to regulate visitors, such as service or maintenance personnel.

The size of the facility, type of cargo handled, and complexity of the operation will determine the type of system to be used. These systems range from personal recognition to a photo identification badge system. The manager of a facility requiring an identification card system can prescribe a basic identification card for all personnel that will allow access to areas that are administrative in nature, contain no cargo, and are not in the controlled area category. Individuals who need access to controlled areas can be issued separate, distinct cards or badges with a photo. Access to areas requiring a high degree of security (e.g., high-value cages and cribs at a large airport cargo terminal) within a facility can be indicated by color coding or otherwise marking the card or badge. Identification devices should be designated as simply as possible while providing for control of personnel movement. Increased security for cargo is provided by limiting the number of people who have access to it.

The provisions for identification by pass or badge should be a part of the security plan. Definite instructions should be prepared covering

1. Designation of the areas in which passes or badges are required
2. Description of the identification devices in use, with authorizations and limitations placed upon the bearer
3. Methods of identification upon entering or leaving the area
4. Details of when, where, and how the identification device should be worn
5. Procedures to be followed in case of loss or damage to an identification device
6. Procedures for the disposition of identification device upon suspension or termination of employment
7. A procedure to issue new identification devices if more than 1% of those in use are unaccounted for

Identification systems may use either passes carried on the person or badges worn on the outer clothing.

Identification Devices

Single Pass. With a single pass or badge system, authorization to enter specific areas is indicated by letters, numerals, or colors. A weakness of the system is that passes or badges frequently remain in the bearer's possession during off-duty periods. This provides an opportunity for loss, alteration, or duplication.

Pass Exchange. The pass exchange system requires the use of two passes or badges. One is presented at the entrance and exchanged for the other, which is identical except for certain coding allowing access to specific areas. In this system the second badge or pass never leaves the controlled area, thereby decreasing the possibility of forgery or alteration.

Multiple Pass. The multiple pass system is a further development of the pass exchange system. Instead of markings on the facility badge indicating authorization to enter various areas, an exchange is made at the entrance to each area. Exchange badges are kept at each area only for those who are authorized to enter. Because of the localized exchange requirements, this is the most secure system.

Identification devices should be designed and constructed in a manner that will make them virtually tamper-proof. To protect the systems, strict accountability of all identification device components, including engravings or special paper, must be maintained at all times. To be effective, this control must extend to the manufacturer or supplier. The identification device control should be maintained by the security officer so that a minimum time elapses between a change in the status of a pass or badge and notification of the guard force. Care must be exercised to assure that passes or badges are returned and destroyed upon termination of employment. Lost or mutilated identification devices must be invalidated immediately.

In addition to passes and badges, there are other methods of personnel control. Primary among these is maintenance of an access list of all persons authorized by management to enter a controlled area. When a permanent addition or deletion is made the old list should be destroyed and a new one prepared. Current verified lists should be issued to access control points. Admission to other than those individuals on the authorized access list is subject to specific approval by the facility manager.

A person whose name is not on the access list must be escorted from the entrance to a controlled area to his destination. The escort may be either a guard or a representative of the person visited. The surest method of positive identification is a personal recognition system. It can be used with an access list if the work force is small enough to be known to the guards personally. Personal recognition can also be used in controlled areas where large groups are admitted at one time. This is done by having the group enter and leave the controlled area with a responsible supervisor who personally identifies all members to the security guard.

A uniform method of handling or wearing identification devices should be prescribed. A pass should be removed from the wallet or pocket and handed to the guard. A badge should be conspiciously displayed on the outer clothing.

Controlled entrances and exits should be so arranged that personnel are forced to pass in single file in front of the guard. At times, it may be advisable to use turnstiles to assist the guard in maintaining control. Artificial lighting should illuminate arriving and departing personnel and be of sufficient intensity to allow the guard to see the pass or badge clearly.

Enforcement is the most vulnerable part of an identification system. Lax performance of duty by a guard will invalidate the most carefully planned program.

Visitors

The screening and control of visitors is a necessary precaution against pilferage, theft, and vandalism. This can be accomplished by establishing the need for a visitor's admission and any limitations placed upon him. Positive identification should be made of a visitor by personal recognition, a visitor's permit, or other identifying credentials—not a business card. Visitor's passes or badges should be numbered serially and contain the following information:

1. Bearer's name
2. Areas authorized for access
3. Escort requirements
4. Time period for which the visit is authorized
5. Signature
6. Photograph, if desired and available.

Racks at control points for passes issued to visitors should be located so they are accessible only to guard personnel.

The enforcement of an identification and control system is primarily the responsibility of the guard force. However, guards should have full cooperation from other employees who should be instructed to consider every unidentified or improperly identified person a trespasser.

Service and Maintenance Crews

Particular care has to be exercised in the admission of service and maintenance personnel. No group of occupations has been used as successfully or as often as a cover for unauthorized entry. Appropriate clothing, a tool kit, and a smattering of technical knowledge are all that is needed to pose as a telephone repairman, an electrician, a plumber, a cleaner, or a business machine maintenance man. Legitimate employees of public utilities and some commercial service organizations carry company identification. They should not be admitted until a telephone check has been made to establish their identity and the request for service. Do not rely on the vehicle they are driving, even if it looks like a telephone truck or any emblem on them, as they can be easily duplicated. Their movement within a controlled area is subject to the same escort procedures prescribed for other visitors.

The guard force should maintain a logbook in which is recorded the name, pass or badge number, and the departure time of anyone who remains in a controlled area after normal working hours. Such a record will serve as a deterrent to a pilferer or thief. It will also provide the names of potential witnesses if they are needed.

Package Control

A package control system is an invaluable aid to preventing or minimizing pilferage, theft, and vandalism. No packages, except those with proper authorization, should be admitted into controlled areas without inspection. If practical, all outgoing packages should be inspected. If this is not possible, frequent unannounced spot inspections should be made. For the convenience of employees and visitors, a package checking service can be provided at the entrance to a controlled area.

3. Basic Cargo Protection

BARRIERS

The most basic protection for cargo is a barrier that prevents the would-be thief from approaching the cargo target. Physical and mechanical barriers are the subject of this section, with a discussion of recommended procedures to be followed outside the terminal facility.

Types

Barriers can be used to create physical and psychological deterrents to accidental entry; to prevent deliberate unauthorized entry; to delay intrusion, making detection and apprehension by guards more likely; to make guards more effective; and to direct the flow of pedestrian and vehicular traffic.

There are two kinds of physical barriers: natural or structural. Natural barriers include rivers, marshes, or terrain difficult to negotiate by vehicle. Structural barriers include fences, walls, buildings, grills, bars, and gates. A barrier should be under physical or electrical surveillance to be fully effective.

The kind of barrier used depends on the size of the controlled area, the flow of traffic during the busiest and least busy periods, and the most prevalent local hazards.

This chapter is adapted from U.S. Department of Transportation *Guidelines for the Physical Security of Cargo*, P5200.2. Washington, D.C.: U.S. Government Printing Office, May, 1972.

The perimeter of a larger controlled area may be protected by a combination of natural and structural barriers. A limited area, however, generally must be protected by a structural barrier.

Fencing

Fences should be chain link no. 9 gauge or heavier wire, no less than 8 feet high, with mesh openings no larger than 2 inches per side and with a twisted, barbed selvage at the top (some prefer razor ribbon with the barbed wire). It should be stretched taut and securely fastened to metal posts set in concrete. The bottom should be within 2 inches of hard ground or paving. On soft ground, it should extend below the surface to compensate for shifting soil or sand. Culverts, troughs, or other openings larger than 96 square inches in area should be protected by fencing or iron grills to prevent unauthorized entry yet allow proper drainage.

A top guard should be attached to perimeter fences and interior enclosures for greater security. A top guard is an overhang of barbed wire along the top of a barrier facing outward and upward at an angle of 45 degrees. The supporting arms are at least 2 feet long and are attached to the top of the fence posts. Four strands of standard barbed wire are tightly stretched between the supporting arms. Some fences have a double overhang facing outward and inward, which makes it more difficult to enter or leave the facility by scaling the fence.

The top guard can be firmly fixed or mounted on springs. The spring type guard further increases the difficulty of scaling the fence. If a building less than three stories high forms part of the perimeter, a top guard should be used along the coping to deny access to the roof.

The fence line should be as straight as possible to provide ease of observation by the guard force. If practicable, fences should be located no closer than 50 feet to buildings or cargo in a controlled area. Twenty feet of clearance should be allowed between the perimeter barrier and exterior features, such as buildings or parking areas, which would offer concealment to a thief.

Fencing for *limited areas* should conform to the same specifications as for controlled areas. It is recommended, however, that the height be increased to 10 feet and that a top guard be used.

Exclusion areas should be located in secure buildings and consist of separate cribs, cages, or vaults. If fencing is used, it should be at least 10 feet high, extend to the ceiling or be topped by a wire mesh roof, and be under observation by a guard.

If a wall serves as the barrier, or a part of it, it should be constructed to provide protection equal to that specified for each of the areas discussed above. If it is less than the height specified, it should be topped with chain link fence and barbed wire to match the minimum requirements. If a fence connects with a building, it should extend to within 2 inches of the wall of the building.

A body of water, whether a river, lake, or ocean, does not in itself constitute an adequate barrier. Additional measures, such as a fence and frequent security patrol and floodlighting, usually are necessary and recommended.

To be effective, barriers must be well maintained. Breaks or damages to the structure should be repaired as soon as they are discovered. Frequent inspections of the barriers must be made by the guard force to locate defects. In addition, the security officer should periodically tour the barriers, giving particular attention to cuts or openings in the barriers that may be camouflaged.

If the perimeter barrier encloses a large area, an interior all-weather road should be provided for guard force vehicles. The road should be in the clear zone and as close to the barrier as possible. Its use should be limited to guard and emergency vehicles.

Entrances

The number of gates and entrances to controlled areas should be limited to the minimum required for safe and efficient operation of the facility. A top guard, equal to that on the adjoining fence, should be attached to each gate. The bottom of the gate should be within 2 inches of hard ground or paving. Adequate lighting should be provided for fast and efficient inspection.

When gates or doors are not manned by guards so that all those entering will be challenged, they should be securely locked, illuminated during hours of darkness, and periodically inspected by a roving guard.

Semiactive entrances, such as railroad siding gates, or gates and doors used only during peak traffic flow periods, should be locked except when actually in use. Keys to these entrances should be in the custody of the security officer or the chief of the guard force and should be strictly controlled. Periodic inspection should be made of these entrances.

Inactive entrances, which are used only occasionally, also should be kept locked. They are subject to the same key control and inspection as semiactive entrances.

Emergency exits should be alarmed and breakout hardware installed on the inside.

Sidewalk elevators and other unusual entrances that provide access within controlled area barriers should be locked and patrolled.

Control signs stating the conditions of entry to a facility or controlled area should be erected at all entrances. They should inform the entrant that he is subject to search of his person, vehicle, or packages and of any prohibitions against packages, matches, smoking, or entry for reasons other than business. The signs should be legible under normal conditions at least 50 feet from the point of entry.

To maintain the integrity of the barriers to controlled areas, guard control stations should be established at all entrances in service.

LOCKS

Locks are an essential and integral part of barriers and the security they provide. To be effective, however, keys and combinations to locks must be strictly controlled. If they are compromised, the security of the entire facility is compromised.

Regardless of their quality or cost, locks can only be considered as delay devices. They are not positive bars to entry. Many ingenious locks have been developed, but equally ingenious means have been devised to open them surreptitiously. Some locks require considerable time and expert manipulation to open but will eventually succumb to force and the proper tools. The protection afforded by a well-constructed lock can be measured in terms of the time the locking mechanism will resist picking, manipulation, or drilling.

Determination of a facility's lock requirements demands expertise. Few security officers, and fewer transportation managers, have the necessary training. When selecting the equipment to be used, it is advisable to consult a professional locksmith.

Locks commonly used in the transportation system include

1. Keylocks, some of which can be opened by an expert in a few minutes. The ease with which a key may be lost and compromised or with which an impression may be made should be considered when determining the security value of a key lock.

2. Conventional combination locks, which may be opened by a skillful manipulator able to determine by touch and sound the settings of the tumblers of a common three-position dial-type lock. Although some combination locks may require

several hours to open, a skilled intruder can open the conventional combination lock in a few minutes.

3. Manipulation-resistant combination locks, which are designed so that the opening lever does not come in contact with the tumblers until the combination has been set. This lock provides a higher degree of protection for important material.

4. Other combination locks with four or more tumblers that afford still greater protection for very important items.

5. Relocking devices, which furnish an added degree of safety against forcible entry to a safe or vault door. This device increases the difficulty of opening a combination lock by punching, drilling, or blocking. It is recommended for heavy safes and vaults.

6. Interchangeable core locks, which have a core that can be removed and replaced by another using a different key. The cores can be replaced quickly, instantly changing the matching of locks and keys if their security is compromised. Other advantages are that all the locks in a facility can be keyed into an overall master-keyed system. Interchangeable core locks are economical, involving lower maintenance and new locks expenses. The system simplifies recordkeeping, is flexible, and can be engineered to the needs of the facility.

7. Kingpin locks, which are placed on the kingpin of a trailer or container chassis to make it impossible to connect a tractor. They provide a medium to high degree of security, depending on the type of lock. Although expensive, one lock can protect a number of trailers simultaneously if the locked trailer is parked in a blocking position.

Since a proper lock can provide positive security, it is recommended for use in an area where only periodic surveillance rather than constant observation is possible.

For effective control of locks, keys, and combinations, accurate records must be maintained and periodic physical inventories made. Combinations and keys should be issued only to those whose official duties require them.

Combinations to safe locks and padlocks securing containers should be changed at least once during each 12-month period, immediately following the loss or possible compromise of a combination or key, after the discharge, suspension, or reassignment of anyone who knows the combination, or upon receipt of a new container with a built-in combination lock.

The facility key and combination control should be exercised by the security officer. Records containing combinations and keys should be securely stored, with only limited and controlled access allowed. Lists of persons authorized to draw keys to controlled areas should be kept in the key storage container. Key containers should be inventoried at the end of each shift and all keys accounted for. Above all, keys should not be issued for permanent retention or removal from the facility. Keys should be logged out at the beginning of each shift and logged in at the end.

Each facility will have its own requirements for key and lock control systems. A survey should be conducted to determine the actual need for additional protection afforded by locking devices. When this determination has been made, an annex to the security plan can be drafted, showing

1. The location of key depositories
2. The keys (by building, area, or cabinet number) to be held in each depository
3. The method of marking or tagging keys for easy identification
4. The method of control for issue and receipt of keys, including register maintenance and identification of personnel authorized to receive keys
5. The action required if keys are lost, stolen, or damaged
6. The frequency and method of lock rotation
7. The assignment of responsibility and accountability by job or position title
8. The availability of emergency keys to the guard supervisor
9. A list of persons to whom this plan is made available

LIGHTING

At night, a protective lighting system enables the guard force to maintain a level of security approaching that observed during the day. Adequate lighting is relatively inexpensive. If it cannot be provided, management must consider other more costly alternatives, such as additional guards, sentry dog patrols, or expanded alarm systems.

The amount and intensity of light needed will vary from point to point within the facility. Designing a system for a large facility is a specialized task. Material is available from the manufacturers of lighting equipment that will assist management, but consultation with an expert in the field will save time and expense and will undoubtedly produce a more satisfactory lighting system.

Protective lighting will permit the guard to observe activities around or inside a facility. It is achieved by providing even light on areas bordering the facility, directing flaring light into the eyes of a potential intruder, and maintaining a low level of light on guard patrol routes.

Planning a Protective Lighting System

When planning a protective lighting system, the creation of light contrast between an intruder and the background is a primary consideration. The ability of a guard to distinguish a darkly clothed man against a dark background improves significantly as the level of illumination is increased. Predominantly dark, dirty surfaces require more light to facilitate observation than those of clean concrete or light-colored paint. This is also true inside buildings where ceilings and walls redirect and diffuse light.

Generally, lighting should be directed downward and away from the structure or area to be protected, and away from the guards assigned to patrol the facility. It should create as few shadows as possible.

Units for lighting perimeter fences of controlled areas should be located within the protected area and above the fence. The light pattern on the ground should include an area both inside and outside the fence. Adjacent highways, waterways, railroads, or residences may limit the depth of the light pattern.

Similarly, piers and docks forming part of the facility perimeter should be safeguarded by illuminating both the pier area and the water approaches. The area beneath the pier flooring should be lit with low-wattage floodlights arranged to dispel shadows.

Movable lighting that can be controlled by the guards is recommended as part of the protective system for piers and docks. Lighting in these areas cannot be allowed to violate marine rules. The United States Coast Guard should be consulted to ensure that proposed lighting systems adjacent to navigable waters do not interfere with aids to navigation.

The lighting of open areas within a perimeter should be the same as the illumination required at the perimeter. Lighting units in outdoor storage areas should be so placed as to provide an even distribution of light in aisles and recesses to eliminate shadows where an intruder may be concealed.

Special Terms

Special terms used in describing lighting must be understood in order to discuss and develop a protective lighting system.

One candlepower is the amount of light emitted by one international candle.

One footcandle is the amount of light on a surface 1 foot from the source of one candlepower. The amount of light varies inversely with the square of the distance between the source and the surface; so the footcandles decrease rapidly as the distance is increased.

Horizontal illumination is the amount of light expressed in footcandles on a horizontal surface. *Vertical illumination* is the amount of light expressed in footcandles on a vertical surface.

Continuous lighting (stationary luminary) is the most common protective lighting system. It consists of a series of fixed luminaries arranged to flood a given area continuously with overlapping covers of light.

Glare projection lighting provides a band of light with great angular dispersal. It directs the glare at an intruder while restricting the downward beam. It is a strong deterrent to a potential intruder and protects the guard by keeping him in comparative darkness. It should not be used if it would interfere with adjacent facilities.

Controlled lighting allows adjustment of a lighted strip to fit a particular need. If a highway, airport, or railroad adjoins the perimeter, this method will permit illumination of a narrow strip outside the fence and a wide strip inside the fence. The weakness of this method of lighting is that it often illuminates or silhouettes guards as they patrol their routes. *Standby lighting* (stationary luminary) is similar to continuous lighting. The luminaries, however, are not continuously lit but are activated manually by the guard force or automatically by the alarm system only when required.

Movable lighting (stationary or portable) consists of manually operated movable searchlights that can be lighted during hours of darkness or only as needed. The system is a supplement to those described above.

Emergency lighting can duplicate any or all of the above systems. Its use is limited to emergencies which render the normal system inoperative. It needs an alternate power source such as installed or portable generators.

Incandescent lamps are common glass light bulbs that produce light by the resistance of a filament to an electric current. Special purpose bulbs are manufactured with interior coatings to reflect the light or with a built-in lens to direct or diffuse the light. A regular bulb can be mounted in a shade or fixture to secure similar results.

Gaseous discharge lamps are of two kinds: mercury vapor and sodium vapor. They are limited in their use for protective lighting as they require a two- to five-minute period to light when cold and a slightly longer period to relight after a power interruption.

Mercury vapor lamps emit a blue-green light caused by an electric current passing through a tube of conducting, luminous gas. They are more efficient than incandescent lamps of comparable wattage. They are used widely for interior or exterior lighting where people are working.

Sodium vapor lamps are made on the same general principle as mercury vapor lamps but emit a golden yellow glow. They are more efficient than mercury vapor or incandescent lamps and are used where the color is acceptable, such as on streets, roads, or bridges.

Normally, the primary *power source* for a transportation facility is the local public utility. The concern of the security force begins at the point at which power feeder lines enter the facility. Feeder lines should be located underground or, in the case of overhead wiring, inside the perimeter to minimize the possibility of vandalism to the lines.

An alternate source of power should be available to supply the system in the event of interruptions or failure. Standby gasoline-driven generators that start automatically upon the failure of the primary source will ensure continuous lighting. They may, however, be inadequate for subtained operation. Generator or battery-powered portable or stationary lights should be available at key control points for use by the guards in case of a complete power failure that makes the secondary power supply inoperative.

Circuit Design

Both parallel and series circuits can be used to advantage in protective lighting systems. Care should be taken, however, to arrange circuits so that the failure of one lamp will not leave a large portion of the perimeter or a segment of a critical area in darkness.

The design should be simple and economical to maintain. It should require a minimum number of shutdowns for routine repair, cleaning, and lamp replacement. It should facilitate periodic inspections to replace or repair worn parts, tighten connections, check insulation, and clean, focus, and aim lights.

ALARMS

Intrusion detection devices can be used as a supplement to, but not a substitute for, the facility security force. They are intended to alert guards to an intrusion or attempted intrusion into the facility. Their effectiveness depends on the reaction time of the guard force once an alarm has been activated.

Management responsible for physical security must understand the strengths and weaknesses of the equipment available if it is to be effectively incorporated into the security plan. If an effective alarm system is installed, management may conserve work hours by using smaller, mobile, responding guard units instead of a larger number of patrols and fixed guard posts. In drafting a plan, however, alarm systems must be treated for what they are—aids to, not substitutes for, an alert, well-trained guard force.

Systems

There are a variety of commercially manufactured devices available that are designed to detect intruders. Certain systems are available only for external protection, while others can be used only inside a structure. Although an alarm system can be neutralized or circumvented by a resourceful individual, consultation with a reputable expert in the field will help assure the most tamper-proof system design for a particular situation.

An alarm system consists of

1. Detection elements located at the protected area designed to initiate an alarm upon entry of an intruder into the area.
2. Transmission lines that conduct signals to a signaling device in the immediate area or to a control annunciator panel that can be continuously monitored.
3. A panel that indicates by visible and/or audible signals the structure in which an alarm is activated.
4. Fail-safe features to provide a signal at the annunicator panel if any part of the system is malfunctioning.

Many types of alarm systems are in common use. Two or more different systems frequently will be installed in the same facility.

A *local alarm system* is one in which the protective devices activate a visual and audible signal in the immediate area to be protected. The light or sound device should be mounted on the exterior of the building and protected against weather or vandalism. It should be visible or audible for a distance of at least 400 feet. Although response to the alarm is made by facility guards or other employees, it can also be answered by the local police and fire departments.

A *police connection system* is one in which the facility-owned system is a direct extension of the police and fire alarm systems. The disadvantage of such a system is the administration of the consequent dual responsibility for maintenance.

The *central station system* is leased by the facility from a commercial agency. The agency designs, installs, maintains, and operates the system to safeguard against fire, theft, or intrusion. Alarms are transmitted to a control station outside the facility. When the alarm sounds, the agency takes appropriate action, such as notifying the police or fire department. Most agencies also have their own private guard force that is dispatched to the scene upon receipt of an alarm. Audible signals can be provided to alert employees or guards at the facility.

A *proprietary system* is similar to a central station system, except that it is owned or leased by, and located entirely within, the facility. Its main controls should be in or near security headquarters. Response to an alarm is by the facility's own security personnel. This system can also be connected to a central control station for immediate notification of appropriate authorities.

Detection Devices

A variety of devices are available to activate alarms. Although they employ different principles, each one will transmit an immediate warning signal to the security force.

Points of entry to buildings or enclosures can be protected by an alarm activated by breaking an electrical circuit. For this purpose, electrically charged strips of foil or wire can be used on window panes. Doors and windows can be equipped with magnetic or spring-activated contacts that sound an alarm if they are opened. Such devices consistently provide the most trouble-free service and cause few nuisance alarms. They may be costly to install at a large number of entry points. Sometimes they can be defeated by bridging, or jumping, the circuit.

A photoelectric device uses a light sensitive cell and a beam projected by a light source. If an intruder crosses the beam, contact is broken with the photoelectric cell, which activates the alarm. The light source may be hidden and/or an infrared filter over it may make the beam invisible to intruders. The beam can be crisscrossed in a protected area by means of mirrors until it strikes the light-sensitive cell. A projected beam of visible light can be effective for approximately 500 feet.

When properly installed, the photoelectric device affords effective, reliable notice of intrusion. There are certain disadvantages, however. Some kind of permanent installation is necessary. Mirrors must be locked into very precise adjustment. Sufficiently dense smoke, fog, rain, or dust will cause activation of the alarm. Frequent inspection is needed to assure that the system's components have not deteriorated.

A protective device that detects sound and vibrations can be used to safeguard vaults, special security storage bins, or warehouses. Extremely sensitive microphones are installed in the area on the walls, ceilings, and floors. Sounds or sound vibrations caused by an attempt to force entry will activate the alarm. The device is economical and easily installed. When an alarm is received, the amplifier can be adjusted to monitor further sounds from the protected area. It can be used only in vault-like installations or other enclosed areas where a minimum of extraneous sound is encountered. It cannot be used effectively out of doors, or in proximity to heavy construction or rail or vehicular traffic.

Another device that can detect motion indoors uses ultrasonic waves traveling at approximately 1130 feet per second with a frequency of about 19,200 cycles per second. The high pitch of the sound is inaudible to the average person. The transmitter is a small metal case mounted on the wall or ceiling. The receiver, mounted similarly, responds continuously to the sound pattern broadcasted by the transmitter. The device "hears" what is issuing from the transmitter as well as the echoes that bounce from the walls, furniture, and other objects in the enclosure. When motion disturbs the sound pattern, the change in ultrasonic frequency activates the alarm.

As much as 4000 square feet of floor area can be protected by a single transmitter and receiver unit. The device can be installed relatively easily by unskilled personnel. However, the unit sensitivity controls must be carefully adjusted and frequently serviced. Nuisance alarms may lead security personnel to reduce the systems's sensitivity, thus destroying its usefulness. It is not adaptable for use in areas where quantities of absorbent materials are stored as they do not reflect sound waves.

An electromagnetic or capacitance alarm can be used for point protection of specific objects requiring a high degree of security, such as safes, file cabinets, or other metal storage containers. The system may be connected to windows or door grids of metallic tubing to provide protection for such openings.

A capacitance alarm forms an electromagnetic field around the object to be protected. The field is tuned by achieving a balance between the electronic capacitance and the inductance. An intruder entering the field unbalances the electromagnetic energy of the field, which activates the alarm. The field cannot be penetrated without triggering the alarm. An electromagnetic device is easily installed at moderate cost.

A contact microphone has been developed for the protection of masonry structure fitted with heavy steel doors. It is capable of detecting the attempted penetration of any part of the enclosures as a result of explosive, hammering, cutting, drilling, or burning attacks. The contact microphone detects vibrations caused in the walls of the structure by attempted penetration. It amplifies the vibrations and sounds an alarm in security headquarters. Because the contact microphone senses wall vibrations rather than sound, the system is not affected by ambient noise.

Although closed circuit television (CCTV) is not an alarm device, it is frequently used to complement an alarm system. This may be accomplished by placing fixed television cameras at critical locations to provide direct visual monitoring from a central vantage point, or a simple camera remotely controlled by the monitoring guard can sweep across a wide area. Television is particularly useful to provide direct monitoring of very sensitive or exclusion areas and to observe gates equipped with electrically operated locks. CCTV can also be used with image sensors or video motion detectors to signal unauthorized entrance to a facility. An alarm can be sounded and a video tape recorder activated.

Care should be taken when choosing CCTV equipment so that the type of lighting used, (e.g., gaseous discharge or incandescent) is compatible with the cameras selected.

Protection

Protection for an alarm system can be provided by built-in technological features or by simple physical security measures. If the system is made more sophisticated to protect itself, greater ingenuity is needed to breach or violate it. As the system becomes more advanced technologically, however, its cost and the cost of maintenance increase accordingly.

Physical security measures usually cost less but afford less protection. Such measures may involve locating transmission lines high above ground or burying them deep below ground, recessing detection devices in armored boxes or walls, and rigid control of access to communication centers. Through a combination of technological and physical security measures, a balance should be achieved in which the maximum time is required to defeat the system and the lowest cost is experienced in its construction and operation.

Maintenance

Intrusion detection devices should remain in continuous operation during nonoperational hours if they are to be effective security aids. Therefore, preventive and corrective maintenance must be performed promptly.

Manufacturers will train and advise designated security personnel on the maintenance of the equipment. To prevent malfunctions, trained personnel should inspect and test components as recommended by the manufacturer and should be capable of effective immediate minor repairs. Spare parts recommended by the manufacturer must be kept in stock. A contract, providing service on a 24-hour basis, should be negotiated with the manufacturer of all other service parts. Plans, diagrams, and data charts for all alarm systems installed should be kept in a locked file in the custody of the security officer.

Standards

The transportation facility manager or security officer developing an alarm system can receive guidance from the standards established by Underwriters Laboratories, Inc. Detailed system requirements are given in the following publications:

- UL 609 — *Local Burglar Alarm Units and Systems*
- UL 611 — *Central Station Burglar Alarm Units Systems*
- UL 634 — *Connectors and Switches for Use with Burglar Alarm Systems*
- UL 639 — *Intrusion Detection Units*
- UL 681 — *Installation, Classification, and Certification of Burglar Alarms Systems*

COMMUNICATIONS

Allied with, but independent of, the alarm system is the protective communications system, which will vary in size and complexity with the importance, vulnerability, size, and location of a specific facility. Its design is subject to local determination. Normally, the regular communication system is not adequate for protective security purposes. Security forces should have a separate system with direct lines outside and an auxiliary power supply.

Although dependence is placed on the telephone, teletype, and automatic alarm systems, internal and external radio communications may play an important part in the security program plan of large facilities. One or more of the following means of communication should be included in the protective system:

1. Local exchange and commercial telephone service.
2. Intrafacility, interfacility, and interoffice telephone systems using rented circuits and equipment that is not interconnected with commercial exchange telephone service.
3. Radio telephone facilities for either point-to-point or mobile service.
4. Hand-carried portable radios or receivers, with transmitters strategically placed throughout the facility.
5. Key-operated electric call boxes located throughout the facility for guard supervision. By inserting a key in the call box, a guard can make a routine tour report or summon emergency assistance.

Alternate communications systems must be restricted to the use of the security force or to report emergencies. The wiring for alternate communications systems should be separate from other lines and placed in underground conduits. For emergency communication with agencies outside the facility, leased wires or a radio that can be tuned to police and fire department frequencies should be available.

The facility communications center, and the nerve center of the entire security program, should be designated a controlled area and access to it closely restricted.

All alarm and communication circuits should be tested at least once during each eight-hour period, preferably when a new shift comes on duty. At small facilities that do not employ guards, a test should be made just before closing for the night.

GUARDS

No matter what structural, mechanical or electronic supplements are employed, the human element in the security program is the enforcement arm of the program. It should be specifically organized, trained, and equipped to protect the security of cargo in the transportation system.

Authority

The authority of facility guards varies with the location and ownership of the facility and must agree with applicable federal and state laws. Complete legal advice should be obtained before guards are instructed in their duties.

In all instances where civilian guards are employed, their power of arrest is limited to that of a private citizen. If they are deputized under federal or state law, their arrest authority is only that specified in the deputization.

Investigations of pilferage or theft frequently require search and seizure actions. Unpleasant social, political, and legal consequences can be suffered by the company and/or guard if an individual is subjected to an overlyzealous assumption of authority.

Duties

Acting within the scope of its authority, the guard force should have standing order to

1. Safeguard cargo, material and equipment against sabatoge, loss, theft, and damage.
2. Enforce the personnel identification system.
3. Patrol designated perimeters, areas, structures, and activities.
4. Apprehend intruders attempting to gain unauthorized access to the facility or persons in possession of stolen merchandise.
5. Determine that vaults, rooms, buildings, and access points are locked and secure during other than working hours.
6. Enforce the system of control governing the entry or exit of cargo, property, and documents at facility access points.
7. Respond to alarm signals or other emergencies.
8. Take all necessary action required in emergency situations affecting the security of the facility.
9. Enforce regulatory traffic controls to expedite the flow of cargo and prevent or reduce the numbers of accidents.
10. Report all matters affecting the security and safety of the facility.

QUALIFICATIONS

Management has the responsibility to determine that guards are screened, selected, or disqualified, based on rigorous mental and physical standards. Most of the qualities desired in a security guard are developed through training and become instinctive with experience.

More than any other quality, alertness will determine the effectiveness of a security guard. Even though hundreds of individuals show proof of the right and need to enter a restricted area, one contact could be with a person who should *not* enter. To detect this one exception, the guard must be constantly alert.

Sound judgement is essential to a guard. It is more than the application of common sense: it is the ability to arrive quickly at a wise decision. It involves the comparison of an unfamiliar situation with a similar situation of known values. The ability to compare, discriminate, and decide must be developed by the guard. Security instructions cannot cover every situation. They can only provide guidelines, as each situation is unique and must be treated accordingly. Guards should be trained to call security headquarters when in doubt about a particular event.

The *courage* required in a security guard is more than bravery when confronted with potential physical assault. It involves the moral courage to apprehend an acquaintance caught thieving, to carry out duties in the face of threats or ridicule, and to report all threats or offers of bribes.

Confidence is a state of mind free from doubt or misgivings. Confidence means faith in one's self and in one's abilities. Nothing can inspire self-confidence as much as a thorough knowledge of the job. An effective security guard must also have confidence in the leaders and other members of the security force. It is best achieved through training and competent supervision.

Physical fitness is indispensable in a security guard. The duty is arduous and demanding. The guard is exposed to all kinds of inclement weather and may be subject to physical attack by an intruder. The security of the facility and the life of the guard depend upon physical fitness.

Tact, the ability to deal with others without giving offense, is a valuable trait. A guard must be able to give instructions clearly and concisely, firmly and authoritatively, but without arrogance or discourtesy.

Security-guard duty requires constant *self-control*. The security guard must be impersonal in the performance of duty. If temper is lost, then control of the situation is lost.

Loyalty is one of the most important qualities of a security guard. An uncompromising commitment to the interests of the employer is essential. Supervisors must be alert to any change in this attitude that might affect the guard's performance. Only a person of known integrity, responsibility, and trustworthiness should be assigned as a security guard.

Organization

Guard forces will differ organizationally from facility to facility. In every case, however, one guard must be placed in charge of each shift, and that guard's authority must be clearly understood by all concerned.

Divided authority can lead only to chaos and evasion of the security program. Usually the guard force is organized on the basis of three or four shifts of eight hours each. *Shift changes should be made before peak periods of activity in the normal operation of the facility.* The requirement for guard personnel on each shift is determined by dividing the total number of work hours needed by the hours on the shift. To this figure must be added sufficient personnel to provide relief, which is normally based on one-half hour per guard per shift.

The high cost of establishing a guard force dictates that care be taken to ensure that posts and patrols are used only where necessary. If less expensive security measures will suffice, they should be used. To determine the posts and patrols necessary at the facility, consideration must be given to the criticality, sensitivity, and vulnerability of the terminal and the cargo it processes.

A stationary guard post will be required where cargo is so critical and vulnerable that loss or damage may occur if it is left unattended, where continuous human observation is required, or where mere access by authorized personnel is prejudicial to cargo security.

Motor or foot patrols will be required if two or more security areas are protected by passive security measures yet need periodic inspection by guards. If one or more guard posts exist that require a periodic reinforcement, a mobil patrol can provide it. Similarly, such a patrol can provide periodic traffic control, emergency aid, and reliefs as required.

Some posts and patrols need to be operational one hour or less per day, while others must be manned all 24 hours. When determining the requirements for specific hours of operation, factors to be considered are:

1. The operational hours of the facility
2. The periods when employees are not present in certain buildings or areas
3. The peak hours of vehicular and pedestrian traffic
4. The hours of limited visibility
5. The schedules of incoming and outgoing shipments
6. The movement of critical items within the facility
7. The scheduled activities that require special security measures
8. The weekends and holidays when the facility will be non-operational
9. The passive security measures that are in effect

Patrols are normally the most flexible segment of a guard force. If sufficient personnel are not available to fulfill all requirements, it is often possible to consolidate patrol functions. For short periods of time, one patrol may perform the duties assigned to two patrols without seriously affecting overall security. If two-guard patrols are used, one guard can be assigned to other duties temporarily.

It is more difficult to reassign a guard from a stationary post. If a post is manned by two or more guards, however, one guard can assume other duties for a short time during slack periods in the movement of personnel, cargo, and vehicles.

Personnel Requirements

The security officer must determine personnel requirements in a systematic manner, with regard for the capability of the force in both normal and emergency situations. The amount of personnel needed for the guard force can only be determined by a detailed study of the posts, patrols, and escorts necessary, the times during which each job must be performed, and the amount of supervision required. Allowances must be made for reserves, leave, sickness, and other contingencies. The security officer seldom will have sufficient personnel to provide all of the guards desired; therefore, care must be taken to program for their economical and efficient use. Annual requirements for posts and patrols are expressed in a work hours per year. The work hours required to operate a post or patrol are obtained by multiplying the number of guards required, the number of hours per day, the number of days per week, and the number of weeks per year.

The number of work hours per year that will be performed by one guard must be based on personnel practices of the employer. If a guard is allowed two weeks vacation and averages one week sick leave, then he can be expected to be on the job 40 hours a week for 49 weeks, or 1960 hours per year.

Some examples of personnel requirement computation are shown below:

Post #1 required two guards, is operated 24 hours per day, seven days each week:

2 (guards) $\times$ 24 (hours) $\times$ 7 (days per week) $\times$ 52 (weeks per year) = 17,472 (work hours per year), divided by 1960 = 8.9 guards.

Post #3 required one guard, 16 hours per day, five days per week:

1 $\times$ 16 $\times$ 5 $\times$ 52 = 4,160, divided by 1969 = 2.1 guards.

Sentry Dogs

While the requirement for physical protection of cargo facilities continues to increase, funds for manpower and availability of competent personnel is always limited. Use of properly trained sentry dogs helps to relieve personnel shortage. The mission of the sentry dog is to detect intruders, alert his handler and, if necessary, pursue, attack, and hold a trespasser. A sentry dog patrol is particularly effective in areas of little activity, such as isolated perimeters, remote storage areas, pipelines, and open storage areas.

The dog and the handler work as a team. As the outstanding qualifications of a sentry dog are his senses of smell and hearing, he can be used to best advantage during the hours of darkness or when the guard's vision is restricted. The dog keeps the guard on post more alert, increases his self-assurance, and relieves the monotony and loneliness of patrol duty.

The dog can be used as a warehouse guard. He can be placed in the building at the close of the working day and removed before the start of the next. This eliminates the need for a guard, requiring only a moving patrol to check on the dog. The dog will alert the guard force if an intruder attempts to enter his guard area.

There are advantages and disadvantages to the use of sentry dogs. The presence of sentry dogs is a strong psychological deterrent to intruders. A dog is more effective during inclement weather than a guard and is better able to apprehend intruders during hours of darkness. Finally, there is less chance of a fatality through the release of a dog than through firing a weapon at the intruder.

The disadvantages are that attrition of personnel trained as handlers reduces the efficiency of a sentry dog program. The training period that enables a guard and dog to work as a team results in many unproductive hours. Personnel who like and understand dogs are not always available as handlers. Those who do volunteer may suffer a morale problem as most of the work is at night. The odor of petroleum will decrease the effectiveness of a dog's sense of smell, just as noise will affect his hearing. Many people disapprove of the use of dogs for sentry duty, and the public relations impact of this practice cannot be ignored.

Although these problem areas cannot be disregarded, the value of the sentry dog should not be underestimated. Used as a supplement to other physical safeguards, the dog can be an invaluable asset to the security program.

CARGO SECURITY CHECKLISTS

The checklist below may be used for many different types of facilities. It permits each facility manager to select those elements pertaining to his establishment and location in making his own security survey.

Barriers

a. Is the perimeter of the facility or activity defined by a fence or other type physical barrier?
b. If a fence or gate is used, does it meet the minimum specifications?
  1. Is the top guard strung with barbed wire and angled outward and upward at a 45 degree angle?
  2. Is it at least 10 feet total height?
  3. Is it located so that it is not adjacent to mounds, piers, docks, or any other aid to surmounting it?
c. If building walls, floors, and roofs form a part of the perimeter barrier, do they provide security equivalent at least to that provided by chain link fence? Are all openings properly secured?
d. If a masonry wall or building forms a part of the perimeter barrier, does it meet minimum specifications of perimeter fencing?
e. If a river, lake, or other body of water forms any part of the perimeter barrier, are security measures equal to the deterrence of the 10-foot fence provided?
f. Are openings such as culverts, tunnels, manholes for sewers and utility access, and sidewalk elevators that permit access to the facility properly secured?
g. List number, location, and physical characteristics of perimeter entrances.
h. Are all portals in perimeter barriers guarded, secured, or under constant surveillance?
i. Are all perimeter entrances equipped with secure locking devices and are they always locked when not in active use?
j. Are gates and/or other perimeter entrances that are not in active use frequently inspected by guards or management personnel?
k. Is the security officer responsible for security of keys to perimeter entrances? If not, which individual is responsible?

l. Are keys to perimeter entrances issued to other than facility personnel, such as clearing, trash removal, or vending machine service personnel?

m. Are all normally used pedestrian and vehicle gates effectively and adequately lighted so as to ensure
    1. Proper identification of individuals and examining of credentials,
    2. That interiors of vehicles are clearly lighted, and
    3. That glare from luminaries is not in guard's eyes?

n. Are appropriate signs setting forth the provisions for entry conspicuously posted at all principal entrances?

o. Are clear zones maintained for the largest vehicles on both sides of the perimeter barrier? If clear zone requirements cannot be met, what additional security measures have been implemented?

p. Are automobiles permitted to park against or too close to perimeter barrier?

q. What is frequency of checks made by maintenance crews of condition of perimeter barriers?

r. Do guards patrol perimeter areas?

s. Are reports of inadequate perimeter security immediately acted upon and the necessary repairs effected?

t. Are perimeters protected by intrusion alarm devices?

u. Does any new construction require installation of additional perimeter barriers or additional perimeter lighting.

Lighting

a. Is the perimeter of the installation protected by adequate lighting?

b. Are the cones of illumination from lamps directed downward and away from the facility proper and away from guard personnel?

c. Are lights mounted to provide a strip of light both inside and outside the fence?

d. Are lights checked for proper operation periodically and inoperative lamps replaced immediately?

e. Do light beams overlap to provide coverage in case a bulb burns out?

f. Is additional lighting provided at vulnerable or sensitive areas?

g. Are gate guard boxes provided with proper illumination?

h. Are light finishes or stripes used on lower parts of buildings and structures to aid guard observation?

i. Does the facility have a dependable auxiliary source of power?
j. Is there alternate power for the lighting system independent of the plant lighting or power system?
k. Is the power supply for lights adequately protected? How?
l. Is the standby or emergency equipment tested periodically?
m. Is emergency equipment designed to go into operation automatically when needed?
n. Is wiring tested and inspected periodically to ensure proper operation?
o. Are multiple circuits used? If so, are proper switching arrangements provided?
p. Is wiring for protective lighting securely mounted?
    1. Is it in tamper-resistant conduits?
    2. Is it mounted underground?
    3. If above ground, is it high enough to reduce possibility of tampering?
q. Are switches and controls properly located, controlled and protected?
    1. Are they weatherproof and tamper resistant?
    2. Are they readily accessible to security personnel?
    3. Are they located so that they are inaccessible from outside the perimeter barrier?
    4. Is there a centrally located switch to control protective lighting? Is it vulnerable?
r. Is the lighting system designed and locations recorded so that repairs can be made rapidly in an emergency?
s. Is adequate lighting for guard use provided on indoor routes?
t. Are materials and equipment in shipping and storage areas properly arranged to permit adequate lighting?
u. If bodies of water form a part of the perimeter, does the lighting conform to other perimeter lighting standards?

Alarms

a. Is an alarm system used in the facility?
    1. Does the system indicate an alert only within the facility?
    2. Does it signal in a central station outside the facility?
    3. Is it connected to facility guard headquarters?
    4. Is it connected directly to an enforcement headquarters outside the facility proper? Is it a private protection service? Police station? Fire station?
b. Is there any inherent weakness in the system itself?
c. Is the system supported by properly trained, alert guards?

d. Is the alarm system for operating areas turned off during working hours?
e. Is the system tested prior to activating it for nonoperational periods?
f. Is the alarm system inspected regularly?
g. Is the system tamper resistant? Weatherproof?
h. Is an alternate alarm system provided for use in the event of failure of the primary system?
i. Is an alternate or independent source of power available for use in the event of power failure?
j. Is the emergency power source designed to cut in and operate automatically?
k. Is the alarm system properly maintained by trained personnel?
l. Are periodic tests conducted frequently to determine the adequacy of response to alarm signals?
m. Are records kept of all alarm signals received to include time, date, location, action taken, and cause for alarm?

Communications

a. Is the security communications system adequate?
b. What means of communications are used?
   1. *Telephone.*
     (a) Is it a commercial switchboard system? Independent switchboard?
     (b) Is it restricted for guard use only?
     (c) Are switchboards adequately guarded?
     (d) Are there enough call boxes and are they conveniently located?
     (e) Are open wires, terminal boxes, and cables frequently inspected for damage, wear, sabotage, and wire-tapping?
     (f) Are personnel cautioned about discussing cargo movements over the telephone?
   2. *Radio*
     (a) Is proper radio procedure practiced?
     (b) Is an effective routine code being used?
     (c) Is proper authentication required?
     (d) Is the equipment maintained properly?
   3. *Messenger.* Is the messenger always available?
   4. *Teletype.* Is an operator available at all times?
   5. *Public address.*
     (a) Does it work?
     (b) Can it be heard?

6. *Visual signals.*
   (a) Do all guards know the signals?
   (b) Can they be seen?
c. Is security communications equipment in use capable of transmitting instructions to all key posts simultaneously?
d. Does the equipment in use allow a guard to communicate with guard headquarters with minimum delay?
e. Is there more than one system of security communications available for exclusive use of security personnel?
f. Does one of these systems have an alternate or independent source of power?
g. Has the communications center been provided with adequate physical security safeguards?

Personnel Identification and Control

a. Is an identification card or badge used to identify all personnel within the confines of the controlled areas?
b. Is the identification medium designed to provide the desired degree of security?
c. Does the identification and control system include arrangements for the following:
   1. Protection of the meaning of coded or printed components of badges and passes?
   2. Designation of the various areas requiring special control measures to which the badge holder may be authorized entrance?
   3. Strict control of identification data?
   4. Clear explanation and description of the identification data used?
   5. A clear statement of the authorization and limitations placed upon the bearer?
   6. Details of where, when, and how badges shall be worn?
   7. Procedures to be followed in case of loss or damage to identification media?
   8. Procedure for recovery and invalidation?
d. If a badge exchange system is used for any restricted area, does the system provide for:
   1. Comparison of badge, pass, and personnel?
   2. Physical exchange of restricted area badge for general authorization badge at time of entrance and exit?
   3. Logging a record of each badge exchanged?

4. Inventory of badges issued by security personnel at the start and completion of tours of duty?

5. Location of personnel who have not checked out of the area at the close of each tour of duty?

6. Security of badges not in use?

e. Are messengers who are required to traverse areas of varying degrees of security provided with special identification?

f. Are the prescribed standards for access to exclusion areas supplemented with arrangements for the following:

1. At least one representative of management or security in the area at all times when work is in progress?

2. No other persons permitted to enter the area until one representative of management or security has entered?

3. A representative of management or security remaining until all others have departed?

g. Are personnel, who require infrequent access to a critical area and who have not been issued regular security identification for the area, treated as "visitors" thereto, and issued either (1) a visitor's badge or pass, or (2) a special pass?

h. Are all personnel required to wear the security identification badge while on duty?

i. Do guards at control points compare badges to bearers both upon entry and upon exit?

j. Is supervision of personnel charged with checking identification badges sufficient to ensure continuing effectiveness of identification and control system?

k. Are badges recorded and controlled by rigid accountability procedures?

l. Are lost badges with one bearing a different number or one that is otherwise not identical to the one lost?

m. Are procedures relative to lost, damaged, and/or forgotten badges adequate?

n. Are temporary badges used?

o. Are lists of lost badges posted at guard control points?

p. Are badges of such design and appearance as to enable guards and other personnel to recognize quickly and positively the authorizations and limitations applicable to the bearers?

q. How long ago were currently used badges originally issued?

r. Do existing procedures ensure the return of identification badges upon termination of employment?

s. Are badges similar to or identical to employee badges issued to outside contractor employees working within the installation?

t. Have local regulations governing identification and control been revised in any material respect since first established?

u. Are all phases of the system under supervision and control of a security officer?
v. Is an effective visitor escort procedure established?
w. Are visitors required to conspicuously display identification on outer garments at all times while on installation?
x. When visitors leave the installation, are they required to turn in their identification badges, and is the departure time in each case recorded on the visitor's register?
y. What procedures are invoked when visitor identification badges are not turned in prior to departure of the visitor?
z. Is there a central receptionist?
    1. If "yes," specify functions.
    2. Are functions performed under the supervision of a security officer?
aa. Are receptionists (or guards) stationed at different focal points to maintain visitor control?
bb. Are there special procedures applicable to visitors requiring access to cargo handling documents?
cc. Are special visitors, e.g., vendors, tradesmen, utility servicemen, or special equipment servicemen issued a special distinctive type of visitor badge?
dd. What measures are employed, other than the issuance of identification badges, to control the movements of personnel from other transportation companies working within the perimeter of the facility?
ee. Does the system used for identification of truck drivers and helpers conform to security regulations?
ff. Is the security officer the single responsible official for all aspects of visitor control?

Package and Material Control

a. Is there standard procedure on control of packages and materials?
b. Are all guards conversant with the package control measures?
c. Are notices on restriction and control procedures prominently displayed at each active entrance and exit?
d. Is there a checkroom where employees and visitors can leave their packages?
    1. Is an adequate receipt system in effect?
    2. Are packages inspected in the owner's presence before a receipt is issued?

3. Is access to the checkroom restricted to authorized personnel only?

4. Is a policy established for disposition of items left beyond a specified period?

e. Are spot checks of persons and vehicles conducted and, if so, are frequency and scope thereof indicated?

1. Regular search
2. Spot search
3. Special search

f. Are detection devices used?

1. X-ray or other similar device
2. Metal detector
3. Other; evaluate effectiveness

g. Is a property removal slip, signed by an authorizing official, required when property is being removed from the facility?

h. Are removal slips available in the security office for signature by officials authorizing property removals?

i. Are property removal slips surrendered to guards at exit points?

j. Are special rules established for package and material handling?

1. Is package and material pass used to exempt bearer from search?

(a) Is time, date, bearer's name, using agency, and description of the contents properly recorded thereon?

(b) Is preparation and issue rigidly controlled?

(c) Is it serially numbered?

(d) Does it provide for signature of validating officials?

(e) Is signature card readily available to guards for comparison?

2. Is a trustworthy and identified courier used at all times?

k. Are special clothing issued for wear in the facility to prevent the introduction or removal of unauthorized items?

l. Is an effective procedure used for control and search of special vehicles?

1. Emergency vehicles
2. VIP vehicles
3. Special courier vehicles
4. Vendor's vehicles
5. Vehicles with loads that are impracticable to search

m. Is there close coordination between security headquarters and the activities that handle cargo movements?

n. Are new employees given appropriate instructions relative to the handling and safeguarding of cargo?

Vehicle Control

a. Are vehicles that are allowed regular access to the facility registered with the security officer?
b. Have definite procedures been established for the registration of private cars, and are they issued in writing?
c. Do the vehicle registration requirements apply also to motor vehicles owned or operated by employees of any individual, firm, corporation, or contractor whose business activities require daily or frequent use of vehicles on the facility?
d. Is annual or more frequent registration required?
e. What information is incorporated in registration application forms?
f. Do the prescribed prerequisites for registration include a valid state registration for the vehicle and a valid state operator's license?
g. Is mechanical inspection of vehicles and/or proof of financial responsibility required as a prerequisite of authority to operate a vehicle within the facility?
h. Are decalcomania or metal permit tags affixed to all vehicles authorized to operate within the facility?
i. Do registration permits bear a permanently affixed serial number and numerical designation of year of registration?
j. Do the regulatory controls for registration include:
    1. Prohibition against transfer of registration permit tags for use with a vehicle other than the one for which originally issued?
    2. Replacement of lost permit tags at the registrant's expense?
    3. Return of tags to the security officer when the vehicle is no longer authorized entry into facility?
    4. Destruction of invalidated decalcomania or metal tags?
k. What is the nature and scope of registration records maintained by the security officer?
l. Do the gate guards make periodic checks to ensure that vehicles are operated on the premises only by properly licensed persons?
m. Is a specified system used to control the movement of commercial trucks and other goods conveyances into and out of the installation area?
n. Are loading and unloading platforms located outside the operating areas, separated one from the other, and controlled by guard-supervised entrances?

o. Are all trucks and other conveyances required to enter through service gates manned by guards?

p. If trucks are permitted direct access to operating areas, are truck drivers and vehicle contents carefully examined?

q. Does the check at entrances cover both incoming and outgoing vehicles?

r. Are truck registers maintained?

s. Are registers maintained on all company vehicles entering and leaving the facility?

t. Are escorts provided when vehicles are permitted access to operating or controlled areas?

u. Does the supervision of loading and unloading operations ensure that unauthorized goods or people do not enter or leave the installation via trucks or other conveyances?

v. Are company trip tickets examined?

w. Is a temporary tag issued to visitor's vehicles?

x. Are automobiles allowed to be parked within operating or controlled areas?

y. Are parking lots provided?

z. Are interior parking areas located away from sensitive points?

aa. Are interior parking areas fenced so that occupants of automobiles must pass through a pedestrian gate when entering or leaving the working area?

bb. Are separate parking areas provided for visitors' vehicles?

cc. What is the extent of guard surveillance over interior parking areas?

dd. Are there restrictions against employees entering private vehicle parking areas during duty hours?

ee. Are automobiles allowed to park so close to buildings or structures that they would be a fire hazard or obstruct fire fighters?

ff. Are automobiles permitted to be parked close to controlled area fences?

gg. Are parking facilities adequate?

Lock Security

a. Has a key control officer been appointed?

b. Are the locks and keys to all buildings and entrances controlled by a key control officer?

c. Does the key control officer have overall responsibility for issuance and replacement of locks and keys?

d.   Are keys issued only to authorized personnel?

e.   Are keys issued to other than facility personnel?

f.   Is the removal of keys from the premises prohibited?

g.   Are keys not in use secured in a locked, fireproof cabinet?

h.   Are current records maintained indicating:
1.   Clear record of person to whom key is issued?
2.   Time of issue and return of keys?
3.   Buildings and/or entrances for which keys are issued?
4.   Number and identification of keys issued?
5.   Location and number of master keys?
6.   Location and number of duplicate keys?
7.   Location of locks and keys held in reserve?

i.   Is a current key control directive in effect and understood?

j.   Are locks changed immediately upon loss or theft of keys?

k.   Are inventories and inspections conducted by the key control officer to ensure compliance with directives? How often?

l.   If master keys are used, are they devoid of markings identifying them as such?

m.   Are losses or thefts of keys promptly investigated by the key control personnel?

n.   Must all requests for reproduction or duplication of keys be approved by the key control officer?

o.   Are locks on inactive gates and storage facilities under seal? Are they checked periodically by guard personnel?

p.   Are locks rotated within the installation at least semiannually?

q.   Where applicable, is the manufacturer's serial number on combination locks obliterated?

r.   Are measures in effect to prevent the unauthorized removal of locks on open cabinets, gates, or buildings?

Guard Forces

a.   Is a guard force provided? Is it responsive to management authority?

b.   Indicate authorized and actual strength, broken down by positions.

c.   Have there been changes since the last survey in either the authorized or actual guard force strength?

d.   Is present guard force strength commensurate with the degree of security protection required?

e.   Is the use of guard forces reviewed periodically to assure effective and economical use?

f. Is supervisory responsibility for guard force operations vested in the security officer?

g. Is a guard headquarters provided?

h. Does the guard headquarters contain control equipment and instruments of all alarm, warning, and guard communications systems?

i. Are guards familiar with the communications equipment used?

j. Does the guard headquarters have direct communication with local municipal fire and police headquarters?

k. Do members of the guard force meet the minimum qualifications standards?

l. Are guards armed while on duty? If so, with what type of weapon?

m. Are the weapons kept in arms racks and adequately secured when not in use?

n. Are ammunition supplies properly secured and issued only for authorized purposes?

o. Is each member of the guard force required to complete a course of basic training and take periodic courses of in-service or advanced training?

p. Are the subjects included in the various training courses adequate? Does the training cover:

  1. Hand-to-hand combat?
  2. Care and use of weapons?
  3. Common forms of pilferage, theft, and sabotage activity?
  4. Types of bombs and explosives?
  5. Location of hazardous materials and processes?
  6. Location and use of fire protective equipment, including sprinkler control valves?
  7. Location and operation of all important steam and gas valves and main electrical switches?
  8. Conditions which may cause fire and explosions?
  9. Location and use of first aid equipment?
  10. Duties in the event of fire, explosion, natural disaster, civil disturbance, blackout, or air raid?
  11. Use of communication system?
  12. Proper methods of search?
  13. Observation and description?
  14. Patrol work?
  15. Supervision of visitors?
  16. Preparation of written reports?
  17. General and special guard orders?
  18. Authority to use force, conduct searches, and make arrests?

q. Are periodic examinations conducted to insure maintenance of guard training standards?
r. Are activities of the guard force in consonance with established policy?
s. Is supervision of the guard force adequate?
t. Are general and special orders properly posted?
u. Are guard orders reviewed at least semiannually to ensure applicability?
v. Are periodic inspections and examinations conducted to determine the degree of understanding and compliance with all guard orders?
w. Do physical, functional, or other changes at the installation indicate the necessity for, or feasibility of, (1) establishing additional guard posts, or (2) discontinuing any existing posts or patrols?
x. Is two-way radio equipment installed on all guard patrol cars?
y. Are duties other than those related to security performed by guard personnel?
z. Are guard patrol cars equipped with spotlights?
aa. Does each guard on patrol duty carry a flashlight?
bb. Do guards record or report their presence at key points in the installation by means of (1) portable watch clocks, (2) central watch clock stations, (3) telephones, or (4) two-way radio equipment?
cc. Are guard assignments and patrol routes varied at frequent intervals to obviate an established routine?

Internal Recommendations

a. All terminals should be equipped with safes for the adequate protection of cash and valuable documents.
b. All pickup drivers should be required to make daily settlements of cash and bills to the cashier or duly appointed employee, matching proceeds on driver's manifest returned bills and cash.
c. Change in safe combinations should be synchronized with turnover of personnel holding such data. Alternatively, it should be done once a year, regardless of employment status.
d. Night or weekend carry over of cash in local safes should be kept to an absolute operating minimum (as authorized by management). This can be accomplished by utilizing night depositories.

e. In all new construction of terminals, time clocks should be installed in positions where employees will be channeled through one corridor to provide surveillance and inspection privileges.

f. All office file cabinets containing personnel files or important documents should be secured by locking devices. Cabinets should *not* be marked "Confidential" or "Classified," etc.

g. All company tools should be stamped (power tools on inner plates) and card records maintained for identification in the event of theft.

h. Inventory should be maintained on all materials and parts by purchase order and record control.

i. Direct allocation of parts and materials should be maintained for direct cost and stock purposes.

j. All company owned garage power equipment should be issued through a charge-out system.

k. Work tickets covering both allocation of labor and materials for each vehicle should be posted on an operations cost sheet, etc.

l. Dispensing of gasoline and oil should be controlled by supervision and use of tickets (meter reading versus dip stick versus tickets).

m. All freight picked up, loaded, unloaded and delivered must be checked accurately for proper controls.

n. All company tools should be kept in a secured tool crib.

Dock Recommendations

a. If possible, ignition keys and rings should be removed from all overnight parked trucks and tractors in the yard.

b. All dock areas should be provided with a locked security section for value traffic (with key control confined to supervision and held to minimum allocation).

c. All damaged traffic should be either repaired immediately or placed in a security area.

d. All terminals should reevaluate their respective operations as to the necessity of line drivers entering the premises at more than one point (to building, office, dock, etc.).

e. Carryover or undelivered traffic by pickup and delivery drivers, should be physically checked (bill against traffic) at time traffic is returned to the dock.

f. All strangers wandering about the dock area should be immediately challenged.

g. All interlines traffic should be checked out by an employee.

h. Drivers should not load out or break out their own vehicles.

i. Dock doors should be kept closed at all times when not in use.

j. Dock areas should not be void of supervision during breaks and lunch periods.

k. Traffic should not be stacked near ends of dock or in unlighted areas where ready theft can be accomplished.

l. Tailgate checks should be conducted at random, covering pickup and delivery freight (bills against freight).

m. Closed out line trailers will be sealed by supervision and seals properly recorded.

n. Seals should be applied and numbers recorded on all empty trucks and trailers moving between terminals.

Perimeter Building Protection

a. All exterior doors with hinge installations on the outside should be changed to inside mountings, or have the pins spot-welded to prevent easy entry.

b. All doors protecting a secured area, where excessive space exists between door and casing, should be either shimmed or have a flange cover installed to prevent latch manipulation.

c. Poles or structures of any nature erected near a building, and which might provide a roof approach, should be hooded or fenced to prevent access (flood lights will also protect approach).

d. All dock doors should be periodically checked for operational security, and repaired as conditions warrant. Docks not equipped with doors should be installed with roller screens and hooks for security of doors not in use.

e. All exterior or security doors should be re-keyed every two years or as conditions warrant (evaluate use of many keys versus one master key.)

f. All buildings should be installed with roof lighting adequate for both security and safety in yard and immediate dock operations.

g. All office or security areas where classified or value documents are stored should check for security breaches such as unbarred windows at ground level, skylight openings, etc.

Perimeter Terminal Protection

a. All terminals should be protected by perimeter fencing, preferably an eight-foot chain link cyclone fence with a three-strand angled barbed wire apron.
b. All existing fences and gates should be repaired as warranted.
c. The number of gates should be kept to an absolute minimum for control purposes.
    1. Gate control by lock, electronic systems, or guard.
    2. Key control (key allocation be kept to absolute minimim).
d. The perimeter fencing should be supported by flood lighting to the extent that any intrusion can be observed.
    1. Spot lighting
    2. Cluster lighting
    3. Flood lighting
e. Intrusion factors
    1. Placing of materials or equipment near fencing, which provides easy entrance or egress, must be discontinued immediately. Present material so stacked must be removed.
    2. Where fence is eight inches or more above ground level, the open area should be closed.
    3. Perimeter fencing should be periodically checked for any security-compromising factors such as joint control of gates, streams running through yard, a breach in fencing, etc.

Yard Operations and Security

a. All pickup and delivery units should be equipped with rear gate padlocks and the key spot welded to ignition key ring.
g. Employees should not be allowed to park their automobiles within the operating yard area.
c. If company parking is permitted in adjacent yard area, car control can be realized through assignment of company windshield stickers.
d. Loaded or partially loaded units parked in the yards at night should be protected by seals. Local seal records to be maintained.
e. On completion of duty, where possible, all ignition keys to tractors and trucks should be removed from units and turned into dispatcher, who will place such in locked glass cabinets and release on an as needed basis.

f.   Yard traffic flow should be confined and channeled through specific gates. Gates in use should be reduced to an absolute operating minimum.

g.   All strangers or questionable units in the yard area should be immediately investigated on observation.

h.   All loaded or partially loaded units should be parked in lighted yard area to fullest extent possible.

i.   In instances where high-value cargo is parked overnight in the yards, units should be parked close to operations and provided with door padlocks and pin locks.

j.   Loaded units should not be parked at points away from terminal where adequate protection is not provided.

k.   In yards having fence and gate protection, gates should be so operated to provide the maximum in-yard security.

l.   Terminals equipped with walkie-talkies will maintain a sign-in and sign-out record control reflecting both unit number and name of employees involved.

4. Warehouse and Dock Security

CARRIER OPERATIONS AND SERVICES

A significant amount of theft takes place before and after transit. Certain security steps taken by the carrier before the shipment leaves the plant or warehouse will help in reducing its vulnerability to theft and pilferage. The basic principles to be observed in establishing procedures for the supervision and accountability of shipments are as follows:

1. Persons physically assembling shipments should not be those responsible for security.
2. Regular spot check of procedures should be maintained.
3. There should be no delay in taking any necessary corrective actions.

The shipper or receiver can take a number of useful precautions when selecting pick-up and long-haul carriers. The shipper or receiver should not choose a pick-up carrier on the basis of price alone, but should examine the carrier's claim history with regard to producing loss and damage and payment of claims. If the former does not have a professional traffic manager, it can obtain skilled traffic advice and service from a traffic consultant, certified carrier, freight forwarder, or customhouse broker.

This chapter is adapted from U.S. Department of Transportation. *Cargo Security Handbook for Shippers and Receivers*. P5200.5. Washington, D.C.: U.S. Government Printing Office, September, 1972; and from U.S. Department of Transportation and the Airport Security Council. *Roles of Packing and Handling in Cargo Security*. Washington, D.C.: U.S. Government Printing Office, September, 1978.

Other factors to be taken into consideration in evaluating management and operation of the carrier are:

1. The amount of business subcontracted and its effect on security
2. Insurance coverage for third party liability and provision for cargo loss and damage liability
3. Reputation in the settlement and payment of claims
4. Efficiency in expediting traffic through the carrier's terminal
5. Limitation of access to the terminal premises and to cargo
6. Adequate lighting, fencing, watchmen, and security systems
7. Provisions of special storage areas for high-risk, high-value cargo
8. Any apparent conditions suggestive of inadequate premises or inefficient management
9. Condition of the carrier's equipment
10. Use of locks and other suitable anti-intrusion devices to restrict access to containers, vans, and railcars
11. Use of alarm systems
12. Provisions for identifying vehicles from the air.

Another important element in affording greater protection to cargo is the precautionary measures the carrier can take in conjunction with the shipper or receiver at the time of shipment and of delivery. Among desirable measures at the time of shipment are:

1. Schedule pickup so that the shipment will arrive at the carrier's terminal during business hours.
2. Provide a continuous seal record or hand-to-hand receipt service.
3. Provide direct routing with a minimum of stopoffs and transfers.
4. Exercise special precautions with respect to high-value merchandise, including armed guard and escort services, delivery to the ship's master or other responsible carrier personnel as determined prior to shipment, and provide reports on the status of the cargo at all stages of transit.
5. To avoid "hold" or "on hand" status, assure that proper documentation accompanies the shipment when it is turned over to the carrier.

Similar precautions should be taken to assure security of the cargo at the point of destination. These should include:

1. Notification of the receiver as to the exact disposition of the cargo

2. Provision for immediate receipt, protection and delivery of high-value cargo.

There will be occasions when the shipper or receiver will be dissatisfied with the carrier's performance in safeguarding goods entrusted to him. In such case, the shipper or receiver may have recourse to the carrier's management, for many of the larger carriers have special shipper or customer relations staffs to receive and investigate complaints from firms using the carrier's services.

There is, however, another means of recourse for the shipper or receiver. The three federal transportation regulatory agencies, Civil Aeronautics Board, Federal Maritime Commission, and the Interstate Commerce Commission, have informal complaint procedures open to shippers and other users of transport services. Under these procedures these three agencies receive, consider, and seek to adjust complaints by users on a wide range of subjects. These subjects include the carrier's cargo security performance. They do not, however, extend to the settlement of claims for loss or damage to cargo, which are subject to the terms of the contract of carriage and the liability rules applicable to the mode of transport in question.

If a shipper or receiver wishes to make use of these procedures, he may direct the complaint to the nearest field office of the agency concerned or he may refer it directly to the agency headquarters in Washington, D.C.

RECEIPT OF SHIPMENTS

The receiving function at a warehouse or terminal is particularly vulnerable to theft and pilferage. In addition to security of the physical area and effective control of personnel, however, there are other safeguards that can improve security. Whether it is a truck or a railcar that arrives with cargo, certain common actions should be taken to assure that the total quantity of merchandise ordered is received, located, and stored safely. An inbound register should be maintained, recording carrier name, commodity, quantity, time of arrival, time of departure, driver's name, truck van or railcar number, and any note of discrepancies. In addition to the inbound register, the receiver may find it advantageous to maintain special control procedures for trucks:

1. Refuse to spot a truck at the dock until receiving personnel are available. A receiving clerk or warehouseman should meet the driver and request the bills of lading or way bills. He should examine these documents against the purchase order

to assure legibility, authenticity, and completeness. All discrepancies should be corrected immediately or the cargo refused.

2. Check the driver to see that he has a valid gate pass and retain it until ready to sign the release. Note the date and hour of release on the pass so that gate security personnel can ascertain normal time lags in travel from the receiving area to the gate.

3. Examine door seals, if called for by the documentation. If the numbers of the seals are at variance with those on the documents, notify the supervisor immediately so that he can notify the shipper and the receiver's security office.

4. Assure that the receiving clerk safeguards the documents through the checking, unloading, and storage process, taking care not to deface or lose them. Require the receiving clerk's signature on the documentation, with date and time information.

5. If a full truckload of the same cargo is moved to a location other than the receiving dock for unloading, do not break the seals until the truck is ready for unloading. Have an employee of the receiver accompany the truck while moving from the receiving area to the unloading point.

6. If a truck cannot be fully unloaded before the close of business, close all doors with suitable locking devices until the next work day.

7. Assure that the supervisor checks the interior of the truck after unloading and before the receiving clerk goes to the next vehicle. Then require the driver to depart immediately.

Similarly, the receiver may wish to maintain special control procedures for railcars:

1. Assure that the documents are legible, complete, and authenticated before issuing the cargo receipt. Require immediate correction of any discrepancies.

2. Inspect the seals on loaded railcars and check against the numbers recorded on the documents. Where possible, assign an employee of the traffic section to check the seals as the cars are spotted by the rail carrier. Notify the carrier of discrepancies immediately.

3. Where discrepancies are found in the seals, make a physical check of the contents of the railcar, with a representative of the rail carrier present. Notify the receiver's security office.

4. If a railcar is spotted in a holding area within the facility and later moved to the unloading area by the receiver's equipment, lock the railcar while in the holding area, using the receiver's locking devices.

5. Assure that the supervisor checks the interior of the railcar after unloading and before the receiving clerk goes to the next railcar. Then close the railcar doors immediately.

The security of sensitive or high-value cargo or other goods requiring storage in security rooms calls for additional safeguards. They should be moved directly from truck or railcar to the security room, and the receiving clerk should require a signed receipt from the security room employees who receive the cargo.

Through lack of supervision, control, and checks during the cargo receiving process, the thief or pilferer gains his opportunity. A large receiving facility is a complex and active place with much movement of merchandise, personnel, and equipment. Unless the devices of the thief are known and adequate controls are maintained, theft is bound to occur. An informed knowledge of the methods of the thief will help the receiver to adopt and apply more effective controls. Some examples follows.

The Partially Emptied Carton

Opening a carton, removing part of the contents, filling the void with some type of waste material, and resealing the carton hides the theft unless someone handling the carton notices the weight differential. The carton, however, is not always resealed. Therefore, the receiving clerk should immediately check the contents and reseal any open cartons. A strange sound from a carton should also alert the receiving clerk. Substitutes such as rocks and bottles that can create sound have been found. If possible, make frequent spot checks at receiving platforms by opening a small percentage of cartons not otherwise subject to loss or damage notations.

Lunch and Break Periods

Leaving the receiving area unguarded and cargo doors open during lunch and break periods is an invitation to the thief to load checked cargo back on the truck. Cargo doors should be closed and at least one employee should remain on duty in the receiving area during these periods.

Pallet Patterns

After pallet pattern and count have been established, a thief who knows pallet patterns can easily change the pattern by putting one less carton per layer on the pallet. Visible evidence of this change is minimal, and several cartons can be extracted from a full truck or carload. These cartons are difficult to see when slipped into dark confines of the truck van or railcar. The receiver should periodically check the pallet load count and inspect the inside of the van or railcar before signing the gate pass or closing the car doors.

Falsified Document

Large quantities of cargo are lost through theft in receiving activities by receiving employees who falsify the quantity received and leave merchandise in the truck or railcar to be hauled out of the terminal. A receiving clerk in collusion with a driver or a rail employee can steal much cargo simply by leaving the quantity he desires in the truck or railcar and certifying on the documentation that the full quantity was received. There are two simple procedures that will do much to control this problem.

1. Require each receiving employee to call the supervisor for a final check of truck or railcar to assure that no merchandise is left in the vehicle. If dock lights are insufficient to illuminate the interior of vans and railcars, the supervisor should use a flashlight or lantern. He should assure that merchandise is not concealed under trash or in the cab of the truck. In damage-free railcars, he should check behind the bulkhead doors.
2. Take a 100% inventory periodically of the stored receipt counts of each receiving clerk for one day's receipts.

Trash

Dropping valuable items into trash bins and later retrieving them from the dump is a common practice. In some cases, the employee has an agreement with the dump attendants. Alert observation of employees by supervisors will do much to prevent this type of theft, but also it is desirable to apply trash collection and removal controls such as establishing timetables for placing trash in bins. Crushing or shredding the contents of trash receptacles prior to removal from the premises will discourage thieves from depositing stolen items in refuse.

Lunch Boxes, Clothes, Lockers, and Automobiles

A "search and seize" agreement signed by employees and enforced by periodic checks can do much to dampen the thief's desire to try these methods of concealment.

Trailers

Unattended trailers and trailers remaining overnight at a receiving point offer an excellent means for the illegal removal of merchandise. Failure of supervisors to make at least one check of each trailer during unloading and, when empty before releasing it, can result in the loss of an entire trailer load. Simply by signing the documents and the cargo receipt, a receiving employee may be able to steal an entire trailer without bringing it to the receiving area. This type of theft can be prevented when supervisors insist on checking each carrier vehicle before release. When trailers are left unattended by receiving personnel, the driver has a blank check for loading cargo. Lock or seal empty and unattended trailers remaining overnight or for weekends or holidays to prevent them from being filled with stolen goods.

Pallet Exchange

If there is collusion between the receiving employee and the driver, empty pallets can be quickly loaded into the van to conceal cargo. Falsifying the cargo receipt showing that the entire quantity was received will cover up the theft. Close supervision is the only answer.

Serious Oversight

A few cartons used to support the end of an unloading conveyor can be conveniently left on the truck. If noticed by receiving personnel, the driver claims that it was an oversight. Checking carrier vehicles before release can prevent this type of theft.

Seal Switches

If seals are left in a readily accessible place, carrier personnel can steal them, break the existing seal, and substitute a stolen one after going to another area and loading illicit cargo before going to the perimeter gate. There are cases where a receiving employee has furnished to the driver in collusion a second seal, the number of which has been entered on the gate pass. This seal is placed on the door of the vehicle after illicit cargo has been loaded elsewhere.

TECHNICAL INNOVATIONS

The growing incidence of cargo theft has led manufacturers of security equipment to give particular attention to the development of devices that can be applied to reduce security hazards. There are now available an encouraging number of new devices that can be used to good effect in the shipper's and receiver's terminal areas. These devices fall into four categories:

1. Access control systems
2. Surveillance systems
3. Locks and seals
4. Alarm system components

New access control systems include:

1. A positive identification system based on an electronic reading of an individual's hand geometry.
2. A laser access control system operating through use of an encoded personnel identification card. The laser provides control by comparing the code on the card with that punched into the recording machine by the employee.
3. A laser hologram locking device which will unlock a door for 90 seconds when the employee's encoded card matches the information punched in the employee keyboard.
4. A remote controlled electric lock to swing open gates up to 20 feet wide.
5. A remote control steel lock that fits standard borings.
6. A double-bolt police lock of heavy construction that moves bolts or locking bars into both right and left-hand door frames and keeps the door secure even after hinge pins have been removed.
7. A boxcar door lock using a brace bar with heavy steel fittings and pick resistant pin tumbler cylinder.
8. A trailer king-pin lock that prevents unauthorized hook-up by a tractor.
9. A keyless padlock and seal for trucks, railcars, and containers. The lock must be destroyed to open.

Among new developments in alarm systems are:

1. A laser intrusion alarm system for perimeter protection. This system throws a fence of laser pulses about a given area and actuates an alarm if the beam is broken at any point.
2. A mobile long-range cargo protection device, which can be installed in trucks, containers, etc., and transmits an alarm to security personnel or a central station.
3. A blanket-type of alarm, which is placed over boxes or cartons and transmits an alarm to a central station if either the blanket or the boxes are disturbed.
4. Motion detection devices that fill an enclosed area with a pattern of ultrasonic waves or microwaves and transmit an alarm if an object moves in that area.

New surveillance systems include:

1. A proximity operated surveillance camera with no external connections and which takes multiple pictures of any movements within 10 to 30 feet.
2. A weatherproof, tamper-resistant surveillance camera with a 50-foot range at night and a 1-mile range in bright sunlight.
3. A computerized facility surveillance system with a stored program digital computer and central monitoring station. The system continuously interrogates up to 10,000 points of interest and notifies the user of any undesirable conditions by printout.
4. Night-vision devices, including a low light-level television camera that produces a daylight picture at nighttime illumination levels, and a direct-viewing device similar to a small telescope, to which a television camera with special eyepiece lens may be attached.

New developments in the area of locking and sealing devices include:

1. A dead bolt lock and a highly sensitive battery-power electric alarm that actuates a siren if an attempt is made to force entry.
2. Magnetic locks, with a magnetically coded key, which must bring both magnetic tumblers and conventional pin tumblers into a uniform shear line before the core will rotate in the cylinder.

DOCUMENTATION

Much of the cargo loss can be traced to poor documentation practices attributable to the volume of paperwork necessary to control both large and small shipments. Nevertheless, documentation is one of management's most important methods for controlling cargo handling and combatting the increasing sophistication of thieves and pilferers. To reduce cargo theft, shippers and receivers should be familiar with the security hazards associated with documentation and the ways in which documentation practices can be improved to increase cargo security.

The purpose of documentation is simple. Documentation gives the characteristics of the cargo, tells how, when, and where a shipment is to move, provides accountability, and forms a basis for carrying out the financing of individual shipments. Documentation, while essential to the movement of cargo, tends by its very nature to expose the cargo it covers to risk of theft. It creates serious security hazards that can be minimized only by stringent control measures.

Accessibility

Many persons have almost unlimited access to the detailed information required to document cargo shipments. The origin, carrier, route, destination, description of commodities, weight cube, value, and time of shipment can be obtained from various shipping documents. The large number of document-processing points associated with each shipment magnifies the problem. Because of easy access to detailed information, shipments can easily be set up for theft and pilferage by company or carrier employees or even by outsiders.

Errors

Errors in documentation constitute a security hazard because they lead to cargo theft. The large number of subsidiary documents that duplicate data found on source documents often contain errors in transcription. Consequently, shipments are misrouted, delayed, or frustrated. The cargo often ends up lying unattended and unaccounted for in terminals, piers, or warehouses where it becomes a target for thieves. The longer cargo is delayed at any given point along its route the more susceptible it is to theft.

Falsification

Company and carrier employees can falsify documents and steal cargo without the theft being readily detected. This is particularly true when large volumes of cargo are being shipped and supervisors are lax in their duties. The spot audit is a useful safeguard against falsified documents.

Late Submission

Failure of shippers and receivers to forward documents promptly to the necessary parties delays the processing of cargo, and cargo delayed in transit is extremely vulnerable to theft.

There are a number of practical measures that shippers and receivers may find advisable if they wish to reduce theft and pilferage caused by poor documentation practices.

1. Maintain a continuing review of the company's documentation procedures and change them where necessary to improve cargo security.
2. Analyze records of incidents and losses to determine causes and direct necessary corrective action.
3. Limit access to documentation. Maintain strict controls over the storage and distribution of invoices, shipping orders, manifests, and other vital materials.
4. Avoid wide dissemination of documents. Do not make excess copies of documents. Discourage transmission of information by telephone or telegram, particularly concerning high-value items.
5. Transcribe information carefully from source documents to subsidiary documents and check the transcription closely.
6. Forward shipping documents promptly, especially those needed at foreign destinations.
7. Limit the number of persons having knowledge of cargo shipments.
8. Maintain strict control of information on the shipment's routing, time of dispatch, time of arrival, and carrier.
9. Give security personnel advance notice of cargo requiring surveillance and protection. Inform the carrier when special protective services are required on its part.
10. Ensure that documentation procedures provide for a clear audit trail of all cargo shipped and received. Require cargo checkers to use self-inking identification stamps to facilitate audit by overcoming the problem of illegible signatures on receipts. Maintain close control of such stamps.
11. Inspect cargo immediately upon receipt. Note shortages on receipt documents and notify carrier. If theft is suspected, notify the proper law enforcement authorities.

12. Enclose a packing list in each shipping container or package, if practicable, to facilitate prompt and complete survey if pilferage occurs. Do not put the packing list on the outside of the container or package.
13. Select documentation employees carefully, ensure thorough training, including instruction in the security hazards of documentation, and require close supervision.

TERMINAL SECURITY INSPECTION

The effective security director will never rest on his laurels after completing his security plan and training curriculum. He will realistically take note of the fact that problems within the industry change from time to time. A constant updating of the security program can best be accomplished by occasionally conducting an inspection. The following form, developed during the Cargo Theft Program at the National Crime Prevention Institute, Louisville, Kentucky, by consultant Harlan Flinner, is an excellent tool for such purposes.

The thoughtful security director needs to constantly monitor all areas of the overall security plan. It means setting up a checklist of possible problem areas which he foresees as troublesome. As a result of this forethought, many security directors have a tendency of developing a form of "tunnel vision" and often miss problems developing in so-called "safe" areas. A checklist of the type suggested here is of great importance to pick up on areas that are too easily overlooked. Setting a regular schedule to cover this checklist is all that is necessary; everything else follows logically. Potential problem areas are being monitored on a regular basis, and small isolated areas are routinely covered. If vigilance is the watchword of all security, this check list is an excellent systematic method of maintaining that vigilance.

TERMINAL SECURITY INSPECTION REPORT

_____ Terminal

_____ Date

_____ Inspector

PURPOSE: A periodic security check should be made of each terminal to determine whether standard security and operating procedures are being followed: to check the handling of freight, vulnerability of the terminal to theft by outsiders: the condition of the fencing and lighting, to provide a vehicle for evaluating the overall security of the terminal, and to make possible specific recommendations.

1. TERMINAL BUILDING (Exterior)
    a. Condition of the building _____
        _____

    b. Outside doors _____
    c. Windows clean and in good repair? _____
    d. Lighting _____
    e. Company identification sign _____
    f. Condition of parking area _____
    g. Employee and guard cars parked in proper parking area? _____

2. TERMINAL BUILDING (Interior)
    a. Reception area for visitors? _____
    b. Condition of offices _____
        _____

    c. Condition of store rooms and supply rooms _____
    d. Arrangements for janitorial/cleaning services _____
        _____

    e. Condition of restrooms _____
3. TERMINAL OFFICE
    a. What are bank deposit arrangements and/or are they satis-
        factory? _____
    b. How are paychecks distributed? _____
        _____

    c. Checks and drafts secured at all times? _____
    d. Petty cash locked up? _____
    e. Is a safe available? In use? _____
    f. Are keys assigned? _____
        _____

    g. Are keys redeemed if key personnel leave? _____
        _____

    h. Are locks changed as warranted? _____
    i. D/R file _____
    j. Term 64 file _____
    k. Term 51 file _____
    l. Pud manifest file _____
    m. Summary manifest file _____
    n. Photo file _____
    o. Fingerprinting equipment _____
    p. Fingerprinting policy compliance _____
    q. Polaroid camera _____
    r. Photographic policy compliance _____

4. CITY DRIVE CHECK-IN
    a. Non-Delivery Report (Term 31) used properly? _____

    b. Over/Damage Report (Term 31) being used properly? _____

    c. Do bills of lading reflect driver's signature and number of
        pieces picked up? _____
    d. Tally sheets attached to bills in the morning? _____

    e. Tally sheet attached to bills when they are turned in? _____

    f. Exceptions being listed in accordance with company policy?
        _____

5. OS&D RECORDS
    a. Shortage files being properly maintained? _____
    b. "ALL SHORT" bills filed in pre-twx file? _____
    c. "ALL SHORT" Bills reported on (Term 80) Control Report?
        _____

    d. Security Reports made to Regional Security Chief? _____
        _____

    e. Over freight processed per policy? _____
    f. Any bills over 30 days old on the Control List? Why? _____
        _____

    g. Refused shipments properly safeguarded? _____
        _____

6. DOCK AREA
    a. What is general appearance of dock? _____
        _____

    b. Is the dock striped? _____
    c. Are doors and bays clearly identified? _____
    d. Adequate storage for OS&D freight? _____
        _____

    e. Hot room (or cage) available and in use? _____
    f. Are any dock lights burning during daylight hours? _____
    g. Are dock door locks in good condition? _____
        _____

    h. Fire extinguishers available? Inspected? _____

    i. Recooping equipment available? _____

    j. Are there any damaged shipments on the dock? _____

    k. Are OWB shipments written up promptly and placed in OS&D

        bay? _____

    l. Seal procedures
        (1) Seal procedure being followed? _____

        (2) Are seals adequately controlled? _____

        (3) Discrepancies reported to supervisors _____
    m. General condition of trailers and loads during this inspection

    n. Trash receptacles available? In use? Need emptying? _____

    o. Reward posters displayed on bulletin board? _____

    p. Are locks assigned to city units? Policy being followed?

7. FREIGHT BILLS PROCEDURES
    a. Bill boxes available on dock? _____
    b. Freight bills handled in accordance with established procedures?

    c. Does break-out man account for all bills given him? _____

    d. Are "security shipments" given proper treatment? (firearms,

        clothing, etc.) _____

    e.   Are shortages, overages and damaged freight brought to fore-man's attention _____

8. GUARD SERVICE
    a.   Hours of service? _____
    b.   Written reports submitted by guard? _____
    c.   Are there written instructions for the guard? _____
        _____
    d.   Is the service adequate? Specific problem areas? _____
        _____
    e.   Is the guard performing other than security-related duties?
        _____
    f.   Is supervision by guard company adequate? _____
        _____
    g.   Are complaints processed to a satisfactory and speedy solution?
        _____
    h.   Are emergency phone numbers available? _____

9. YARD AREA
    a.   Yard fenced? _____
    b.   Fence condition? _____
        _____
    c.   Grass kept cut on either side of fence? _____
        _____
    d.   Are gates locked at night? _____
    e.   Are high value loads protected? _____
    f.   Signs posted on or near gates prohibiting cars from entry?
        _____
    g.   Is employee access controlled? _____
    h.   Lighting
        (1) Adequate? _____
        (2) Controlled by timer? _____
        (3) Any burned out? _____
        (4) Would additional lights help? _____
    i.   General condition of yard _____
        _____
        _____

10. MAINTENANCE AREA
    a.   Gas pumps locked when the terminal is shut down? _____
        _____

   b.   Fire extinguishers available? Inspected? _____

   c.   Maintenance work area orderly? _____

   d.   Appear well organized? _____

   e.   Parts and tools properly secured? _____

   f.   Inventory method used? _____

_____

_____

This report was discussed with _____ by _____

at _____ on _____ 19__.

SECURITY INSPECTION REPORT
MASTER LOG
YEAR:

TERMINAL	REGION	DATE OF INSPECTION

5. Packaging, Pallets, and Containers

Shipping goods in the right kind of package or container is essential to good cargo security. Good shipping practice requires that packaging be suitable to protect cargo against all hazards of transportation, and theft has become a serious hazard. Inadequate packaging is not only a major reason for damaged shipments, but weak or damaged packaging invites pilferage by making it easy to steal the goods. Most often goods are stolen from broken packing cases in small quantities either in the warehouse or during cargo-handling operations.

There are a number of precautions that shippers and receivers may take to curb losses by increasing difficulty and risk for the thief or pilferer.

1. Select shipping containers strong enough to protect the load from damage and to hold together without breaking open under stress or rough handling.
2. Select shipping containers that are so difficult to breach and closes so tightly that the thief must destroy the case to get at its contents.
3. Reinforce heavy shipments with strap, normally applied girthwise.
4. Examine wooden containers to assure that all nails are driven home and reinforced strapping used.

This chapter is adapted from U.S. Department of Transportation, *Cargo Security Handbook for Shippers and Receivers.* P5200.5. Washington, D.C.: U.S. Government Printing Office, September, 1972; and from U.S. Department of Transportation and the Airport Security Council. *Roles of Packing and Handling in Cargo Security.* Washington, D.C.: U.S. Government Printing Office, September, 1978.

    5. Avoid using second-hand packaging materials where possible. Marks of previous nails and straps and obliterated addresses make it difficult to determine on inspection whether pilferage has occurred.

    6. Adopt the unitized load principle through use of pallets and van containers to the greatest extent feasible.

The object of the unit load principle is to give greater speed, security, flexibility and economy to cargo movement by consolidating small packages into unitized loads of optimum size for the use of mechanical cargo-handling equipment. The main applications of the unit load principle are the pallets and van container.

The pallet affords security to cargo by assembling small packages in units held to the pallet by heavy strapping and various forms of covering. Consolidation in a palletized unit reduces the danger of loss or pilferage of individual packages. To reach a package, the thief ordinarily must cut the strapping or slash the covering or otherwise leave visible evidence of having disturbed the load. There are several variant forms of palletization:

    1. Consolidation of packages on a standard wood, plastic or fiberboard pallet secured by strapping.

    2. Consolidation of packages in a fiberboard container sealed and strapped to a skid.

    3. Consolidation of packages on a standard pallet, with the load secured by transparent shrink wrapping—a heavy plastic coating formed to the shape of the load by application of heat and by consequent shrinkage upon cooling.

The van container normally offers an even greater measure of security to cargo. Its security attributes are substantial because:

    1. It usually is constructed of steel, aluminum, or plywood; it is difficult to break without leaving visible marks.

    2. It can be padlocked and sealed, affording security equal to that of truck trailers and railcars. If seals of good quality and design are used, their removal is difficult without signs of tampering.

    3. Entire pallets can be accommodated in the van container. This materially increases the degree of protection against pilferage afforded to the goods.

    4. Containers are adapted to intermodal movement and can be transported door-to-door with minimum delay and opening

for inspection of the contents. Each opening thus eliminated reduces opportunities for theft.

Experience has shown that theft or pilferage is most likely when containers are open at the shipping and receiving dock. This calls for the same security procedures for personnel, documentation, and physical controls as for trucks. Pilferage while containers are en route is most likely if the container has been damaged or is not properly maintained. Proper attention to sealing, with use of reliable, tamper-proof seals and maintenance of accurate seal records, including noting seal numbers and the reasons for any breaking of seals, will do much to reduce the incidence of pilferage en route. Good maintenance practices are the first line of defense against such pilferage, and the shipper should be careful to reject a damaged or defective container if it is offered for the transportation of his cargo.

PACKING CONSIDERATIONS

FORCE is the genesis of most loss and damage to product and shipping containers. A primary function of protective packing is to eliminate or inhibit the action of destructive force. Inadequate packing design can result in loss and damage. The ideal package provides proper safety and security, avoiding excesses that do no more than increase cost. The shipper must know the packing needs of the product in order to deliver it securely.

Arriving at the desired level of protection necessitates intelligent evaluation of a product in relationship to the various hazards of trans-portation. This chapter is intended to assist shippers and carriers by suggesting sound packing guidelines and practices.

Carriers have rules and regulations on packing and handling, which the shipper should be aware of when preparing goods for shipping. These rules and regulations are published in the tariffs of the carriers. Terms and conditions, some of which limit the liability of the carrier for loss and damage, appear in the contract of carriage, such as the bill of lading. Shippers should also be aware that most carrier packing regulations pertain to the exterior shipping container, not the interior packaging.

Packing includes the exterior shipping container, closure system, and when necessary, blocking, bracing, cushioning, waterproofing, strapping, and container marking. The container alone cannot be blamed for all losses or damages. Inadequate blocking, bracing and cushioning, or none at all, may also be major causes of losses or damage. Efficient use of available packing aids will improve the shipper's economic posture through secure delivery of his product.

By experience, inspection, and common sense the shipper should know the more obvious hazards against which the goods require protection. For instance, breakage, which is of major concern for fragile articles, requires only casual consideration in the case of soft goods. If the product is an instrument, machinery, or a special device, specifications of the component materials should be obtained in order to determine the extent of protection needed.

Method of product distribution should be considered in determining the type of packing needed. Packing designed for point of sale frequently imposes criteria different from those applicable for an item intended for additional treatment or multiple movements before point of sale.

Knowledge of port conditions and facilities to be encountered is a primary requisite for overseas shipping. Savings may be gained on export goods by dispatching in a domestic container to a seaport, where the merchandise is then repacked for overseas transportation. Goods exported to undeveloped areas of the world usually need greater protection than goods shipped to industrialized countries.

Packing must be styled to the modes of transportation to be used and the market being served.

Price of product is a determining factor as to amount of funds available for packing, since competitive pricing is intense. Value in this context is set by appearance and quality of product at point of sale. A penny unwisely saved in packing may reduce product salability.

Energy Considerations

The type of energy and forces encountered in transportation causing the most damage are mechanical and chemical in nature.

Mechanical energy, arising from movement, exists in all modes of transportation. Abrupt starts and stops and the vibrations and jolts of vehicles are potentially destructive forces. Handling forces, these involved in loading and unloading, are significant. Some may be applied accidentally, some maliciously. In any event, the affected package may be ripped open, exposing it to damage, theft, or loss. Adverse storage forces most commonly experienced are those resulting from the crushing effect of superimposed weights through stacking.

Chemical energy affecting shipments is chiefly the result of contamination by foreign materials or weathering from external conditions, such as humidity, rain spray, extreme heat, and cold.

These tend to cause breakdown of the container and deterioration of unprotected contents. Exposure resulting from packing failures can cause goods to be susceptible to damage, theft, or loss.

Mechanical forces in movement of product are counteracted by the use of rigid containers and bracing and cushioning. Chemical forces are counteracted by cleaning the product prior to packing and using water-resistant containers and waterproof barrier materials.

Shape of Product

Irregularly shaped items, especially those with projections of any size, generally need more intricate blocking than regularly shaped pieces. Keeping the article immobile is important. So, too, is the distribution of forces affecting it. Long pieces, particularly when heavy, generate great stress on the ends of containers. Problems are increased when odd-shaped, heavy items must be cushioned as well as blocked. The general solution is to even out the surface with pads and blocking.

Weight and Size

Energy developed by the abrupt stopping of an object in motion is directly proportional to its weight. Therefore the weight of the item is most important in relation to blocking and cushioning requirements. As the item is studied, consider the distribution of the weight in connection with size and bearing areas. Concentrated weight should be distributed, where necessary, over a larger area by transferring it from one container face to the edges or corners of the container by the use of blocks at the ends of the item.

Strength and Fragility

Many items are rugged enough or of such a nature as to withstand most transportation forces, with the result that packing functions primarily are for material handling purposes.

Articles which need some form of cushioning are classified as fragile. The amount of cushioning needed is determined by the ability of the piece to withstand shipping and handling forces.

When fragile components of an item cannot be removed from an otherwise rugged article, the entire unit must be treated as fragile, even though this may result in a large, cumbersome pack.

If disassembly is desirable for packing, it should not be done until it is known that reassembly requires no technical skills or special tools.

Types of Loads

Loads are classified as "easy," "average," and "difficult" in terms of the degree of support they give to the faces of the container. Single items capable of completely supporting all faces of a package are classified as easy loads. A shipment of radios, shoes in boxes, packaged hardware—all transmitting vigorous support to the faces of the box—are characterized as average loads. Clothes, wigs, bolts of cloth, machine parts of varied and irregular shapes—since they obviously do not uniformly support the faces of the package—are characteristically difficult loads. Patently then, a shipper who gives no consideration to the nature of the load in selecting packaging for shipment, will frequently expose the cargo to unnecessary damage.

INDICATORS OF WEAKNESS

It is to be observed, that weaknesses in packing will be common to more than one package. Shippers should evaluate their packing through experience tests to assure that their goods in movement are bearing up as well as expected.

Load Bulge

A supplemental problem, associated with load type and general carton quality, is load bulge, of which there are three groupings: filling, compression, and settling. Briefly (since the matter is rather obvious), and over-loaded carton of loose wearing apparel bulges by overstuffing; a carton with side bulges caused by over-tightening of straps bulges by compression; settling is self-evident. But while bulging weakens a carton, its greatest detriment is to handling and to loose unit loading in particular.

Load Collapse

The opposite of load bulge is the caved-in or collapsed load, which reveals itself in a crease or crush inward of at least one of the faces of the carton. While container cave-in, like bulge, causes loose loads, its greater significance is that it evidences an oversized box for the load, inadequate interior packing, compression, or the container being hit. Care in the selection of the carton to be used reduces the risk of such failures.

Inadequate Interior Packing

There are no published commercial specifications as to what constitutes adequate interior packing. How goods are blocked, braced, and cushioned within the carton is a judgmental responsibility of the shipper. They should be packed so that they cannot move. Any item that can move within a container invariably damages itself, the container, or both.

Improper Closure

Improper closure occurs when the top and bottom flaps are not tight together and square. This results from poor or inadequate application of closure devices, such as staples, adhesive or tape.

TYPES OF CONTAINERS

The weight of the product to be packed is a major factor in the selection of the proper carton to be used in transportation. Avoid loading cartons beyond their rated capacity.

American-made cartons usually show the gross weight limit in the manufacturer's certificate on the bottom of the carton. Weighing the carton and comparing its weight with that of the certificate will show if the container is overweight and, therefore, improperly packed.

Bags and Sacks

Many bulk products are economically shipped in flexible containers, such as bags and sacks. The chief advantages of these are their relatively light weight in relation to the weight of the contents they carry, plus flexibility, filling and handling ease, minimum storage space required, and low cost of manufacture.

There are five basic types of bags and sacks: cotton mailing bags; cushioned paper sacks; burlap, cotton and waterproof textile bags;

polyethylene or other plastic materials; and the paper shipping sack. This latter sack is the most common and can be manufactured to suit a wide range of bulk products.

Aside from selection of the appropriate shipping sack, proper storage and filling and handling strongly influence the serviceability of these containers.

Brittleness of paper sacks causes ruptures and usually results from storing bags in too dry an atmosphere. Paper sacks should be stored in areas of high humidity.

The wrong filling equipment can damage paper shipping sacks. Care must be exercised also in properly closing the mouth of the bag. Common problems involving closures are poor stitching, not allowing sufficient gathering for good application of wire ties, and failure to tuck valves into their correct position. Regardless of how well the bag construction and filling are performed, sacks cannot withstand certain mishandling practices.

Certain precautions should be observed when handling sacks:

1. Sacks should be lifted with hands under both ends and carried at waist height or on the shoulder.
2. When stacking on platforms, skids, or two-wheeled hand trucks, sacks should be laid on flat sides. Use only trucks with wide and extended noseblades.
3. Examine every sack in bottom tier before lifting. Carry damaged sacks with torn side up.
4. Maintain plenty of aisle space to prevent snagging.
5. Avoid dragging sacks on floor or over other cargo.
6. Drop sacks only on the flat.
7. Don't jab bags with truck blades.
8. Avoid bags overhanging on pallets.
9. Don't walk over or dig heels into sacks.

Bales

Bales are either compressed, such as those used for raw cotton, wool, and scrap paper, or loose, for shipment of soft goods including textiles, clothing, furs, rugs, and so forth.

Products susceptible to dirt, water, chafing, cutting, and hook damage require interior protection, usually in the form of waterproof barrier material, fiberboard wrap and, to minimize hook damage, "ears" at the corners of the bales. Handling and cautionary markings should be stenciled legibly and large on the bales.

Cans, Pails, and Drums

Cans, pails, and drums are adaptable to many uses. For instance, they can handle liquids, semiliquids, powder, and flaked and granular chemicals. They provide considerable protection for fragile and precious instruments. They are common for the handling of dangerous, flammable, corrosive, and acid materials.

These containers are dustproof, waterproof, and may be made vaporproof. They likewise serve as a deterrent to pilferage. Construction may be of fiberboard, paperboard, paper composite, plywood, steel, aluminum, or plastic. A number of possible closure techniques are available.

Cans, pails, and drums are broadly classified as exterior or interior containers and reusable or nonreusable.

The propensity of the consumer is to reject dented cans, even if they are not ruptured. The principal causes for can denting are oversized shipping containers and poor closures. In the case of a carton, the fault is the result of not tightly butting and squaring the top flaps, or too large a box.

Dented pails and drums usually are less vulnerable to consumer resistance, unless the container is ruptured. Here, too, the cause is container shifting, resulting in body, seam, or lip dents. Tight loading and adequate dunnage minimizes load movement.

Wood Boxes

The durability of wood and its ability to withstand shock and impact stresses are valid reasons for selecting wood containers. Woods used in container construction are either soft or hard. The characteristics of the soft woods are that they do not split easily and have moderate nail-holding power, strength, and shock resistance. The hard woods have a greater tendency to split. Wood grain often deflects nails, but hard woods have greater nail-holding power, strength, and shock resistance then soft woods.

Nailed Wood Boxes

There are seven basic styles of nailed wood boxes, which are distinguishable by their cleats or lack of cleats.

The chief advantage of these containers are:

1. Maximum protection to contents against damage due to puncture, distortion, and breakage.

2. Ability to support loads during transit and storage.
3. They contain difficult loads without undue distortion.
4. Adaptability to complex wood blocking and bracing.
5. Adaptability to varying strengths by adjusting the style of box, thickness of material, and group of wood.
6. They are easily workable and of simple construction.

Disadvantages of nailed wood boxes are:

1. High tare weight to cube
2. Not water-tight
3. Tendency to wrack

Tables describing board thicknesses for the different wood groups, box styles, load types, and weight of contents are available. In general, when the weight of the contents is less than 100 pounds, 1/2" thick boards are used for the sides, tops, and bottoms. Board thicknesses increase to 3/4" when the weight of the load is 400 to 600 pounds. End boards are 1/4" thicker than those of the girth. For heavier loads, cleats should be about 3/4" by 2 5/8". These boxes should be reinforced with strapping.

Cleated Panel Boxes

Cleated boxes have an assortment of uses. They may be used as complete containers or for paneling items secured to a load-bearing base. The panels may be of plywood, fiberboard, or paper-overlaid veneer.

These containers may fail when overloaded, installed with insufficient intermediate cleats, or split or broken cleats, or if assembled panels are improperly nailed. Avoid reused boxes.

Apply strapping over cleats and hold straps in position with staples.

Wirebound Containers

Wirebound boxes are resilient engineered containers, deriving both strength and economy from the substitution of steel wire for a considerable portion of wood. The sides, top, and bottom are stapled to several binding wires and are fastened to a framework of cleats at each end by staples driven astride the end binding wires. The ends are nailed, stapled, or wired to the framework to form the container.

In using these boxes, care should be exercised to select the box designed for the type of load to be shipped.

Line boxes with waterproof barrier material when necessary. Apply strapping when pilferage is a factor, or when the load weighs over 150 pounds.

Pallet boxes and crates are containers having an attached base designed to carry substantial loads and to be easily and efficiently handled by mechanical handling equipment. The sidewalls and base of this container may be of tight or open construction and may or may not have tops of tight or open construction. This type of packing has grown remarkably since the end of World War II, simultaneously with the development of mechanical handling equipment and the design of high-ceiling warehouses to accommodate heavy floor loading.

The use of lightweight wirebound pallet containers has resulted in substantial economies to the users:

1. By reducing the tare weight and thus transportation costs;
2. By the reduction of cube, permitting the loading of more containers in a given conveyance, thus further reducing transportation costs;
3. By permitting maximum cube utilization in warehousing at origin, as well as at destination and in transportation vehicles.

When requirements are for extreme stacking, pallet containers with corner posts can be designed. Such designs have sustained maximum compression tests of 27,000 pounds to over 30,000 pounds.

Crates—Open and Closed

When an item is too large to be shipped in a box, crating is used. To select the proper crate, it is necessary to consider certain basic factors that may influence the selection.

1. To manipulate a crate without excessive tilting, the size and weight should be limited to 30' by 9' and 11,200 pounds. These weights and measurements permit the crate to be handled by standard material handling equipment. Larger and heavier pieces usually require special handling arrangements with the carrier.
2. Protection requirements depend upon the nature of the contents and handling and shipping hazards. If no protection is required against weathering, use an open crate.

3. Disassembly of item permits a reduction in container cube. However, do not disassemble the item to the point where special tools or personnel are needed to reassemble it.
4. Weight distribution should be such that the center of gravity coincides with the geometric center of the crate. When this is not possible, mark exterior of crate where the points of balance are located.
5. Anchor the load securely to the base of the crate. All loose parts must also be secured within the crate.
6. Clearance of at least 1 inch should be allowed between the item and the interior faces of the crate to allow for container distortion.
7. Bases of crates are designed to support the contents. The two types of bases are the sill base, frequently used to save cube, and the skid base.

Crate design basically conforms to building construction. For instance, studs are vertical frame members; horizontal members are the lower edge pieces of the side and end panels; joists support the top and prevent crushing; sheathing is the shell; floor boards together with load-bearing boards form the flooring; diagonals provide rigidity; and headers are cross members attached to the ends of the skids that hold the skid together.

Unit Loads

Although the unit load is basically designed to reduce packing and material handling cost, it does provide significant benefits in reducing cargo loss and damage when handled properly.

The greatest advantage accrues when the unit load is assembled as early in the transportation cycle as possible and disassembled as late as possible.

In addition to the typical application of the unit load, some units are designed for special purposes such as being reusable and providing pilfer-proof protection. Also, many carriers make available to shippers containers and pallets that are either captive or intermodal.

Fiberboard Containers

Advanced technology in transportation contributes significantly to reduction of hazards of loss and damage. It has made possible the development and use of light-weight, low cost, and easily handled packing, which is exemplified in the fiberboard box or carton.

Although fiberboard is adaptable to a great variety of packaging and packing conditions, five principal factors affect its capabilities:

1. Resistance to compression
2. Strength of score lines (creased edges)
3. Resistance to puncture
4. Ability of the fiberboard to resist the weakening effects of moisture
5. Weight of product to be packed

Resistance to Compression   A carton's capacity to resist compression is, in general terms, inversely proportionate to the length of its corrugations. This principle holds, however, only when the carton is stacked with the corrugations vertical to the base upon which it rests. If the carton selected has corrugations too long to sustain the weight of the merchandise, or if the carton is placed on its side, crushing and the consequent opening of closure is inevitable. The relative humidity is also a factor in determining resistance to compression.

Score Lines (Creased Edges)   If the closures of the carton remain secure, most pressure and breakage will occur along the score lines. Score line joints vary considerably in their capacity to withstand pressure; however, it has been observed that foreign-made cartons, particularly those boxes in which the body joint is lapped and stitched, are the most likely to fail. Handlers should be most pointedly made aware of this fact.

Resistance to Moisture   The effects of moisture on the strength of a box at different relative humidities are variable and should not be relied upon without wire bracing.

SOLUTIONS

The function of the exterior shipping container is to protect its contents and to provide ease in handling. With those objectives, container selection is based upon the physical characteristics of the product: whether it is to be a domestic or overseas shipment, type of load, cost of package versus value of product, its criticality, its weight and cube, and ease of assembly and closure.

Blocking and Bracing

Blocking and bracing is intended to prevent the movement of an item within the container and to transfer the impact of concentrated loads to larger areas or other faces of the container. Although the choice of materials used for blocking and bracing varies widely, from heavy lumber to fiberboard, it must be stiff and strong in relation to the size and shape of the areas against which it will be placed, as well as the size and weight of the contents.

Cushioning

The purpose of cushioning is to absorb the energy of shock and vibration through a gradual but increasing resistance to the movement of the load. The energy is absorbed as the cushion is compressed, resulting in a damping or minimizing of the force on the load.

Cushioning may also be used to prevent rupture of barriers or containers, prevent abrasion, and to absorb liquids, as well as distribute forces.

Waterproofing

Most carriers make every reasonable attempt to protect goods from water damage when they are handled during bad weather. Where it is known or predictable that equipment and facilities are poor, some weathering seems inevitable. Products susceptible to moisture or sweating require waterproof barriers when such exposure is expected. It must be remembered also that certain packing materials absorb and retain moisture. Water, more than any single element, causes fiberboard materials to lose much of their strength, exposing the contents to damage, theft, and pilferage.

Waterproof barriers exclude entry of water (not water vapor) or divert water. Barriers also afford protection against dust, dirt, and other foreign matter. Waterproof barriers take the form of crate liners, crate liners, shrouds, or wraps. The atmosphere within crates lined with waterproof material frequently causes sweating. Condensation is counteracted by desiccants and by providing vents and drainage holes in the crate. Holes should be designed and located so that water runs out of the crate.

Cargo in open-top vehicles may require shrouds. Cars and containers should be inspected for leaks prior to loading.

Closure Systems

Most materials used in packing are supplied by manufacturers and vendors. The function of the shipper thus becomes one of assembling these materials and proper closure of the finished package. Aside from good workmanship in assembling, the type, quality, and skill in performing the closure operation is of paramount importance. The cliché that a shipping container is no stronger than its closure is fundamental to successful packing. This makes it vital that gluing, stitching, taping, stapling, nailing, and the like be as good as the packing.

Moreover, a carrier looking for a packing defense for use in the event of a claim for loss or damage will examine the closure system of a package to determine its adequacy. Too much stress, therefore, cannot be placed on the need for a proper packing closure system.

The first requisite for the shipper is to ensure that the type of closure used is correct for the package: that is, that it meets the needs of the container and contents. The employees performing the closure must be properly trained and provided with correct equipment that is kept in good order. Establish a quality-control procedure, which will monitor the output and ensure that it is in the shipper's interest to analyze his own claims experience to see if he is contributing to losses by failures of his own closure operation.

Strapping

Although strapping is used as a reinforcement for blocking and bracing, its widest use is for reinforcing the exterior shipping container. The principal strapping materials are metal or plastic. Strapping is particularly useful in strengthening wooden boxes and crates and in minimizing nail pull. Strapping adds by about 10% to the strength of a fiberboard box, particularly along the score lines. With an overloaded carton (obviously something to be aovided), the strap is often the difference between failure of the box and successful delivery.

Care in Stacking

As indicated, superimposed weights may result in container crushing. Exercise care, therefore, in stacking tiers squarely, limiting weight of tiers to the stacking strength of packages. Prevent containers from overhanging edges of shelves and pallets. Provide adequate aisle space to prevent damage by material handling equipment.

Markings

Marks identifying the shipment are required on all packages. Distinct, legible, complete, and accurate marks minimize handling errors. If an error occurs, clear markings assist in locating and correcting the mishandling.

ALL old markings, except shipper's and manufacturer's marks, must be obliterated.

In addition to identifying the shipment, all restricted articles must be specifically labeled. When necessary, appropriate cautionary symbols should be applied, located where they will do the most good. Warning marks for international cargo should be in the language of the countries of transit.

Marks revealing the contents are to be discouraged, especially if the item is valuable, desirable, and readily portable. A box that does not advertise its tempting contents is less likely to catch the eye of a potential thief.

Sealing

Where practical, vehicles and containers should be sealed. There are two basic classes of seals: those mainly providing evidence of tampering, and high-security seals.

Proper application of seals to containers and vehicle doors protects shipper and carrier against loss from theft or error. Record seal numbers on shipping documents for purposes of verification.

The value of the seal was demonstrated during a test of 873 rail cars provided with high-security seals. The program reported shortages in 43 cars, of which 39 had undisturbed seals. This demonstrates that the security seal protects the goods while in transit, and that all shortages are not attributable to the carrier.

TRANSPORTATION HAZARDS

The laws of motion cause most damage to goods in transit. It can be said, therefore, that aside from outstanding exceptions such as seawater for marine shipments and atmospheric pressure for air, transportation loss and damage hazards are generally common to all modes. Any variations are principally a matter of degree.

Ocean

Forces at work on cargo aboard a vessel are beyond the control of a shipper but can vary according to such factors as the tightness and security of the load, height of stow, and weight distribution of a given stow, as well as the weight distribution of the cargo throughout the vessel. In addition to the forces generated by the method of ship stowage are the external forces of speed and state of the sea. A combination of these forces may cause the ship to roll, dive, pitch, pant, and vibrate whenever the propeller comes out of the water. All of these events obviously increase the possibility of cargo damage.

Rail

Changes in the direction of force caused by abrupt starts and stops result in load shifting. The condition of the roadbed will influence the degree of vibration. A poor bed, even at minimal speed, results in considerable car sway and load disruption. It cannot be overly emphasized, in loading rail cars, that the load be tight, adequately blocked, and braced. Incomplete layers require support. Dunnage should be used when stacks of containers are of different levels and density. Car doors must also be protected in order to prevent cargo from falling into the opening.

Motor Carrier

Changes in direction of force, caused by abrupt starts and stops, result in load shifting. Vibration, created by the surface over which vehicles travel, may cause damage. A vehicle will sway and jerk, depending upon the condition of the highway, speed, and the cushion action of the vehicle. Loads should be tight, balanced, blocked, and braced to minimize load shifting.

Air

Ground handling of air cargo will experience the forces comparable to those involved in the mode of transportation used to move a shipment to and from an airport. Hazards in the air are primarily the result of changes in atmospheric pressure and temperature.

Handling

The most common cause of damage during handling operations is from dropping of goods. Packages may be manually dropped or fall from handling equipment. Contact between a heavy item and a light piece may result in damage to the light article; this probably would occur on a chute, conveyor, or when a load shifts in a vehicle. Other handling hazards are caused by forklift trucks, broken pallets, and pushing. At some seaports, where nets and slings are used, damage may occur while lifting packages or when they are dumped. Some handling damage may be malicious.

Storage

Weight of superimposed packages in storage may cause crushing. Failure to keep stacks plumb, or allowing them to hang over edges of racks or pallets, causes similar damage. Long-term storage may result in container crushing.

Weathering

Any cargo handled during inclement weather may be subjected to water damage. Cargo moving on open-top vehicles will get wet unless packing is designed for outside storage. Cars and containers should be inspected for leaks prior to loading. Bottom layers of cargo on aircraft unit load devices become wet when not fully covered and/or not supported off the ground during rains.

MARKING AND LABELING

The purpose of marking and labeling is to identify shipments sufficiently to enable carriers to forward them to the ultimate consignee. When marks and labels are not clear or have come off packages, shipments are delayed or misrouted and become prime targets for pilferage and thieves. Only those markings and labels that are necessary to move a shipment should be placed on containers or packages. Old marks and signs should be obliterated.

The following recommended actions can help shippers reduce theft and pilferage caused by poor marking and labeling practices:

1. Do not identify the contents of valuable or easily pilferable shipments such as cameras and portable radios by advertising or other external marks. Company advertising, particularly of well-known brand names and articles attractive to pilferers, is an open invitation to theft of products.

2. Make certain that every shipment is plainly, legibly, and durably marked with the name and address of only one shipper and one consignee before it is tendered to a carrier.

3. Stencil or tag each package or loose piece of freight as required by the carrier's classifications and tariffs.

4. Mark fragile articles with noticeable labels to indicate their fragile nature.

5. Do not order containers with precautionary markings unless they are necessary.

6. Identify shipments consigned "to order" or "COD" by marking each package. Also mark each package with an identifying symbol or number and show it on the shipping order and bill of lading.

7. Show the name and address of the broker or agent at the point of export as well as consignee for export shipments.

8. Attach labels securely with good adhesive.

9. Avoid using secondhand containers if possible. If secondhand containers are used, remove or obliterate all old labels and old markings.

10. Do not use small mimeograph or stencil-type imprinting devices for addressing shipments. Printing by these devices usually results in addresses that are difficult to read.

11. Properly mark containers holding commodities requiring special handling or stowage. This information should also appear on the bill of lading.

12. Provide training classes for employees. Basic training of employees should include loss prevention education with proper instruction regarding marking, labeling, materials handling, obedience to cautionary labels, making notations on bad-order packages, and disposition of such packages, such as where or how they should be repaired.

13. If precautionary markings are necessary, mark containers TOP, UP, THIS SIDE UP, GLASS, KEEP DRY, PERISHABLE, KEEP FROZEN, or other special handling instructions of a similar nature. Arrows should be employed to indicate or supplement the words UP or TOP. These markings should be affixed only when essential. Such markings should not obscure other markings.

14. Instruct forwarders when new markings are required. For
export shipments, consider marking handling instructions
in two languages (particularly that of the country of destination) on the outside of the container. Use of symbols in
international trade is more effective than words.

CONCLUSION

Except for damage resulting from poor packing design or a weakness
of the product, most damage attributable to packing results from
poor closures, overloading, voids, inadequate blocking, bracing,
and cushioning.

When a shipper performs the loading and unloading function of
a rail car, a trailer or a container, he may cause the identical damage
a carrier can cause if rough handling or loose load are permitted or if
the load is not properly blocked and braced.

A shipper should trace cargo movements to determine consistent
patterns of damage. Consistent patterns, clearly indicating faults in the
strength of the product or packing, must be corrected before further
shipping so that unnecessary shipping costs can be avoided.

Clearly these matters are mutual problems of shippers and transportation companies.

Damage to goods in transit means financial loss. Theft or pilferage
resulting from damage or package weakness compounds that loss.
The nature of a product's packing may be a major factor in transportation loss through theft and/or damage.

Reduction of such losses can be accomplished through recognition
and implementation of practical packing guidelines and principles.

This chapter has been prepared as a guide to packing and handling
of goods in transit, to assure them safe, secure delivery. It is not
meant to cover the technical aspects of packing, but to illustrate
packing principles. For further information on the subject, shippers
are strongly urged to obtain the services of a recognized package
testing laboratory or a reputable packaging consultant.

The references that follow are excellent sources for further
guidance in packing and handling.

Federal Transportation Regulatory Agencies

Office of Consumer Affairs, Civil Aeronautics Board, Washington,
D.C. 20428

Office of Informal Complaints, Bureau of Enforcement, Federal Maritime Commission, Washington, D.C. 20573
Bureau of Operations, Interstate Commerce Commission, Washington, D.C. 20423

Publications

Distribution Packaging, Freidman and Kipness
Robert E. Kreiger Publishing Co., 645 New York Avenue, Huntington, N.Y. 11743

Fibre Box Handbook, Fibre Box Association
Obtain from your supplier of corrugated materials or request from the Society of Packaging and Handling Engineers (SPHE).

Packaging For The Small Parcel Environment,
Available from United Parcel Service, or order from SPHE Office.

Principles of Package Development, Griffin and Sacharow
Avi Technical Books, Inc., P.O. Box 831, Westport, Conn. 06880

AMCO 706-121 Engineering Design Handbook Packaging and Pack Engineering, 3/72
Order from Technical Information Service, Department of Commerce, Springfield, Va. 22151

Packaging Production Management, Raphael and Ollson
Rochester Institute of Technology, College of Continuing Education
One Lomb Memorial Drive, Rochester, N.Y. 14623

Functional Plant Planning Layout and Materials Handling, Merle C. Nutt
Exposition Press, Inc. 50 Jericho Turnpike, Jericho, N.Y. 10016

Materials Handling Systems Design, James M. Apple
The Ronald Press Co., 79 Madison Avenue, New York, N.Y. 10016

Societies and Associations

American Management Association
International Material Management Society
Packaging Institute U.S.A.
Society of Packaging and Handling Engineers (SPHE)

6. Motor Carriers

In motor carrier management, have years of conditioning and exposure developed an acceptance level of claim losses? Has a tolerance been developed because published claim loss figures indicate a particular company meets or exceeds the industry average? If there is an acceptance level above zero claim losses, it should be reviewed. In claim losses, whatever management allows will be the level, whether small or large. If a rebirth of the concept of zero claim losses is needed, then this position must be faced squarely and answered. It is hard to motivate a "win" attitude if the opposition is conceded automatic points. Realistically, there will be claim losses, but these losses must be restricted to honest human error or laxity that cause a loss or damage. Knowing that an opportunity or exposure for a claim loss exists and failing to minimize that exposure will surely invite an economic drain of profit dollars.

A second concept is that the staff handling loss prevention must be professional and have the experience and expertise needed to develop and implement system procedures and individual programs tailored to the requirement.

A PROGRAM OF LOSS PREVENTION

Applicant Screening

A business entity is made up of people. If a person with a problem is hired, the business will have a problem. If the problem is a thief, there certainly will be theft. If the problem is lax attitude and unreliable behavior traits, there certainly will be mishandling and damage.

Careful selection, screening, and investigation of each new employee is an integral part of loss prevention. Points to consider in applicant screening include:

1. Any falsification or discrepancies are reasons to investigate and question further.
2. Attitude, past and present.
3. Financial problems.
4. Excessive layoffs, terminations.
5. Criminal activities.

Immediately following the offer and acceptance of employment, each new employee should be fingerprinted and photographed at the hiring facility location and these records forwarded to the loss prevention department for processing and investigation.

In the long range, the quality, honesty, and integrity of employees will be reflected in the reduction of claim losses.

Good applicant screening affects employee morale. Pride in the company and identification with fellow employees are easier if good employees are hired. The desire and motivation to produce and to do a good job are enhanced when a majority of employees personally become a part of a winning team.

Facility Security

Each location must be surveyed for its own particular requirements. Factors that directly affect or potentially influence the facility should be evaluated, including:

1. Criminal theft activities in the community
2. Adjacent businesses and surroundings
3. Socioeconomic patterns of the community
4. Physical access to the facility
5. Operational hours and activity
6. Major type of potential customers

Based on this survey, minimum physical security measures should be considered, such as perimeter fencing, lighting, access control by vehicles and employees or pedestrians, and the use of physical guard service or electronic alarms.

Storage in lock-up rooms for the protection of high value, theft-susceptible freight is a basic consideration.

Private vehicles should be restricted from the terminal yard area whenever possible by providing separated employee and visitor parking. Protection and surveillance of the employees' private cars also are necessary in facility security and will prove that the company is interested and is concerned with the welfare of individual employees.

A terminal security survey checklist should be maintained for each facility, updated at least once a year, and reviewed during visits by loss prevention personnel.

Management Information System

Timely and accurate reporting systems will help to identify the claim loss and damage problem. Two basic types of reporting systems will provide the data necessary:

1. Field reports of known and suspected theft incidents, recording location, dates, times of discovery, description of loss, identifying factors, and narrative remarks provide an information flow.

2. Computer reports on claims filed and paid are helpful analytical data. If data processing reports are not available, sample analysis of manual data can be used.

Information so received should be analyzed to identify the types of commodities lost or damaged, the shippers of those commodities, locations involved, and the dollar value. This will provide visibility to identify problem areas so that intensive investigation can be made of the internal control system and the external factors that are contributing to the loss or damage. In most cases, it will be found that a breakdown in procedure has provided the opportunity for a claim loss to occur. When these exposures are identified, an update or procedure or new controls can be effected to eliminate the opportunity.

Employee Training in Loss Prevention

All employees need to know their specific job duties and what is expected of them. Also, each employee must comprehend the rationale behind his job description. If an employee understands how his job adds to and contributes to the overall operation, he is less likely to question and devise shortcuts that may conflict with the system. This also applies to loss-prevention training and education designed to encourage individual employee involvement in loss prevention. Methods to accomplish education and training include:

1. Posters, using themes and cartoons. Mix the themes between security and proper handling to avoid damages. Posters should be distributed at regular intervals, usually once each quarter.
2. Periodic meetings held both by terminal management and claim prevention personnel.
3. Hand-out reminder pamphlets with a single topic. A driver is only interested in driver reminders—so, too, for office or dock personnel.
4. Special bulletins of interest, such as reprints of newspaper articles and federal and state legislation affecting transportation.

The purpose of education is to heighten the awareness of loss prevention of every employee. If the employee knows the policies, understands the risks if dishonesty is in mind, and realizes the effect on job security, then opportunity, exposure, and carelessness will be minimized as each employee becomes a team member and individually contributes to the goal of loss prevention.

Internal Controls

Probably the biggest singular contributor to claim losses is the failure to follow procedure. Counting and checking procedures are liable for the vast majority of errors, wherein the physical accountability of freight is documented against the controlling documents. A constant review of these procedures will discover the exceptions, failures and, consequently, the exposures. If we examine the shortages, they can occur only when:

1. There is a failure to pick up the correct number of pieces,
2. There is an improper delivery involving either a consignee or connecting line carrier, or
3. Theft.

If we examine the majority of damage claim losses, which are visible damages, they usually result from careless or improper loading or handling.

Several specific internal controls that can minimize exposure to loss and damage are cited below.

1. Random check of city units to inventory freight against documents. Exceptions should trigger investigation of causes.
2. Daily review of delivery receipt exceptions to identify commodities and responsible individuals. Suspicious exceptions should be investigated at once. Many times patterns or trends can be detected and opportunity for theft identified.
3. Trailer seals applied promptly on trailer closeout under supervision ensures integrity. Also, inspection and recording of seals at the time of break prevent undetected entry and loss.
4. Trailer and city unit locks prevent opportunists from theft. It is relatively easy to equip units with locks or to issue locks but, again, usage procedures must be monitored constantly. Many devices for locking and seal locking are available, and should be used on claim loss-susceptible freight.
5. Regular review of source documents—the bill of lading and delivery receipt—will provide insight on the accuracy of checking procedures, the readability of equipment numbers, and the ability to pinpoint responsibility by identification of names or initials.
6. On known high-value commodities or specific shipments, the use of a special stamp or sticker highlights that shipment as loss-susceptible to the person handling it. Procedure on these designated shipments should be that a supervisor is immediately notified when the shipments are to be handled so a supervisor verification of count and handling can be made.

Other specific situations may call for a control procedure tailored for that particular type of shipment. The question is often raised whether such controls are time-consuming and costly or will disrupt the normal operation. This certainly is a consideration, but as a rule, the potential saving versus the uncertainty of susceptible loss is worthwhile in terms of reducing claim losses.

Loss and Damage Investigation

To be effective, active investigation of a known or suspected theft or "mysterious shortage" incident must be carried out immediately upon discovery. This implies that the procedure for detecting and reporting such incidents must be followed up by the responsible supervisor involved. This is also true of reported damage incidents. Immediate investigation is important: probably the source of greatest failure is when time is allowed to lapse because memories dull, management gains a "not concerned" image, and the confidence of the thief or careless employee grows. When a suspicious or known incident is discovered, the worst course that management can follow is inaction. The mere fact that questions are asked and a search is made acts as a tremendous preventive tool because it reflects the concern and awareness of management.

The purpose of active investigation of theft is to:

1. Gather information.
2. Document and confirm the criminal act of theft.
3. Identify the person(s) responsible.
4. Aid in the apprehension and conviction of those responsible.
5. Actively deter future thefts.

Effective investigation is planned, directed by one responsible individual, and documented in a factual manner. It should be aggressive and continuous until brought to a logical conclusion.

Concerned law enforcement agencies and management should be notified immediately. Each facility should maintain a record of the name and telephone number of the person to notify, and all supervisors should have this information. When management reflects a willingness to accept some responsibility for the course of the investigation and is able to gather quickly the necessary source documents and basic facts, then concerned law enforcement agencies will respond with equal vigor.

TYPES OF INDUSTRIAL THIEVES

According to published sources, the nation's bonding company representatives have categorized and described industrial thieves as follows.

True Criminal Type. The genuine, unreformed criminal element to whom larceny is as a normal way of life as breathing. They have no compunctions against stealing to benefit themselves at whatever cost to others. In cases where in-plant thievery is being carried on by a gang, the originator and leading spirit almost always turn out to be a criminal with a prior record.

Susceptible Type. Individuals who are not "true criminals," but are easily led, or who readily succumb to temptation when suddenly faced with financial emergency. Such persons may be only intermittent thieves.

Aggrieved Type. An element which steals to "get even" for some real or fancied wrong, and who sometimes takes the property of others as a "gag" or to "break the monotony." They occasionally turn out to be "pack rats," repetitively stealing, continuously concealing, and not disposing of the loot!

These same sources have also emphasized that "The inclination to steal is not particular to any level of society . . . and the educated person is just as vulnerable to said inclination as the uneducated one!"

In the delivery of freight, a driver is faced on many occasions with taking an exception to the quantity or quality of the shipment. Vague or unqualified exceptions such as "one carton short" or "one carton torn" literally provide the shipper/consignee with a license to claim loss or damage of the highest value. Definitive exception notations are more helpful. If one carton is short, which carton is OS&D looking for? If a carton is torn or crushed, are the contents actually damaged? In most instances the consignee, if asked, can identify which exact carton is short, so the exception notation can read this way. An inspection at the time of delivery will determine if the contents are actually damaged and whether a notation is appropriate with proper description.

Upgrading the quality of exception delivery notations is a professional way of doing business, eliminates the opportunity for unchallenged claims, and provides better information to process and settle just claims. The authority for accepting any delivery exception notation should be a member of management, not the driver. It is management's responsibility to provide service and delivery freight and to guarantee the quantity and quality of freight.

Investigations should always be designed to analyze the weakness that allowed the loss or damage to occur. This is problem definition, and usually just knowing a problem provides the basis to correct it.

Liaison Activities

It is important that loss prevention personnel conduct a systematic program of liaison with various outside agencies, such as law enforcement, other government offices, and associations. This function acquires intelligence data and new security device market data that enables better evaluation of local conditions.

Emergency Action Plans

At the moment of emergency, such as riots, strike action, civil disorder, natural disaster, or bomb threats, rumors and facts are greatly distorted. Such conditions can cause panic or chaotic response, all of which tend to jeopardize operations and possibly expose personnel and facilities to unwarranted danger. Having a prepared emergency action plan available can greatly lessen these dangers. An emergency plan should include:

1. The organization chain of command.
2. Communication provisions to supplement normal methods. This also includes a listing of both business and residence numbers of key management and external agencies such as police, fire, ambulance, and the hospitals.
3. Priority of tasks to be accomplished and assignments to specific key individuals.
4. Provisions for photographic documentation, catering service, and secondary skills of personnel as back up on switchboards, first aid, and other necessary operations.

Loss prevention must be cost effective when weighed against goals and objectives. Considered as an investment, it is a profit contributor. It takes a team approach to a continuous effort, and its success depends on the awareness and involvement of every employee. No one program by itself is effective; loss prevention requires the integration of simple, planned programs.

A SEAL IS A SEAL IS A SEAL*

Let's talk about seals. Not the ones that balance a ball on the end of their noses or that play the horns, but the seals that we are so dependent upon to determine whether or not the doors have been opened on your units. Contrary to some opinions, the simple seal is not a lock, but rather a numbered control from point A to point B. A simple seal will not deter someone who is determined to get into the unit physically, but proper control of seals will deter someone who is thinking of taking freight without anyone's knowledge. And yet we see so many loaded trailers on streets without seals or locks.

Seals and locks go back to the cave man who rolled a giant boulder in front of his cave against marauding animals and to the wax impression on the edges of a document or any envelope that was sent by courier in the days of the Roman Empire or Merry Robin Hood. Over the years the physical shape or material has changed, but the purpose is still the same: to produce evidence of entry.

There are several reputable firms manufacturing seals. Some are metal; some are plastic; some are prettier than others; some are more expensive than others, but it all boils down to the fact that most of them will do the job that was intended for them to do if proper use

*Reprinted from *Claims Forum*, "A Seal is a Seal is a Seal" by Harry W. Goodwin, January/February, 1977. Permission obtained from the author.

and control is maintained. It has been proven that seal control sometimes is very lax. One sees seals lying around the dispatcher's table
or desk, hanging on a nail in the dock, hung on the handle of a trailer
while it is being loaded. Why? We certainly don't leave our money
lying around like that. But we do with the company's money—because
an uncontrolled seal, subject to tampering prior to use, is the company's
money' claim dollars "right off the top." Sad indeed.

Here are a few time-tested tips that may assist you in seal procedures and control:

1. Ordering and Storage. One person only should be charged
   with the responsibility of buying protective seals from the
   manufacturer. The manufacturer should be instructed to ship
   the seals to one person's attention only at the home office
   or another designated place.
   When ordering, the company's name or initials should be
   embossed onto each seal. It is also recommended to code
   each terminal by letter, numeral, or color.
   If unissued seals are not kept in a locked area, unauthorized
   people may obtain them for illegal use. For this reason, all
   seals and security devices must be kept under lock and key.
2. Distribution and Outbound Recording. One person for each
   shift should be charged with the responsibility of dispensing
   seals. It is not recommended that drivers be given seals to
   secure the trailer they drive out of the terminal yard. Effective control is only possible with accurate records of pertinent
   data. The information suggested for recording in the outbound
   mode is on the manifest or load sheet which will be retained
   for some time to compare numbers from origin to destination
   in cases of shortages from unit.
3. Information to Record:
   a. Date and time seal is applied.
   b. Load destination.
   c. Number of the trailer.
   d. Name of person applying seal.
   e. Drivers making pickups involving shipper's load and count
      can be furnished with a seal to be applied at time of
      closing of the doors by a shipper's representative. The
      driver will show on the bill of lading or shipping order
      the seal number applied at the shipper's dock.
4. Application. Unless seals are properly applied, control is lost
   over your sealing system. The procedure to follow in closing
   are simple, safe, and fast:

    a. Seal all doors—not only the rear ones.

    b. Run seal through hasps only once.

Seals wrapped around several times become illegible.

    c. To ensure positive closure, tug down on seal with sufficient pull to make sure it is locked.

5. Gate Procedures. If gate operations are part of your organization, the guard should record the following information:

    a. Tractor number.

    b. Trailer or container number.

    c. Seal number, color, and coding.

    d. Driver's name.

    e. Date and time.

On high security shipments it is also suggested that the guard apply a second seal. Some low valued shipments should also be double-sealed to prevent an obvious pattern from developing.

6. Broken Seals. At times it may be necessary to break a seal between terminals or between terminal and final destination. An occurrence of this nature must be reported and the following information recorded:

    a. Name of person breaking seal.

    b. Reason for breaking seal.

    c. Time and date seal was broken.

    d. Serial number of broken seal and serial number of the replacement.

    e. Whoever has been instructed to break the seal should do so in the presence of a witness. If witnesses are present, their names must also be included in the broken seal report.

The broken seal report must be filed with the terminal. This procedure must be followed no matter how far the driver may be from the point of origin.

7. Seal Removal and Inbound Recording. Many shipments are received and assumed intact if the seal is seen swinging from the door latch. Nothing could be further from the truth. There is only one way to make certain seals have not been violated and that is by a physical check. The recommended procedures for seal removal are as follows:

    a. Authorized personnel only should remove seals.

    b. The name, serial number, and all coding information appearing on the seal must be checked against the corresponding shipping papers and recorded on inbound documents or manifests.

    c. Prior to breaking the seal, pull down, making sure it has not been shortened or faked.

       d. Any discrepancies in information on the seal or on the shipping documents should be reported to persons assigned to accept such statements. Should a shipment be received with a broken seal or a seal violated in any way, reports must be turned in as previously described. Any evidence of theft should be reported to the security department and investigation begun immediately, irrespective of the time of day or night.

8. Other Procedures. There are other steps which can be taken to beef up your seal control program. Some of the suggestions could be part of your security system while others are optional:

       a. The door hinges and locking handles must be such that removal cannot be made without violating the seal.

       b. Sealed loads discovered to be tampered with while in transit should be immediately reported to the nearest terminal location or location assigned to receive such reports.

       c. Loads in the yard should be inventoried and controlled.

9. Cable Seal Locks. The conventional seal is no longer respected in several areas of the world. The flagrant abuse of seals during the last several years led to the development of a heavy-duty, self-locking, initialed, and serial-numbered cable seal lock. The unit is recommended for all shipments traveling through known problem areas. The same procedures outlined in previous paragraphs for ordering, storage, application, and removal apply to the use of cable steel locks.

Cable steel locks provide physical security as well as undisputed seal integrity. This dual security device should be carefully considered for certain phases of transportation operations. TD 77–30 makes mandatory the use of custom-approved high security seals on "in bound" shipments, effective April 25, 1977. Dispensing of cutting tools should be carefully controlled. Drivers should not be allowed to carry cutters except for special occasions.

10. Audit Procedures. As you have read the above, I am sure that some of you do most of this with your eyes closed. Yep, maybe some really do! When is the last time you checked to see that the seal procedure is being followed to the letter? How about a spot check at the gate? Ever see any unused seals lying on the dock floor? What does the switcher do with the seal when he opens the units and has to swing and pin the doors back before he backs into the dock? Are the

seal numbers going on documents or do some terminals get blamed for shortages because no seal number is available from origin?

I guess we could examine the system at any time and find human error! So, in essence, control your seals at all times—treat them as money. Maintain good seal records. Check your seal numbers against documents. Come down hard on anyone not complying with seal procedures.

MOTOR FLEET SECURITY

Major vulnerabilities in most fleet operations are the vendor trucks and company trucks that move in and out of the terminal yard. This can be met to a degree by performing occasional and random spot checks on the contents of the vehicles as they exit the yard.

Most terminal yards should have a list of approved vendors that visit the yard more or less frequently. The yard has no control over who is driving these vehicles and cannot generally control the need or reason for their entering the yard. Thus, spot checks on vehicles and their contents would act to deter the drivers of nonfleet vehicles from being involved in cargo theft.

Gate guards should be instructed to check trucks for valid names permanently displayed on the side in paint or decal. Non-permanent type placards (i.e. Tape, card sign, magic marker) should be further checked to ensure that the driver can produce valid documentation showing an affiliation with the carrier of record. Rental trucks, especially, should be reviewed closely. Trucks with permanent markings, but from unfamiliar carriers, should also be scrutinized carefully.

Proper documentation in the hands of the wrong party poses a serious threat to cargo security. It is a simple matter to rent or borrow a truck. It is more difficult to acquire a ligitimate carrier vehicle. Security procedures which verify the propriety of the truck, the driver, and the drayage company are needed for the highest level of loss prevention. In any instances of unfamiliar carrier, rental trucks, temporary truck markings, the truck registration should be examined and matched to the license plates by the gate guard. Drivers with leased equipment should possess lease papers and a driver's license for personal identification before being admitted to the yard. Any drayman who does not comply with any of the procedures should be refused admittance to the terminal, and the security supervisor should be notified of the occurrence. All too often, a driver and helper will drive into a fleet yard in a rental truck and the helper will climb into a fleet truck and they will both pull out of the yard getting away with a valued cargo, unchallenged.

When higher levels of security are required, as when actual fraudulant pickups have been experienced, carrier cooperation in terms of phone verification of truck and driver legitimacy should be arranged for.

Truck Pass

The gate guard should verify the accuracy and completeness of the truck pass as a vehicle exits the by:

1. Comparing the truck pass chassis and truck number to the actual chassis and truck number.
2. Examining the signature/initials for propriety.
3. Making sure all required information is on the truck pass.

All truck pass information should be written in ink. Some terminals prohibit any alterations to the originally recorded truck pass information. If alterations are required for any reason (e.g. clerical error, incorrect waybill), a new truck pass is issued. Each terminal should establish its own clear procedures concerning changes to the originally recorded truck pass information.

Truck passes, ideally, should be serially pre–numbered. Management should review the passes on a reasonable time cycle for:

1. Numerical sequence.
2. Clerical accuracy and clarity of written information.
3. Completeness of the information.
4. Truck turnaround time (time-in and time-out).

An analysis of truck turnaround time will enable management to assess operating efficiency and possibly highlight security weaknesses. The more time a truck is in the terminal yard, the greater the possibility of a theft occurring; a drayman has more time to talk with yard personnel, alter documents, switch containers, or tamper with seals.

Always spot check weekly under normal circumstances. More often if high losses become evident.

Unusual Occurrence Reporting

All unusual security occurrences should be reported to the "next level" supervisor. This includes discrepancies in areas such as:

1. Cargo count and/or condition.
2. Container or chassis damage.
3. Injuries to employees.
4. Presence of persons in unauthorized areas.
5. Other occurrences not always classified as "security-related".

Management often possesses a knowledge of security problems which it cannot discuss with terminal employees or drivers. Therefore, activities which may not, on the surface, seem to be security related may in actuality be very important to the loss prevention program.

Notification to the "next level" management should not be confined to security guards but should apply to all employees. This recommendation is intended to provide management with more knowledge and expedite security measures when necessary. Reporting relationships should be clearly understood, and failure to notify the next level management should be questioned. The reasons may vary from carelessness, to cover up and collusion.

Another problem facing many fleet owned trucks today is the theft of equipment from vehicles while in the yard. Vehicles are stored in the yard in the open, and radios, tapedecks, C B units, spare tires are the victims of attack. Locking vehicles and periodic spot patrols would do much to discourage these thefts.

Yard Saturation

When the facility receiving or delivering capability has reached the saturation point there should be a planned method to deny access to additional traffic. Both security procedures and normal business operations become difficult and to some extent inefficient or impractical if the number of draymen allowed to enter is more than can be handled by the staff on duty. A situation of this type seriously increases risk of thefts, misdeliveries, accidents, inaccurate records, and frauds.

The Containerized Yard

In the containerized environment, large cargo thefts will probably require drayman involvement. A *Regiscope* is a photographic device which can be placed at the entry gate to take a picture of the driver and cargo documents. The equipment is easy to operate and will not slow down cargo movement. The regiscope is widely used in the retail industry and is a valuable tool for deterring theft. An unauthorized driver attempting a theft would have to assume the risk of being photographed and subsequently investigated. (Note: The applicability of this recommendation would be determined by the labor and union environment of each particular operation.)

A tractor is necessary to move containers out of any terminal; trailers can be obtained at the yards with sufficient cunning and knowledge of operations. If a motor carrier has equipment or cargo hijacked or stolen, it should notify three other carriers and various officials. The three carriers initially notified should call three others and continue this pyramid notification process until a sufficient segment of the motor carrier system and drivers are aware of the equipment and/or cargo loss.

In addition, federal, state, and local police should be notified. The success of the system depends on cooperation between all parties involved and instant communications originating from the carrier suffering the hijack or cargo loss. An effective theft information exchange network would permit the community to quickly respond to an equipment or hijack/cargo theft situation.

Employee Identification Cards

All terminal employees should possess an identification card so only authorized personnel are allowed into the terminal premises. Each employee should display the identification card in a visible manner at all times. (Spring clip, pocket-flap, etc.). Each card should be assigned a control number with a perpetual log maintained of card number and employee name. Cards should be collected from terminating employees to maintain good control. Information listed on the card should include:

1. Color photograph of employee.
2. Name and home address.
3. Social Security number
4. Union affiliation.
5. Date of birth.
6. Employee signature.
7. Expiration date.

(Note: The applicability of this recommendation would be determined by the labor and union environment of each particular operation.)

Draymen Identification Cards

Intermodal cargo security would be strengthened if drayage company drivers possessed identification cards. The possibility of an unauthorized driver receiving cargo from a terminal would be significantly reduced. Drayman would be required to present the identification card and appropriate cargo documents to the gate guards for admittance into the terminal. Each card should contain a control number with a perpetual log maintained of card numbers and drayman name. Cards should be collected from terminating draymen to maintain good control. Information on the card should include:

1. Color photograph of drayman.
2. Drayage company affiliation.
3. Name and home address.
4. Social Security number.
5. Union affiliation.
6. Date of birth.
7. Drayman signature.
8. Expiration date.

Owner operators driving for a drayage company should present a copy of their employment contract to the gate guard. A drayman identification system would increase security ranging from pocket-theft or major container hijacking. (Note: The applicability of this recommendation would be determined by the labor and union environment of each particular operation.)

LIABILITY AND CLAIMS

In arranging for the movement of cargo, the shipper or receiver must be prepared to accept that on occasion even good security measures may fail, and theft or pilferage may occur. It is at this point, after the harm is done, that liability and claims procedures come into play. Knowledge of the rules of carrier liability and of claim procedures will prove indispensable to the shipper or receiver if the entitled indemnity is to be paid. Actual loss, however, should give shippers and receivers an incentive to go beyond indemnification and consider how to prevent recurrence.

From the standpoint of cargo security, the most important aspect of liability and claims is claims prevention. Every safeguard the shipper or receiver adopts is an act of claims prevention. Moreover, the shipper or receiver can obtain professional help in taking preventive measures on a systematic basis. Many insurance companies have claims prevention specialists who can survey a shipper or receiver's operation and recommend ways in which greater security can be attained. Use of consultative services of this kind is a prudent course of action even for the shipper or receiver with relatively good loss experience.

Carrier Liability for Loss to Cargo

When loss occurs through theft or pilferage, the shipper or receiver is in a situation with many variable elements. Since there are no uniform rules of carrier liability, the amount of the shipper's indemnity, if it is paid at all, depends in large measure on the mode of transport used to ship the cargo. Each mode of transport operates under differing rules with wide variation in limits of liability and in the defenses available to the carrier. For the informed shipper or receiver, these variations among modes of transport determine whether the carrier's liability is relied upon whether there should be additional protection by cargo insurance to cover the shipment.

Stated in their broadest terms, the present monetary limits of carrier liability may be summarized as follows:

1. Within the United States, rail and highcarriers, except household goods carriers, are liable for full actual loss, air carriers up to 50 cents a pound, and water carriers up to the limit agreed to in the contract of carriage, but these limits may be modified by agreement between shipper and carrier under a released rate arrangement.
2. In international transportation, airlines are liable to up to $8.16 a pound and water carriers up to $500 a package. A container is considered a package, but recent court decisions suggest that this rule may be modified.
3. Surface transportation in foreign countries usually is subject to local law. Most countries in Western Europe, however, are parties to international conventions that limit the liability of highway carriers to $3.70 a pound and railways to about $15 a pound.

In air transportation the shipper may obtain an increase in the carrier's limit of liability by paying an additional charge. The same is usually possible in water transportation by agreement between the shipper and carrier.

In view of the numerous defenses available to the carrier, these monetary limits on carrier liability offer only partial assurance of indemnity to the shipper. Commonly, the fault of the shipper or owner of the goods is a valid defense. For example, defective packing frequently exonerates the carrier. The low limits of carrier liability and uncertainty as to recovery have led shippers as a common practice to obtain cargo insurance on goods they ship by air or water carrier. For shipments moving by rail or motor carrier, the need to obtain such insurance may be less compelling, but the shipper may find it prudent to consult his underwriter especially if the shipment is of high value or would be unduly exposed to theft or pilferage. Additional assistance may be obtained from the carrier's claims prevention section.

Claims Procedures

When loss from thefts or pilferage occurs, the shipper or receiver should take care to observe the requisite claims procedures, especially as to notification of loss of the carrier, the formal filing of claims, and, if need be, the institution of suit. As a matter of law or under the contract or carriage, these actions ordinarily must be taken within specified time limits. Failure to comply may foreclose the shipper or receiver's right to indemnity, regardless of the merits of the claim.

Claims Prevention

From a practical standpoint, claims prevention is the most important element of liability and claims. The shipper or receiver must have a reasonable assurance of indemnity if goods are pilfered or stolen, but it is much more in his interest to reduce theft or pilferage to a minimum. The best way is through systematic claims prevention measures. Many of the measures recommended elsewhere in this book are in actuality basic claims prevention measures, for their aim is to remove opportunities for theft or pilferage and thus reduce the incidence of claims. These recommendations deserve the most serious consideration.

It is desirable to go about a claims prevention program in a systematic way. Even if loss experience is relatively good, the shipper or receiver usually will find it to his advantage to make a thorough survey of his operations from beginning to end, with the specific objective of locating weak spots. Such a survey should cover all parts of the operation; documentation, communications, procedures, personnel, and physical facilities. One method could be to trace a variety of individual shipments step by step. Another might be a concentrated examination of each single element such as documentation or physical security.

Some shippers or receivers have the capability of making such surveys with their own staff. If a shipper or receiver lacks this capability or wishes to have the objectivity of an outsider, professional help can be obtained easily and quickly. He should turn first to his insurance underwriter or broker, whose interest in claims prevention coincides with his own. Many will be able to conduct security surveys with their own staff. Others will prefer to call in specialists from the particular insurance company or association with which they are affiliated.

A single survey, while useful, probably would not suffice in most instances. The prudent course might be to repeat at suitable intervals. In this respect the shipper or receiver could be guided by his loss experience. It would be a sound practice, however, to order a security survey whenever an important new operation is being set up, as, for example, when a firm is entering the export business for the first time.

In addition to such surveys, shippers and receivers may find it useful to review their claim files periodically to see if there is a pattern with respect to the number and types of claims resulting from the operations of other shippers and receivers with whom they do business. Examples would be repeated instances of faulty packing or count discrepancies.

TRUCKING NOMENCLATURE

Aggregated shipments   Several shipments from different shippers to one consignee that are consolidated and treated as a single consignment.

Assign   The transfer of property to another, such as transfer of a freight bill to transport clearings or a bank.

Assignee   One to whom a right or property is transferred.

Astray freight   Freight bearing marks indicating origin and destination, but separated from the waybill.

Axle load   The amount of gross weight transmitted to the highway by one axle.

B.L. or B/L   Bill of lading.

Back haul

    a.   Traffic moving in direction of light flow when a carrier's traffic on a route is heavier in one direction than the other.

    b.   To haul a shipment back over a part of a route it has traveled.

Bill of lading   The written transportation contract between shipper and carrier (or their agents).

Blocking Supports used to prevent shipments from shifting during transportation.

Bobtail Tractor operating without a trailer; also a straight truck.

Bogey A two-axle assembly.

Bond of indemnity An agreement made with a transportation line relieving it from liability for which it would otherwise be liable.

Box Trailer or semitrailer; also, the transmission of a motor vehicle.

Break bulk To separate a composite load into individual shipments and route to different destinations.

Bulk commodities Liquids or solid materials hauled in bulk, such as petroleum products, asphalts, steel ingots or structural members, liquid fertilizers, molasses, etc.

Bulk freight Freight not in packages or containers.

Cargo The freight carried by a vehicle.

Carrier An individual, partnership, or corporation engaged in the business of transportating goods or persons.

Cartage (local) Hauling between locations in the same town or city or contiguous municipalities.

Casuals Employees (teamsters) who have not obtained seniority under one or more of the various labor contracts.

Certificated carrier A common carrier of dry or liquid freight subject to rate regulatory powers of the Public Utilities Commission and operating over a route specified by the Commission.

Chocks Any block put in front of or behind wheels to keep unit from rolling.

Claims A demand made upon a transportation company for payment on account of loss damage alleged to have occurred while shipment was in possession of carrier.

Claimant Person or company filing a claim.

Class 1 license An operator's license allowing the holder to drive any combination of vehicles. Classes II and III are restricted to single vehicles drawing a trailer under 6000 pounds gross.

Classification rating The class to which an article is assigned for the purpose of applying transportation charges.

Clean bill of lading A bill of lading signed by the carrier for receipt of merchandise in good condition (no damage, loss, etc. apparent), and which does not bear such notation as "shipper's load and count."

Clearing house An organization set up to process and collect bills for participating trucking companies.

Cleat A strip of wood or metal used to afford additional strength and to improve warping; to hold in position.

Combination Motor truck or truck tractor coupled to one or more trailers (including semitrailers).

Commodity   Any article of commerce; goods shipped.

Concealed loss   Loss or damage that cannot be determined until the package is opened.

Concealed damage   Freight damage that cannot be ascertained until exterior packaging, casing, or other appurtenances are removed.

Connection carrier   A carrier that has direct physical connection with another for interchange of cargo.

Consignee   One to whom something is shipped.

Consignor   The person by whom articles are shipped.

Container   A specially constructed reusable box or shell into which cargo may be packed to be transported from point-to-point as a unit.

Continuous seals   A term denoting that the seals on a truck remained intact during the movement of the truck from origin to destination; or, if broken in transit, that it was done by proper authority and without opportunity for loss or occur before new seals were applied.

Contributory negligence   A carrier's failure to use reasonable diligence or care to remedy an error made by another carrier, or an act of negligence that contributes materially by additional error to any loss or damage.

Convertible   A truck or trailer that can be used either as a flatbed or open top by means of removal of side panels.

Coupled-vehicle combinations   Two or more vehicles connected together to be operated by a single power source.

Cry sheet   A report to be completed by a driver at the end of his run. Required by federal and most state regulations. It is used to report mechanical irregularities or failures.

Customhouse broker   An individual or firm who handles documentation and receipt of inbound international shipments in return for a fee or commission.

Deadheading   Running empty.

Demurrage   Detention of a freight vehicle or container beyond a stipulated time; also the payment made for such delay.

Dispatcher   Employee whose duty it is to dispatch trucks from a terminal to deliver or pick up cargo.

Dock   A platform where trucks are loaded or unloaded.

Dolly   An auxiliary axle assembly equipped with a fifth wheel used to convert a semitrailer to a full trailer. This is called a *trailer converter dolly.*

Doubles   A tractor and two trailers connected by an auxiliary dolly.

Double bottom   Combination consisting of a truck tractor, a semitrailer, and a full trailer coupled together.

Drag line   A method of moving freight carts around a carrier's terminal. Refers to moving cable (the line) that operates either from a suspended position overhead or in a slot in the floor. The line supplies the motive power (drag) to the carts when they are attached to the line.

Drayage   The charge made for hauling freight on carts, drays, or trucks.

Dunnage   The material used to protect or support freight in trucks. The weight of dunnage is shown separately on the bill of lading since it is material used around a cargo to prevent damage. Often it is transported without charge.

F.O.B.   Free on board. Usually indicated place where responsibility for expenses and risk for goods is passed from seller to buyer.

Frt   Freight.

Feeder service   Short transportation lines running from a truck line into nearby areas to collect and distribute freight for the main line. Usually 25 to 35 miles long.

Fifth wheel   A device used to connect a truck tractor to a semitrailer.

Flatbed   A semitrailer with no sides.

Forklift   A machine used to move goods loaded on pallets or skids.

Free-astray   A shipment miscarried or unloaded at the wrong terminal is billed and forwarded to the correct terminal free of charge because it is astray.

Freight bill   Document for a common carrier shipment. Gives a description of the freight, its weight, charges, rates, taxes, and whether collect or prepaid.

Freight claim   A claim by the shipper against a carrier to recover the value of damaged freight.

Freight forwarder   An individual or firm who arranges for shipment of documentation in return for a fee or commission.

Full railer   Truck trailer with wheels on both ends (as compared to a semitrailer in which the front rests on the rear of the power unit).

GBL   Government bill of lading.

Gladhand   A connecting device on the end of an air hose used to connect air hose to source of air supply.

Grievance   A real or alleged violation of the labor contract between an employer and a union.

Grievance committee   A group of persons specially chosen to attempt to settle grievance disputes.

Gross operating revenue   All revenues earned by a carrier from its motor carrier operations.

Gross weight
    a. The weight of an article together with the weight of its container and the material used in packing;
    b. As applied to a truck, the weight of a truck together with the weight of its entire contents.

Gypsy An independent truck operator who drives his own truck and obtains freight wherever he can.

Hazardous materials Any number of commodities described by state and federal agencies as being hazardous to the public, e.g., poison, explosives, etc.

Hijack
    a. To steal an entire rig;
    b. Forcing the driver out of the cab with a gun.

Hiring hall A service offered by labor unions for temporary help.

Hostler Same as yard jockey; one who moves or spots freight-carrying equipment in the yard or terminal facilities.

Hot load Emergency shipment of cargo needed in a hurry.

Initial carrier Transportation line that picks up a shipment from the shipper.

Interchange Transfer of freight from one carrier to another.

Intermodal Involving more than one mode of transportation, (e.g., ship and train, on air and truck, ship, truck, train, etc.).

Interline Business between two or more transportation lines.

Intermediate carrier A transportation line hauling a shipment between the originating and delivering carrier.

Issuing carrier A transportation line that publishes a tariff or issues a bill of lading or other document.

Joint routes Routes established by two or more connecting carriers for the continuous through movement of traffic over their lines.

King pin A boltlike pin on a trailer unit used to connect to a fifth wheel assembly.

Land-bridge A system of getting international cargoes across an intervening continent from one sea coast to another by special through-trains. Shipments from Europe to Japan, for example, instead of going via the Panama Canal, would be unloaded on the United States or Canadian east coast, taken by train to the west coast, and reloaded on another Japan-bound ship.

Landing gear Device that supports front end of semitrailer when not attached to a tractor.

Lift tailgate A power-operated tailgate capable of lifting a load from street level to the level of the truck or trailer floor.

Line driver A driver qualified to take a big rig on long haul as against a local delivery driver.

Line haul Movement of freight between cities or terminals. Line haul does not include pick up and delivery service.

Loading seal Seal applied at time of initial loading or when freight is checked in transit.

Local cartage carrier A company that transports property entirely within the commercial zone of a municipality (or contiguous cities). This may be pick up and delivery service for a line haul carrier.

Lockout The shutting down of a facility by an employer as the result of a labor dispute.

Log book A book carried by truck drivers containing daily records of hours, route, etc. They are required by Department of Transportation regulations.

Lumper A temporary employee used to help load or unload trucks at warehouses, docks, etc.

Manifest A document describing a shipment of the contents of a vehicle or ship.

Memorandum bill of lading A duplicate copy of a bill of lading.

Negligence Failure to use reasonable diligence or care, such as a careless or erroneous act or omission, or a disregard of duty, resulting in loss or damage.

Operating ratio The relationship of total expenses to total operation revenue.

Over-freight Freight separated from its waybill and bearing no identifying marks.

Owner-operator A person who drives and owns his truck. Usually hires himself out to another trucking company or business.

P.U. & D. Pick up and delivery.

Packing list A detailed specification of packed goods.

Pallett A wooden platform upon which cargo can be stacked and subsequently moved as a unit.

Palletized Stacked on pallets.

Peddle runs Local pick up and delivery operation entailing numerous stops for pick up and/or delivery.

Pick up & delivery (P.U. & D.) This pick up is referring to someone taking something and putting it into a vehicle.

Pig Trailer transported on flatcar.

Pig ramp A ramp used to load and unload piggyback trailers.

Piggyback Transportation of a highway trailer on a rail flatcar.

Pro number Pro is the abbreviation of the word progressive. Pro usually is prefixed to freight bill numbers.

Rag top Open top trailer using tarpaulin for a covering.

Reefer A refrigerated truck or trailer.

Regular common carrier Any company that holds itself out to serve the general public and authorized to transport general commodities over regular routes between fixed terminals.

Rig Truck, tractor, semitrailer, truck and full trailer, or other combinations.

Roadeo A competition between the top drivers for each trucking company (in each type of truck) to determine the best drivers.

Run through train A solid block of cars handled through a junction point, under an operating agreement, without a scheduled stop except for necessary changes in power or crew.

S.L. & C. Shipper's load and count.

Seal A device to assure that truck doors are not opened in transit.

Semitrailer Truck trailer equipped with one or more axles and constructed so that the front end rests upon a truck tractor.

Shipper's load and count Indicates that the contents of a truck were loaded and counted by the shipper and not checked or verified by the transportation line.

Shipping order Instructions to carrier for transportation of a shipment. Usually it is a copy of the bill of lading; used also as a record by the freight agent at origin.

Shipping papers Papers used in connection with movement of freight.

Skid A wooden platform on which heavy articles or packaged goods are placed to permit handling by freight handling equipment.

Sleeper Truck with sleeping compartment in cab.

Tachograph A device used in a cab to automatically record miles driven, number of stops, speed, and other factors during a trip.

Tack Short for tachograph or tachometer.

Tare weight The weight of the truck exclusive of its contents.

Tariff A schedule of commodity classifications and the transportation rates that will be charged for the carriage of each.

Terminal A building for the handling and temporary storage of freight as it is transferred between trucks (from a city pick up to an intercity truck for example).

Towveyor An endless chain conveyor installed beneath the floor of a cargo dock, to which small cargo carts can be attached through a slotted track, so their loads can then be automatically taken to loading doors.

Trace To check the movement of a shipment.

Tracer A request that a carrier locate a shipment to speed its movement or to establish delivery.

Trailer interchange Transfer of trailer with or without load from one transportation line to another.

Truck A self-propelled motor vehicle used to carry property, but not necessarily designed for this purpose.

Truck-tractor Motor vehicle designed primarily for drawing truck trailers and semitrailers. Constructed to carry part of the weight and load of a semitrailer.

Truck trailer Freight-carrying vehicle designed to be drawn by a truck or truck-tractor.

Waybill Description of goods sent with a common carrier freight shipment.

Weight sheets Itemized list furnished by shippers to weighing bureaus itemizing articles in each consignment.

Yard jockey Person who operates a yard tractor or yard mule, a small tractor used to move semitrailers around the terminal yard.

Yard mule Small tractor used to move semitrailers around the terminal yard.

7. Marine Cargo

MANAGEMENT SYSTEM ANALYSIS TECHNIQUES

This involves analysis of the entire maritime port operation, its cargo flows, paper flows, computer networks risk-points, marketing and competitive factors, operating constraints, staffing factors, union and labor considerations, federal, state and locally available law enforcement and prosecution resources, and the characteristics of local criminal activity.

Efforts underway by the maritime community to reduce the loss of freight entrusted to it do not appear to be having a significant impact on either the incidence or value of cargo loss. In short, there is no coordinated maritime industry approach to the cargo loss problem. It is hoped that continued study can encourage such a coordinated approach and provide a cost-effective tool to reduce such cargo losses within our nation's transportation system.

Access to a terminal data base, a stationery supply cabinet, a high-risk cargo list or detailed manifests can be far more valuable in terms of theft and fraud than the keys to the front gate.

This chapter covers findings and recommendations on less than truckload (LTL) thefts-of-opportunity and on the exposures to the systems thefts and frauds of the future.

Recommendations

In all cases, recommendations and advisory guidelines made in this book weigh carefully each of these factors:

This chapter is adapted from U.S. Department of Transportation. "Maritime Cargo Loss Prevention" Volume 1, P5200.17. Washington, D.C.: U.S. Government Printing Office, October, 1979.

1. Cost. Is the cure worse than the disease?
2. Operations. Does it slow cargo movement unacceptably?
3. Marketing. Does it complicate paper/convenience to the degree that shippers will go to the competition?
4. Human factors. Will the management, employees, and unions accept it and make it work?
5. Is it adaptable? Can it be put in place (or escalated) when actually needed, and removed when not? A key criterion.

General Findings

Cargo loss exposures fall into three general classes:

- The traditional "pocket, lunchbox, over-the-fence" thefts. Prevention systems for these are, to various degrees, reasonably workable in most ports. Losses here tend to be of an LTL nature. This type of loss appears throughout the United States and foreign port environments.
- The organized crime, collusion, theft, bribery, persuasion thefts and frauds. These are more complex—more difficult to head off or detect. Prevention systems are not as evident, nor as effective as those for pocket thefts. Losses here can be major, and can continue over considerable periods of time. This type of loss tends to concentrate in certain specific ports and/or coastal areas.
- The systems theft and fraud. Here forged papers, false documentation, pseudocargo (short shipments), computer record alteration, false shipment diversions and the like are the methods employed.

Losses can easily overshadow the previous two classes and can involve multicontainer losses over extended periods of time.

White collar, and particularly systems and computer crime and fraud, is increasingly evident in the general business scene. It can, and most likely will, become equally evident in the maritime community in the near future.

Prevention systems are sparse. Although ample opportunity for systems crime is evident, as yet it is making no great inroad in the general port environment.

Summary

In view of the above findings, this chapter focuses on all three loss areas.

- *The Pocket Theft/Fraud.* The prevention systems now usually in place concentrate on this area. More is known about this type of loss. Dollar exposure, per incident, is less than for other loss types. In addition, a great many guides and documents relating to loss prevention for traditional pocket crimes are already available in various operator and port environments. It is not the intention of this book to add significantly to the body of information already available in this area.
- *The Organized Theft/Fraud.* High loss exposure; complex; less than effective prevention systems now are in place.
- *The Systems Theft/Fraud.* Exposure is highest; little is known about it. It appears to be the most evident future point of vulnerability. Current prevention systems are few.

CARGO LOSS

The recommendations made in this chapter consider loss in its broadest terms, not only from direct theft, pilferage, and fraud.

If responsibility for the delivery of a particular piece of cargo is accepted on paper, and if the cargo is later found to be undeliverable, and if it cannot clearly be determined that nondelivery is caused by fire, loss overboard, damage and similar clearly identifiable non-theft-related circumstances, then it is a cargo loss for all intents and purposes. Some loss examples are theft, pilferage, fraud, hijacking, unknown disappearance, pseudo-cargo (it existed only on paper), unexplained shortages, etc.

The terms *terminal operator*, *operator*, and *tenant* as used throughout this chapter also include stevedores, pier operators, agents, and similar organizations involved in handling cargo.

The term *organized* as used throughout this book includes collusion, temporary alliance, computer-knowledgeable individuals with fraudulent intent, and individual professional criminals, as well as the more traditional meaning of the term—members of organized and disciplined criminal associations.

THE TOTAL SYSTEM APPROACH

These chapters consider loss prevention from the point of view of the total maritime port system. Emphasis is placed on (1) the analyses of cargo operations and documentation procedures at the terminal areas, (2) how those operations and documentation procedures relate to and impact on each other, (3) to related land transportation modes, and (4) to the overall seaport. This is preferable to a "security system only" approach since loss risk is increasingly complex and is possible from all directions within the system from

1. The cargo-flow system (traditional theft)
2. The paperwork and administrative system (theft, fraud, false claims)
3. The computer system (computer fraud)
4. The before and after terminal system of rail, motorfreight, agents, brokers (theft, fraud, hijacking)

In addition, as the terminal business grows more complex, and as cargo moves faster and in greater volumes, a single loss-prevention procedure can have profound effects on marketing, competitive positions, administration, computer systems, management, contractors, union relations, liability, and finances. A step-by-step procedure was developed for the conduct of such a total system analysis: *the security systems analysis (SSA)*. It is, in fact, one of the major recommendations of this chapter that such an analysis be conducted by the individual terminal operator.

The Security Systems Analysis (SSA)

The SSA method, developed for the conduct of this study, analyzes successive layers of a maritime port operation until major risk points are identified.

The *risk points* are the holes, gaps, or weak spots in the operation *where losses are occurring, or reasonably could occur, if discovered by someone intent on theft or fraud.* Once these risk points are isolated, the SSA proceeds to develop levels of loss prevention. *Routine levels* are sufficient, for normal operations, to discourage routine theft/fraud attempts and to detect escalation of attempts above routine levels.

Special-response levels can be brought into play if unusual loss activity is detected in a particular area of operation these are designed to de-escalate to routine levels once the problem is effectively reduced.

In this way loss-prevention costs and efforts are proportional to the size of a particular problem at a particular time. They do not go on forever. In addition, this special-response planning creates useful "in case" scenarios. Response to a problem is faster when plans are already developed; the potential for loss is reduced.

SSA, Specific Steps

STEP 1: Flowchart, on a photo or yard layout, the actual flow of the cargo through yard, terminal shed.

STEP 2: Break the flow into understandable elements that fit your operation. (Examples: gate entry, gate to weigh station, etc. See figures 7–1 through 7–5 for guidance.)

NOTE: If you have charted operations before it is easy to get sidetracked into unnecessary detail. Show ONLY SECURITY-ASSOCIATED OPERATIONS. (If it is not important that containers move via straddle carrier, crane, or lift as far as security is concerned, do not bother to show which of the methods is used.)

STEP 3: Flowchart (or make notes) on the SECURITY and LOSS-RELATED paperwork (forms, tags, computer terminals) that is currently used in each of the elements developed in Step 2.

NOTE: Again, do not sidetrack into nonsecurity paperflows.

Identify in particular all paper that can show the location of high-value cargo.

STEP 4: Identify staffing considerations for each element in these categories:

- Who handles the cargo?
- Who handles the paper?
- Who is responsible for the operation (supervision)?
- Who is responsible for security?
- Who, if anyone, is prohibited from entry to this element/area?
- What types of persons, not involved with the element, can gain access to it for possible theft or fraud purposes?

STEP 5: Identify, as far as possible, what the past loss experience has been for each element. Recognizably, this will be very approximate and gross if your operation is typical. Use claims records, security reports and folklore as best you can.

THOUGH IT MAY BE NECESSARY TO RECHECK ONE OR MORE OF THE ABOVE STEPS AS THE ANALYSIS PROGRESSES, PRELIMINARY DATA-GATHERING IS NOW COMPLETE. ACTUAL RISK ANALYSIS IS NOW POSSIBLE.

STEP 6: THE KEY STEP—RISK ANALYSIS. Organize your flows, notes, findings into sets—one for each element. Then proceed as follows:

STEP 6A: Digest the material for this element gathered from all prior steps. Become thoroughly acquainted with, and get the feel of, what goes on in the element.

STEP 6B: Approach the element AS A THIEF, *NOT* as an employee of the terminal. Develop scenarios (as detailed as possible, as many as possible) depicting ways in which to:

- Steal cargo,
- Misdirect cargo to where it can later be stolen,
- Falsify paper to allow fraudulent claims for non-existent cargo,
- Persuade, bribe, force someone to do it for you,
- Use any other method by which a cargo loss, for your benefit, can be arranged. Document these scenarios.

NOTE: Scenarios are most beneficial if developed by two or three individuals separately and then discussed further as a group. Preferably, such a group should represent backgrounds from management, operations, and security.

MAJOR CAUTION: We have waited until this point in the SSA to stress the importance of PROJECT SECURITY and SSA STAFF SELECTION. The risk involved should by now be very obvious:

- CARE IS VITAL!
- THE SSA METHOD IS A SURPRISINGLY POWERFUL ONE!
- GENUINE AND VERY DANGEROUS SCENARIOS CAN BE DEVELOPED!
- THEY WILL WORK!

- MAJOR LOOPHOLES CAN BE FOUND IN YOUR OPERATION!

The project paper/findings, and especially risk analyses, must be treated with utmost security. Selection of the staff, and particularly the scenario-team, requires careful thought and continual high-management monitoring.

STEP 6C: Again approach the element from the point of view of theft and fraud potential, but with this change:

- How can this element be used to set the stage for thefts/frauds that will be actually executed in some other element?
- What preparations may be needed in other elements (OR BEFORE CARGO IS EVEN IN YOUR HANDS) to allow theft/fraud in this element?

RISK ANALYSIS (IN THE FORM OF DOCUMENTED THEFT AND FRAUD SCENARIOS) IS NOW COMPLETE, AT LEAST IN PRELIMINARY FORM.

NEXT, LOSS PREVENTION RECOMMENDATIONS ARE DEVELOPED.

STEP 7: Classify the scenarios in order to establish ROUTINE LEVEL and SPECIAL-RESPONSE categories:

- If a scenario *matches* known thefts/frauds that have happened in the past (as determined by Step 5) class it for ROUTINE prevention procedures (i.e., in-place at all times).
- If a scenario seems to explain losses that have occurred in the past, for which there was not an apparent explanation, class it as ROUTINE.
- Class all remaining scenarios as SPECIAL-RESPONSE.

STEP 8: Develop the necessary loss prevention or loss reduction procedures called for by each scenario. For example (note that the categories below approximate those surveyed during steps 1 through 4):

CARGO FLOW:
- Restrict access to certain area.

- Restrict travel to certain pathways.
- Identify the purpose of a truck (truck pass/stickers, etc.).
- Identify the destination of a container/shipment (pass/tag/sticker).
- Put high-risk cargo in easily seen locations.

DOCUMENTATION
- Alter documentation.
- Add documentation.
- Eliminate documentation.
- Restrict unauthorized access/sighting.
- Signatures/initials.
- Audit and checking (type/frequency).
- Document security (storage).

STAFFING
- Clear responsibility for all high-risk elements.
- Minimal handling of high-risk paper.
- Minimal access to high-risk areas of the yard/shed etc.
- Public access restrictions.
- Guarding (Who? How often?).
- Inspection (Who? How?).
- Counting.
- Weighing.

STEP 9: Weigh each loss prevention/reduction procedure carefully in light of these considerations:

- Cost versus benefit.
- Marketing/Competition: (Pro) Can it be used as a sales-plus to potential shippers? (Con) Is it so restrictive that it will drive business away?
- Operations: Does it have an unacceptable effect on cargo handling speed/efficiency?
- Human Factors: Will management, employees, and unions accept it and work with it?
- Is it the simplest solution, or is there a simpler, cheaper, and more acceptable one?

REVIEW THE ABOVE WITH ALL DEPARTMENTS/UNITS THAT WILL OR MAY BE AFFECTED.

STEP 10: Implement the ROUTINE LEVEL procedures. Document, and hold for use as required, the SPECIAL-RESPONSE

LEVEL procedures. Develop and implement the necessary warning procedures that may alert you that a special-response may be needed.

EXAMPLE: "Insurance Department, please let me know if you begin to get abnormal claims for shortages in hide shipments."

(A scenario showing that by stowing moldy hides across the doorspace, counts and inspections would be severely discouraged. False claims could be filed.)

EXAMPLE: "Let me know if claims from meat-box second and third consignees start to climb."

(A scenario showing that the first consignee in a multiple-consignee container could substitute old or second-grade meat for that destined for second and third consignees.)

STEP 11: Revise, adapt, refresh the findings whenever a significant change is made in your operation/location/cargo patterns or OVERALL LOSS EXPERIENCE.

Actual examples of the methods, findings, risk points and recommendations of an SSA are covered in detail in section III "Analysis by Element". These, along with the above coverage of the SSA steps, should provide a reasonable guide to the conduct of such an analysis.

A Typical Cargo Flow

The study of a variety of container yards and freight stations led to the identification of a typical or model cargo flow. This was checked against a further number of operations and proved valid. It can, in fact, be used as the basis for steps 1 and 2 of your own SSA, although a more exact replica of your own operation probably would be more effective. Your own flow, however, should not contain very many more elements than shown in the model flow.

The typical flow uses a simple schematic of a yard and freight station as shown in figure 7-1 following. Note that the operation is highly idealized, abstracted, or modeled. It is organized for analysis convenience and DOES NOT MAKE ANY ATTEMPT TO BE GEOGRAPHICALLY CORRECT for any actual live operation. It is fully effective for SSA purposes, in fact, it is more effective than many of the actual geographically accurate plots this project has used. It is clearer and simpler, allowing for concentration on security and not on whether straddle carriers turn right or left at the end of aisleway B. For example, whether your yard uses one gate (not two) for entry and exit is not material for systems security analysis purposes. There are still two distinct security functions and the model flow makes it easier to show them, think about them, and develop procedures for them.

Examples of the Flows

The figures that follow show the elements of the model or typical cargo flow that was used for all actual findings and recommendations presented in this chapter. Figures 7-2 through 7-5 represent outbound and inbound cargo flow in the container yard (CY) and the container freight station (CFS). As with the CY and CFS schematic shown in figure 7-3, these flows were used and verified in some 14 live operations for SSA purposes.

This chapter is also valid for planning noncontainer operations, for which flows and schematics for containers should be omitted. Vessels should be placed alongside what is now the CFS to CY gate. The SSA applies.

Figure 7-6 is designed to show a break-bulk schematic of use in SSA work.

In general, break-bulk flows in very similar patterns to those shown for containerized cargo (i.e., in gate, into storage across stringer, etc.). As such, it is subject to a majority of the security vulnerabilities and loss-preventatives described in this chapter. All are well worth reviewing even in a purely break-bulk environment.

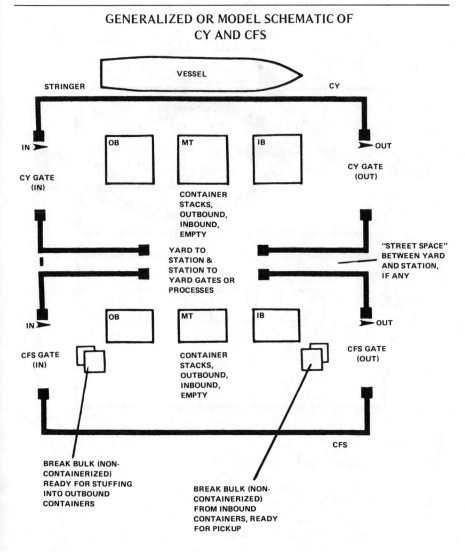

GENERALIZED OR MODEL SCHEMATIC OF CY AND CFS

Legend for Figures 7-1 through 7-7.

CY	— Container Yard
CFS	— Container Freight Station
OB	— Out Bound
IB	— In Bound
MT	— Empty Container

Figure 7-1. Generalized or model schematic of CY and CFS.

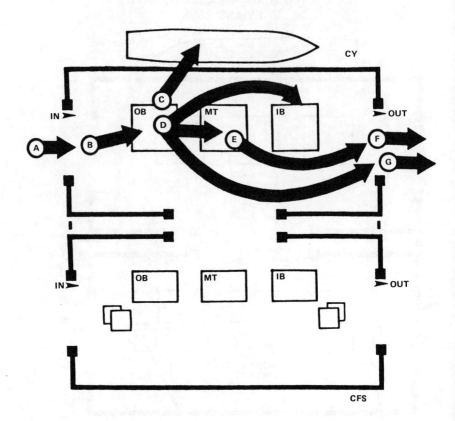

Element	Container Yard—Outbound
A.	Gate entry with full outbound container
B.	Drayman moves toward the container storage area
C.	Container moved from the CY to the vessel
D.	After delivery of an outbound container, the drayman moves toward the container storage area or the gate.
E.	Drayman with an empty container moves toward the gate.
F.	Drayman with an empty container exits the CY
G.	Drayman without a container exits the CY

Figure 7-2. Container yard—outbound.

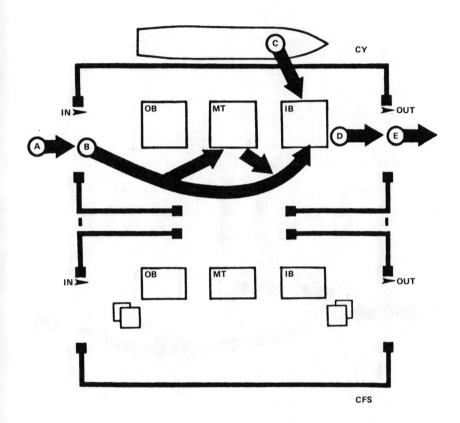

Element   **Container Yard – Inbound**

   A.   Gate entry to pick up a full inbound container
   B.   Drayman with a container moves toward the container yard storage area
   C.   Container discharged from the vessel and moved to the inbound stack
   D.   Drayman picks up an inbound container and moves toward the gate
   E.   Gate exit with a full invound container

Figure 7-3. Container yard – inbound.

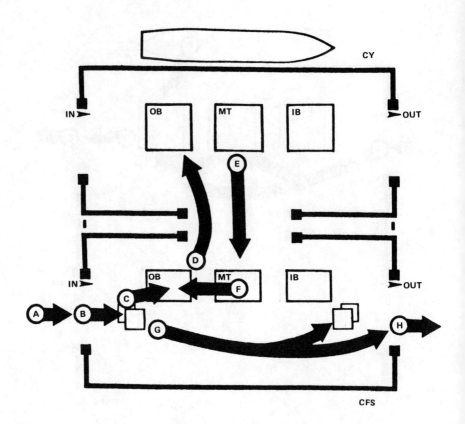

Element	Container Freight Station – Outbound
A.	Gate entry with outbound CFS cargo
B.	Drayman moves towards CFS outbound break bulk area
C.	Outbound break bulk placed into container
D.	Outbound container moved from CFS to CY
E.	Empty container enters the CFS from the CY
F.	CFS empty container moved to the CFS dock
G.	Drayman proceeds to pick up inbound CFS cargo or depart CFS
H.	Drayman without inbound break bulk exits the CFS

Figure 7-4. Container freight station – outbound.

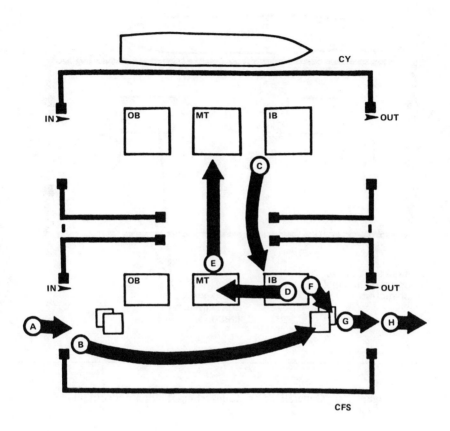

Element	Container Freight Station – Inbound
A.	Gate entry to pick up inbound CFS cargo
B.	Drayman moves toward CFS inbound break bulk area
C.	Inbound container moved from the container yard to the CFS
D.	Container moved from CFS inbound stack to empty stack
E.	Empty container moved from CFS to CY
F.	Full container unloaded at CFS dock
G.	Drayman picks up inbound CFS cargo and moves toward the gate
H.	Drayman with inbound cargo departs from the CFS

Figure 7-5. Container freight station – inbound.

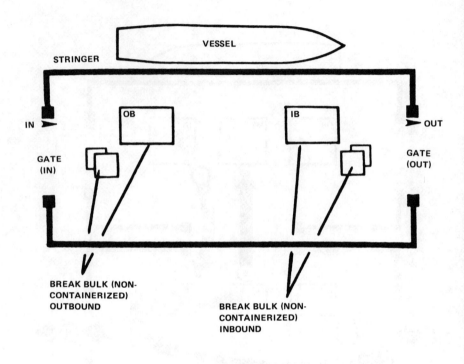

Figure 7-6. Generalized or model schematic of a noncontainer.

Analysis by Element

The following container yard (CY) and container freight station (CFS) models are presented with the knowledge that all of the individual elements certainly will not apply to every terminal operation.

Factors such as the type of yard equipment used, the manner in which cargo is stored (e.g., decked, on wheels), the type of cargo handled (e.g., break-bulk, containerized), the degree of computerization in effect, and others will determine the portion of each model that applies to a specific terminal.

Each element illustrates a unique link of physical cargo movement, documentation requirements, employee responsibilities, and security procedures in the chain of events. Each element characterizes a segment of terminal operations with security considerations probably quite different from any other.

In addition to the abbreviations CY and CFS, other terms in figures 7-1 to 7-7 appear as OB (outbound), IB (inbound), and MT (empty container).

Model 1
Container Yard - Outbound

Element	Description
A.	Gate entry with full outbound container.
B.	Drayman moves toward the container storage area.
C.	Container moved from the CY to the vessel.
D.	After delivery of an outbound container, the drayman moves toward the container storage area or the gate.
E.	Drayman with an empty container moves toward the gate.
F.	Drayman with an empty container exits the CY.
G.	Drayman without a container exits the CY.

CY OUTBOUND

ELEMENT:(A)   GATE ENTRY WITH A FULL OUTBOUND
              CONTAINER

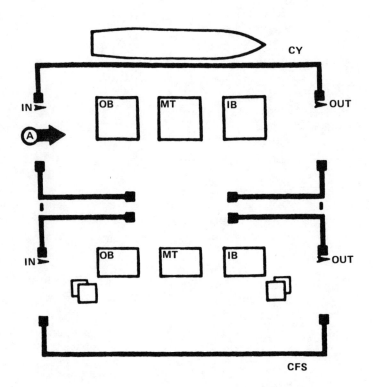

The Operation

Truck (with full container) enters the yard gate. A guard controls this function. In addition to the guard's traditional security role, he performs valuable claims-prevention, equipment control, and insurance functions.

His major operating document is a truck pass. Content of a typical truck pass, and uses of the pass data are:

Truck Pass Data	Use
Vehicle registration #	Claims
Time/date IN	Claims
Tractor license #	Claims/loss trace
Company	Claims/loss trace
Seal number	Claims/loss trace
Chassis number	Claims/equipment control
Container number	Claims/equipment control
Purpose of visit	Security/loss prevention
Time/date out	Claims

Claims. The truck pass information listed above is invaluable to the claims department when the need arises to determine the WHO, WHEN, WHERE, and WHY of an insurance claim. A terminal operator assumes responsibility and liability for the container and cargo when the drayman enters the container yard. Examining the seal for intactness and recording the seal number on the truck pass will limit a terminal operator's cargo liability to the period of time extending from gate entry to cargo aboard ship. *Properly maintained seal records provide the most useful information for handling claims brought against the terminal operator.*

Equipment Control. Recording the chassis number and container number on the truck pass verifies that the information on the drayman's handtag is correct, or if no handtag is available, provides the receiving clerk with a document which can be used in preparing the equipment interchange and safety report. This document is used by equipment control to monitor and plan movements of physical equipment. The process of having the guard visually examine and physically record the container number and chassis number on the truck pass aids the receiving clerk in processing draymen.

Outbound shipments are not always accompanied by a waybill and the amount and type of information on a waybill varies among trucking lines. A truck pass which contains chassis number and container number enables the receiving clerk to obtain equipment information from a standardized document.

Purpose of the Visit. Recording the purpose of the visit on the truck pass technically authorizes the drayman to perform a particular function (and no other) within the container yard. The truck pass provides a means by which yard personnel can determine the nature of a drayman's visit for security purposes or to provide assistance. It also alerts yard personnel to draymen who are confused as to directions within the yard or who were deliberately in the wrong area.

Accuracy of the Truck Pass. The responsibility for recording the information on the truck pass rests with the gate guards. Management, however, can help ensure that the desired procedures are followed by (1) providing the guards with a clear written set of procedures and (2) conducting both scheduled and spot reviews of truck passes for completeness.

Risk Analysis

The major cargo-loss risk derives from unauthorized entry onto yard premises by:

1. A drayman, a tractor
2. A drayman, a tractor/chassis
3. A drayman, with empty container
4. A drayman, with probably full (and/or sealed) container

Point 4 is the least risky. The other points, 1 through 3, represent somewhat greater security risks. It is easier for an unauthorized person to acquire a tractor only than to acquire an entire tractor/chassis/container combination.

Risk should be reduced to an acceptable level:

- If the truck is authorized,
- If the container is apparently full/sealed,
- If proper data is recorded for possible insurance/claims use.

ELEMENT:Ⓑ DRAYMAN MOVES TOWARD THE CONTAINER STORAGE AREA

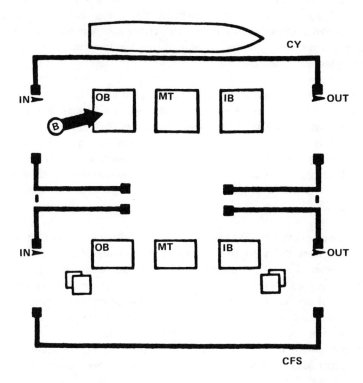

The Operation

After the drayman enters the gate, but before he enters the outbound container stacking area, terminal employees perform (1) equipment control functions (inspection and weighing) and (2) operating, claims/insurance functions (receiving document preparation). The terminal inspection of the container and chassis verifies the soundness of the equipment.

Weighing the container enables the terminal to verify the "on paper" weight of the container. This is necessary to satisfy Occupation Safety and Health Act (OSHA) requirements and also to properly bill the customer. Failure to detect shipper paperwork indicating a weight lower than the actual weight results in a terminal underbilling the shipper and a monetary loss—possibly deliberate.

Inspection Station. After the gate guard determines that the outbound container in fact belongs in the container yard, the terminal conducts an inspection of the container and chassis. Any damage or deficiency in the equipment is agreed upon between the terminal and the drayman and clearly marked on the equipment interchange. The inspection clerk also records the container number, chassis number, and seal number on the equipment interchange and physically pulls on the seal to make certain of its intactness. The equipment interchange serves as the terminal record for control of equipment, maintenance of equipment, and establishing terminal liability.

Weighing Station. All containers entering the yard are weighed prior to terminal preparation of the outbound container manifest. The weighing station verifies the accuracy of the weight information listed on the drayman's handtag. The cargo weight is a factor in determining the proper billing to the shipper; thus, carefully performing this function ensures the terminal of proper revenue collection and blocks an avenue for both fraudulent reduction of shipping/insurance charges—and fraudulent claims for nonexistent cargo. (i.e., listed on paper but never shipped.)

Receiving Documentation. The most secure method for ensuring that only authorized cargo enters the yard is to accept only shipments with a valid terminal booking number. The sales department daily forwards a booking list to the receiving clerks. The booking number listed on the drayman's documentation is verified with the booking list to determine validity. Following the verification of the outbound shipment and the physical condition of the container and chassis, the container manifest is prepared from the trucker's handtag.

If the drayman delivers a container without proper documentation, the terminal might assume custody of an improper container, which might result in unnecessary and time-consuming legal and clerical work. The processing of a container without documentation creates a burden on the receiving clerks and slows down operating efficiency. Some terminal operators establish standard receiving procedures for containers which arrive without proper documentation to ensure the propriety of the shipment while not overburdening the clerical operations.

The container manifest contains all the pertinent information concerning the movement and contents of a container. Terminals should safeguard this document restricting its access to only a few employees and storing this document in a secure location when not in use.

Yard Design and Traffic Patterns. Traffic patterns within the yards provide the best security, safety, and operating efficiency when they are designed to minimize confusion within the yard and allow quick truck turnaround time.

An orderly flow of traffic through the yard is possible when containers are clearly segregated into inbound, outbound, and empty areas; and the drayman possesses knowledge of the yard. However, segregation of containers might be impossible because of the manner of container storage (e.g., decked, on-wheels) and/or the physical size of the yard. Terminals that operate small container yards often do not possess the capability to segregate containers according to their destination. Regardless of the type of storage used, every terminal operation possesses the ability to direct the drayman to the proper area for unloading. The directions can be given in the following ways:

- Receiving clerk orally provides direction.
- Truck pass contains a map.
- Receiving clerk gives the drayman a yard spot card which indicates the row and spot within the row, or row only.
- Yard directional markings/colored lines/signs.

After the drayman departs from the receiving office area, a yard clerk can also be assigned to assist the drayman in locating the proper storage area.

Container Yard Storage. After the container is placed in the yard, the terminal needs to obtain the exact storage location to facilitate the loading process, determine the safety of the storage area and institute additional security procedures for high-risk cargo.

The verification of the container storage location can be determined at the time of initial delivery or after delivery. A daily inventory of all full containers might be performed by a security guard or terminal clerk before beginning yard operations. The nature of this inventory and the employee responsible should be determined by the terminal management so that it does not require an increase in payroll expense.

Risk Analysis

A terminal can incur damage and/or loss claims, revenue loss, and legal claims by improperly performing the procedures covered in this element. The terminal operating procedures and the possible types of loss which might result are listed below:

1. Inspection: Loss and damage claims
2. Weighing: Revenue loss, claims on nonexistent cargo
3. Receiving: Loss claim, legal claim
4. Vehicle control: Loss and damage claims

Risk should be reduced to an acceptable level:

- If all containers are properly inspected,
- If all containers are weighed and the weight cross-checked against the shipper documentation,

- If proper documents accompany all cargo,
- If terminal receiving documents are properly completed and controlled,
- If traffic patterns within the yard minimize confusion and allow quick truck turnaround time and reasonable observability by security and supervisory personnel, and
- If high risk cargo receives special security considerations.

CY OUTBOUND

ELEMENT: Ⓒ CONTAINER MOVED FROM THE CY TO THE VESSEL

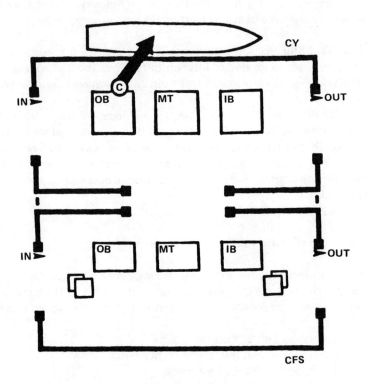

The Operation

When cargo is moved from the stack to the ship, security procedures should ensure that a driver picks up the proper container, and it is loaded aboard ship in the location designated by stowage documentation.

When the container is removed from an outbound stack, a terminal employee should verify the container and seal number against a master cargo list and physically test and seal for intactness. This point in yard operations provides the final opportunity for the terminal to document its handling of the container. The examination of the seal before the container is loaded provides a means by which theft or damage to the box while in storage at the container yard can be detected. The ship generally has the responsibility for ensuring that containers are stowed in the proper location.

Automobiles. Many ports handle the movement of automobiles. They present special problems, of course, and it is in this element that the yard should make a final examination of the condition of the vehicle and note high risk parts that were accepted within the vehicle for shipment.

For example, at the time the vehicle enters the yard an examination is made and scratches, dents, and other damage are noted on a form. These conditions should be reviewed when loading the vehicle and any new ones entered in a separate place on the form. Note should also be taken of radios, tape decks, and CB radios that might have been included in the shipment.

Risk Analysis

This element is the final point in the outbound terminal process. Proper precautions taken will allow a terminal to determine if a loss occurred while the cargo was in the container yard or while it was aboard the ship.

Risk should be reduced to an acceptable level:

- If the container is sealed,
- If the seal is physically tested for intactness,
- If special security procedures are applied to high risk cargo.

ELEMENT: ⒟ AFTER DELIVERY OF AN OUTBOUND CONTAINER,
THE DRAYMAN MOVES TOWARD THE CONTAINER
STORAGE AREA OR GATE

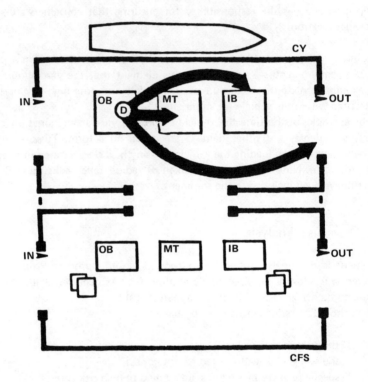

The Operation

The truck pass should indicate the nature of a drayman's visit to the container yard. The pass authorizes the drayman to travel within the yard and provides personnel with a means for determining his authenticity. It also enables yard personnel to direct a drayman who is unfamiliar with the yard to the proper area.

After delivering the outbound load the drayman should be directed to the proper area by any of the means previously mentioned in CY OUTBOUND ELEMENT B.

Empty Container—Prior to Drayman Arrival. The empty delivery clerk should receive daily an empty container list from the inbound freight department. This indicates the containers to be released by:

- Type of equipment
- Vessel and voyage
- Shipper
- Booking number

Empty Container—Drayman Arrives. When the carrier arrives at the empty delivery window to pick up a container, his truck pass will already state the nature of his visit, (pick up empty, recorded by the gate guard).

If the trucker is a house carrier, he will present a release slip obtained from the terminal dispatcher. If an interline trucker requests a container, he will provide a booking number. The empty delivery clerk will check the daily empty container list to validate the booking and the fact that it has not been previously covered.

After the request to pick up an empty has been verified, the delivery clerk will indicate approval on the truck pass and note the release on the empty container list. If the above procedures cannot be followed because of lack of information, release of a container will be denied, and the driver will be instructed to (1) contact his dispatcher for further information or (2) receive verbal authorization from the terminal documentation supervisor.

After the carrier has been authorized to pick up an empty container, the empty delivery clerk will initiate the equipment interchange and delivery report (EIDR). The carrier may not be assigned a specific empty container at this point. Therefore, container information for the EIDR may need to be recorded later when the drayman actually receives the empty as mentioned in the next element, CY Outbound Element E.

Risk Analysis

A truck stopping in the yard poses a risk to cargo security. The following theft possibilities arise during this element:

1. Stolen loose cargo placed in a tractor
2. Stolen loose cargo placed in an empty container
3. Full container theft by a drayman

Risk should be reduced to an acceptable level:

- If draymen are not permitted unauthorized stops in the yard,
- If traffic patterns minimize confusion and allow quick turnaround time and reasonable observability by security and supervisory personnel,
- If yard personnel assist or question nonmoving drayman.

ELEMENT: Ⓔ DRAYMAN WITH AN EMPTY CONTAINER MOVES TOWARD THE GATE

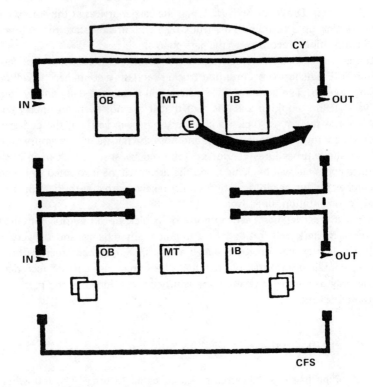

The Operation

A trucker (with proper authorization to pick up an empty container) arrives at the empty storage area. Yard personnel examine his truck pass to verify his authority and issue an empty container. The yard personnel initial the truck pass, and the drayman proceeds toward the gate. Security procedures for the issuance of empty containers are the responsibility of the gate guard. The truck pass serves as his operating document.

Empty Container Pick Up. In order to release a container, terminal personnel verify the nature of drayman's visit and his authority to receive a particular container. After a container has been provided to the drayman, the terminal personnel initial the truck pass to indicate their approval of the pick up. Empty containers should be opened to make sure no loose cargo remains. Full containers should be examined for proper container number. If the yard personnel are unable to perform the container examination procedures, they should be part of the gate guard responsibilities.

Empty Container Moving Toward Gate. While an empty container is moving there is virtually no possibility for theft. However, if a driver with an empty container stops in the yard, a possibility exists for placing stolen cargo in the box. The chance of this occurring is minimized when draymen are provided clear exit directions upon leaving the outbound area. Directions can be provided orally by the yard personnel and visually through use of a truck pass or a well-marked container yard.

Yard personnel should be instructed to remain alert for draymen with empty containers at rest in the yard and periodically examine the container of any drayman at standstill. Crane operators and straddle carrier drivers seated high above ground operations have an ideal vantage point from which to notice parked trucks.

Before reaching the gate, the drayman will stop and have his equipment tested for roadability at the inbound inspection station. The container and chassis will be examined for any physical defects and the exceptions noted on the equipment interchange. Empty container inspection procedures usually have the mechanic enter the box and look for damage in the top and sides. This provides an opportune time for the mechanic to perform a security function in that he can also look for loose cargo.

Risk Analysis

Cargo loss can be incurred during this element when

1. Stolen cargo is placed inside the draymen's tractor.
2. Stolen cargo is placed inside an empty container. Security from these potential loss situations is achieved when (1) the empty-yard personnel examine all empty containers before they are released and (2) the drayman moves to the gate without intermittent stops.

Risk should be reduced to an acceptable level:

- If all empty containers are examined for loose cargo,
- If yard personnel assist or question nonmoving drayman,
- If drayman are not permitted unauthorized stops in the yard,
- If empty yard personnel review truck pass information and then initial the pass.

ELEMENT:(F)   DRAYMAN WITH AN EMPTY CONTAINER
EXITS THE CY

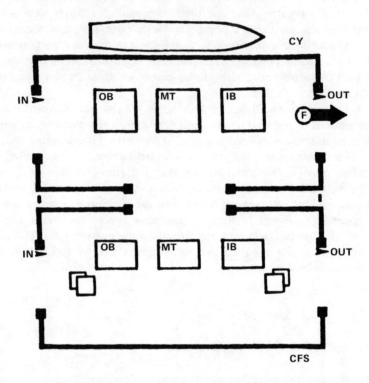

The Operation

A tractor/chassis with an empty container exits the container yard. A potential for cargo loss exists in that loose cargo can be placed in the empty container for transport out of the yard. The gate guard has security responsibility for this element, and the truck pass is his main operating document.

Gate Procedures. The exit gate guard provides the final security check of empty containers leaving the terminal. The guard will perform the following procedures:

- Examine the empty box for loose cargo.
- Examine the truck pass for completeness, accuracy, and proper signatures.
- Record the time out.

Container Examination. Loose cargo could remain in the container through an unloading error or stolen cargo could be placed in the box. For these reasons the guard needs to visually inspect the empty container. Instructions for the guard as to container examination will have to state who is going to open the container. In some instances, the guard will do this and the drayman will remain in his tractor. In other instances, the drayman will leave his tractor and open the container himself. Whether the guard or drayman actually opens the container will depend on the contact between the yard and the security force, and union considerations.

Truck Pass Examination. The gate guard verifies the accuracy and completeness of the truck pass by:

- Comparing the truck pass chassis and container numbers to the actual chassis and container numbers
- Examining the signature/initials for propriety
- Making sure all required information is on the truck pass.

All truck pass information should be written with ink. Some terminals prohibit any alteration to the originally recorded truck pass information. If alterations are required for any reason (e.g. clerical error, incorrect waybill), a new truck pass is issued. Each terminal should establish its own procedures concerning changes to the originally recorded truck pass information.

Since the guard may not be a steady terminal employee, it is a good security procedure to have signature cards of authorized clerks available in the gatehouse. When signature cards are maintained in the gatehouse, they should be stored in such a manner that the information is not available to unauthorized persons.

Record Time-Out. After the exit security procedures have been performed, the truck pass should be stamped with the time out and a copy given to the drayman. Terminal management reviews the truck passes daily for numerical sequence, completeness of information, and truck turnaround time.

The truck pass provides the terminal with a reference record, which is needed when a claim for stand-by time is filed by a motor carrier. An analysis of turnaround time might also provide information on operational bottlenecks and potential areas of vulnerability in the security system.

Risk Analysis

The possibility of stolen cargo being placed in an empty container or tractor for transport out of the container yard is the security risk in this element. Since the empty container is previously examined at the empty yard and at the inspection station, the only opportunity for such theft is when the truck is traveling between the inspection station and the gate. Stolen cargo placed in a drayman's cab is difficult to detect for union contracts might prohibit a security guard from actually entering the tractor.

Risk should be reduced to an acceptable level:

- If the drayman is not permitted unauthorized stops in the yard,
- If the empty container is examined,
- If the truck pass is examined for completeness and accuracy,
- If the truck pass is reviewed by management.

CY OUTBOUND

ELEMENT: Ⓖ DRAYMAN WITHOUT A CONTAINER EXITS THE CY

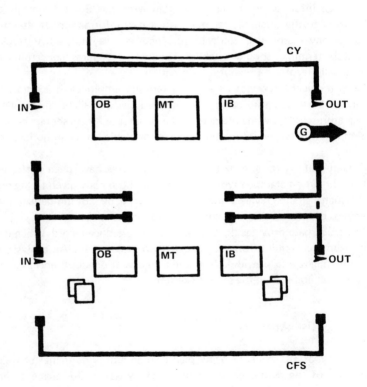

The Operation

A tractor or tractor with a chassis exits the container yard. The terminal faces only the risk of "pocket theft" during this element. Stolen small cargo might be transported out of the yard with the trucker. The gate guard has security responsibility for this element and the truck pass is his main operating document.

Risk Analysis

The security procedures and risk analysis for this element are similar to CY Outbound Element F—drayman with an empty container exits the yard.

Model 2
Container Yard - Inbound

Element	Description
A	Gate entry to pick up a full inbound container.
B	Drayman with a container moves toward the container yard storage area.
C	Container discharged from the vessel and moved to the inbound stack.
D	Drayman picks up an inbound container and moves toward the gate.
E	Gate exit with a full inbound container.

CY INBOUND

ELEMENT:(A)   GATE ENTRY TO PICK UP A FULL
               INBOUND CONTAINER

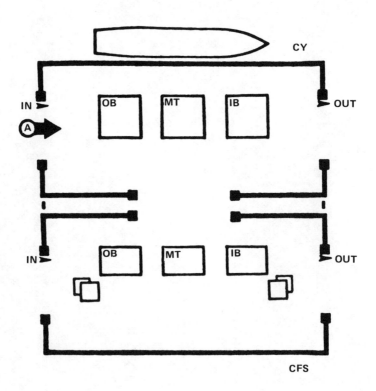

The Operation

Tractor without a container enters the yard to pick up a full or empty box. A gate guard is responsible for this function. While performing his security duties the guard is also gathering information for claims prevention, insurance, and equipment control functions. The gate guard procedures during this element are the same as those previously mentioned in CY Outbound Element A.

Required Documentation. The gate guard should record the container number to be released on the truck pass. This information can be obtained from the drayman's copy of the bill of lading (delivery order) that usually accompanies the driver.

If the drayman does not possess the proper documentation for receiving inbound cargo, the guard should direct the driver to the terminal delivery clerk for further assistance.

Having the guard responsible for only directing drivers without documents does not slow down gate traffic. Terminal management should establish documentation and information standards for the pick up of inbound containers and make sure terminal guards are following these rules. A list of authorized motor carriers and required delivery documentation and information should be maintained in the guard house as a reference.

Risk Analysis

Risk of cargo loss derives from containers being released from the yard without proper documentation being requested from the drayman. If the terminal delivers containers based on verbal information or a scrap of paper, there is a high probability for an entire container theft.

Risk should be reduced to an acceptable level:

- If the drayman presents a copy of the bill of lading (delivery order),
- If the motor carrier company is authorized by the terminal to transport inbound cargo,
- If proper data is recorded on the truck pass for future reference.

ELEMENT: Ⓑ DRAYMAN WITH A CONTAINER
MOVES TOWARD THE CONTAINER
YARD STORAGE AREA

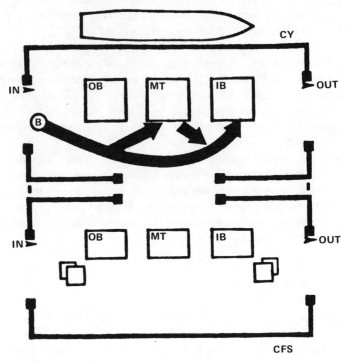

The Operation

After clearance by the gate guard, the drayman proceeds to the delivery window to obtain authorization to pick up a container. The delivery clerks are responsible for approving the drayman's request for a container. Thus, they perform the main security function in the movement of inbound containers.

A copy of the bill of lading (delivery order) is the document presented by the drayman. It establishes his right to pick up a container. If the drayman desires a foreign container, a customs entry must be on hand before pick up authorization is granted. After the delivery documents are in order, the drayman proceeds towards the container storage area.

Two situations are covered in this element: (1) a drayman entering with the sole purpose of picking up a full inbound container, and (2) a drayman with a dual mission, delivering an empty and receiving a full inbound box. The process of delivering an empty container to the yard poses no risk to cargo security; therefore, this element covers only the pick up of a full inbound container.

Full Container—Prior to Drayman Arrival. Prior to vessel discharge, terminal delivery personnel prepare the equipment interchange-out and delivery record (EIDR) for each container. (For this analysis it is assumed that the equipment and delivery information are combined on one document. However, terminals may desire to use separate documents for the equipment interchange and the delivery record).

If customs entries for foreign cargo are received, delivery personnel record the entry number on the EIDR and container control listing and forward the entry to customs. Every bill of lading is covered by a customs entry.

After the vessel has completely discharged its cargo, the exact yard location is recorded on the EIDR and the EIDRs are then filed awaiting delivery of the container.

Full Container—Drayman Arrives. When the carrier arrives at the delivery window to pick up a full container, the truck pass should already state the container number desired (recorded by gate guard from the delivery order, see Inbound Element A). If the truck pass is not completed, this indicates to the receiving clerk that the carrier does not possess a delivery order. The delivery order is the shipper's authorization to the terminal to release a container to the drayman.

This document is usually physically handed to the motor carrier by the customs broker or delivered by the broker's courier directly to the terminal.

Requiring that the drayman present a valid delivery order to the terminal when he arrives to pick up a container is a critical security procedure for preventing large scale container theft. One customs entry may clear (and one bill of lading may contain) from one to any number of containers. But one delivery order should be required for each container exiting the yard. Demanding that a delivery order be presented by the drayman for *every* container leaving the yard provides the maximum protection against cargo loss from employee collusion or fraudulent paperwork.

Full Container—Documentation. When the paperwork is approved by the delivery clerk, the yard location will be noted on the truck pass. If the cargo requires customs clearance, the customs entry, truck pass, and EIDR will be returned to the driver. He will be directed to the customs office prior to picking up the container listed on the truck pass and/or EIDR. If the cargo does not require customs clearance, the truck pass and EIDR will be returned to the driver, and he will be directed to the pick up location indicated on the truck pass and/or EIDR.

The security procedures for a truck moving to receive a container are indicated in CY Outbound Element D.

Risk Analysis

The possibility of a full container theft being initiated during this element exists. If a terminal authorizes release of a full container without receiving proper documentation from the drayman, it assumes considerable security risk. This must be weighed against operating efficiency.

A terminal can operate at different levels of security in performing the delivery function, based on the documentation requirements established.

- HIGH: Delivery order must be presented by the drayman.
- MEDIUM: Delivery order not presented by the drayman but mailed by the customs broker to the terminal. Drayman presents some form of documentation.
- LOW: Delivery order not presented by the drayman but mailed by the customs broker to the terminal. Drayman orally provides container information.

The appropriate level of security depends on terminal operating procedures and cargo loss history.

Risk should be reduced to an acceptable level:

- If appropriate requirements for issuance of a container are established and monitored,
- If the equipment interchange and delivery record are properly completed by terminal personnel.

ELEMENT: Ⓒ

CONTAINER DISCHARGED FROM THE VESSEL AND MOVED TO THE INBOUND STACK

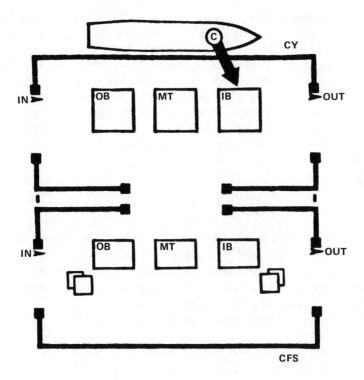

The Operation

Containers are discharged from the ship to the container yard. The supercargo, supervisor, hatch clerk, and walking boss control this function. Their main duties are operational, to move the cargo off the ship as fast as possible. In addition to this primary function, these employees perform valuable security functions when they examine the cargo for container number, seal number, and seal intactness. This information is invaluable to the claims process and loss prevention program.

Examine Containers. Discharged containers should be examined at the stringer or at the yard spot soon after storage for the proper container number, seal number, and seal intactness.

Examining the container at this point isolates the terminal's liability to the period of time in which the container is physically on terminal premises. This inspection informs management of containers that have been broached before they reach the yard. Determining the intactness of a container at the stringer or when it is initially placed in the yard is invaluable when a claim arises from an overseas shipper or terminal operator.

Storage of Containers. Containers should be stored in the yard in a manner which maximizes security without causing an unnecessary delay in operations. After the container is placed in the yard the terminal needs to obtain the exact storage location to facilitate the release of an inbound box, determine the safety of the storage area, and institute additional security procedures for high risk cargo. The storage location of each container can be determined before the vessel discharges cargo or verified after the fact through a physical inventory. A daily inventory of all full containers might be conducted by a security guard or clerk if the time and cost permit. The terminal should establish special security procedures for "high risk" cargo entering the yard.

Risk Analysis

The major cargo loss risk arises from container numbers and seals not being examined when cargo is discharged from a vessel. If the container number, seal number, and seal intactness are not examined it becomes impossible for the terminal to pinpoint WHEN, WHERE, WHY and HOW inbound cargo losses occurred. Special security measures should be used for high-risk cargo.

Risk should be reduced to an acceptable level:

- If the container and seal are examined at the stringer or in the CY immediately after storage,
- If special security procedures are used with high risk cargo.

ELEMENT:Ⓓ DRAYMAN PICKS UP AN INBOUND
CONTAINER AND MOVES TOWARD
THE GATE

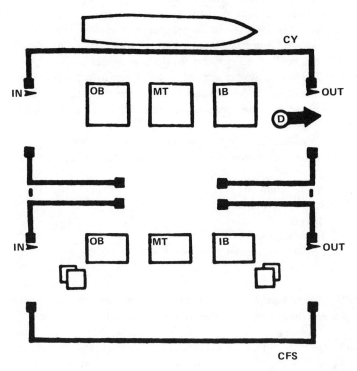

The Operation

The yard personnel release a container to the drayman as directed by the truck pass and/or equipment interchange. They initial or sign the truck pass and direct the drayman to the roadability equipment inspection area. After the container and chassis have been examined, and delivery paperwork completed, the drayman heads toward the gate with the full inbound box.

Yard Releases Container. A drayman arrives in the container yard with proper documentation and desires to pick up a full container. The yard personnel are responsible for delivering the correct box to the drayman as specified by the truck pass and/or container release document (equipment interchange-out) prepared by the delivery clerk. The yard personnel perform the delivery, and sign or initial the truck pass or release document.

Equipment Inspection. The drayman with a full inbound container will proceed to the roadability inspection station. Mechanics will examine the equipment and note any deficiencies on the EIDR.

United States Customs. After the roadability inspection the trucker may proceed to the United States Customs area to have the cargo examined. When this situation occurs, the original seal is broken by the drayman, the container contents examined, and a customs seal is given to the drayman for resealing the box.

The equipment interchange and delivery record should indicate the number of the old seal broken at customs and the new seal applied after the cargo is examined. The seal is usually applied by the drayman in the presence of customs personnel. A record of the broken seal is valuable to the terminal operator because it establishes proof that the container was not broached before reaching customs.

Final Delivery Procedures. The trucker then proceeds to the delivery window area where the following EIDR information is verified or completed if necessary:

- Container number
- Required signatures
- Chassis number
- Tractor number
- Truck license number
- Seal number

The EIDR is then signed by a terminal employee and the drayman and a copy given to the drayman. The driver then proceeds toward the exit gate.

Terminal Documents. The terminal should maintain a permanent record of delivered cargo. The container control list and EIDR should contain all the information necessary for cargo tracing and proof of delivery. A file should be maintained (by vessel and voyage) of the container control list and the EIDR.

Risk Analysis

The risk to cargo security in this element involves yard personnel releasing an incorrect container to the drayman and this error not being caught by the delivery clerks. Yard personnel and the delivery clerk perform the security procedures in this element.

Risk should be reduced to an acceptable level:

- If yard personnel indicate their approval of the release of a container on the truck pass,

- If the equipment roadability inspection is performed properly,
- If a record is maintained of the original seal number broken at customs and the new seal number applied to the box,
- If the terminal operator retains the necessary information for cargo tracing and proof of delivery,
- If the EIDR-out is properly completed and the information verified before the drayman reaches the gate.

CY INBOUND

ELEMENT:Ⓔ GATE EXIT WITH A FULL INBOUND CONTAINER

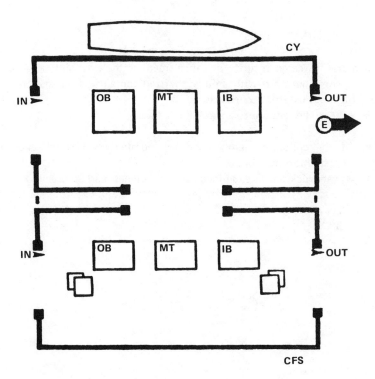

The Operation

The main security procedure for inbound cargo has already been performed. Therefore, the gate guard should double check the container number, seal number, and physically test the seal for intactness.

Final Security Procedure. The guard at the exit gate provides the final opportunity for the terminal to verify the security over inbound cargo. The guard will perfrom the following procedures:

- Compare the truck pass container number to the actual container.
- Compare the seal number to the actual seal on the container.
- Physically pull the seal to test intactness.
- Examine the truck pass for the required signatures.
- Record the time out.

Signature cards of authorized clerks should be maintained in the gatehouse containing name, signature, and initials. A substitute guard would find such cards useful. The signature cards should be filed in such a manner that this information is not available to unauthorized persons.

Risk Analysis

The main risk to cargo security in this element is the possibility of a drayman exiting the container yard with an unauthorized container. Final gate procedures should protect against this occurrence.

Risk should be reduced to an acceptable level:

- If the container number and seal number are verified, and the seal is tested for intactness,
- If the truck pass is examined for completeness and accuracy.

Model 3
Container Freight Station - Outbound

Element	Description
A	Gate entry with outbound CFS cargo.
B	Drayman moves towards CFS outbound break bulk area.
C	Outbound break bulk placed into container.
D	Outbound container moved from CFS to CY.
E	Empty container enters the CFS from the CY.
F	CFS empty container moved to the CFS dock.
G	Drayman proceeds to pick up inbound CFS cargo or depart CFS.
H	Drayman without inbound break bulk exits the CFS.

CFS OUTBOUND

ELEMENT: Ⓐ GATE ENTRY WITH OUTBOUND CFS CARGO

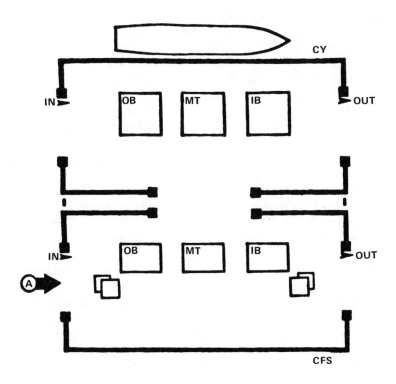

The Operation

The CFS operation is more prone to cargo theft than a container yard, but the possible dollar exposure is generally smaller per incident (break bulk cargo loss versus full container loss).

Therefore, the cost of security procedures must be weighed against the potential benefits, and they must especially be weighed in light of a terminal's actual CFS dollar loss history. A terminal should also consider the marketing and advertising benefits of having a secure CFS operation.

A guard controls this function and in addition to his traditional security duties performs valuable claims-prevention and insurance functions.

The possible contents of a typical truck pass and the uses of the pass data are expressed in the table below.

Truck Pass Data	Use
Vehicle registration #	Claims
Time/date IN	Claims
Tractor license #	Claims/loss trace
Company	Claims/loss trace
Seal number	Claims/loss trace
Chassis number	Claims/equipment control
Container number	Claims/equipment control
Purpose of visit	Security/loss prevention
Time/date out	Claims
Full or partial load	Claims

Note: The difference between this and the truck pass example for a CY (full or partial load added.)

Nature of Truck Visit. Trucks may enter the yard for one of four possible purposes:

1. Delivery partial load to CFS and exit.
2. Deliver partial load to CFS and pick up inbound cargo.
3. Deliver full load to CFS and exit.
4. Deliver full load to CFS and pick up inbound cargo.

Situations 1 and 2 pose the most risk of cargo theft from a security viewpoint. It is almost impossible to determine if extra stolen cargo has been placed in the container. Union contracts may prohibit the security guard from actually entering the container to examine the contents.

Recording the purpose of the visit on the truck pass technically authorizes the drayman to perform a particular function (and no other) within the CFS yard. It allows yard personnel to determine the nature of the visit for security purposes.

Full or Partial Delivery. Indicating on the truck pass whether an entire or a partial load is to be delivered allows yard personnel to determine if cargo aboard a container is authorized. Many trucks entering the CFS will have cargo for more than one terminal; therefore, the container will not be sealed. This fact makes CFS operations considerably more prone to pocket theft than a container yard.

Security Procedures. The main security procedures performed by the gate guard are:

1. Determine if the truck is authorized to deliver CFS cargo. (Does the waybill contain a booking number?)
2. Properly record information on the truck pass.

A complete description of the use of truck pass information is given in CY Outbound Element A.

Risk Analysis

The main loss risk in this element derives from a truck entering the CFS to deliver a partial load and exiting with stolen cargo in addition to the remainder of the load. A drayman entering without documentation or with incorrect documentation poses another major security risk.

Risk should be reduced to an acceptable level:

*   If the truck is authorized,
*   If whether a container is "full or partial" is determined at the gate,
*   If proper data is recorded on the truck pass.

ELEMENT: Ⓑ   DRAYMAN MOVES TOWARD CFS OUTBOUND BREAK BULK AREA

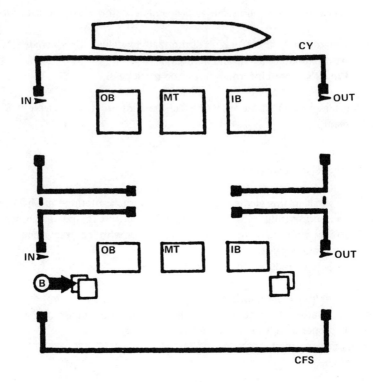

The Operation

The gate guard directs the trucker to the outbound (receiving) area of the CFS terminal. The trucker's paperwork should contain a booking number, or the terminal, ideally, should not accept his cargo. Assuming the cargo is accepted, the drayman or a lumper unloads the cargo onto the dock. A CFS checker then physically tallies the cargo, verifies the count to the trucker's waybill, and prepares a dock receipt. *At this point the CFS assumes liability for the cargo.* Thus, the CFS checker performs procedures vital to both security and liability.

Waybill. After the drayman reaches the proper area for unloading, the CFS checker examines the waybill for a proper booking number. The waybill booking number is compared to the daily list of booking numbers received from the outbound freight department. If the trucker does not have documentation which includes a booking number, the dock supervisor should be contacted. Depending on company policy, a terminal may or may not accept CFS cargo that arrives without a booking number.

Dock Receipt. When the cargo is on the dock, a CFS checker will physically tally the load and compare the actual count to the trucker's waybill count. If exceptions are noted, the dock supervisor is contacted and the situation is resolved to the satisfaction of the trucker and the CFS.

The dock receipt establishes acceptance of the cargo and claims liability. This document contains all the information necessary to ship the cargo and bill the customer. Information from the dock receipts is used to prepare the outbound container manifest, which will eventually accompany the cargo aboard the vessel. After the cargo delivery has been approved, the checker signs the trucker's waybill indicating acceptance of the cargo, and the drayman departs.

High Risk Cargo. Cargo attractive to theft is usually placed in a security corral or sealed inside a container set aside for that purpose. Good security over high risk cargo is also obtained by shipping the cargo as quickly as possible.

Final Paperwork. After all of the above procedures have been completed, the final paperwork is forwarded to the proper departments. The dock receipt is distributed as follows:

- One copy into a file by port of destination.
- One copy plus a copy of the trucker's waybill to documentation clerk/ department.
- Hard copy attached to the cargo.

Risk Analysis

The physical tally and comparison to the trucker's waybill is the main security procedure of this element. If the procedure is performed accurately and then monitored, the following types of cargo loss can be prevented or drastically reduced:

1. Short-shipments by the shipper
2. Acceptance of damaged cargo
3. Acceptance of unauthorized cargo
4. Acceptance of incorrect amounts of cargo
5. Employee theft (employee steals part of shipment but records correct amount)

Unfortunately, security procedures to counteract thefts brought about by collusion between the CFS counter and the drayman, are difficult to implement. Some possibilities: (1) frequent rotation of CFS counter employee. (2) reviewing for the same CFS counter employee and drayman signatures (or initials) appearing frequently on paperwork, (3) spot checks by security or operations management.

Risk should be reduced to an acceptable level:

- If the cargo is authorized,
- If the physical counts are performed accurately,
- If documentation is complete and accurate.

CFS OUTBOUND

ELEMENT:© OUTBOUND BREAK BULK PLACED INTO A CONTAINER

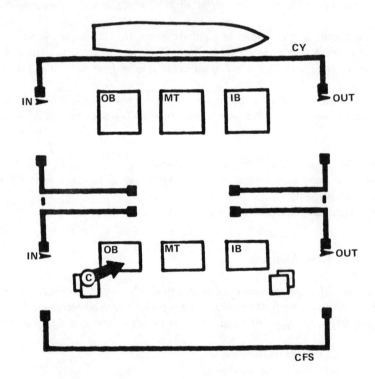

The Operation

Break bulk shipments are consolidated into container loads and placed inside an outbound container. The dock supervisor plans container loading by reviewing the dock receipts for all cargo destined for a particular port. He then preplans the stowage based on weight, cube, and nature of the cargoes, (hazardous, incompatible). A loading checker then counts the cargo during the loading process and the container is sealed by the supervisor. Opportunities for theft arise during this element when:

- Cargo is physically loaded into a container. Loading checker has security responsibility.
- Break bulk cargo rests in a partially loaded and unsealed container (either during normal working hours or after). CFS supervision or patrol guards have security responsibility.

Break Bulk Loading. After the dock supervisor has prepared the container loading preplan, CFS personnel are authorized to begin loading the container. The container loading preplan indicates the dock receipt numbers of break bulk cargo for a particular container.

When a break bulk shipment is loaded into a container, a loading checker removes the dock receipt from the cargo and counts the freight during the loading process. He records the count totals and the container number on the dock receipt and delivers all the dock receipts applicable to a certain container to the CFS office. If the loading count differs from the receiving count, the exception should be immediately reported to the dock supervisor. Special problems arise in counting because of the different units of measure used for describing the same quantities (one pallet may contain 30 cartons). Therefore, care must be taken to record receiving and loading counts in the *same* unit of measurement.

Break Bulk in a Partially Loaded Unsealed Container. This situation poses a unique problem to security in that cargo has already been tallied and any theft occurring at this point might not be detected until the container is unloaded overseas. The design of the CFS dock may prohibit the closing of container doors at the end of operations, unless the container is actually moved far from the loading location. The best security for a partially loaded container at the dock is achieved when the doors are closed and the box is sealed. However, operating practicalities and cost may prohibit this procedure. During normal working hours all CFS employees have access to a partially loaded container, unless management has established specific rules limiting the personnel allowed entering a container to the actual loading crew.

Sealing Container. After reviewing the dock receipts applicable to each container and examining the load for proper bracing, the dock supervisor affixes a seal to the container and records the seal number in his log. All seal numbers are accounted for and stored in a secure location while not in use.

Risk Analysis

The physical loading tally (when compared to the dock receipt receiving tally) is the main security procedure for this element. If the loading tally differs from the receiving tally, any of the following situations may exist:

1. Cargo loss undetected by the receiving process
2. Cargo loss while in CFS storage
3. Cargo loss during the loading process.

Therefore, unless loss prevention procedures are strictly maintained for the receiving and storage of CFS cargo, it is difficult to determine the WHO, WHY, and WHERE involved with missing cargo.

Safeguarding cargo in a partially loaded unsealed container is critical. Any losses during this stage of cargo movement might remain undetected until the container is unloaded overseas.

Risk should be reduced to an acceptable level:

- If the physical loading count is performed accurately,
- If the loading personnel are properly supervised,
- If cargo in partially loaded unsealed containers is safeguarded,
- If containers are sealed immediately after filling,
- If proper claims and cargo tracking records are maintained.

ELEMENT: ⓓ OUTBOUND CONTAINER MOVED FROM CFS TO CY

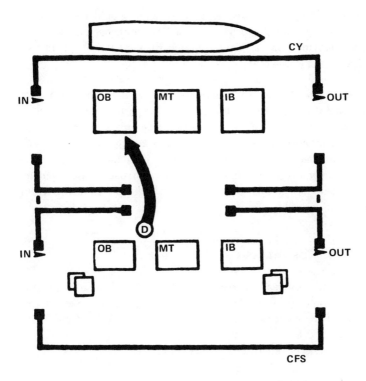

The Operation

The container is transported from the CFS to the CY. The CFS prepares a container manifest from the information listed on the dock receipts and forwards a copy to the container yard for use in preparing the vessel manifest. The main security related document used during this process is a CFS receipt. This contains shipping and cargo information similar to a trucker's waybill. This document accompanies the shipment and provides the authorization for the CFS container to enter the CY. The house jitney driver or outside drayman has responsibility for the cargo during transit between terminal areas.

Cargo Handling. The CFS may be physically located within the terminal area or off terminal premises. The second situation is more vulnerable to cargo theft because the drayman has the opportunity to sidetrack cargo before it reaches the container yard. For this reason a time log might be used that indicates:

TIME-OUT — CFS
TIME-IN   — CY

Any drivers taking an unusual amount of time should be questioned and seals closely inspected. When a driver with a CFS container enters the CY, the gate procedures are the same as CY Outbound Element A, except that a CFS receipt replaces the trucker waybill.

Documents. The CFS sends a copy of the container manifest and equipment interchange to the CY before the container departs from the CFS. This enables the CY to prepare the vessel manifest and determine a proper storage location before the container arrives. The CFS retains a copy of the dock receipt, trucker waybill, container manifest, and equipment interchange. The CY keeps a copy of the container manifest and equipment interchange. These documents, retained in a permanent file, contain the information necessary for cargo tracing and proof of delivery information.

Risk Analysis

The major and very real security loophole in this element is the possibility of a driver removing cargo from the container in the process of moving it from the CFS to the CY. This risk is especially critical if the CFS and CY are widely separated, or if non-house draymen are used.

Risk should be reduced to an acceptable level:

- If the container is properly sealed,
- If the transport time is checked.

ELEMENT:Ⓔ EMPTY CONTAINER ENTERS CFS FROM THE CY

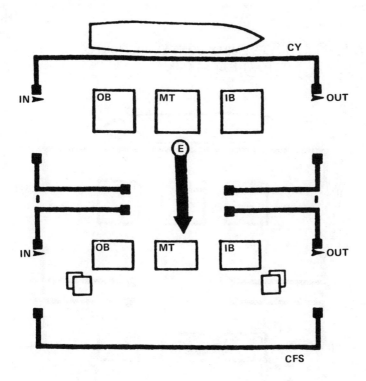

The Operation

An empty container is moved from the CY to the CFS. The main security consideration is the actual emptiness of the container. Checking the supposedly empty container for freight before it departs from the CY and before it enters the CFS will satisfy this security requirement. For equipment control purposes the movement of the container should be properly documented. A complete discussion of an empty container exiting the CY is presented in CY Outbound Element F.

Risk Analysis

Empty container can be used to transport stolen cargo; therefore, verifying that the container is actually empty becomes necessary.

Risk should be reduced to an acceptable level:

- If the container leaving the CY is actually empty,
- If the container entering the CFS is actually empty.

ELEMENT:(F) CFS EMPTY CONTAINER MOVED TO THE CFS DOCK

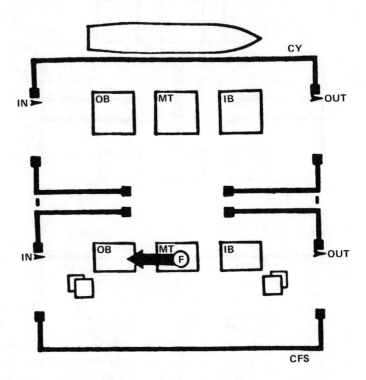

The Operation

The empty container is moved from the empty storage area to the CFS dock. Examining the container at the dock to ensure that it is empty precludes the possibility of stolen cargo being transported in the box during this element. While a container is in storage at the CFS, having the doors sealed prevents cargo from being placed in the box.

Risk Analysis

Risk should be reduced to an acceptable level:

- If the containers stored at the CFS are sealed,
- If the empty containers are examined at the CFS dock.

ELEMENT: Ⓖ DRAYMAN PROCEEDS TO PICK UP INBOUND CFS CARGO OR DEPART CFS

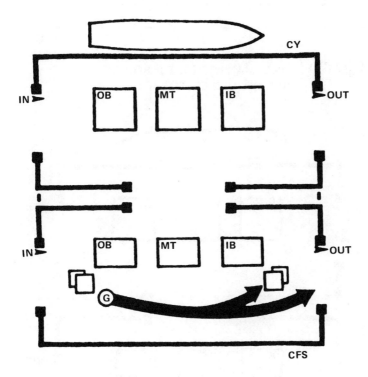

The Operation

After a drayman has delivered an entire or partial load to the CFS, he departs to pick up inbound break bulk or to exit the CFS. The truck pass indicates the nature of the visit; therefore, yard personnel have the means for determining if a truck is in the proper location.

Risk Analysis

The main threat to cargo security during this element is:

- A truck stopping to pick up stolen freight.
- Stolen freight placed on the truck, without the drayman's knowledge, before it departs the CFS outbound dock area.

Risk should be reduced to an acceptable level:

- If CFS employees are properly supervised,
- If the CFS yard is designed in a manner which permits vehicles to move without stopping in the yard, or being unduly hidden from sight.

CFS OUTBOUND

ELEMENT: Ⓗ DRAYMAN WITHOUT INBOUND BREAK BULK EXITS THE CFS

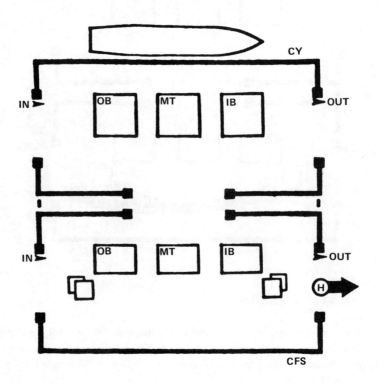

The Operation

A vehicle exits the CFS after delivering inbound break bulk to the CFS. The vehicle may be of the following types:

1. A tractor with an empty trailer; see CY Outbound Element G.
2. A tractor without a chassis/container; see CY Outbound Element H.
3. A tractor with a partially loaded trailer.

Situation 3 is the most risky situation in regard to cargo security. It is difficult to determine if all the cargo in a partially loaded trailer is authorized to leave the CFS. In addition to the authorized cargo destined for delivery at other terminals, the container might contain stolen CFS cargo.

Therefore, final security procedures must check this theft possibility as thoroughly as possible.

Final Security Procedures. The guard at the gate performs the final security function for the outbound CFS process.

- Record the time-out.
- Examine the truck pass for the required signature.
- Observe the contents of partially loaded container, looking for stolen cargo when a partial load is indicated on the truck pass.

The guard might be restrained by union contracts from actually entering a partially loaded trailer, but giving the appearance of looking for stolen cargo is a strong deterrent in itself. This small security procedure will discourage theft to some extent. Unfortunately, a high-risk-exposure still remains. We know of no truly effective preventative for this situation.

Risk Analysis

Partial loads exiting the CFS pose the main risk to cargo loss. Even though CFS theft is mostly of the pocket theft variety, continuous small dollar thefts can amount to a significant loss total.

Risk should be reduced to an acceptable level:

- If the truck pass contains proper signatures and is complete.
- If the guard views all partial loads.

Model 4
Container Freight Station - Inbound

Element	Description
A	Gate entry to pick up inbound CFS cargo.
B	Drayman moves toward CFS inbound break bulk area.
C	Inbound container moved from the container yard to the CFS.
D	Container moved from CFS inbound stack to empty stack.
E	Empty container moved from CFS to CY.
F	Full container unloaded at CFS dock.
G	Drayman picks up inbound CFS cargo and moves toward the gate.
H	Drayman with inbound cargo departs from the CFS.

CFS INBOUND

ELEMENT: (A) GATE ENTRY TO PICK UP
INBOUND CFS CARGO

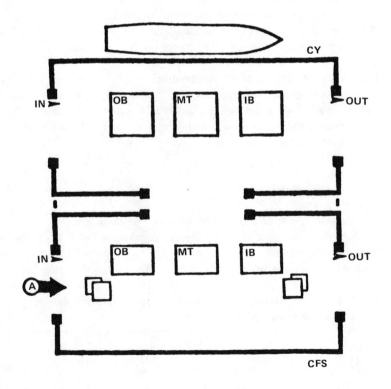

The Operation

The drayman enters the CFS yard to pick up a partial or full container load of inbound CFS cargo. A gate guard controls this function and records information on the truck pass which is valuable for security, claims-prevention, insurance, and equipment control. The possible contents of a typical truck pass and the uses of truck pass data are shown in the table below.

Truck Pass Data	Use
Vehicle registration #	Claims
Time/date IN	Claims
Tractor license #	Claims/loss trace
Company	Claims/loss trace
Seal number	Claims/loss trace
Chassis number	Claims/equipment control
Container number	Claims/equipment control
Purpose of visit	Security/loss prevention
Time/date out	Claims
Delivery-full or partial load	Claims

Note: The variance with the truck pass example for CY (full or partial load has been added).

Required Documentation. All draymen entering the CFS to pick up cargo should present a copy of the bill of lading (delivery order) to the gate guard. If the drayman does not possess the proper documentation for receiving inbound cargo, the guard should direct the driver to the CFS delivery clerk for further assistance.

Therefore, the gate guard either quickly examines the driver documentation or directs the drayman to a clerk who will provide further assistance. Having the guard responsible for simply directing drivers without documents does not unnecessarily slow cargo movements. Terminal management should establish documentation and information standards for the pick up of inbound CFS cargo and should make sure terminal guards are following these rules.

Nature of Truck Visit. Trucks may pick up inbound cargo under these conditions:

1. Pick up a partial container load of cargo after delivering a partial container load.
2. Pick up a full container load of cargo after delivering a full container load.
3. Pick up a partial container load of cargo without making a delivery.
4. Pick up a full container load of cargo without making a delivery.

Situations 1 and 3 pose the most risk to cargo security. At the exit gate, it is virtually impossible to determine if a partially full container holds stolen cargo in

addition to its proper cargo destined for other terminals. Union contracts may prohibit the security guard from actually entering the container to physically examine
the contents. Therefore, detection of this type of theft is extremely difficult.

The security procedure of recording the purpose of the visit on the truck
pass is an aid for detection of stolen cargo placed in a partially full container. The
truck pass authorizes the drayman to perform a particular function (and no other)
within the CFS yard. It also permits yard personnel to determine if a drayman is
actually performing his proper function.

Full or Partial Delivery and Pick Up. Indicating on the truck pass whether the
entire cargo load or only a partial load is to be delivered allows yard personnel
to determine if cargo abroad a container is authorized. Many trucks entering the
CFS will have cargo for more than one terminal; therefore, the container will not
be sealed. This fact makes CFS operations more vulnerable, from the standpoint
of pocket thefts, than a container yard.

Stolen cargo placed into a container along with authorized inbound cargo
is difficult to detect. This presents a major CFS security loophole.

Security Procedures. The main security procedures performed by the gate guard are:

1. Determine if the truck is authorized to pick up CFS cargo. (Does the
    drayman possess a delivery order?)
2. Properly record information on the truck pass.

A complete description of the use of truck pass information is provided in CY
Outbound Element A.

Risk Analysis

Risk of cargo loss derives from CFS freight being released from the terminal without proper documentation being presented by the drayman. If a CFS delivers
containers based on verbal information or a slip of paper received from a drayman,
there is a high exposure to theft.

Risk should be reduced to an acceptable level:

*   If the drayman presents a copy of the bill of lading (delivery order),
*   The proper data is recorded on the truck pass for future reference.

ELEMENT: Ⓑ DRAYMAN MOVES TOWARD CFS INBOUND BREAK BULK AREA

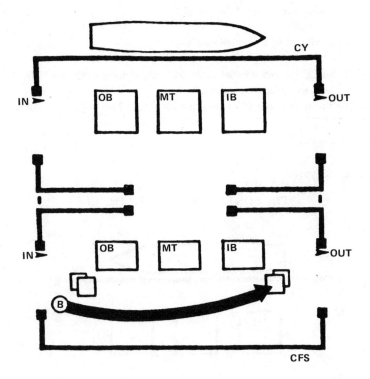

The Operation

The gate guard directs the drayman to the inbound (delivery) area of the CFS terminal. Providing clear directions to the inbound area of the CFS is the main operational, safety, and security procedure performed in this element. While a drayman is moving, there is little risk of stolen cargo. A CFS with separate outbound (receiving) and inbound (delivery) areas facilitates the operating function and also increases security.

Risk Analysis

The threat to cargo security during this element is:

- A truck stopping to pick up stolen cargo
- A truck proceeding to an area other than that authorized by the truck pass, and picking up stolen freight

Risk should be reduced to an acceptable level:

- If the CFS is designed in a manner which permits vehicles to move to the CFS docks without stopping,
- If gate guards properly perform their traffic function.

ELEMENT: Ⓒ INBOUND CONTAINER MOVED FROM THE CONTAINER YARD TO THE CFS

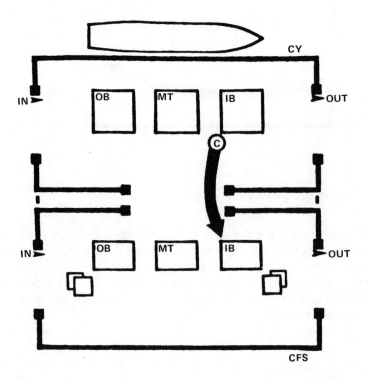

The Operation

The container is transported from the CY to the CFS. Two or three days before the vessel arrives the terminal operator will receive from the steamship lines the:

1. Inbound container list
2. Container manifests (cargo load plans)
3. Delivery records

The inbound container list and/or the container manifest indicate which containers should be released to the CFS. These documents authorize the CY to release a container to the CFS. The house jitney driver or outside drayman has responsibility for the cargo during transit between terminal areas.

Cargo Handling. The CFS may be physically located (1) within the terminal area or (2) off terminal premises. The second situation is more vulnerable to cargo theft because the drayman has the opportunity to sidetrack cargo before it reaches the CFS. For this reason a time log might be used which indicates:

TIME-OUT — CY
TIME-IN   — CFS

Any drivers taking an unusual amount of time should be questioned and seals closely inspected. When a driver with a CY container enters the CFS, the gate procedures are the same as indicated in CFS Inbound Element A. If the CFS gate guard discovers a broken seal, the CFS supervisor or security supervisor should be contacted immediately.

Documents. Before a container is released from the CY to the CFS, the CY needs to have on file an equipment interchange and a customs permit to transfer (P/T) (if the cargo is received from a foreign port of loading). This element assumes that the CFS is part of the terminal operation; therefore, no formal delivery or receiving documents are necessary.

The terminal maintain seal records which indicate intactness when:

- The container is discharged from the vessel.
- The container exits the CY.
- The container enters the CFS.

The seal records, container manifests, and equipment interchanges should be retained in a permanent file to permit cargo tracing and claims prevention.

Risk Analysis

The major security consideration of this element is the possibility of a driver removing cargo from the container in the process of moving the box from the CY to the CFS.

Risk should be reduced to an acceptable level:

- If the container is sealed,
- If the transport time is checked, and drayman taking an unusual amount of time are questioned.

CFS INBOUND

ELEMENT: Ⓓ CONTAINER MOVED FROM CFS
INBOUND STACK TO EMPTY STACK

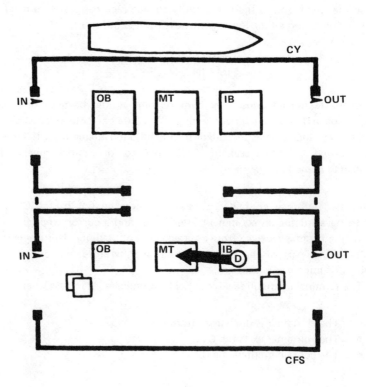

The Operation

After the cargo has been unloaded from an inbound container the empty box is moved away from the CFS dock to the empty container storage area. When the container is completely unloaded, the dock supervisor should inspect the box and arrange for the yard jitney driver to move it away from the CFS.

The empty containers stored at the CFS should be inventoried daily by the security guard or CFS personnel. A good security measure is to seal every empty container to preclude the possibility of stolen cargo being placed in the box. However, if this procedure is not used, the person performing the daily inventory should inspect each container for possible stolen cargo.

Risk Analysis

The main risk to cargo security in this element is the possibility of using an empty container to transport stolen cargo. Stolen cargo might be placed in the box while the container is at the CFS dock or while it remains in the CFS yard.

Risk should be reduced to an acceptable level:

- If the container is inspected before it is removed from the CFS dock,
- If empty containers stored at the CFS are sealed,
- If frequent inventory of CFS empty containers is taken.

ELEMENT:Ⓔ EMPTY CONTAINER MOVED
FROM CFS TO CY

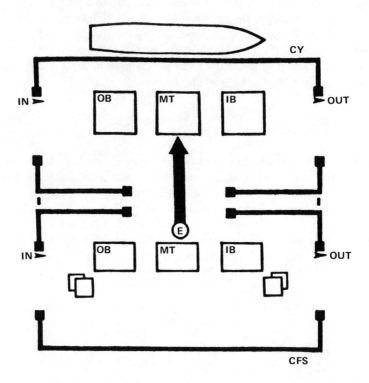

The Operation

The empty container is moved from the CFS to the CY. A yard jitney driver or an interline drayman has security and equipment control responsibility for the empty container during this element. The container should be inspected for emptiness when it exits the CFS and when it enters the CY. A log of empty containers should be maintained by both the CFS and the CY and the physical condition of all empties entering the CY should be thoroughly inspected.

Risk Analysis

The risk to cargo security during this element is relatively slight. Stolen cargo should be placed in the empty container or the drayman's tractor for transport out of the CFS area.

Risk should be reduced to an acceptable level:

- If the empty container is inspected upon exit from the CFS,
- If gate guard gives the appearance of examining the tractor for stolen cargo,
- If the CY and the CFS maintain accurate empty inventory records.

ELEMENT:(F) FULL CONTAINER UNLOADED
AT CFS DOCK

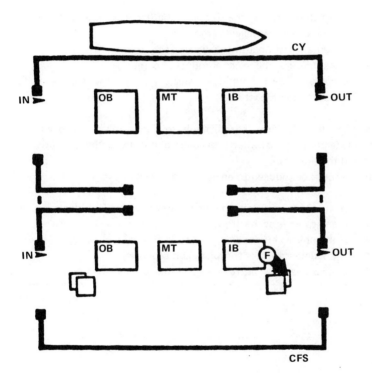

The Operation

A full container of inbound cargo is unloaded at the CFS dock. Before the container arrives at the CFS, the CFS should have received from the CY or steamship line a copy of the bill of lading (delivery record) and container manifest (cargo load plan). A CFS checker then counts the cargo as it is unloaded and records his tally on the container manifest.

If an exception to the paperwork count is noted, it should be brought to the immediate attention of the dock supervisor. A CFS clerk should also record the CFS storage location on each container manifest and make sure high risk cargo receives proper security storage as determined by the CFS management.

Risk Analysis

The physical unloading tally and comparison to the container manifest is the main security procedure of this element. If this procedure is performed accurately and then monitored, the following types of cargo loss can be prevented or reduced:

1. Short-shipments by the shipper (whether accidental or deliberate)
2. Acceptance of damaged cargo
3. Acceptance of unauthorized cargo
4. Acceptance of incorrect amounts of cargo
5. Employee theft (employee steals part of the shipment but records the correct amount)

However, for this element, it is difficult to design security procedures that will provide protection against thefts brought about by collusion between the CFS checker and the drayman.

Risk should be reduced to an acceptable level:

- If the container is sealed when it arrives at the CFS dock,
- If the cargo is authorized,
- If the physical unloading tally is performed accurately,
- If documentation is complete and accurate,
- If CFS checkers are rotated to other duties when collusion is suspected.

ELEMENT: Ⓖ DRAYMAN PICKS UP INBOUND CFS CARGO AND MOVES TOWARD THE GATE

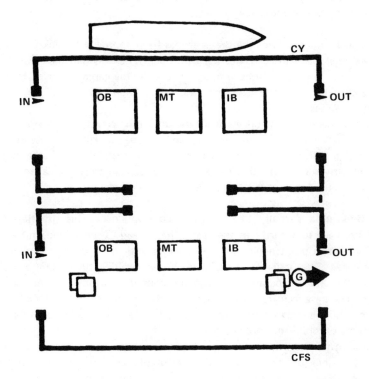

The Operation

The CFS personnel release cargo to the drayman as directed by the container manifest and delivery order. As the cargo is loaded into the container, a CFS checker tallies the load and records his count on the dock delivery record. The drayman signs the delivery record indicating his acceptance of the cargo and then moves toward the CFS exit gate. A copy of the delivery record is also retained by the CFS to provide a historical record of inbound freight movements.

Delivery Order. The delivery order (DO) is the shipper's authorization to the terminal to release cargo to a motor carrier. The delivery order may be presented by the drayman when he arrives to pick up the cargo or may be mailed directly by the customs broker to the terminal operator. The delivery order is first examined by office personnel, who record the location of the freight on the DO to assist the CFS loading personnel.

In situations where the drayman does not present a delivery order, the CFS should determine his authenticity through other documentation or procedures. A CFS should have formalized documentation requirements and terminal procedures covering the release of cargo.

CFS Cargo Loading. After the drayman has been approved to pick up cargo, the CFS personnel move the cargo to the CFS dock. The drayman then actually loads the cargo into his van or uses lumper services. As the cargo is moved to the CFS dock, a checker tallies the load and records his count on the delivery order and container manifest.

If the loading count differs from the unloading count, the exception should be immediately reported to the dock supervisor. Special problems arise in counting because of the different units of measure used for describing the same quantities. (one pallet may contain 30 cartons). Therefore, care must be taken to record receiving and loading counts in the *same* unit of measurement.

Break Bulk in a Partially Loaded Unsealed Container. This situation poses a unique problem to security in that cargo has already been tallied and any theft occurring at this point might not be detected until the container is unloaded by the consignee. The design of the CFS dock may prohibit the closing of container doors at the end of operations, unless the container is moved from the loading location. The best security for a partially loaded container at the dock is achieved when the doors are closed and the box is sealed. However, operating practicalities and cost may prohibit this procedure.

During normal working hours all CFS employees have access to a partially loaded container unless management has established specific rules limiting the personnel allowed into a container to the actual loading crew.

Final Documentation. The final paperwork maintained by the CFS and CY should contain all the necessary information for cargo tracing and proof of delivery. The CFS usually keeps a file by vessel/voyage which includes the permit to transfer, copy of the bill of lading, delivery order, and delivery record. The CY usually maintains a copy of the permit to transfer and the equipment interchange.

Risk Analysis

The terminal can operate at different levels of security in performing the delivery function, depending on the documentation requirements established. The appropriate level of security depends on the CFS cargo loss history and management's security objectives. A complete description of the different levels of security possible is given in CY Inbound Element B.

The loading tally with comparison to dock receipt unloading count is a strong security procedure for this element. If the loading tally differs from the receiving tally, any of the following situations may have occurred:

1. Cargo loss undetected by the receiving process
2. Cargo loss while in CFS storage
3. Cargo loss during the loading process

Therefore, unless loss prevention procedures are adequate for the receiving and storage of CFS cargo, it is difficult at the point of loading to determine the WHO, WHY, and WHERE involved.

Safeguarding cargo in a partially loaded unsealed container is critical, for any losses during this stage of cargo movement might be undetected until the container is unloaded overseas.

Risk should be reduced to an acceptable level:

- If appropriate requirements for issuance of cargo are established and monitored,
- If proper records of delivery are maintained to ensure cargo tracing,
- If the loading count is performed accurately,
- If the loading personnel are properly supervised,
- If cargo in partially loaded unsealed containers is safeguarded.

ELEMENT: (H) DRAYMAN WITH INBOUND CARGO
DEPARTS FROM THE CFS

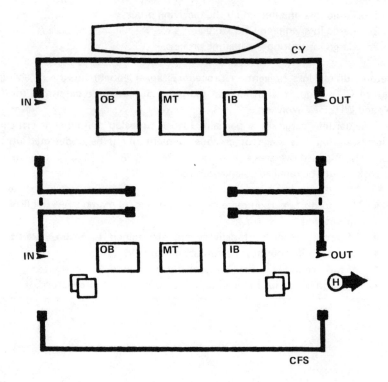

The Operation

After picking up CFS cargo, a drayman exits the CFS. The container may hold only cargo picked up at the current CFS or it might contain cargo previously received at other CFS operations. The latter situation is more risky in terms of cargo security. It is difficult to determine if all the cargo in a container is authorized to leave the CFS. In addition to the authorized cargo, the container might contain stolen cargo. Final gate procedures must check this theft possibility.

Final Gate Security Procedures. The CFS gate guard will perform the following procedures:

- Record the time-out.
- Examine the truck pass for the required signature.

- Observe the contents of partially loaded containers, looking especially for stolen cargo when a partial load is indicated on truck pass.

The guard might be restrained by union contracts from actually entering a partially loaded trailer, but giving the appearance of looking for stolen cargo is a strong deterrent in itself. This security procedure will discourage theft to some extent.

Risk Analysis

Less-than-container-load (LCL) shipments exiting the CFS present the main risk to cargo security. The detection of stolen cargo among authorized cargo is a difficult task. Although CFS theft is usually of the pocket theft variety, continuous small dollar thefts can amount to a significant loss total.

Risk should be reduced to an acceptable level:

- If the truck pass contains proper signatures and is complete,
- If the guard is especially alert to all less-than-container-load shipments.

CARGO TO AND FROM THE TERMINAL

The increasingly intermodal nature of cargo flow between motor carriers, rail carriers, marine terminals, and steamship lines increases the need for security controls and procedures to prevent cargo loss.

The freight carriers and the preparers of freight documentation (i.e., shipper, broker, forwarder) all perform security procedures during the course of their operations. The accuracy of the information they maintain and the type of security procedures used determines their ability to quickly settle claims and investigate and prevent losses.

By neglecting certain security procedures freight carriers can intentionally or inadvertently pass claims responsibility to another party. When this situation takes place, all parties involved incur unnecessary cost. Additional administrative cost has the same effect as a physical loss of cargo on financial statements. Both cause a decrease in profits.

Cargo to the Terminal

The "cargo to the terminal" portion of the intermodal cargo flow involves those concerns which move the export cargo and documentation *from* the shipper *to* the terminal operator. Those involved with this stage of the shipping process are the shipper, freight forwarder, trucking line, and rail carrier. The manner in which they impact cargo security is detailed below.

Domestic Shipper.   The shipper establishes the first point of liability for cargo security by sealing the container and recording the seal number on the inland bill of lading. Although sealing is not mandated by law, this simple and inexpensive security device will reduce cargo loss. When a trucking company receives cargo from the shipper, the company driver will usually insist that the container be sealed and the seal number recorded on the bill of lading.

However, rail carriers because of the large volume of cargo handled and the vast geographic area covered, cannot economically have an employee physically present to inspect the seal and sign for every container. The rail companies must rely on the shipper to perform this function. In addition, the shipper can assist the freight carrier with cargo security by not highlighting the nature of the cargo with a seal bearing the company name (e.g., Ajax Scotch 96431).

The shipper should maintain accurate seal records and, if possible, have the freight carrier sign a receipt for the cargo. Cargo security is increased and marine terminal operations are more efficient when the shipper provides the carrier with a handtag containing all the pertinent shipping information in easy-to-use format.

A handtag with the correct information, especially booking number and vessel/voyage, allows (1) a terminal operator to quickly receive containers and (2) permits a drayman to move quickly in and out of the yard.

The shipper initiates the export process when he requests an empty container from the terminal operator. The shipper informs the terminal of the size and type of container the date required, and the vessel/voyage desired. A terminal booking number is issued to the shipper.

Freight Forwarder.   The shipper may decide to employ a freight forwarder to prepare the necessary shipping documentation and coordinate the physical movement of cargo. The forwarder will:

1.   Arrange the booking with the steamship line.
2.   Arrange for cargo movement with the truck and/or rail lines.
3.   Prepare the necessary document masters. (Clients of the forwarder usually prepare the desired number of copies from the master).

The document masters prepared by the forwarder contain all the information available concerning a particular cargo movement. Keeping the paperwork secure is absolutely necessary to ensure cargo security. A bill of lading in the wrong hands makes a full container theft relatively simple and very difficult to prevent.

Trucking Company.   Moving cargo quickly increases a trucking company's profits and strengthens cargo security. Delays in getting trucks in and out of the yard notably decreases cargo security since drivers idle in the cargo areas. Thus, they have more time to observe container content and terminal security procedures.

After the shipper has obtained a terminal booking number, a drayman is hired to pick up an empty container. When the driver arrives at the terminal he should possess a document stating the size and type of container. shipper, vessel, and booking number. The empty box is inspected before it leaves the terminal yard and the driver receives an equipment interchange. The equipment interchange is the trucking company's record of the equipment condition. The marine terminal operator should maintain a record indicating the date, empty container number, and shipper to whom the box was released for equipment control and vessel stowage planning. The drayman then takes the container to the shipper.

After the empty container has been loaded by the shipper, the drayman arrives to transport the container to the marine terminal. Before the drayman signs a receipt for the cargo, he examines the seal applied by the shipper and makes sure the bill of lading indicates the correct seal number. The signed receipt indicates that the drayman has assumed responsibility for the cargo.

The shipper should provide the trucker with a copy of the bill of lading (waybill) to present to the marine terminal. A waybill informs the terminal that the cargo is authorized for shipment and facilitates the receiving process. When a drayman accepts cargo from a shipper, it is a good security practice to insist on receiving a waybill covering the freight. A proper waybill:

1. Increases overall cargo security
2. Permits more efficient truck and terminal operations
3. Decreases trucking company claims exposure
4. Decreases terminal operator claims exposure.

After the terminal has accepted the cargo the receiving clerk signs the waybill and equipment interchange. A copy of each of these is given to the drayman. These documents record that the responsibility for the cargo has passed from the drayman to the marine terminals.

Rail Carriers. Rail carriers typically do not deliver cargo directly to the marine terminal but to the port vicinity where it is subsequently moved by truck. The main risk of cargo loss to the rail carrier occurs when (1) a shipper does not seal a container (previously discussed under shipper segment) and (2) when a train is stopped outside a congested yard. Rail claims/loss records indicate most cargo losses are by theft of opportunity. High security seals might prove beneficial in reducing this type of theft. The extra time and equipment needed to break a high security seal might deter these thefts of opportunity.

Railroads should maintain seal records and documentation which provide a record of cargo movement and responsibility. Rail personnel should examine the container seal and verify the seal number against paperwork whenever a container enters or exits the rail yard. Adequate records enable a carrier to limit its liability to the actual period of time in which it was in possession of the cargo. The point of transfer between the rail carrier and the trucking line is particularly vulnerable to cargo theft. Security is best achieved when both parties clearly document seal integrity and cargo transfer.

Railroads are especially susceptible to theft at points in the shipping process when cargo is at rest. Cargo on hand in rail yards and cargo aboard a train at rest is attractive to theft attempts. A rail carrier maintains many terminal locations and it can not physically inspect and guard containers at all stopping points. Therefore, it is extremely important that rail yards maintain strong security over vehicular and pedestrian traffic. Terminal personnel should remain on the alert for unauthorized vehicles or persons. If shipments to particular locations are experiencing undue losses, the railroad should consider the use of high security seals on shipments through those areas.

Railyards serving port locations should specify the security procedues they will perform. The obligations of each party regarding seal and container inspection should be agreed upon. Security procedures to be performed by the rail carrier should be written in the contract. For operational efficiency the railroads should request that cargo for outbound shipments be delivered to the yard a predetermined time in advance of train departure. Cargo destined for the marine terminal should be picked up within a specified time period after train arrival.

Intermodal cooperation is needed between the rail carrier, truck carrier, and marine terminal to ensure safe shipment and isolate claims responsibility. Complete and accurate documentation verified by inspection at the cargo transfer points is necessary to isolate and prevent theft occurrences.

The rail carrier, truck carrier, and marine terminal should maintain records accessible by container number.

These records should clearly indicate the seal number attached to each container. If a receiver replaces a seal for any reason, the new seal number (along with the old number) should be recorded on the interchange. Information concerning the new and old seal should be forwarded to the previous delivering party so their records can also be updated. The seal records provide the audit trail for establishment of claims responsibility.

IT SHOULD BE NOTED THAT THERE IS A GREAT DEAL OF SIMILARITY BETWEEN THE MARITIME OPERATION AND A RAIL FREIGHT HANDLING SYSTEM (see figure 7-7).

- Breakbulk cargo being placed in containers is similar to freight being placed in railcar.
- Containers being placed on a vessel are, for security analysis purposes, generally similar to a container being placed on a railcar.
  Many of the processes, risk-points, loss-preventatives, and security procedures are identical.
  Thus the SSA, and many of the guidelines and recommendations contained in this book may prove of direct use in a rail environment.

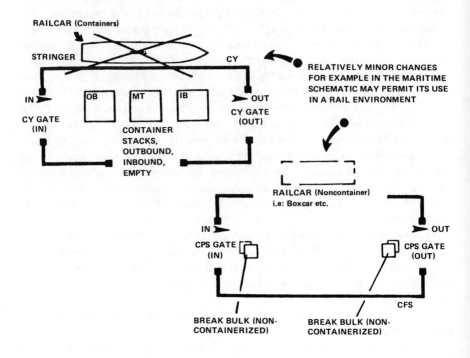

Figure 7-7. Relatively minor changes in the maritime schematic may permit its use in a rail environment.

Risk Analysis

Opportunities for theft and fraud exist in the movement of marine export cargo before the freight actually reaches the marine terminal. Unless cargo security procedures are applied by all the parties in the intermodal cargo flow system, determining the WHEN, WHERE, WHY, and HOW of cargo loss becomes impossible. The following are examples of some of the simpler types of cargo theft that can occur in the cargo "to the terminal" portion of the cargo flow. An imaginative mind with a bit of collusion can invent even more exotic scenarios.

- The shipper applies a damaged seal to the container, under-loads the box, and then files a claim against the drayage company. (All seal records are in order.)
- The freight forwarder provides a fradulent drayman with the documents necessary to pick up a container from the shipper.
- The trucking company is in collusion with a shipper; the container is not sealed until after part of the freight has been removed from the box.
- Rail carriers can provide same scenario as the trucking company.

Cargo from the Terminal

This portion of the intermodal flow involves movement from the foreign shipper to the marine terminal and then on to the consignee. The foreign shipper, customs broker, motor carrier, and rail carrier work together in this stage of the shipping import process. They impact cargo security as follows.

Foreign Shipper. The foreign shipper (like his domestic counterpart) establishes the first point of liability for cargo security by sealing the container and recording the seal number on the bill of lading. The bill of lading and a copy of the invoice are then directed by the shipper to the customs broker.

Customs Broker. A foreign shipper usually hires a custom broker to prepare the necessary paperwork and coordinate the physical movement of cargo for import shipments. The customs broker will:

1. Arrange to have an insurance company underwrite a bond for customs.
2. Coordinate arrangements between the steamship company, motor carrier, rail carrier, and shippper.
3. Ensure that the customs duty is paid, possibly advancing funds to the importer.
4. Prepare the customs entry form and other shipping documents.

After the broker receives the ocean bill of lading and invoice, the customs entry is prepared. If the importer does not designate a drayman, the broker selects the drayman and prepares a trucking bill of lading. A package of documents consisting of the customs entry, invoice, and delivery order is either picked up by the drayage company at the broker's office or sent by mail or courier to the terminal operator.

Trucking Company.   The trucking company is hired by the consignee or broker to pick up the inbound cargo. If the trucking company does not receive a delivery order for the freight, it is good practice to phone the terminal and find out if the proper documentation is on hand.

The trucker should present documentation from the shipper, to the marine terminal, authorizing pick up of a particular container. This document should state the container number, seal number, bill of lading number, and vessel/voyage for the cargo. The best security over the inbound movement of cargo is achieved when the drayman presents a delivery order to the marine terminal.

After the drayman has received a container, the box may be inspected by customs. When this situation occurs the drayman should observe the customs inspection and apply a new seal to the container in the presence of customs. The marine terminal then gives the drayman a copy of the record of delivery and equipment interchange. Both of these documents should state the old and new seal number and be signed by the driver and the terminal operator.

The drayman should not exit the container yard with an unsealed container. The signed equipment interchange and delivery record of cargo leaving the container yard transfers claims responsibility from the marine terminal to the trucking company.

Rail Carrier.   The rail carriers usually do not pick up cargo directly from the marine terminal, but receive the inbound freight from a trucking company. Cargo security and claims prevention is best achieved when the rail carrier and drayage company sign an agreement verifying the seal integrity and cargo transfer. The rail carrier should inspect the seal on each container it receives and make sure that the number is recorded on trucker's paperwork. If the seal is broken or missing, it should be documented and a new seal applied to the container. The marine terminal can assist the rail carrier by providing advance notice of shipments to the rail yard and by giving the drayman a complete set of paperwork covering the cargo movement.

Risk Analysis

As with the export cargo risk analysis, all parties involved with the import cargo flow can execute or be part of a cargo theft. The following are examples of some simple theft scenarios:

- The foreign shipper short ships goods and then files a claim based on a complete shipment.

- The customs broker makes a copy of the delivery order, rents a truck, applies a false drayage company placard to the tractor, then steals a container.
- The trucking line driver calls the terminal to verify that all documents are at the terminal (including delivery order) and then receives a container by presenting a valid container number written inside a match book cover or on a similar piece of scrap paper.
- The rail carrier container arrives from the drayman with a broken seal, rail personnel steal part of the freight and then reseal the container.

COST EFFECTIVE PROGRAM FOR A MULTI-OPERATOR PORT

A straightforward five-part program is recommended for consideration for those ports having more than one terminal facility. Its cost effectiveness is literally built in. No major expense is incurred until the program itself determines that specific circumstances and/or security penetration requires such expense.

STEP 1. SSA REVIEWS/TUNEUPS: based on individual operator SSA reviews of their own operation, institute appropriate low-level security recommendations as outlined in this book.

STEP 2. FAMILIARITY WITH ESCALATION PROCEDURES: operators to become thoroughly familiar with the higher-level security recommendations outlined herein, as well as any others that may emerge in the future as a result of individual SSA activity or security experience.

STEP 3. MONITORING FOR LOSS ESCALATION: create and *seriously maintain* an ongoing detection process to alert the port and through them, the operators, to any escalation of loss experience. Anonymity is the key to the success of this program.

STEP 4. ACTIVATION OF HIGHER LEVEL PROCEDURES: institute on an individual operator discretion basis, appropriate *temporary* higher security recommendations prepared by Step 2 as and while needed. Notify authorities.

STEP 5. DEACTIVATION: based on further monitoring (Step 3), remove the escalated security mechanisms as soon as losses reduce to acceptable levels.

STEP-BY-STEP DETAILS

Step 1—SSA Reviews/Tuneups

It is recommended that copies of this book be made available to all interests involved in the transport of maritime cargo, including related rail and motor carriers.*

Discussion of the SSA technique would be appropriate at a joint operators/port meeting.

Tenants are encouraged to conduct their own SSA reviews to the depth practical for their particular operation and resources.

Security gaps uncovered by the SSA should be corrected.

Step 2—Familiarity with Escalation Procedures

The port and each operator is encouraged to earmark the higher-level security recommendations appropriate to their individual operation should increased-risk conditions appear.

They should go so far as to prepare simple but written escalation procedures for the various SSA risk points uncovered. These should, of course, be restricted to "need-to-know" individuals and stored securely.

A sharing of knowledge on techniques and results should be encouraged.

Step 3—Monitoring for Loss Escalation

It is here that most maritime security efforts have been only partially effective. Marketing considerations, reputation with shippers agents, insurance costs, and the like provide very real "disincentives" to the sharing of loss data among operators.

For this reason, we recommend consideration of a monitoring technique that avoids these disincentives:

Anonymous Loss Reporting. It is recommended that the port prepare a stock of LOSS SITUATION FORMS of simple design and distribute same to the operators.

Spaces for date/approximate time/type of loss/value range of loss/description of circumstances/pattern with prior losses if any, should be provided on the form.

---

*The book should also prove to be an effective cargo loss prevention tool for air, rail and motor transportation industries not involved with the maritime community.

At the top of the form should appear the legend "No indication of origin is to appear on this form. Its use and storage will be under strict security precautions."

"Use plain envelope to mail to XXX"

Based on these, the port should conduct a continuing review to detect patterns, trends and the need for general security escalations.

Verbal reports of these should be given operators when appropriate. Written material should be kept to a minimum.

STRICT SECURITY IS MANDATORY FOR THE HANDLING, DISTRIBUTION AND STORAGE OF ALL REPORTS/NOTES/ FORMS.

Selection of the port person or persons involved is critical.

A "leak" of a sudden escalation in losses could have massive marketing implications.

Without this key monitoring step, however, the port and its operators are highly vulnerable to some rather impressive losses before typical informal monitoring methods can react and "spread the word."

Verbal comment on trends is to be considered useful in port coordination efforts with outside agencies.

Step 4—Activation of Higher Level Procedures

The earmarked recommendations (Step 2) are selectively activated when monitoring indicates the need.

Joint port/operator meetings (called by the port) are a reasonable vehicle for notifying tenants of an undesirable loss pattern—and the need for higher level security procedures.

Again, verbal handling is desirable.

Security, for marketing and competitive reasons, is paramount.

Invitations should be verbal, meetings private, notes and agendas nonexistent.

Step 5—Deactivation

This is, in simplest terms, Step 4 in reverse.

Joint meetings, based on the monitoring of a drop in the previously detected loss pattern, serve to reduce tenant security levels to normal once more.

Other Recommendations

The SSA technique, though described largely in cargo security terms, applies equally well to:

- Port facilities, non-port real estate and equipment security.
- Operator equipment and asset security.
- Rail, air and motor freight security.

It, and many of the specific recommendations covered in this book, may prove worthwhile in the above noncargo environments.

In addition, the cost effective program may prove applicable in the motor carrier association, or rail association, context with only slight modifications.

OTHER AGENCIES

Investigation and Prosecution

When cargo theft occurs maritime operators generally have the services of both local and federal agencies available to assist with investigation and prosecution. These agencies possess different ranges of jurisdictional power, different priorities, and will provide various levels of assistance depending on the nature of the particular case and the working relationship that has been developed.

Operators can receive assistance with the investigation of cargo thefts from the local Police, United States Customs Office of Investigation, and the Federal Bureau of Investigation. When a case is developed against a cargo thief, it can be prosecuted by the United States attorney, or the state, or the county District Attorney. A brief description of the typical jurisdictional responsibilities and procedures of each of these agencies is provided below.

Office of the United States Attorney. The Attorney General has given high priority to the prosecution of:

1. White collar crimes
2. Organized crime
3. Foreign counter-intelligence
4. Narcotics

Thefts of maritime cargo are subject to prosecution by the United States Attorney according to the federal statute authorizing them to conduct legal proceedings in cases involving thefts from interstate or foreign shipments (TIFS) and interstate transportation of stolen property (ITSP). However, United States attorneys adhere to the above mentioned priorities established by the Attorney General and these officials do establish policy guidelines for the prosecution of cargo theft crimes committed within their respective districts.

Federal Bureau of Investigation.   FBI agents have the authority to investigate waterfront crimes by federal statute. The law authorizes investigation of theft from interstate or foreign shipments (TIFS). The agency has shifted emphasis during the last few years as a result of the Attorney General's selection of certain priority areas for federal investigation and prosecution. The following areas were granted high priority status:

1. White collar crimes
2. Organized crime
3. Foreign counter-intelligence
4. Narcotics

United States Customs Service.   The Customs Service will generally investigate cargo thefts of merchandise under their jurisdiction as follows:

1. All imported shipments from foreign countries
2. Export shipments which are under customs bond or control

The Customs Office of Investigation is assisted by the Customs Patrol Officers and Customs Inspectors on the waterfronts. Thefts reported to customs but outside of their jurisdiction will be directed to the proper investigative agency.

Customs stresses the need for immediate reporting of thefts so that customs personnel can prepare their theft information system (TIS) reports (Form 153) and make necessary investigations. The customs service TIS is a valuable tool in the investigation of cargo thefts.

State and Local District Attorney.   State and county district attorneys will typically prosecute cargo theft cases regardless of the dollar amount. However, these agencies do not generally pursue cargo theft cases which should be handled by federal prosecutors.

State and Local Police Departments.   Police Departments, including State Police, when they receive calls from operators will proceed with routine investigative procedures. If the theft is not within their jurisdictional area, they will forward the case to the proper agency. Police generally desire to be informed immediately upon discovery of a theft, especially if the theft is in progress.

RECOMMENDATIONS

Port operators generally have significant resources available from federal state and local law enforcement agencies to investigate and prosecute cargo thefts. However, the focus of law enforcement has changed over the years, and the operators must develop cargo security programs and practices that are workable in the current environment.

Regardless of the agency performing the investigation, port operators can provide assistance by keeping a detailed log of all loss/theft occurrences and by continuously providing information to the police, United States Customs, and the FBI. This will serve two purposes: (1) to alert the investigating agency of any recurring loss patterns and (2) to provide documented evidence as to the cumulative effect of the thefts. If loss/theft incidents increase dramatically continuous reporting will focus the attention of investigative agencies on the seriousness of the problem.

Some port operators feel that law enforcement agencies have not been responsive to their needs. Because of this they prefer to investigate the theft internally, collect the available evidence, and only then call in an investigative agency. The agencies generally do not appreciate this method and would prefer to be called into the situation early. Notification of the theft permits the agency to assist the operator with the investigation or in some cases tie the theft in with similar occurrences, unknown to the operator, that may be taking place elsewhere in the port or at other ports.

In summary, operators should consider the local practicality of:

1. Appointment of a single individual to act as liaison with law enforcement agencies.
2. Establishment of documentation guidelines concerning theft reporting and the desired level of detail relative to various loss dollar values.
3. Establishment of guidelines for the distribution of loss/theft statistics to the various agencies as appropriate to the particular loss.
4. Establishment of guidelines for immediate notification of the appropriate agency when a theft occurs.
5. Development of investigation procedures for various types of theft.

As with other recommendations in this chapter, the level of detail and complexity of these efforts will depend on the degree of crime current at any given time and location, the cost/benefit practicalities of the situation, and the federal, state, and local law-enforcement climate.

8. Air Cargo

The air cargo industry moves only about 2% of all the freight within the United States, even with the growth the industry has experienced over the past two decades. Year-end reports indicate that the revenue ton-miles have continued a recent deteriorating trend in the domestic market—the volume cropping almost 6% during 1981.

Whether airlines make money on freight operation is almost impossible to determine. Methods of allocating air freight costs vary, making industry freight revenue results unclear and comparisons between individual airlines almost impossible. It is generally felt that the recent years have produced lean profits for the air freight industry as fuel and labor costs have soared, cargo carrying capacity has risen, and shipper demand has been down. This is in direct contrast to the 10% to 12% expansion in the sixties and early seventies.

Most of the air freight handled today is in combination passenger/freight flights during the day. Truck carriers have cut the use of all-freighter aircraft to concentrate freight on passenger-freight flights.

Small shipments continue to show a tremendous growth curve with most carriers. Estimates indicate that over 20% of all shipments consist of packages weighing less than 25 pounds. Handling costs vary directly with the number of pieces handled, but only marginally with per package weight. Lighter packages do not necessarily mean more revenues. More packages mean more revenue, but more labor costs and increased chances for theft and pilferage.

Today, forwarders attempt to become airlines while the existing airlines have gone into ground handling. The forwarders thus lose their

This chapter is adapted from U.S. Department of Transportation and The Airport Security Council. *A Study in Loss Prevention*. Washington, D.C. and Long Island, New York: 1980; and from Airport Security Council. *Reducing Opportunities for Crime*. Long Island, New York: 1980.

flexibility, and the airlines step into the many problems of handling freight. Forwarders now handle about 50% of all domestic air cargo business. This has come about since the passage of the deregulation act, which gave the forwarders the right to fly their own planes, and a large number of them have taken advantage of this authority.

The effects of the recent deregulation trends have been troublesome; many different things have happened and, not all the effects have been determined for the carriers or their customers. Many new carriers have entered the field and they may not have as much interest in security awareness as others have had—and still do. Carriers must still advise the Civil Aeronautics Board of their intentions or new route and rate, but CAB decisions are now made more quickly. Schedule approvals are no longer required, and many all-cargo flights have been cancelled. Such changes worry some shippers and some now consider using other modes.

The majority of air freight shipments will continue to be confined to time-sensitive goods, perishable items, and goods with high value per unit of weight. These criteria are the very ingredients for the heavy theft-related losses that have occurred in the industry during the last 20 years. Over the years, however, the airlines have concentrated on security awareness so that theft-related losses are now the lowest per dollar of revenue than any other domestic transportation mode.

AIR CARGO SECURITY: A STUDY
IN LOSS PREVENTION

Recent figures show that Airlines are losing $.36 of every $100.00 of cargo revenue as a result of claims of undelivered cargo. While not an astronomical figure, it does represent $5 million of lost profit each year in an industry that has to count every profit dollar carefully. Most of these losses are caused by theft or pilferage, and they can be prevented.

At least one city, New York, has an effective program of prevention that has reduced theft-related losses to a fraction of their 1969 level. This was accomplished despite a sharp rise in the value of cargo handled at New York's airports. Losses now are just $.03 for each $1000.00 worth of cargo carried, about 1/10 of the amount of loss in 1969.

This dramatic improvement did not come about just by apprehending criminals, or by implementing new and expensive security systems. It happened from within, as a natural part of operations, and was the result of increased efficiency and tighter procedural controls.

Loss prevention starts with the acceptance of a shipment. The cargo agent is the first person to have exposure to the cargo, and the way he does his job can have a lot to do with whether the cargo reaches its destination.

Since freight is most vulnerable during the interface between ground and air transportation, it is important that trucks be off-loaded carefully. During this process the cargo agent should verify the count and check for several key items. He should make sure the packaging is adequate so that cartons won't break open during transport; such breakage could lead to pilferage. Also, packages must be properly labeled, and lot labels should be prepared for all shipments.

The agent must make sure the commodity and value information is shown on the shipping documents and that any special handling instructions are clearly understood, since this is how the agent determines the handling of the shipment. The waybill is one of the two basic elements of cargo control, so accuracy is essential.

The other element is physical accountability, which means using signature service whenever possible to assign responsibility to an individual employee. The cargo agent should be required to sign and time-stamp the waybill before giving a copy to the driver. By this act the airline officially accepts the shipment.

Next, the agent should separate another copy for the origin station's records, making it possible for the airline to verify that the shipment is in the terminal. The remaining copies of the waybill are attached to one of the cartons for domestic cargo, while for international flights they are assembled and shipped separately. Where computer facilities are available, the waybill information can be put on line immediately, and then the airline has an in-house record that the shipment has been accepted.

Any employee can trace movements of the cargo. Experience has shown that it is better for everyone involved to have access to this information so that proper security precautions can be taken. Otherwise, there is a risk that essential personnel will not be alerted to the presence of vulnerable or high-value cargo. Regardless of whether a computer system is used, it is important to make sure the origin station's copy of the waybill is physically separated from the other copies and from the freight as quickly and efficiently as possible. This protects a shipment from disappearing without a trace, and it is a key element in the audit trail.

After a shipment has been accepted, it usually enters the airline's warehousing system, where it becomes vulnerable to a different set of potential loss situations. The key here is to limit the number of times cargo is handled. The most secure shipment is one that arrives at the receiving dock already contained in a unit. It can usually be sealed and the seal number recorded on the waybill.

Since loose cartons are most subject to theft, it is a good practice whenever possible to assemble this freight in carts on unit loads close to the receiving dock. Of course, as long as freight is near the dock, it must be closely watched.

When cargo is not packaged by the shipper, or when the cargo load is assembled near the receiving dock, the cargo must decide which assembly area to send it to. Care should always be taken to avoid mistakes, since misrouted freight becomes more accessible to theft.

Besides considering the destination, the agent must make decisions based on the kind of equipment the cargo will travel on. It may be added to a 747 container, or possibly a pallet, igloo, or bin. On the other hand, maybe it will be put on a cart for loose loading in a belly compartment.

It is also important to consider if the shipment is going on a cargo plane, or it will be transported to a passenger terminal for loading. Also, the agent must check to see if the shipment is reserved for a particular flight.

It is important that the cargo and documents arrive at the staging area together. The agent responsible for assembly should carefully check the shipment again for accuracy, making sure that the piece count is still correct, as well as the destination. The efficiency of the agent's work is another element in the protection of the freight. He must be responsible for verifying what cargo is loaded in a container or on a pallet or igloo, since his list becomes the record of the contents of the container. An error here can cause cargo to be unaccounted for, and therefore to become susceptible to theft. When the unit load is completed, documents go to the cargo dispatcher, or load control, for preparation of the manifest.

Whether manually or by computer, the dispatcher has to balance considerations of space, weight, special handling, and reserve status before making his decision. Once again accuracy is critical. The dispatcher must be sure to enter the correct flight information on the records in order to avoid causing lost or misdirected freight.

The shipment will be handled another time when it is loaded. If it is going to a freighter or wide-bodied aircraft, it probably will be palletized or placed in a container. This greatly limits the danger of theft. But if the shipment is dispatched on a passenger flight, it usually has to be transported to another terminal, and often it is carried loose on a cart. It is critical for security that this cargo move in closed vehicles. Whenever possible, ground transportation vehicles should be sealed, and the seal number documented. This is especially important for high-value cargo.

Strict time standards should be set and enforced for movements between terminals. Drivers must be directed not to deviate from the prescribed route, nor should they pick up any unauthorized passengers along the way. As an additional precaution, ground vehicles should be prominently marked with airline identification, as well as with a vehicle number on both sides and the back.

When a shipment arrives at its destination, or at an intermediate point, some of the same operating security problems need to be taken into consideration. In addition, there are new situations to deal with.

Arriving freight that has not yet been checked in is vulnerable. One of the ways operating efficiency can improve security is by making sure this process takes place as soon as practicable. Meanwhile, the cargo should be under constant observation.

There are various systems for checking in freight, and one of the most accurate is to have the checker count pieces without knowing how many he should find, then check findings against quantities listed in documents. Another method is to check each shipment against a copy of the waybill. Whatever system is used the final tally should always be double checked against the flight manifest.

Errors occurring prior to arrival can complicate the handling of off-loaded cargo. It's important that the overages and shortages be caught immediately and entered on a form that will allow corrective action to be taken. This form might be an irregularities report, exception report, OS&D, or any other form that serves the same purpose. Damaged cargo should also be noted on the sheet and then moved quickly to a special crib or restricted area.

When the freight has been checked in, it must be stored in preparation for pickup. It's important that the storage location be carefully noted on the air waybill, or some other appropriate record, since this is a point at which a shipment can be misplaced. If cargo is moved within the terminal, the new storage location also should be recorded.

Whenever possible, separate inbound and outbound cargo storage areas should be used. This will help avoid the misdirection of a shipment, which once again would make it accessible to theft.

The consignee must be notified that the shipment has arrived and provided with the waybill number and other information about the shipment.

In the case of international cargo, the consignee's messenger will be given documents allowing clearance of the shipment through customs. Since the papers control valuable merchandise, it is essential to verify the identity and authority of the runner.

The final element in the cargo transport cycle is delivery to the consignee, and this may be an area where security is most important. Statistics have shown that most freight thefts involve shipments weighing 50 pounds or more, and these usually leave the terminal by truck, under the guise of normal cargo.

One simple device that can help prevent this kind of loss is to place a physical barrier or to paint a line 10 feet back from the edge of loading and unloading docks. Drivers and other unauthorized persons should be prevented from going past this point, and cargo should never be left unattended outside the line or barrier.

Another important precaution is to make sure cargo doors are closed and locked when they are not in use. Also, employees should not be allowed to park their personal vehicles near the terminal building.

It is the responsibility of the airlines to deliver cargo only to the consignee or his authorized agent. The driver must establish his identity and authority to pick up the shipment. For domestic cargo, he should be able to supply the waybill number and flight information. If there is any doubt about the driver, it's best to make a phone call to the consignee for verification.

Equipment is available that can simultaneously photograph the driver and the delivery receipt or other documents. This is an important final safeguard that should be taken before releasing a shipment.

If possible, let one agent pull the cargo from storage, and a second person release it after getting a signed delivery receipt from the driver. This way the second agent can verify that the right shipment and only the right shipment has been released.

If the driver or the agent discovers an irregularity, the supervisor must be called. His job is to make careful note on the delivery receipt, or on an exception report, of any damages or shortages, thus protecting the airline against claims for theft or pilferage that may take place after the shipment is released.

Since the supervisor plays an important role in maintaining good operating procedures, he should spend as much time as possible on the floor, monitoring the work and providing assistance.

Special handling is called for whenever high-value cargo, hazardous materials, perishable items, or live animals are received for shipment. This freight requires separate arrangements and security safeguards in addition to normal operating procedures and practices. Cargo that qualifies for high-value security treatment includes such items as currency, stocks and bonds, gold and silver, gems, furs, jewelry, and watches. These comprise the major part of the value of all cargo losses.

When a high-value shipment is received, it should be counted immediately and moved to a secure vault or cage. As an added precaution, a log should be kept that identifies the cargo and indicates when it entered and left the security cage, as well as who brought it in and who took it out. Signature service is especially important here. A physical inventory of this storage area should be taken periodically. This will help guarantee maximum security.

High-value cargo should remain in the vault or cage until time for loading. If the total of such items scheduled for one flight is particularly high, police, whenever possible, or a security guard should accompany the cargo to the plane and observe the loading process. A good rule-of-thumb might be that $25,000 or more in high-value goods warrants a security escort.

Pick up and delivery should both be restricted to the time between 0800 and 1700 hours, Monday through Friday.

It pays to keep in mind that many items other than high-value cargo are particularly attractive to the potential thief.

If a shipment includes goods that are very portable and easily fenced, security can be improved by storing in an inaccessible location.

Cutting back on air cargo theft losses is not an impossible job, or even a particularly expensive one, as these procedures have shown. All that is required is a realization that theft and pilferage occur when errors are made. Cargo is vulnerable when procedures break down and rules are not followed.

Airlines lose valuable profit dollars when inefficiencies creep into the system. The object is to tighten operational procedures and monitor them, and cargo losses can be dramatically cut. Remember that the key to cargo loss prevention is a well-run cargo terminal.

How Law Enforcement Guided the Airlines

Law enforcement know-how has been enormously helpful to the airlines. The airline industry in metropolitan New York and New Jersey had the good fortune to receive police guidance during the formation of the Airport Security Council at Kennedy, La Guardia, and Newark airports in 1968. The law-enforcement agencies at the airports analyzed the cargo thefts and losses that the airlines were experiencing. On the basis of this study, they proposed to the airlines 24 law enforcement points, which identified in quite specific terms the problems causing air cargo losses and made specific suggestions for corrective action. Here we have a significant departure from the "catch-the-perpetrator" philosophy, substituting instead a loss-prevention approach that has led to industry stopping thefts, not just police catching thieves. The 24 law enforcement points are:

1. Each airline should assign a security officer to cargo activities.
2. Do background checks of cargo applicants.

3. Install a photographic identification badge system.
4. Supervisors to question presence of unidentified persons in cargo area.
5. Restrict cargo area to authorized employees.
6. Hold supervisors accountable for whereabouts of employees.
7. Fix responsibility for signing freight in and out.
8. Do not allow employee vehicle parking at cargo terminal.
9. Gate guards to control and record movements in and out of cargo area.
10. Keep unauthorized persons away from cargo unless supervised.
11. Prohibit parallel parking of trucks in front of bays.
12. Keep trucking firm vehicles out of airline parking lots and segregate them from private vehicles.
13. Strictly limit access of brokers' runners and supervise their movements.
14. Do not allow any private vehicles to park near loading areas.
15. Do not permit pickups without valid orders; clear any doubts with consignee.
16. Establish burglar-proof high-value storage areas.
17. Consider silent alarms connecting vital cargo areas with Port Authority Police desk.
18. Keep loaded mobile equipment secure at all times.
19. Install key operated positive locking devices in all mobile equipment.
20. Do not allow keys to be left in ignition locks of unattended vehicles.
21. Cargo containers, empty or loaded, should always be locked.
22. Contents of cargo trains should not be open to view.
23. Watch forklifts so they won't be used to force doors.
24. Lock gates and doors of trucks containing cargo.

Airline Response

Recognizing the validity of the law enforcement position, the airlines responded by certain mandatory procedures to protect their cargo from theft and loss. Following are the first mandates:

1. Theft reporting system. Council members are required to record thefts, pilferages, and losses of air cargo under the Airport Security Council Uniform Reporting System and report these matters to appropriate law enforcement agencies and to the council.

2. Employee badging system. All employees working in air
    freight facilities at or near the airports are required to wear
    identification badges.
3. Reward program. A reward program was established for
    information leading to arrest and conviction of cargo thieves.

AIRLINE STUDY TRIGGERS ACTION

With law enforcement's 24 points in hand and the new mandates in
place and working, an in-depth study of the airport theft/loss problem
was begun by the airlines. The 24 points were anchors for specific
security rules; what was needed next was development of the detailed
data necessary to tailor these rules to operations. An airport in the
New York metropolitan area is a complex facility, not adaptable to
operating as an armed camp. The airlines had to study the economics
of the 24-point program with a view to adapting it to a highly competitive industry in which financial profitability is the key to survival.

The study pooled data from law enforcement, from knowledgeable
airline security personnel who combine industry and law enforcement
experience, and from cargo operations people who understand the
intricacies of freight movements. In the words of the late Peter A.
Marcus, a former chairman of the Airport Security Council, "this
combination represented an excellent marriage of skills." With knowledge and staff as their basic resources, the airlines turned to the newly
implemented loss-reporting program to develop the specifics required
to establish a sound system of security. Analysis of the loss reports
proved the key to solving the problems. It provided numbers and
values to assess the costs of their loss experience. More important,
as each theft and loss was tallied, the results provided details about
the what, where, when, why, and how of the total experience. The
kinds of information the loss reports showed were:

1. The value of cargo losses versus cargo revenue.
2. To protect high value cargo, special handling procedures
    are necessary.
    a. Valuable cargo accepted no more than three hours before
        departure at the origin station.
    b. As the flight goes to the destination, the destination
        station is notified of the shipment.
    c. The shipment is met at the destination station.
    d. It is off-loaded under supervision and moved in closed carts.
    e. It is then moved to the terminal security cage/vault.
    f. It is then released to the consignee.

3. Cargo is stolen by persons authorized to be on the premises, using vehicles authorized to be there. Reports of loss, theft, or pilferage over a five-year period show that 79% of all theft was accomplished by persons authorized to be on the premises (see table).

Analysis of Cargo Loss

Source	%
Terminal	73
Transit	11
Pilferage	9
Interline	4
Truck or cart	2
Hijack	1

4. The weight of missing cargo is an indication that most stolen goods go out on the trucks in the guise of normal cargo movement. Of all missing shipments, 52% weighed more than 50 pounds; 48% weighed less than 50 pounds. Of missing shipments, 33% weighed between 1 and 25 pounds, 15% weighed 25 to 50 pounds, 17% weighed 50 to 100 pounds, and 35% weighed more than 100 pounds.

5. High value security systems reduce losses; systems breakdown leads to high value losses. For example, the origin station did not always give high value warning to the receiving station; some valuable shipments in igloos were not received promptly; the destination station did not always follow high value handling procedures despite high-value warning from the origin station; and insufficient control of the value cage or vault led to some cargo losses. These types of system failures caused more than 60% of all cargo losses over 10 years.

6. Armed robberies and hijackings, while relatively infrequent, are costly to airlines. In 11 years only 12 thefts, less than 1/2 of 1% of all airline cargo thefts, were the result of an armed robbery or hijacking, but the value of cargo lost through these crimes was $8,221,000 and represented 39% of all airline cargo lost for that 11-year period.

Exact Information

Even before the installation of the reporting system, the airlines had good, general off-the-top-of-the-head type intelligence, but the specificities in reports to law enforcement had not yet been extracted, analyzed, and synthesized for further use. The new reporting system enabled them to gather the scattered building blocks of sad experience and stack them in revealing columns that show exactly what, where, when, and why the goods were being stolen. It identified their vulnerable commodities, pinpointed the areas where most of the losses took place, suggested the times when losses were most likely to occur, and exposed the points in the system where protection was inadequate and required bolstering.

Closing the Gaps

With this kind of knowledge available, it became possible for the airlines to recommend economically viable deterrents that would close the gaps in security.

All measures are not necessarily appropriate in all terminals, but the major proposals were adaptable to some acceptable form for all of their operations. Universally suitable procedures were mandated for use by all member airlines. Proposals requiring more flexible application were advanced as recommended procedures.

The reporting system, by correlating for examination the experience contained in the airlines' reports relating to thefts and losses, enabled them to identify and pinpoint dangerous conditions, practices, and areas. It also highlighted the type of cargo most frequently sought by thieves. Bits of knowledge, accumulated in patterns, like pieces in a puzzle, form pictures of each problem, which may be studied in depth.

As further studies added to their understanding of the problems, airlines were able to add to their mandated procedures. The new mandates developed were:

1. Loading/unloading platform doors in cargo terminals must be kept closed, except while in use.
2. Barriers or painted lines are required to separate public terminal areas from segregated areas in which only authorized persons are allowed.
3. Airlines must not stow or leave cargo in front of such barriers or painted lines, except while attended.
4. Council members must designate prescribed parking areas in and around cargo terminals, segregating employee parking from operating areas.
5. Neither cargo nor documents may be released to anyone without full identification of the recipient.

6. All airlines are required to use the Kennedy form for cargo reported at Kennedy Airport from abroad. This form is a combined document, including carrier's certificate, pick up order and tally, and United States Customs release. By its very nature, it prevents fraudulent pickups of cargo.
7. Airlines must follow specific procedures for protection of high-value cargo.
8. Council members are subject to fines and other penalties for failure to comply with mandates and for action contrary to objectives of the Airport Security Council.
9. Council members must comply with regulations concerning locking and sealing of vehicles moving mail between ramps and airmail facility. This mandate establishes routes for moving mail designated to assure swift and secure delivery between planeside and post office.
10. Periodic inventories should be conducted of air cargo stored in airline cargo facilities at Kennedy, La Guardia, and Newark airports.

Putting Accumulated Data to Use

The original input is important. It permits the synthesis of experience when its elements are collected and pooled in groupings. The catalytic agent, however, is the communication of the accumulated knowledge to the airlines' operations people for use in attacking the problems identified. This is the role of the Airport Security Council at metropolitan airports. In practice, the system works beautifully in specialized areas where there are funds to support this private system.

If this program works, should not law enforcement more fully process its available data concerning losses and thefts for use in all major areas affected by property crimes? Is the system applicable only to property crimes? Are there other areas of police experience where solution rates of cases are so low that developing protective plans might be as important as seeking the elusive criminal? Are court rulings making it ever more difficult to prove the commission of crime, telling us that there must be a better way to prevent crime than the incarceration of the occasional perpetrator caught by the police?

Consider what has occurred in the airline industry: a security system recommended by police has reduced the numbers of crimes by over 61% in 10 years, while the rate of solution of crimes committed has remained virtually unchanged at the 6% to 10% level. Is this kind of product worth the effort? It has proven so at the airports. Since there are fewer crimes, many hours of work are saved for enforcement officers, prosecutors, judges, jailers, and parole officers. Many wasted hours of criminal suspects have been saved. Many families have been spared grief, humiliation, and financial loss because occasions for crimes of opportunity have been reduced. Similar results may well be achieved elsewhere by use of such a crime prevention system.

Should this technique be available only in evidence where private industry is able to foot the bill, as in airlines, jewelry, banking, and the like? Or should the police, who have the same data in hand, set up their own equivalent programs of these private plans in areas where rate of solution or crimes are low?

Law enforcement has blazed the trail for airlines and certain other industries in specialized areas. The loss and damage prevention procedures developed by the airlines through the Airport Security Council are based upon accumulation of knowledge and systematic communication of that knowledge to the operations people who must move cargo in an economically practical manner.

Experience indicates that areas in the public sector also have the potential to move forward by developing similar programs at reasonable cost. Fully utilizing the wealth of knowledge in the accumulated experience and records of law enforcement agencies would pay generous dividends.

Solving crimes is a tedious process, often painfully difficult. It is, in fact, usually more difficult to solve a crime than to prevent it in the first place. There should, therefore, be much more concentration by law enforcement on preventive security in those areas where experience has revealed a low case solution rate; thereby saving the time and expense required to identify, prosecute, incarcerate, and rehabilitate the occasional perpetrators brought to justice.

Reducing the Opportunities for Crime

Every police department is capable of gleaning valuable data from its experience with crimes, solved or unsolved. Distribution to the community of the knowledge thus gathered, for use in defensive efforts aimed at reducing the opportunities for crime, provides protection against criminals. This is truly a service of the police that may be quickly activated at the present level of operations, without great increases of manpower or expense.

Modus operandi files should be aimed not only at apprehending perpetrators, but at uncovering and correcting weaknesses that make crimes easy to commit. This use of readily available end-products of police investigation, aided by computer technology where practical and feasible, is infinitely more productive than the "catch-the-perpetrator" philosophy that dominates most law enforcement special programs. Law enforcement laboratories are almost totally perpetrator-oriented today, although actually our greater need is for means of preventing crimes.

Any police department that is primarily perpetrator-oriented in its efforts ignores its potential for identifying security weaknesses that are causative factors in the great percentage of crime. Juveniles began criminal careers with small-time criminal activities. They go to reform school and come out ready to try new and bigger crimes that promise greater profits or payoffs. Much of the fault and cause of troubles for this age group lies with the average citizen, who has not bothered to protect his property or person adequately. Common juvenile violations, committed simply and seldom planned, are the introductory steps to careers in crime.

Citizens should be more sophisticated about deterrence of household, business, and property crimes and should apply the guidelines derived from police experience. Such an approach may prevent the curious or hungry youngster, as well as others tempted by ready opportunity, from participating in antisocial raids on the property of others.

Experience shows that law enforcement agencies now possess the raw material needed to compile and make available to industry and individual citizens the knowhow they need to protect themselves against crime. Implementation of this capability on a broad scale will reduce the opportunities for crimes against property. Fewer hours will be spent by police on investigations and apprehensions; fewer hours will be spent by prosecutors in preparation of trials and appeals; fewer convicts will crowd our jails.

Law enforcement agencies should be encouraged to develop more creative security programs for public use. These programs should be components of on-going projects and should have the same status as programs aimed at apprehending criminals. Law enforcement agencies should specifically establish units devoted to compiling, analyzing, and disseminating to private citizens and industry criminal intelligence data for crime prevention.

The air cargo industry, working with law enforcement, has developed a truly successful means for the prevention of crime; their success should spread to many other areas. As law enforcement, industry, and private citizens work together in this endeavor, there should be continuing government participation through Law

Enforcement Assistance Administration (LEAA) or a similar support program for crime prevention programs throughout the United States. Such efforts in other segments of industry and society, modeled upon the successful airport approach, will provide a more secure environment in which all of us may live and work.

CARGO LOSS DATA AND TRENDS

The Department of Transportation (DOT) has used data collected by the Civil Aeronautics Board as its primary source for monitoring and projecting trends in air cargo losses. For the period January, 1974 to June, 1977, a detailed quarterly report was required of certain of the major air carriers. This report and its detail provided the bases for the DOT's analyses of air cargo losses. However, in mid-1977, the CAB issued Economic Regulation 996, which reduced the original quarterly reports to semiannual reports and reduced the detail simply to claims received, claims paid, and total freight revenues in both dollars and numbers. And, as discussed earlier, on May 10, 1970, the CAB issued another ruling that eliminated in its entirety part 239, "Reporting Data Pertaining to Freight Loss and Damage Claims," by certified route air carriers. The data used for the 1970 report was the last data collected under the requirement of the CAB.

However, the DOT began discussing with the Air Transport Association the possibilities of the air carriers continuing the CAB's modified or reduced data submission on a voluntary basis. The DOT offered to receive the raw data, process it in whatever form the Air Transport Association desired and publish it for the carriers. In turn, DOT was to use the data to sustain its data base and ability to provide trend information on the extent and magnitude of air cargo losses from theft. A final meeting of the carriers was held, and the decision was that the DOT did not need this information and that it would no longer be submitted. Subsequent meetings with both the statistical and security officers of the Air Transport Association have now indicated that there is little interest on the part of the carriers to provide the data needed by the DOT. As recently as November, 1980, the DOT conferred with air carriers at a Washington meeting. There was little favorable indication with regard to supplying the DOT with data to continue its trend projection capability.

JUDGE SUCCESS THROUGH INVESTMENT*

How do you, or your management, judge success in claim prevention? If it's judged by any formula except as a profit contributor, then you are probably accepting excessive claim losses. The name of the game is "Prevention," and we define "Loss Prevention" as:

> The continuous activity that contributes to the prevention of claim losses resulting from mysterious shortages, thefts, and damages.

To make a profit in loss prevention, an investment must be made— an investment to organize and effectively implement a professional security program; a claim prevention program; a claim investigation program; a salvage program; and an over, short, and damage clearance program. If claim liability is considered a cost by management, then success is measured in dollars paid out and not in profit earned by retention and by minimizing claim losses. One could easily argue, "What's the difference?" There is a great difference because the philosophy of investment means executive management awareness, decision, establishment of goals, monitoring, and measuring return on that investment. The philosophy of cost in loss prevention is a negative approach and eliminates the winning investment spirit.

From an organizational standpoint, the loss prevention function should report to the highest management level of operations. It is operations that cause a claim liability, and it is operations that can make the decision necessary to correct or minimize claim causes.

Applying our investment concept, claim prevention is judged by profit contribution made compared to a base year or prior period as a ratio to revenue. Industry experience has shown that this ratio will rise a much greater percent than corresponding revenue if it is not effectively checked. Many factors must also be considered that can affect claim liability, such as the state of the economy, the type of freight handled, the amount of handling, acquisitions, and mergers.

Investment return can be measured as:

1. Actual dollar pay out decrease compared to the base year or period,
2. Ratio pay out decrease to revenue,
3. Ratio pay out level with revenue increase, or
4. Any combination of the above.

---

*Reprinted from *Claims Forum*, "Judge Success Through Investment," by Harlan C. Flinner, January/February, 1977.

For example, based on current period revenue, using the ratio from the base year or period, x dollars would have been paid. The difference between the current actual pay out and the calculated pay out represents a profit contribution (loss). Your investment is known — hence a measured return.

One should be skeptical of published industry average claim ratio data. Formulas vary, and individual company operations may dictate exposure and claim liability. Based on experience and management philosophy, a claim ratio becomes good or bad. In any event, it is important to not accept a tolerance level.

Claim losses have been soaring at alarming rates in recent years. Analyzing the causes is complex and a separate topic by itself. For the purposes of this book, however, it suffices to recognize that behavioral attitudes of people have changed dramatically, that respect for property and concepts of honesty and integrity have diminished, that vast new horizons of merchandise which constantly tempt individual wants and desires are available — all of which have fueled the soaring problem of claim losses in transportation. What can the individual company do to halt and protect its employees, its customers, and possibly its financial health from the staggering liability of claim losses?

The name of the game is "prevention." To take action after a theft has occurred, or to view the results of damage, is helpful and necessary to pinpoint responsibility and to take corrective action for the future. But the most direct path to retention of profit dollars already earned is the prevention of claim losses.

Objectives of Loss Prevention

When an athletic team takes the field, their one objective is to win the contest. So, too, loss prevention is a team effort in the game of claim loss prevention. Objectives must be clear, simple, and understood by every employee in the company. Every employee has an individual responsibility to know and understand loss prevention objectives and to know why the success or failure of these objectives directly affects individual job security and family security. Loss prevention objectives, simply stated, are to:

1. Prevent the loss of customers' freight due to shortage, theft, damages, or error.
2. Prevent the loss or damage of company property due to dishonesty or error.
3. Aggressively detect, investigate, expose, apprehend, and prosecute individuals responsible for acts of dishonesty.

4. Conduct audit and training programs aimed directly at moti-
   vating individual employee involvement in claim prevention.

To meet these objectives requires systematic planning. Unless
the team has a game plan to win at loss prevention, then the terminal
level and system level are on the defensive.

Loss Prevention Policies

Policies form the foundation of the game plan to win. The team must
know which information will be used in the contest—which field forms
the boundaries. Clear, simple policies, publicized and communicated
to all employees start the game plan. These policies should include
the following statements:

1. Theft of customer freight or company property will not
   be tolerated.
2. Willful negligence or destruction of customer freight or
   company assets will not be tolerated.
3. Individuals engaging in acts of dishonesty, will have their
   employment terminated and prosecuted to the fullest extent
   possible.
4. It is the individual responsibility of every employee to prevent
   claim losses occurring as a result of theft, shortage, or damage.

Communication is the thread that ties the activity of management
together. Loss prevention policies that are known and understood by
all employees will also become known via the grapevine to outside
factors, which potentially can affect the program. The reputation of
a strong loss prevention team precedes it just as a reputation for being
weak and lax will also become known to opportunists and to those
who prey on easy victims.

The Functions of Loss Prevention

In team effort with regional and individual terminal management,
loss prevention activity must perform seven functions:

1. Isolate exposure to claim losses.
2. Develop the means to minimize such exposure.
3. Audit existing loss prevention procedures.

4. Conduct internal loss prevention training and public relation programs.
5. Provide security control standards.
6. Investigate suspicious and questionable incidents.
7. Maintain awareness of new programs and products to strengthen loss prevention controls.

With objectives to win, with policies on which to build, and with functions defined to operate, the team is assembled and ready to learn and practice the plays that will roll up the score of success in loss prevention. Success is measured in net profit dollars. The potential to contribute to profit is perhaps no greater than in the activity of loss prevention, for these are net profit dollars already earned. And, in many instances, the effort needed is much less than the effort to increase sales volume.

Preliminary, but Important Concepts

Before describing various programs, let's put into focus some basic equipment of the loss prevention game plan. First, there must be full executive management awareness and commitment to make a cost-effective investment in loss prevention. The term investment is used purposely—investment precedes a return. If considered a pure cost, then potential returns are hindered almost from the start.

INDUSTRY ACTIONS

The year 1980 was a year of progress in cargo security by the scheduled airlines. The accent was on loss prevention through sound operational procedures and instilling security awareness in personnel. Currently, there is some concern that security will suffer from the increase in the number of airlines, both passenger oriented and all-freight, brought about by industry deregulation. Little if any data exist on the theft-related experience of these new airlines.

Loss statistics for 1980 indicate the theft-related loss ratio for those airlines that have reported will continue to be under $.50 per $100.00 in revenues.

Seminars, conferences, and workshops headed by individual airlines, the Airport Security Council (the security coordination body for Kennedy, LaGuardia, and Newark airports) and the 50 local Air Transportation Association's security committees of the nation's busiest airport highlighted the 1980 industry year with particular emphasis upon all aspects of security, both internally and with law enforcement bodies. The Annual Freight Claims Prevention Seminar, sponsored by the Air Transportation Association Freight Services Department, served as a workshop on the different problems and the solution to those problems.

The booklet, *Role of Packing and Handling in Cargo Security*, published by the Airport Security Council and the DOT, went into a second printing in 1980. The Council also produced in 1980 the second edition of its crime prevention publication, *Reducing Opportunities for Crime.*

The Airport Security Council and the Police Department of the Port Authority of New York and New Jersey, working with the New York/Newark "City Campaign" of the National Cargo Security Program, and the DOT published *Guidelines for the Maintenance of Air Cargo Security* in November, 1980. The booklet provides a blueprint for establishing effective cargo security in the air freight industry. Copies of the guidelines were sent to airport and air carrier managements throughout the country.

The Airport Security Council also developed a slide presentation that was reproduced and disseminated by the DOT, "Baggage Loss Prevention." This slide and tape presentation is available for loan to any airline- or airport-oriented group.

FEDERAL ACTIONS

The Federal Aviation Administration (FAA) enforced mandatory passenger security measures that aid in the protection of air cargo.

The FAA has developed an advisory circular that describes security procedures that indirect air carriers, such as freight forwarders, should follow when dealing with carriers. Federal Aviation Regulations (FARs) prescribe requirements to ensure that certain security procedures are followed in the acceptance of cargo from companies and individuals.

Steps have been taken by FAA to ensure that a comprehensive and viable compliance and enforcement program is implemented to ensure compliance with FARs and the hazardous materials regulations as they pertain to air transportation of hazardous materials cargo.

Deregulation of airlines have taken some long time markets away from carriers, but motor carriers deregulation may aid airlines as it eliminated restrictions on combined truck-air cargo operations.

In 1977, the CAB reduced its collection of freight loss and damage claims data from air carriers. This reduction resulted from an evaluation by the CAB of its need for the reports as opposed to the expense and hardship imposed on both the federal government and the carriers. Data for 1977 were collected in the loss and damage area—not broken down into categories that make up the theft-related losses in previous collections. In December, 1978, the CAB proposed to eliminate the reporting of the data regarding claims for lost and/or damaged cargo.

On May 10, 1979, the CAB adopted a final cancellation of the old requirement that completely eliminated any federal government collection of data needed to analyze and evaluate air cargo loss and damage.

9. Rail Cargo

A DIFFERENT APPROACH*

How do you effectively protect cargo from theft and loss? That question has plagued the railroad industry and its customers from the very beginning. If past experience has taught us anything, it is that cargo theft will always be with us. Just how big the problem is and what can be done about it has been the subject of a great deal of discussion during recent years. When congressional hearings on the matter were first held in the early seventies, the cargo loss problem in the transportation industry as a whole was described as "epidemic in nature, resulting in a loss of billions of dollars annually." Since that time there has been much discussion and disagreement among the "experts" as to the actual cost of cargo theft. But all agree the problem is serious and does in fact cost us millions of dollars each year.

In recent years the railroad industry has increased its efforts to deal with this growing problem. Most of the work has centered around improved physical security. The use of high security sealing devices, the introduction of secondary security hasps (located on boxcar doors 10 feet 4 inches above ground level), and the total enclosure of auto rail cars are some of the more notable efforts. These and other improvements have been shown to be effective, but despite these improvements, the problem of how to identify and deal effectively with cargo loss on a long-term basis persists. In fact, some measurement standards indicate that rather than decreasing because of better physical security, the cargo theft problem is growing both in size and complexity.

This chapter is adapted in part from material provided by the Union Pacific Railroad, Salt Lake City, Utah.

*Permission to reproduce obtained from Union Pacific Railroad.

In recent years, Union Pacific's security department has introduced an approach to cargo security that it feels is the best way to deal with the problem of cargo loss. Judging from their successes to date, they appear to be on the right track.

Their approach is neither complicated nor unique. Since the theft of cargo obviously involves the loss of the customer's goods, it only makes sense to extensively involve that same customer in the solution of the problem. To illustrate the validity of this philosophy, they point to the utilization of the secondary security hasp. When this hasp has been engaged and properly secured by the shipper, the reduction of theft in transit has been dramatically reduced. In fact, when a high security seal has been used in this hasp, not one unauthorized entry in transit has been reported. Unfortunately, the security hasp had only one drawback. It was seldom used! Railroad security personnel discovered that not only was the majority of the shipping public not using the hasp, but in many cases were not even aware of its existence. Because of customer involvement from the beginning, Union Pacific's program tends to avoid such communication breakdowns between the carrier and the shipper.

An excellent example of this carrier/shipper cooperation would be the joint effort of the Terminal Freight Cooperative Association and Union Pacific. Terminal Freight is the nation's largest shippers' association and is headquartered in Chicago. This association operates major consolidation/distribution facilities in major cities throughout the United States.

In 1978, Union Pacific began working with Terminal Freight on loss prevention. During the course of their efforts, they followed a general format that has become a basic guideline to the cargo security program. The format is as follows:

> *There is a problem.* After several preliminary discussions, Terminal Freight and Union Pacific agreed the present level of claims and costs were not acceptable. No specific goals were set as to levels of reductions. They simply reconciled themselves to there being a problem and something that needed to be done. But all too often, loss prevention efforts involve two or more parties: one side who feels there is a problem and the other who doesn't. Unfortunately, these two opposing parties are usually the shipper and carrier.

> *Both parties have a problem.* This step was perhaps the most critical part of the effort. It was mutually agreed that no matter where the physical location of the problem or problems was discovered, both Terminal Freight and Union Pacific would work together to resolve it. Most companies involved in the transportation proceess tend to be somewhat self-centered when it comes to loss prevention. They measure success by the reduction of their

own claim cost and number rather than a reduction of costs for all involved in the movement of a particular commodity. By so doing, they fail to realize that what affects one member of the transportation chain will inevitably affect all members of that chain.

Problem Identification.   In 1978, a study was made in an attempt to identify by location major cargo loss causes. This study was conducted for a period of 90 days on traffic moving between terminals on the coasts. Terminal Freight advised the railroad of the pending railcar movements prior to their release. This information included records of seals applied at origin. The Union Pacific closely monitored these cars as they moved across the rail system. This monitoring included physical inspections at all points. Terminal Freight provided unloading information at destination which included seal records and any noted shortages. The results of the survey were sobering. One of the major problems that surfaced was a very high seal exception rate when the transportation vehicles arrived at destination. This exception rate was totally unacceptable to Terminal Freight. It was felt that if a significant number of railcars were arriving at destination without seal protection, then certainly a sizeable amount of loss was occurring in transit.

The survey also revealed that seal application and recording procedures needed improvement. Several of the seal exceptions noted at the destination terminal were simply misapplied seals which had not been properly applied to the railcar at origin. Flaws in seal recording practices at destination also resulted in erroneous seal conditions being noted on Terminal Freight's unloading reports.

Problem resolution.   Owing to the high seal exception rate noted in transit, Terminal Freight expanded its use of high-security seals. They now apply high-security seals to all railcars and to secondary security hasps when the cars are so equipped. To deal with the procedural problems encountered in the area of seal application and recording, Union Pacific and Terminal Freight jointly developed two sound/slide presentations which illustrate proper sealing practices and procedures. These slide presentations have been shown through Terminal Freight's system in an effort to communicate the important role seals play in loss prevention.

To improve the security of cargo while still in the terminal, and with input from the various consolidation/distribution terminals throughout their system, Terminal Freight developed a distribution manual. The distribution terminal manual endeavors to standardize freight handling procedures and deals with such subjects as document control and freight accountability. It was felt that if procedures were followed as outlined in the manual, freight loss in the terminal could be greatly reduced.

The results.   The claim prevention effort centered mainly on procedural change in the existing operation. Little, if any, increase in ongoing operating costs occurred as a result of these changes; however, Terminal Freight had invested a great deal of time and effort to curb this seal exception rate and reduce claim costs. To measure the effectiveness of their efforts, a follow-up study was conducted in 1979. This follow-up study was identical in nature to the first study. The results were gratifying; the seal exception rate had been reduced 300%.

The best measurement of any loss prevention program is the reduction of claims. In Terminal Freight's case the reduction has been impressive. Actual claim numbers and costs filed against the association were down 30% and 14%, respectively, in 1980 when compared to the same period in 1978. Other factors such as inflation, terminal improvements, and business downturns certainly impacted on these figures. What effect these external factors had on the decline in claim activity is difficult, if not impossible, to measure. But one fact continues to stand out: claims numbers and costs used to go up every year; now they go down.

In addition to reduced claims, Terminal Freight felt it had received residual benefits. Management had experienced first-hand an awareness of loss prevention techniques and the positive impact they can have on the transportation process. Also, communication channels had been opened between all members of the transportation chain which would facilitate the response to future cargo security problems.

Union Pacific plans to continue emphasizing customer involvement in its cargo security program. Such positive examples as Terminal Freight tend to justify the approach. Not only does the program deal effectively with present cargo security problems, but it establishes those communication lines necessary to quickly identify and deal with problems if they arise.

With all the emphasis on customer involvement, one could get the impression that Union Pacific's prevention program would tend to be narrow in its approach. Neither the Union Pacific nor Terminal Freight discount the impact other prevention programs have had on cargo loss. They certainly don't view their methods as the only way to deal with the problem. But they hold fast to their basic tenet, which is the essence of their program: any loss prevention program that does not include meaningful involvement by all members of a transportation chain tends to generate short-term results that fail to identify and resolve the real cause of cargo loss.

FREIGHT FORWARDERS

To be truly effective in controlling cargo theft, it is imperitive to have an understanding of the entire transportation chain and the intermodal network. Although there are many, many facets to be covered, the basic knowledge of freight forwards and the regulations it covers and are covered by, are important in cargo security and the intermodal network as a whole.

When investigating the trail of evidence, use of this background information on the waybill is essential for retracing the trail to pinpoint the origin of the theft.

What is most important is that the Security and Special Service Department and the Claim Department work hand in glove not only to find missing or stolen shipments, but as a loss prevention team.

A freight forwarder is any individual or firm that is available to the general public as a common carrier to transport or provide transportation of property, and that

1. Assembles and consolidates shipments.
2. Assumes responsibility for the transportation of such property.
3. Uses, for the whole or any part of the transportation of such shipments, the services of a rail, motor vehicle, or water carrier.

The freight forwarder cannot perform the physical transportation except in its terminal areas. It assembles shipments, consolidates them, ships them by common carrier (usually a railroad), receives them, and then separates and distributes them to individual consignees. A large portion of the freight forwarder's traffic consists of consolidation of small shipments.

Freight forwarders are regulated by the Interstate Commerce Commission under part IV of their charter. The act establishing the ICC specifically provides that no permit to engage in freight forwarding shall be issued to a common carrier by rail, motor vehicles, or water. But a freight forwarder may be controlled by such carrier, or under common control with it, and the act specifically provides that the commission may not for this reason deny a permit to the freight forwarder.

Freight forwarders publish public tariffs and file them with the ICC. They function as indirect carriers and are authorized to contract from any common carrier. Their profit is generally based on the difference between the LCL/LTL rates they charge and the CL/TL rates they pay the railroad or truck line.

Shippers' Associations

Shippers' associations have been formed to meet the specific transportation needs of their members. While not regulated by the ICC, the activities that a shippers' association may perform are specifically

outlined in section 402 (c) of the ICC act. Shippers' associations
are made up of numbers with a common transportation goal. The
shipper's association operates on funds gathered from membership
fees and service charges per shipment. Since shippers' associations
must be operated on a nonprofit basis, excess revenues after expenses
are returned to members at year's end.

Consignees often employ consolidators to perform consolidation
of small articles into single shipments. Many retail chain stores have
formed associations in the Midwest to utilize consolidations at New
York and other eastern origins to transport small shipments in CL/TL
service and avoid the high cost of LTL truck service.

Commodities

Commodities that have been considered "hot loads" by the Security
and Special Services Departments of the railroads and have been
given extra scrutiny in the yards and at interchanges are cigarettes,
tires, beer, wines, liquor, and meat. However, an examination of
the railroads portion of Freight Claim Payout for shortage packaged
shipment and for robbery, theft, or pilferage indicates that numerous commodities should be added to this list, or that all loads be
considered "hot."

Shipper Association and freight forwarder traffic account for
a large amount of shortage claims. As with miscellaneous mixed shipments, the contents of these loads (in both CL and TOFC) can be
anything and everything. Such shipments will often show on COIN
train sheets as "Mdse" or "FAK" (freight all kinds).

Valid Inspection

Valid and complete inspections of loaded box cars or other enclosed
transportation vehicles, flat cars, and special equipment rail cars
are necessary for the security of cargo moving from the shipper to
the consignee.

Following are procedures for use in making valid inspections.
Records of these inspections should be accurately recorded on the
proper forms for future reference by the Security and Special Service
Department and the Claim Department.

Boxcars, Trailers and Containers.   Exceptions concerning shipment in box-cars, trailers, and containers will initially entail missing, broken, or misapplied seals, Subsequent investigation may disclose a noticeable void in the load and/or possible damages with other cases falling into this void. Without a bill of lading, however, it is impossible to ascertain exactly how many cartons, cases, etc., may have been stolen. Taking photographs of the doorway area would be a valuable tool for determining how much has been stolen and what may have been damaged by a load shift into any void. Should a void exist, arrangements should be made to level or secure the load to prevent future damage. Any load shift into the void should be reported on the exception report.

Record all seals on the car being inspected. This includes unlocked, broken, or misapplied seals and seals remaining from previous ship-ments. The latter may complicate a claim for shortage if there is no record of the seal prior to delivery of the car to the consignee. It is possible the consignee would record the old seal instead of the seal applied by the shipper to protect the current load. All seal records should show all markings as indicated on each seal.

Seal location should be recorded by indicating the right or left side door mechanically. If the car is equipped with primary and secondary doors or inspection doors and all the doors have had seals applied, then all of the seals should be recorded as to their door location. When seal exceptions are noted, the inspection record should indicate the type of door, type of locking device, and condition of same.

Exceptions should be recorded on the appropriate form. If available, information on this form should include complete waybill information, including routing and junction points plus time of arrival, time of inspection, train or connecting line received from, and direction of movement.

Seals applied to correct an exception, and which remain intact to destination, will appear on destination records since both origin and destination seal records must be obtained to determine rail liability for any given shortage. However, the reason for such application must be determined prior to distribution of subsequent claims, which requires accuracy and completeness on all seal exception reports.

Open Top Loads.   Open loads should be inspected for exceptions caused by theft, vandalism, or improper loading or securing of the load to the rail car. Motor vehicles noted to have exceptions must be identified by vehicle identification numbers. Tractors, combines, and other

implements or machinery noted with exceptions should be identified
by serial number and location on the rail car.

Damage must be defined as accurate and completely as possible
to be a usable exception for the Freight Claim Department. As special
agents often are unable to determine exactly the extent of damage,
cameras should be made available at major interchange points. Photos
taken by special agents should be examined by persons more familiar
with any given piece of machinery (shipper representatives, loss- and
damage-prevention personnel, etc.) to determine the exact nature
of damage, or if any parts of a given open top shipment are missing.
Also, photos taken of damaged shipments at interchange points
could be compared with those taken at destination. Should a shipment of machinery be delivered to a railroad at interchange with
obvious apparent heavy damage, loss- and damage-prevention personnel
should be contacted so they may inspect the load prior to the railroad
company movement to determine proper action to be taken. Such
photos may also indicate violations of required loading practices
by the shipper, and such information could be used to deny a subsequent claim.

Usable auto exceptions involve broken glass, missing items, or
heavily damaged vehicles. Again any damage must be accurately
defined in detail. As there may be up to 18 vehicles per rail car
on any given rail car, the recording of the vehicle identification number
is required to properly identify the damaged vehicle. Interiors of
vehicles with glass damage should be checked for missing items (radios,
wheel covers, etc.), as the glass may have been broken to gain access
to the vehicle.

Exceptions to farm implements will also involve glass damage
and/or missing parts, tool boxes, or batteries. Notations should also
be made of damaged or flat tires, along with any heavy damage caused
by load shift or sideswipe.

Transformers should be inspected, especially at interchange
points. They should be inspected for load shifts, proper tie-down and
securement to the rail car, for gauges or other parts missing or damaged,
and for leakage of liquid coolant. The slightest load shift may damage
a transformer.

When load shift, improper tie-down methods, or damage is noted,
the exceptions should be brought to the attention of the mechanical
department at that terminal so corrective measures can be taken and
further damage prevented. This should include covering broken
windows of autos, trucks, and farm machinery.

Exceptions noted should be recorded by the use of cameras
whenever possible. The resulting photographs should be forwarded

with the exception report or narrative report to be filed for subsequent investigative use.

As with enclosed loads, all waybill information should be transcribed to the exception report. Any exceptions that are noted should be recorded on the waybill, if possible.

SIGNED, SEALED, AND DELIVERED*

In the early days of railroading, determined groups of thieves were very successful in relieving the railroads of their high-value cargo. The exploits of such colorful outlaws as Butch Cassidy, the Sundance Kid, and the Wild Bunch have been well documented in law enforcement annals and popular films. Fortunately, the railroads were successful in stopping such thievery. A group of private policemen was organized by the railroads to cope with the rising rate of cargo theft; they weren't very glamorous, but none could fault their effectiveness in eliminating the threat posed to railroad cargo by outlaws. In the late nineteenth century the answer to the cargo security problem was quite simple. A lot has happened since those early days of railroading: cargo transport has become much more complicated, not only for the railroads, but for all modes of transportation. A product moves from manufacturing to the consumer through what is commonly referred to as the transportation chain. The protection of cargo while it moves through this chain has proved to be a difficult task; as the transportation of cargo has become more complex, the opportunities for cargo theft have greatly increased. An indication of the widespread changes that have taken place in the transportation industry is the dramatic increase in intermodal traffic. Rail, truck, and maritime companies now are seldom responsible for total movement of a product from origin to destination. Instead they work in tandem to bring the product from the producer to the consumer. As a result of these and other changes, it is becoming more difficult to deal with cargo security problems. To illustrate this point, follow an imaginary shipment of cargo as it moves through a common transportation chain. Suppose there is a carton of 12 electrical drills manufactured by the Stanley Drill Company of Wadesville, Ohio. This carton is part of a 12-carton shipment destined for Joe's hardware store in Jefferson City, California. Because of the small size of Joe's order, the Stanley Drill Company has engaged the services of a shipper's association. On Monday, Joe's shipment is scheduled to move by truck from the Stanley Manufacturing plant at Wadesville to Superfast Shippers'

---

*Permission to reproduce obtained from Union Pacific Railroad.

Association's consolidation terminal at Columbus, Ohio. Ralph, the truck driver, has the responsibility of counting the product into the truck trailer at Wadesville. Ralph also has the responsibility of applying seals to the trailer hasp once the loading operation is completed. Ralph was a little late getting up and hasn't had his morning coffee, so Ralph asks Jim, the dock foreman at Stanley Drill, with whom he has worked a long time, to handle his count and seal the truck after it is loaded. After all, Jim has to make a count anyway—no sense in duplicating work. Leaving the seals with Jim, Ralph heads for the employer's lounge for his morning coffee. After his coffee, Ralph drives his trailer, carrying Joe's shipment to Superfast Shippers' Association terminal in Columbus. John, the dock foreman at Superfast, has had a rough day. Normally, John records the seals and makes an accurate count of freight coming from Ralph's trailer; however, Ralph is late and decides John has been under heavy pressure to increase his productivity on the dock, so in the interest of saving time the inbound seals are merely recorded from the shipping papers in the dock office, and no accurate count is made. Joe's shipment is then consolidated with 45 other shipments and put in a rail car. The rail car is billed to Superfast's distribution terminal at San Francisco, California. Confusing so far? There's more to come. The dockhand at Columbus, whose job it was to apply the seals to the car, misapplied one of the seals. He applied the seal in such a way that entry could be gained to the rail car interior without breaking the seal. Because of this seal misapplication, the seal was of no real value. During its journey the car moved over four different railroads: Conrail, Chicago and North Western, Union Pacific, and Southern Pacific. Under normal circumstances, no railroad would routinely record the seals on all cars moving over their respective lines. Such was the case with the rail car with Joe's shipment as it moved from Columbus to San Francisco without any seal inspections. When the rail car arrived at Superfast dock in San Francisco, Ed, the dock hand assigned to record all seals on inbound shipments, showed both seals intact—even though one seal had been misapplied since the rail car had left Columbus. When the railcar was unloaded in San Francisco an accurate count was finally made, and Joe's shipment was noted short one carton. When Joe's shipment was delivered to his store in Jefferson City, Joe realized the shortage and was very concerned. After all, he was planning to use those drills for the month's sales promotion. Of course, Joe filed a claim with the appropriate transportation company and waited thinking all the time about the profit lost because he didn't have the drills to sell.

Cargo losses of this type are becoming all too common. Recently completed studies indicate that all forms of cargo theft exceed $1 billion in direct losses annually. An investigation of the loss of Joe's drills should determine at what point in the transportation chain the shortage occurred. Did the theft occur at the manufacturing plant in Wadesville? At the Superfast terminal in Columbus? Or San Francisco? Or maybe on one of the four railroads? Unfortunately, there is no answer; there is no way of knowing. The problem would try the abilities of even the best investigators. Poor seal control and poor seal application were the major causes of inability to track down the exact place where Joe's drills were taken. If the location of the actual theft cannot be identified, the chances of locating the thief are almost nonexistent. To make matters worse, one cannot take measures to stop the same type of thefts from occurring in the future. Imagine Superfast calling the local police department in San Francisco to report the loss of Joe's drills—someplace between San Francisco and Columbus, Ohio.

How easy the investigation would have been if the dock hand in Columbus had realized the importance of properly applying the seals to the rail car. It would have been even better if Ralph had personally counted Joe's shipment into his trailer at Wadesville and then had sealed the trailer. Such information would quickly have led an investigator to the Columbus terminal.

Emphasis so far has been on changing transportation patterns and their impact on cargo security, while neglecting the activities of the cargo thief. The average cargo thief is not as cunning or as glamorous as his historical counterpart, but the cargo thief population certainly has grown.

Today's thief relies on opportunity, stealing the cargo that is least protected. A good example would be the rail car in which Joe's drills were transported. If the contents were like most shipper association movements, it would not be unusual for the value of lading to exceed $20,000. Yet, an utterly inappropriate seal was used by Superfast to protect that lading—a simple, metal strap. It's a modern security paradox. Cargo handling companies have not hesitated in providing adequate security for their terminals and warehouses, such as fencing, access controls, and elaborate alarm systems to protect cargo stored in these facilities; yet when that same cargo leaves the terminal in a transportation vehicle, a serialized metal strap is considered sufficient protection. Changes are coming, however, and an increasing number of progressive shippers have been using high-security seals. These seals come in various shapes and sizes. Some are more effective than others, but they all have one thing in common: they help to eliminate opportunity for cargo theft. The effectiveness of these devices was shown recently by a DOT study indicating that for every dollar spent on these devices, a savings of $14.00 is realized—a sound investment. As illustrated in the example above, development and maintenance of a good seal control program is the foundation of any cargo security effort.

Quality seal application rests on obeying a basic rule: if a transportation vehicle can be entered without destroying the seal protecting it, then the seals are misapplied and are of no value.

Every employee who has been given the responsibility of sealing transportation vehicles should, upon completion of the task, question whether entry can be gained without breaking the seal. If the answer is no, then the vehicle has been properly sealed. This approach sounds simple. Perhaps we should examine a few common types of transportation vehicles to see how the rule applies.

(This first example is the most common hasp that dock employees face: once the seal is applied through the pin and stationary bracket the wedge pin cannot be removed without breaking the seal.) There are two doors. Which one should be sealed? Anyone who has been around a dock very long knows the door on the right must be opened first. Therefore, if the right door is sealed, the car would be properly protected. The same double-door dilemma occurs with truck trailers, and again the right door must be opened first, so proper application would require the right hasp to be sealed. Under normal circumstances the application of this seal would be satisfactory, but just to be safe let's apply our basic rule. Can the vehicle be entered without breaking the seal? In this case the answer is yes. Many trailers have been burglarized by the use of an unprotected side door. Furthermore, truck trailers are not the only transportation vehicle with extra doors.

The extra door on a railcar is called an inspection door, and it is wide enough to remove rather large items. When a seal is improperly applied it may still look like it is properly applied, but there may be a couple of things wrong. First, the seal may be applied in a manner that exposes too much cable, making it easier for the thief to remove the seal. A second problem with application of seals is the misuse of a secondary security hasp, which is located approximately 10 feet from the ground. In 1974, the American Association of Railroads required all new or rebuilt boxcars to be equipped with this hasp. The effectiveness of these hasps has been overwhelming. According to AAR reports, when high-security sealing devices have been placed

in the security hasp, there has not been a single recorded incident
of unauthorized entry in transit.

From these few examples it would be futile to develop specific
seal application rules for every type of transportation vehicle; there
are too many variations. Simply remember the basic rule, and the
sealing practice will become a realiable part of your cargo protection
program. Effective cargo security measures must be taken by all members of the transportation chain. If just one link is weak, then the
whole chain is threatened at all levels.

Remember that if any link in the transportation chain is defective, it should be remedied immediately. Take whatever steps are
necessary to correct it. It is vital to you and your claim costs.

SEALS AND SECURITY DEVICES*

The nations' railroads and shippers and receivers are experiencing
cargo losses representing millions upon millions of dollars per year.
Statistics, as compiled by the Department of Transportation, reflect
a total transportation cost of 150 billion dollars per year for all modes
of transportation. This figure is about as high as our National Budget.
One billion dollars of this cost is directly attributed to cargo loss.
This loss is further expanded when you include the indirect costs
of claims handling and processing, reordering, interruption of cash
flow, lost sales, and of course, customer dissatisfaction.

Cargo losses can be dramatically reduced by the establishment
of policies and procedures of (1) an unbroken chain of freight accountability, (2) proper application and recording of seals, and (3) proper
utilization of available security devices. To achieve this result will
require a collective and cooperative effort on the part of the management of both the carriers and the customers they serve. They must
first work together to identify specific problems and then be jointly
committed to the resolution. The responsibility for the creation and
the maintenance of security awareness within the principal companies
must be assumed by management to ensure that all the goods tendered
by a vendor are received by the ultimate consignee.

The purpose of this section is to demonstrate proper seal application and recording procedures, and to identify the various types of
security seals and devices available for the protection of cargo.

---

*Permission to reproduce obtained from Union Pacific Railroad.

AAR ANTI-THEFT HASP

After considerable research and evaluation of theft deterrent systems for railroad box cars, the Police and Security Section of the Association of American Railroads developed the "anti-theft hasp" and placed it 10 feet above the rail. This "second" hasp on rail cars was tested thoroughly and proved to be the most effective security system ever used.

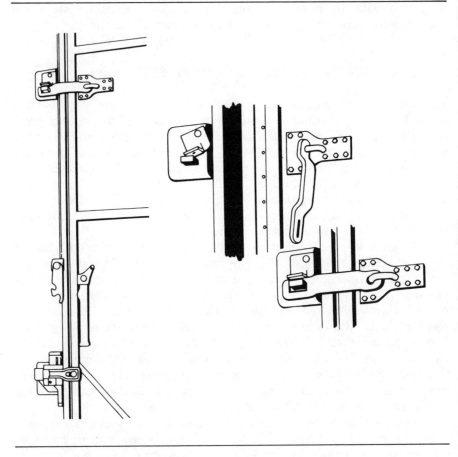

With the assistance of all major railroads, the AAR unanimously voted to make the "anti-theft" hasps mandatory on all new and rebuilt refrigerator and box cars, to be effective July 1, 1974.

PROPERLY LOCKED SEALS

Due to the lack of uniformity in fastening designs for railroad car doors, many problems arise due to improperly applied seals. Whenever seals are not properly applied, the lading is not protected and cars can be entered without evidence of this having occurred. To protect the integrity of your shipments, *seals should be applied in such a manner that they must be broken to gain entry* to the car or trailer. Additionally, full records of prefixes, suffixes, and serial numbers should be recorded and maintained.

The following drawings describe the proper method for applying seals to the most commonly used hasps. The seals demonstrated are the common tyden-ball type. In most instances a high security seal can be utilized.

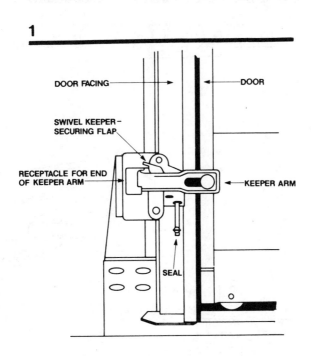

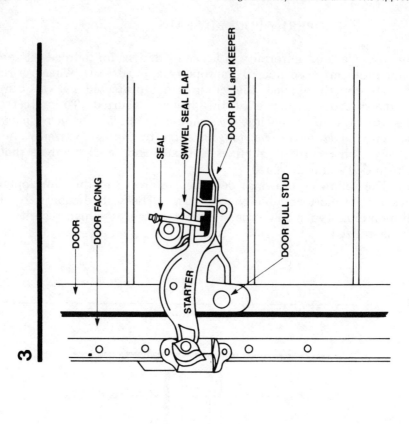

3

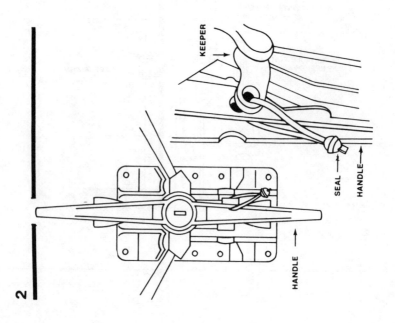

2

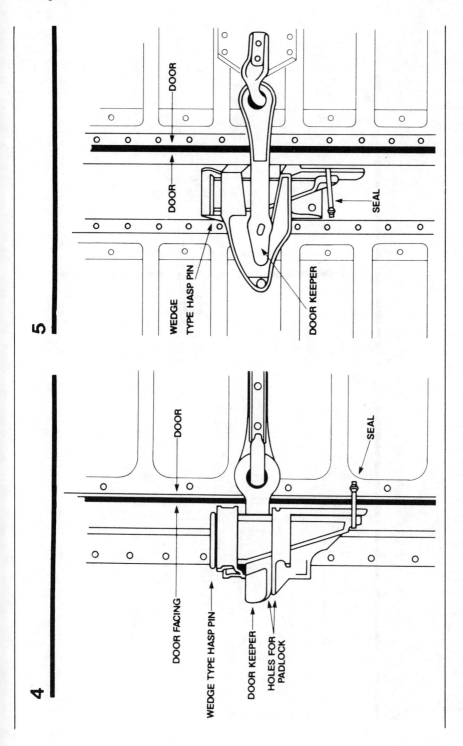

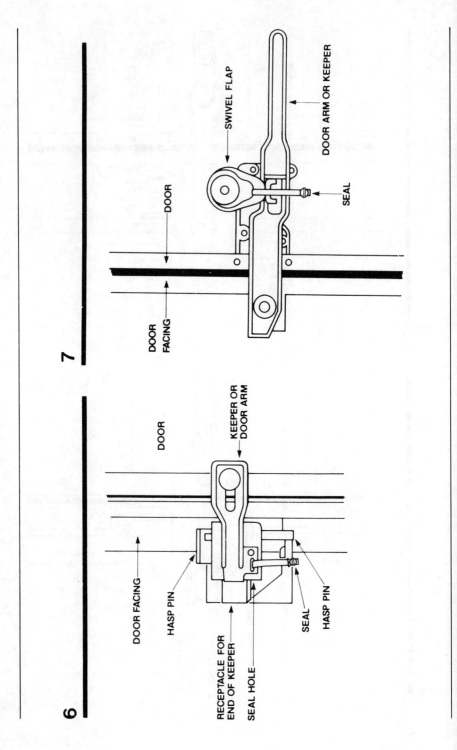

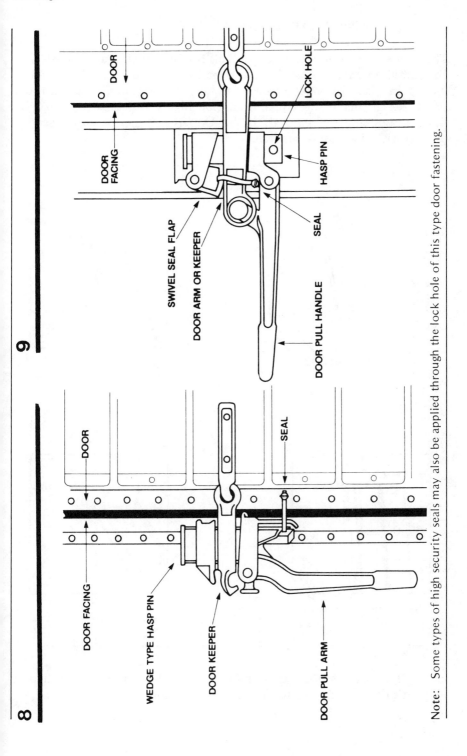

DOOR

LOCK HOLE

DOOR FACING

HASP PIN

SWIVEL SEAL FLAP

DOOR ARM OR KEEPER

SEAL

DOOR PULL HANDLE

9

DOOR

SEAL

DOOR FACING

WEDGE TYPE HASP PIN

DOOR KEEPER

DOOR PULL ARM

8

Note: Some types of high security seals may also be applied through the lock hole of this type door fastening.

UPPER RAIL LOCK "A"

The Upper Rail Loc is a reusable lock for boxcar doors. It consists of an aluminum extrusion which fits over the upper door guide rail and is locked in place by a set screw. The height of installation and the set screw design make the Upper Rail Loc highly resistant to defeat by thieves. Locking or removal of the Upper Rail Loc is easily accomplished with the extension wrench.

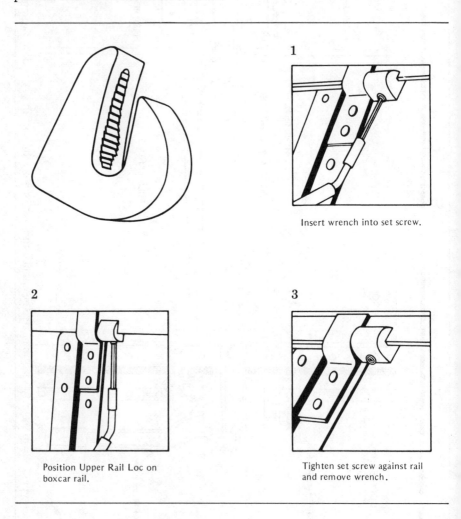

1

Insert wrench into set screw.

2

Position Upper Rail Loc on boxcar rail.

3

Tighten set screw against rail and remove wrench.

Upper runner lock gives maximum protection when applied at shipper's dock, using extension tool from ground.

TWIST-SEAL WIRE

One of the easiest and most economical security devices, it is applied with a "T" tool with a double twist to prevent "slipping". This is of great advantage in tightening up pins in box car hasps to prevent inadvertent opening through pin action. Thieves must come equipped with tools to break wire. Excellent to use in anti-theft hasp, as thieves cannot reach 10 feet in the air.

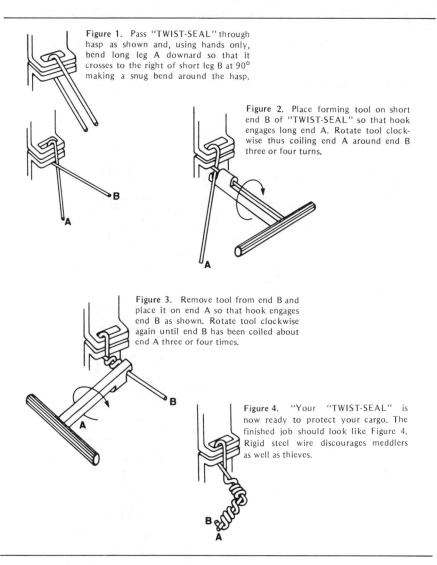

Figure 1. Pass "TWIST-SEAL" through hasp as shown and, using hands only, bend long leg A downard so that it crosses to the right of short leg B at 90° making a snug bend around the hasp.

Figure 2. Place forming tool on short end B of "TWIST-SEAL" so that hook engages long end A. Rotate tool clockwise thus coiling end A around end B three or four turns.

Figure 3. Remove tool from end B and place it on end A so that hook engages end B as shown. Rotate tool clockwise again until end B has been coiled about end A three or four times.

Figure 4. "Your "TWIST-SEAL" is now ready to protect your cargo. The finished job should look like Figure 4. Rigid steel wire discourages meddlers as well as thieves.

CABLE SEAL

The Cable Loc Seal is an inexpensive and simple one-time throwaway—
lock. It is a field-proven method of securing any type of cargo. The
Cable Loc Seal utilizes high tensile strength aircraft control cable with a
simple cold-rolled steel one way lock body for positive cargo protection.

   The Cable Loc Seal can be used by all segments of the transportation industry for locking long-haul truck trailers, boxcar doors,
containers, covered hopper cars, tank cars, and others who want to
secure their cargo.

   Up to six letters and six digits can be stamped on locking body
at no additional cost.

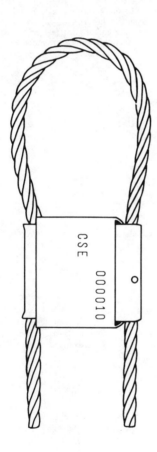

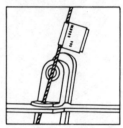

To apply grasp Cable Loc Seal by the
lock body with long end of cable point-
ing downward.

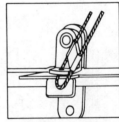

While grasping lock body with one hand,
free long end of cable upward through
opening in locking device with other
hand until a substantial length of cable
protrudes.

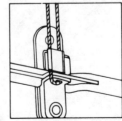

Grasp cable with one hand and lock
body with other. Pull down on cable
tightly to minimize loop in cable.

5/16 CARRIAGE BOLT AND NUT

The 5/16 inch carriage bolt and nut gives good protection to all types of hasp, including anti-theft hasps on box cars, for as little as $.10 per fastening. Easy to apply, difficult for thieves to remove. Can be purchased at local hardware stores.

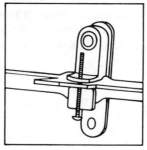

Insert the bolt through the hasp locking holes with the head down.

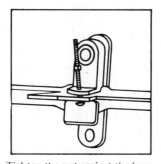

Tighten the nut against the hasp.

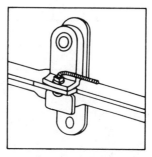

Using tool (or pliers), bend the bolt as close to the nut as possible to a 90° position. Strike the threads at the bend in the bolt with the tool, hammer or pliers.

SEAL-LOK

Excellent protection for all types of hasps. Heavy bolt cutter required to remove.

Each Seal-Lok consists of a hardened-steel shackle and a steel body. Once assembled, the lock must be destroyed to open. Once opened, it can never be reused. There are no keys to lose or duplicate.

Seal-Loks are consecutively numbered and cross-indexed to provide protection against unauthorized replacement. Your own trademark or identification letters can be added at slight additional cost. Shorter or longer shackle lengths are also available.

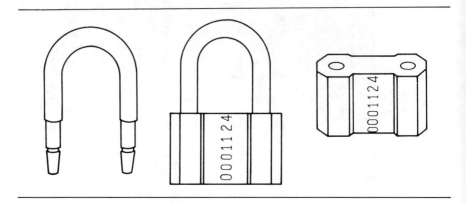

LOOP CABLE SEAL

Loop type cable seal. Comes as shown. Is easily applied to most hasps on railroad box cars and trailers. Can be purchased in narrow diameter. To apply, simply insert male end into barrel until lock snaps.

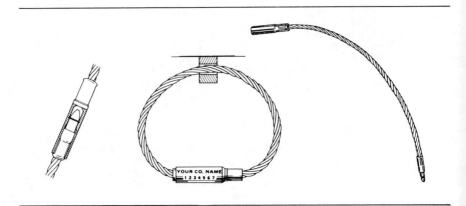

SEAL-BOLT LOCK

Seal-bolt locks offer excellent protection to all types of hasps on railroad cars and trailers, and are easily applied. Large bolt cutters required
to cut off.

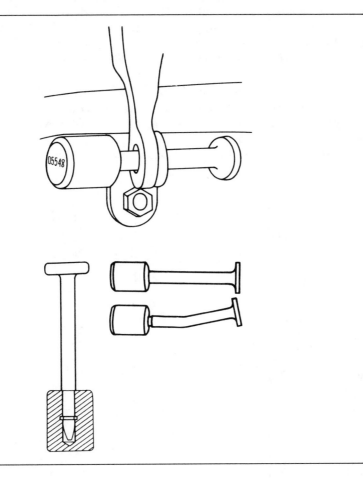

  Each Seal-Bolt consists of only three parts: A bolt, a retaining
ring, and a body.
  The bolt is one-piece steel with a hardened steel retaining ring
crimped onto the pointed end.
  When the bolt is inserted into the one-piece steel body, it can be
snapped shut by hand and securely locked in a moment. When locked,
it requires more than 1½ tons of pressure to separate the bolt from
the body!
  Simple, yes. But amazingly effective for all kinds of storage and
high-value cargo protection.

CONE-LOC SEAL

The Cone Loc Seal is a combination lock and seal specifically designed for the transportation industry. The Cone Loc Seal consists of two pieces, a throwaway flag and reusable locking body. Each flag is stamped with a sequential seal number. The flag is made of high tensile strength aircraft control cable with a rust-proof aluminum flag permanently attached to one end. The reusable cone, or locking body, is made of low-carbon steel and houses the locking mechanism. The cone is zinc-plated to resist corrosion.

The Cone Loc Seal can be used by all segments of the transportation industry to lock long-haul truck trailers, boxcar doors, containers, covered hopper cars, tank cars, and others who want to feel secure when they ship cargo.

Also comes with broad flat base for hasps with large holes.

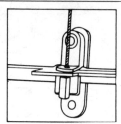

Insert free end of cable through hasp locking hole.

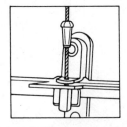

Slide cone locking body over free end of cable. Push the cable into the small end of the cone locking body.

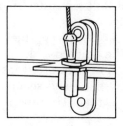

Slide the cone down the cable until the flag and cone are snug against the hasp.

CONCLUSION

A seal by itself will not prevent instances of cargo theft. A high security seal does represent an effective deterrent against cargo loss if properly applied for the proper reasons.

To be effective, a cargo security program must have the involvement and the commitment of both the carriers and their customers. Only then can real problems be identified and resolved.

In rail cargo security, as in all modes of transportation of cargo, the responsibility for success has to be shared.

LOSS AND DAMAGE CLAIMS

According to the law you must establish whether the loss is due to theft or pilferage or whether the loss was sustained by negligence or other means. In doing so, an understanding of rules and causes as set forth by the I.C.C. and other governmental bodies must be adhered to in order to file a claim.

Particular rules are especially important in claims. These rules have been carefully selected for this section because they are particularly pertinent to security. Since there is a "Hand in Glove" relationship between the security department and the claims department, an understanding of these rules by the Security Department is essential in assisting the claims department on loss and damage.

There is not a rule of thumb in determining loss and damage claims as each instance is unique and must be investigated since a mistake can cost the carrier the entire amount of the liability.

Claims must be filed within 9 months, so the carrier must have the Security Department complete their investigation as soon as possible. Some carriers however, have the Claims Department do the investigation themselves so as to avoid loss of time or perhaps mistakes in the definitions of rules. In either case, the trail of evidence must be followed as it pertains to seals and inspections of the cars upon arrival at each destination to determine if a loss occurred enroute.

Rules for Loss and Damage Claims

There are many causes of loss and damage, such as rough handling of cars, defective cars, fires, wrecks, improper loading, failure to protect properly against cold or heat undue delays, and pilferage. When the cause is one for which a carrier is liable, a loss and damage claim usually is filed.

Carriers are bound by law in regard to the payment of claims. Under the provisions of Section 6 of the Interstate Commerce Act, it is unlawful for a carrier to change or receive any greater, lesser, or different compensation for transportation than the rate and charges specified by tariffs; nor may the carriers refund any portions of such rates and charges. The refund or remission of such through the payment of fraudulent, fictitious, or excessive claims is as much a violation of the law as is a departure from the published rates and charges. The ICC also stipulates that any deviation as to the payment of claims before the full facts and measure of legal liability is determined will render both the carrier and claiment liable to the penalties as prescribed by law.

Loss and damage claims must be submitted as provided for in the bill of lading, and should be on the standard form for presentation of loss and damage claims; however, presentation on any particular form is not absolutely necessary. An assertion of loss or damage and a demand for payment is sufficient, regardless of the form of transmittal. The claim should be supported by the original bill of lading, original paid freight bill, and the original invoice, or certified correct copies of those documents, or a properly executed bond of indemnity protecting carriers in the absence of any of those documents. All other documents or evidence needed to substantiate the claim should be furnished to expedite handling.

The pertinent section of the bill of lading states as follows:

> As a condition precedent to recovery, claims must be filed in writing with the receiving or delivering carrier, or carrier issuing this bill of lading, or carrier on whose line the loss, damage, injury or delay occurred, within nine months after delivery of the property (or in case of export traffic, within nine months after delivery at port of export) or, in case of failure to make delivery, then within nine months after a reasonable time for delivery has elapsed; and suits shall be instituted against any carrier only within two years and one day from the day when notice in writing is given by the carrier to the claimant that the carrier has disallowed the claim or any part or parts thereof specified in the notice. Where claims are not filed or suits are not instituted thereon in accordance with the foregoing provisions, no carrier here under shall be liable, and such claims will not be paid.

As noted in this section, claims must be filed within nine months following delivery of the shipment. Settlement of any claim filed after the nine months period would subject both the carrier and the claiment to penalties prescribed by the ICC.

Common carriers can only limit their loss or damage liability according to the terms of that section of the bill of lading contract, or if the lading moves under a released (a cheaper rate secured by specifying a lading value not exceeding a specified amount) rate in accordance with applicable tariff.

Section 1(b) states:

> No carrier or party in possession of any or all of the property herein described shall be liable for any damage from or damage thereto or delay caused by an act of God, the public enemy, the authority of law, the act or default of the shipper or owner or for natural shrinkage, or from riots or strikes.

Claims must be filed with either the origin or destination carrier, or with the carrier on whose line the alleged loss or damage occurred.

Upon receipt of a proper claim, the carriers will acknowledge such to the claimant within 30 days of receiving the claim, unless the carrier has either paid or declined the claim within the 30-day period. The carrier will indicate in its acknowledgement to the claimant what, if any, additional information is required to further process the claim.

Each claim filed in the prescribed manner must be properly and thoroughly investigated to establish liability prior to any settlement. The investigation must disclose a lawful basis for payment before the claim may be settled. The ICC is concerned with the fair and equal treatment of the shipping public, and the commission will bring about the enforcement of laws which prohibit rebates and other discriminatory practices.

At the outset, claims will be examined to ascertain the following:

1. Presentation to the proper carrier.
2. Presentation within the time prescribed in the bill of lading (9 months).
3. Support by original bill of lading.
4. Support by paid freight bill or copy thereof.
5. Support by invoice or other proof of value.
6. Verification of loss.
7. Whether claimant is the shipper or consignee. If not, is claim supported by adequate evidence of interest?

Striving for maximum efficiency in regard to claim handling, the carriers endeavor to settle properly filed claims within 30 days from receipt of such. However, should the carrier not be able to pay, decline, or offer a compromise settlement within 120 days after receipt, the carrier will at that time advise the claimant, and after each succeeding 60-day period, the status of the claim and reasons for delay in making final settlement will be reviewed.

Freight Claim Rules

All freight claims are investigated, paid, and distributed between carriers according to rules agreed upon by members of the Association of American Railroads.

Applicable terms are defined in chapter 6.

Destination Station Records

Destination station records consist of all reports of inspections that have been generated by destination railroad forces; all reports of inspections that have been forwarded to destination agency for inclusion in agency records; the waybill and freight bill; all information accumulated at a central point or points by destination carrier during claimed shipment movement that is available, upon inquiry, without further investigation, from such point or points as specified in the Freight Claim Investigation Directory. The rule numbers and descriptions that apply (see table) are discussed below.

Rule	Description
4	Investigation
20	Imperfect sealing, defined
21	Imperfect seal record, defined
22	Imperfectly sealed cars, seal and record when received
23	Seals not required under certain conditions
24	Opened for inspection or in error, seal and record
25	End door security, seal and record
26	Recording seals
27	Correcting seal record
40	Seal or seal record; imperfect, resulting in loss
50	Claims under $200.00 use destination record only
54	Located loss for damage, not otherwise provided for
56	Open top equipment; loss or damage in or on

Rules

Rule 4 (a) The investigating carrier shall develop all facts necessary to determine liability and apportion responsibility in accordance with these rules by communicating directly with agents or other proper representatives of interested carriers by letter or otherwise.

Inquiries should be addressed to the freight claim officers of the interested carriers after failure to obtain information from the agents or other proper representatives, or when necessary from the nature of the inquiry.

(b) When the agent or other proper representatives of another carrier fails to furnish the specific information requested, or explain why he cannot do so, within 20 days from the date of inquiry, copy of the inquiry with request for reply shall be sent by express, registered mail, or messenger to the freight claim officer of delinquent carrier.

(c) If a reply is not received with 30 days to such request, or to a direct inquiry to freight claim officer regarding a paid claim, the carrier investigating and settling claim may, provided responsibility is not in its opinion located, charge the full amount of claim to the delinquent carrier nearest the investigating and settling carrier in direction of destination and shall forward all papers relating to the claim to such delinquent carrier. The delinquent carrier shall become the investigating and settling carrier and shall complete the investigation and distribution of the claim.

Rule 20 All enclosed transportation vehicles containing freight must be sealed at all openings and will be considered imperfectly sealed under any of the following conditions:

(a) Absence of seal (locks are not sufficient)
(b) Seal improperly applied
(c) Broken seal
(d) Indistinct impression on seal
(e) Blank seal
(f) Seal on insecure car door fastenings
(g) Lack of secure fastenings on inside unsealed end door
(h) When seals are other than those of carriers, shippers, state or national governmental agencies, or other persons acting under authorized arrangements

Rule 21 A carrier's seal record shall be considered imperfect under any of the following conditions:

(a) Absence of any record of seal.
(b) Absence of a record of marks or impressions on seal. Name or initials of carrier applying seal is not alone sufficient; number of other distinguishing marks must be recorded.

(c)   Absence of a record of securing inside fastening of end doors when not sealed as required in rule 25.

Rule 22 When a transportation vehicle is interchanged at a junction point improperly sealed, the carrier receiving the vehicle shall seal it promptly and make a record of the fact. By so doing, the outbound junction carrier is relieved of liability if the records of the subsequent movement show the vehicle to have been sealed properly at all points on its line.

Rule 23 Transportation vehicles do not require seals under the following conditions:

(a)   Transportation vehicles which cannot be sealed are those with doors cleated open for ventilation, those containing coal, coke, or other low grade commodities when a doorway barricade prevents closing of the doors, and those which may be exempted by special arrangements.

(b)   No carrier is required to apply seals or other sealing devices to top hatch or vent covers of refrigerator cars, dome covers or other openings of tank cars nor to similar closure devices on hopper cars.

Rule 24 (a)   When a sealed transportation vehicle is opened by an authorized person for any legitimate reason, it shall be considered as having been under "continuous seals" provided a continuous seal record is maintained.

(b)   When a transportation vehicle is opened in error it shall be considered unsealed unless an affidavit is made on the record at the time the transportation vehicle was opened, that it was opened in error but was under proper continuous surveillance while open and was resealed immediately.

Rule 25 (a)   End doors on railway cars shall be securely fastened on the inside or sealed by the receiving carrier or the carrier loading freight into the car at a transfer point, and a record shall be made of such seals or fastenings at the time of each loading.

(b)   The carrier unloading freight from a car at a transfer point and destination point shall record seals or the nature of the fastening of end doors.

(c)   Sealing, fastening inside, inspection, or recording security of end doors is not required other than provided in paragraphs (a) and (b) of this rule.

Rule 26 (a) Each carrier shall take record of all seals on or placed on doors on openings of transportation vehicles at the time of each loading and of all seals removed at the time of removal. Seals applied or removed by shippers, consignees, or other authorized persons, and records made thereof, shall be considered to be the carrier's records. Each carrier shall also take record of all seals on or placed on side doors or openings of transportation vehicles delivered to or received from other carriers at junction points. Such records shall be taken at the time of interchange (except as provided in paragraph (d) of this rule). An unlocked or defective seal must be removed and a new seal properly applied.

(b) Record must be sufficient to fully identify the seals. The name of initials of a carrier applying seals, without numbers or other distinguishing marks appearing on seals, will not be considered as a valid seal record.

(c) If a transportation vehicle is sealed properly and a proper record is made of those seals, the absence of a record of customs "in transit" of "in-bond" seals shall not be considered a defective record.

(d) Failure to record the seals or other sealing devices on top hatch covers of refrigerator cars, dome covers or other openings of tank cars, or similar closure devices on hopper cars shall not be considered a defective record. Seals applied to end doors of railway cars need to be recorded only at the time of loading or unloading.

Rule 27 A change in statement of seal record will be permitted only when evidence is presented proving that the previous statement was in error.

Rule 40 (a) A claim for loss shall be charged to any carrier having an imperfect seal or seal records. When two or more carriers have imperfect seals or seal records the loss shall be equally divided between such carriers.

(b) No carrier shall be charged with a loss on account of imperfect seal records when investigation shows that the seal was perfect beyond the point having the imperfect seal record.

(c) Imperfect end-door security only will be prorated on a mileage basis from the point of last recording to the point where imperfect security was discovered, except that when side-doors defects also exist the end-door deficiencies become a point of defect and will be charged accordingly. A carrier or carriers may be assessed a defect for end-door security as well as side-door security.

(d) Loss which the evidence shows conclusively to have occurred through top hatches or vents shall be prorated on a mileage basis from point at which the shipment was last checked in full and found to be in good order to the point where loss was discovered.

(e) This rule applies subject to rule 50.

Rule 50 (a) A claim or portion of a claim for damage other than concealed damage which, after deducting salvage or other proper credit, does not exceed $200.00 shall be distributed as follows:

(i) If a destination station records disclose no exceptions en route, the amount shall be prorated on a mileage basis from the initial point to destination point.

(ii) If the destination station records disclose where damage was discovered, amount shall be prorated on a mileage basis from the initial point to point or to the point where the damage was discovered.

(iii) If the destination station records disclose point or points where the damage occurred and places responsibility, carrier or carriers responsible shall be charged the amount involved.

(b) A claim or portion of a claim for loss of a package, or loss from a package, other than concealed loss which, after deducting any proper credits, does not exceed $200.00 shall be distributed as follows:

(i) If the destination station records disclose no exceptions en route, the amount shall be prorated on a mileage basis from the initial point to destination point.

(ii) If the destination station records disclose a defective seal record exists as defined in rules 20 to 27 inclusive, the amount shall be prorated on a mileage basis from initial point to destination point, eliminating from such prorate any portion, or portion of the move in connection with which destination station records show that the seals were perfect.

(iii) If the destination station records disclose the point or points where the loss occurred and places responsibility, the carrier or carriers responsible shall be charged the amount involved.

(c) No investigation other than securing destination stations records shall be required, except that when carload or less than carload freight, including consolidated traffic, was checked or transferred at a point where a new bill of lading was issued, the record at such point must be developed and amount paid, will be distributed in accordance with that record; except further, that when water carriers are involved the record of checking to or from the water carrier shall be developed and will determine the liability of the water carrier.

Rule 56 (a) Claims for loss of freight transported in or on an open transportation vehicle which, from its nature indicates negligence and is not otherwise located, or loss from cars which cannot be sealed (rule 23 [a]) shall be prorated on a mileage basis from the point at which loaded or last checked in full or where the loss was discovered.

(b) If any carrier en route properly seals a transportation vehicle which under rule 23(a) is defined as unsealable and no imperfection in seal record subsequently develops, the claim for loss shall be prorated up to the point at which the seals were applied. Should imperfect seal or seal records develop subsequently, the loss shall be prorated from the point at which such defect was detected, except that if the transportation vehicle was properly sealed during the entire time it was in possession of any carrier or carriers, they shall be exempt from participation.

(c) Claims for damage to freight transported in or on an open transportation vehicle where the nature of the damage indicates negligence, and where the damage is not otherwise located, shall be prorated on a mileage basis from initial point to destination.

Causes of Rail Cargo Loss

1. Shortage, packaged shipment: failure to deliver all or part of a packaged shipment for unknown reasons, includes the unexplained disappearance of all or part of a shipment for reasons other than robbery, theft, and pilferage, chargeable to cause 7.

2. Shortage, bulk shipment: failure to deliver all or part of a bulk shipment for unknown reasons. Includes the unexplained disappearance of all or part of a shipment for reasons other than robbery or theft and pilferage, chargeable to cause 7.

3. All damage not otherwise provided for.

4. Defective or unfit equipment: loss or damage to leaky or defective car roof, floor, side, end or door, defective hoppers, protruding nails, bolts or hooks, dirty or improperly cleaned equipment. Delay due to car defects should be classified in cause 6.

5. Temperature failures: damage due to improper icing, improper manipulation of vents, failure to ice, overflow from drip pipes, defective mechanical units or failure to refuel units. Damage due to freezing, frosting, chilling, or improper handling of heaters causing smoke or soot damage or overheating, etc. Included in this list is all freezing due to improper manipulation of vents, delays during severe weather, or other causes resulting in frost damage.

6. Delay, loss, or damage owing to delay in movement delivery of freight.

7. Robbery, theft, pilferage: *robbery* is failure to deliver all or part of a shipment as the result of stealing, including hijacking, with the use of force or threat of force against person or persons. (Note: claims for physical damage to freight in the same or other shipments resulting directly from robbery should be reported under this cause.) Theft and pilferage are failure to deliver all or part of a shipment as the result of known stealing, under circumstances indicating the probable cause was stealing, without use of force or threat of force against a person or persons, when it is known the freight was in the carrier's custody. (Note: claims for physical damage to freight in the same or other shipments resulting directly from theft or pilferage should be reported under this cause.)

8. Concealed damage: damage to freight discovered after delivery to consignee in apparent good order without evidence of irregularity in handling by carrier or carriers.

9. Train accident: damage due to derailment or collision.

10. Fire, marine, and natural catastrophes: fire or marine casualty, also, loss or damage resulting from catastrophies such as floods, storms, landslides, etc., not directly chargeable to other causes.

11. Error of employees: loss or damage due to error in loading, waybilling, directing or reconsigning, receipting for or delivery of freight, issuing bill of lading or requiring surrender thereof, or failure to make proper report of freight over, refused or unclaimed, etc.

12. Vandalism: damage due to acts of vandals when not a direct result of robbery, theft or pilferage as defined in cause 7.

10. Hazardous Materials

The general public as well as environmentalists are concerned with the problems of hazardous materials: its storage, disposal, and transportation. They have a right to be concerned. Pick up any newspaper and you will read articles about contaminated water supplies, land fill that is leaching toxic waste, railroad cars that leak deadly fumes, truck accidents that spill hazardous materials onto roadways, and commercial aircraft that carry passengers and also carry radio active material in the cargo hold.

More and more material and chemicals are being manufactured today that by themselves are not harmful, but if mixed with another chemical or fire could cause a hazardous materials emergency which could cost lives.

Today we have become more aware of these problems because we read about them and hear about them on television and radio, but how many can identify hazardous materials and their potential dangers?

The goal here is to reduce the harm created by hazardous materials emergencies by providing emergency response personnel with the basic skills with which to:

1. Recognize hazardous materials presence.
2. Identify the hazardous materials problems surrounding your transportation mode or industrial complex.
3. Identify the specific hazardous material(s) and their associated hazard characteristics.

Specific Objectives

1. Determine the extent of the hazardous material potential in the mode of transport and surrounding community.

This chapter is adapted from Union Pacific Railroad Personnel Department's Technical Training Manual, *Recognizing and Identifying Hazardous Materials*. Permission to reproduce obtained from Union Pacific Railroad, Salt Lake City, Utah.

2. Create senario's describing the types of problems associated with emergencies involving hazardous materials within your mode of transport.
3. Establish the function of emergency response personnel in hazardous materials emergencies.
4. Teach your staff the DECIDE process.
5. Know the six clues for the detection of hazardous materials presence.

The next step is to obtain the cooperation and assistance and the information from the following sources:

1. Chemtrec
2. Shipper (Chemical Industry)
3. Transportation Industry
4. Federal Agencies
5. Various emergency action guides

When creating your senario's remember to:

1. Select the situation involving hazardous materials.
2. Identify the specific name of the material(s) involved.
3. List the hazard characteristics associated with that material.

THE HAZARDOUS MATERIALS PROBLEM

I. What is a hazardous material?
    A. According to the Department of Transportation: "any substance or material in any form or quantity which poses an unreasonable risk to safety and health and property when transported in commerce."
        1. Hazardous substance (EPA): any material which when discharged into or upon the navigable waters of the United States or adjoining shorelines may be harmful to the public health or welfare of the United States, including, but not limited to, fish, shellfish, wildlife, and public or private property, shorelines and beaches.
        2. Hazardous wastes (EPA): any material that may pose an unreasonable risk to health, safety or property when transported in commerce for the purposes of treatment, storage, or disposal as waste.

II.   Classification of hazardous materials, DOT classifications
      A. Explosives A
      B. Explosive B
      C. Blasting agents
      D. Explosives C
      E. Flammable gas
      F. Nonflammable gas
          1. Pyrophoric liquid
      G. Flammable liquid
      H. Oxidizer
      I. Organic peroxide
      J. Poison A
      K. Poison B
      L. Irritant
      M. Etiologic agent
      N. Radioactive I
      O. Radioactive II
      P. Combustible liquid
      Q. Flammable solid
          1. Water reactive
          2. Spontaneously combustible
      R. Radioactive III
      S. Corrosives
      T. Other regulated materials A, B, C, D, and E
III. Hazardous materials locations
      A. Production
      B. Transportation
      C. Storage
      D. Use

DETECTING PRESENCE OF HAZARDOUS MATERIALS

I.   D.E.C.I.D.E. process (note initial of each step)
      A. Detect hazardous materials presence.
      B. Estimate potential harm without intervention.
      C. Choose response objectives.
      D. Identify action options.
      E. Do best option.
      F. Evaluate progress.
II.   Clues for detecting hazardous materials presence
      A. Occupancy and/or location
      B. Container shapes

    C. Markings and colors (including the identification number)

    D. Placards and labels

    E. Shipping papers

    F. Senses

III. Identification number

    A. Identification numbers will be required on portable tanks, cargo tank cars after November 1, 1981 (see figure 10-1)

    B. Identification numbers may be displayed on other conveyances.

    C. Methods of display of identification number:

        1. Orange panel adjacent to the placards. Panel is $5\frac{7}{8}''$ $\times$ $15\frac{3}{4}''$ with 4-inch letters.

        2. Combustible placards which have the identification number on the placard will have the bottom of the placard in white.

IV. Placards

    A. Placards are diamond shaped, $10\frac{3}{4}$ inches square. The placard provides recognition information in a number of ways.

        1. Colored background

        2. Symbol at the top

        3. United Nations class number at the bottom

        4. Hazard class or the identification number in the center

           a. Color

              (1) Orange indicates explosive

              (2) Red indicates flammable

              (3) Green indicates nonflammable

              (4) Yellow indicates oxidizing material

              (5) White with vertical red stripes indicates flammable solid

              (6) Yellow over white indicates radioactive material

              (7) White over black indicates corrosive material

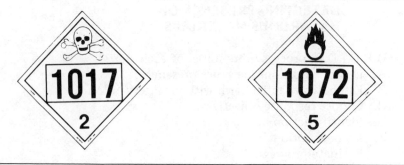

Figure 10-1. Hazardous Materials Placards with Identification Numbers.

    b. Symbols (see figure 10-2 for examples.)
       (1) Bursting ball symbol indicates explosive
       (2) Flame symbol indicates flammable
       (3) Slash W indicates dangerous when wet
       (4) Skull and crossbones indicates poisonous material
       (5) Circle with the flame indicates oxidizing materials
       (6) Cylinder indicates nonflammable gas
       (7) Propeller indicates radioactive
       (8) Test tube/hand/metal symbol indicates corrosive
       (9) Word *empty* indicates that the product has been removed, but a harmful residue may still be present
    c. DOT general guidelines on the use of placards
       (1) Each person who offers a hazardous material for shipment must label the package containing the material, if required, with the appropriate label(s). (Sec. 172.400 (a))

DOT Hazardous Materials Warning Placards

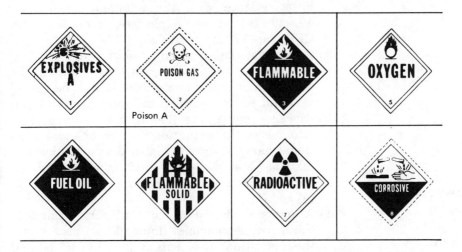

Figure 10-2.   DOT Hazardous materials warning placards (Source: United States Department of Transportation.)

(2) Labels may be affixed to packages even though not required by the regulations provided each label represents a hazard of the material in the package. (Sec. 172.401)

(3) Exceptions to the labeling requirements for limited quantities of certain hazardous materials are specified in the regulations.

(4) The number appearing at the bottom corner of some labels represent the UN and IMCO hazard class number. These are permitted, but not required, by DOT regulations. (Sec. 172.407 (g))

(5) Label(s), when required, must be affixed to or printed on the surface of the package near the marked proper shipping name. (Sec. 172.406 (a))

(6) When two or more different warning labels are required, they must be displayed next to each other. (Sec. 172.406 (c))

(7) When two or more packages containing compatible hazardous materials are packaged within the same overpack, the outside container must be labeled as required for each class of material contained therein. (Sec. 172.404 (b))

(8) Packages containing a sample of a hazardous material other than an explosive must be labeled in accordance with the requirements of Sec. 172.402 (h). (For Explosives, see Title 49, CFR, Part 173, Subpart C)

(9) A material classed as an Explosive A, Poison A, or Radioactive material, that also meets the definition of another hazard class, must be labeled as required for each class. (Sec. 172.402 (a))

(10) Packages containing Radioactive material, that also meets the definition of one or more additional hazards, must be labeled as a Radioactive material and for each additional hazard on opposite sides of the package. (Sec. 172.403 (e) and (f)

(11) A material classed as an Oxidizer, Flammable solid, or Flammable liquid, that also meets the definition of a Poison B, must be labeled POISON, in addition to the hazard class label. (Sec. 172.402 (a) (3))

(12) A material classed as a Flammable solid, that also meets the definition of a water reactive material, must have both FLAMMABLE SOLID and DANGEROUS WHEN WET labels affixed. (Sec. 172.402 (a) (4))

(13) For OXYGEN, the word "OXYGEN" may be used in place of the word "OXIDIZER" on the OXIDIZER label. (Sec. 172.405 (a)) For foreign shipments, the NON-FLAMMABLE GAS label may also be required.

(14) For CHLORINE, a CHLORINE label may also be used in place of the NON-FLAMMABLE GAS and POISON labels. (Sec. 172.405 (b)) For foreign shipments, the NON-FLAMMABLE GAS label may also be required.

   d. United Nations class numbers
       (1) Explosives
       (2) Compressed gases
       (3) Flammable liquids
       (4) Flammable solids
       (5) Oxidizing substances
       (6) Poisonous and Infectious substances
       (7) Radioactive substances
       (8) Corrosive substances
       (9) Miscellaneous dangerous substances
   e. Hazard class or identification number

V. National Fire Protection Agency (NFPA) 704 System
   A. Health (Blue)
       In general, health hazard in fire fighting is that of a single exposure which may vary from a few seconds to an hour. The physical exertion demanded in fire fighting or other emergency conditions may be expected to intensify the effects of any exposure. Only hazards arising out of an inherent property of the material are considered. The following explanation arranged by descending degree of hazard, is based upon protective equipment normally used by fire fighters.
       4. Materials too dangerous to health to expose fire fighters. A few whiffs of the vapor could cause death, or the vapor or liquid could be fatal on penetrating the fire fighter's normal fully protective clothing. The normal fully protective clothing and breathing apparatus available to the

average fire department will not provide adequate protective against inhalation or skin contact with these materials.

3. Materials extremely hazardous to health but areas may be entered with extreme care. Fully protective clothing, including self-contained breathing apparatus, coat, pants, gloves, boots, and bands around legs, arms, and waist should be provided. No skin surface should be exposed.

2. Materials hazardous to health, but areas may be entered freely with full-faced mask with self-contained breathing apparatus that provides eye protection.

1. Materials only slightly hazardous to health; it may be desirable to wear self-contained breathing apparatus.

0. Materials which on exposure under fire conditions would offer no hazard beyond that of ordinary combustible material.

B. Flammability (red)

Susceptibility to burning is the basis for assigning degrees within this category. The method of attacking the fire is influenced by this susceptibility factor.

4. Very flammable gases or very volatile flammable liquids; shut off flow and keep cooling water streams on exposed tanks or containers.

3. Materials that can be ignited under almost all normal temperature conditions; water may be ineffective because of the low flash point.

2. Materials that must be moderately heated before ignition will occur; water spray may be used to extinguish the fire because the material can be cooled below its flash point.

1. Materials that must be preheated before ignition can occur; water may cause frothing if it gets below the surface of the liquid and turns to steam. However, water fog gently applied to the surface will cause a frothing which will extinguish the fire.

0. Materials that will not burn.

C. Reactivity (stability) (yellow)

The assignment of degrees in the reactivity category is based upon the susceptibility of materials to release energy either by themselves or in combination with water. Fire exposure was one of the factors considered along with conditions of shock and pressure.

4. Materials that (in themselves) are readily capable of detonation or of explosive decomposition or explosive

reaction at normal temperatures and pressures; includes materials sensitive to mechanical or localized thermal shock. If a chemical with this hazard rating is in an advanced or massive fire, the area should be evacuated.

3. Materials that (in themselves) are capable of detonation or of explosive decomposition or explosive reaction but require a strong initiating source or must be heated under confinement before initiation. Includes materials sensitive to thermal or mechanical shock at elevated temperatures and pressures or that react explosively with water without requiring heat or confinement; fire fighting should be done from an explosive-resistant location.

2. Materials that (in themselves) are normally unstable and readily undergo violent chemical change but do not detonate. Includes materials that can undergo chemical change with rapid release of energy at normal temperatures and pressures or can undergo violent chemical change at elevated temperatures and pressures; also includes those materials that may react violently with water or may form potentially explosive mixtures with water. In advance or massive fires, fire fighting should be done from a safe distance or from a protected location.

1. Materials that (in themselves) are normally stable but may become unstable at elevated temperatures and pressures or may react with water with some release of energy, but not violently; caution must be used in approaching the fire and applying water.

0. Materials that (in themselves) are normally stable even under fire exposure conditions and are not reactive with water; normal fire fighting procedures may be used.

IDENTIFYING HAZARDOUS MATERIALS

I. Identification activities
   A. Determine the specific name of the material and its hazard classification.
   B. Determine the hazard characteristics of the material.
II. Aid for determining the specific name of the hazardous material involved
   A. Shipping papers and other documents
   B. Markings and colors (including identification number)

III. Resources for determining the hazard characteristics of hazardous
     materials
     A. CHEMTREC—(800) 424-9300
     B. Chemical industry (shippers, manufacturers, etc.)
     C. Rail transportation industry
     D. Bureau of Explosives—(202) 243-4048
     E. National Response Center—(800) 424-8802
     F. Emergency action guides
IV. Common emergency action guides
     A. EMERGENCY HANDLING OF HAZARDOUS MATE-
         RIALS IN SURFACE TRANSPORTATION HAZARDOUS
         MATERIALS—EMERGENCY RESPONSE GUIDE
         1. Available from: Bureau of Explosives
                                Association of American Railroads
                                1920 "I" Street, NW
                                Washington, DC 20036
     B. FIRE PROTECTION GUIDE ON HAZARDOUS MATERIALS
         Contents: Flashpoint Index of Trade Name Liquids
         NFPA 325M: Fire Hazard Properties of Flammable
                               Liquids, Gases and Solids
         NFPA 49:   Hazardous Chemical Data
         NFPA 491M: Manual of Hazardous Chemical Reactions
         NFPA 704:   Recommended System for the Identi-
                               fication of the Fire Hazard of Materials
         Available from: National Fire Protection Association
                               470 Atlantic Avenue
                               Boston, MA 02210
     C. HAZARDOUS   MATERIALS—EMERGENCY   RESPONSE
         GUIDEBOOK
         Available from: Department of Transportation
                               Office of Hazardous Materials Operations
                               2100 Second Street, SW
                               Washington, DC 20590
     D. HAZARDOUS CHEMICAL DATE (U.S. Coast Guard CHRIS
         System)
         Available from: Superintendent of Documents
                               U.S. Government Printing Office
                               Washington, DC 20402
                               Order Number 050-012-00147-2
V.   Identification Project
     A. Definitions
         1. *Boiling point*: the temperature at which the vapor pressure
             of a liquid equals the atmospheric pressure.

2. *Flammable limits*: the highest and lowest percentage or concentrations of a flammable gas or vapor with the oxygen in the air that will ignite.
3. *Flash point*: the minimum temperature at which a liquid gives off enough vapor that will ignite and flash over but will not continue to burn.
4. *Ignition temperature*: the temperature at which a fuel or substance ignites.
5. *Specific gravity*: the weight of a substance as compared to the weight of an equal volume of water; less than 1 indicates that the material is lighter than water and will float, and more than 1 indicates heavier than water and will sink.
6. *Vapor density*: the weight and volume of pure vapor or gas compared to the weight of an equal volume of dry air at the same temperature and pressure; less than 1 indicates the material is lighter than air and may rise and more than 1 indicates heavier than air and means that it will stay low to the ground.
7. *Water solubility*: the ability of a solid or liquid to dissolve or mix with water.

Potential Hazards

I. Health hazards
    A. Poison
        1. May be fatal if inhaled, swallowed or absorbed through skin.
        2. Contact may cause burns to skin and eyes.
        3. Runoff from fire control or dilution water may cause pollution.
II. Fire or explosion
    A. Will burn; may be ignited by heat, sparks and flames.
    B. Flammable vapor may spread away from spill.
    C. Container may explode in heat of fire.
    D. Vapor explosion and poison hazard indoors, outdoors or in sewers.
    E. Runoff to sewer may create fire or explosion hazard.

Emergency Action

III. General precautions
    A. Keep unnecessary people away: isolate hazard area and deny entry.

    B. Stay upwind; keep out of low area.

    C. Wear positive-pressure breathing apparatus and special protective clothing.

    D. ISOLATE FOR 1/2 MILE IN ALL DIRECTIONS IF TANK OR TANKCAR IS INVOLVED IN FIRE.

    E. FOR EMERGENCY ASSISTANCE CALL CHEMTREC (800) 424-9300.

    F. Also, in case of water pollution, call local authorities.

IV. Fire

    A. SMALL FIRES: Dry chemical, CO2, water spray or foam.

    B. LARGE FIRES: Water spray, fog or foam.

       1. Stay away from ends of tanks.

       2. Do not get water inside container.

       3. Cool containers that are exposed to flames with water from the side until well after fire is out.

       4. For massive fire in cargo area, use unmanned hose holder or monitor nozzles.

       5. If this is impossible, withdraw from area and let fire burn.

       6. Withdraw immediately in case of rising sound from venting safety device or discoloration of tank.

V. Spill or leak

    A. No flares, smoking or flames in hazard area.

    B. Do not touch spilled material.

    C. Stop leak if you can do it without risk.

    D. Use water spray to reduce vapors.

    E. SMALL SPILLS

       1. Flush area with flooding amount of water.

       2. Do not get water inside containers.

    F. LARGE SPILLS

       1. Dike far ahead of spill for later disposal.

VI. First aid

    A. Move victim to fresh air; call emergency medical care.

    B. If not breathing, give artifical respiration.

    C. If breathing is difficult, give oxygen.

    D. Remove and isolate contaminated clothing and shoes.

    E. In case of contact with materials, immediately flush skin or eyes with running water for at least 15 minutes.

    F. Keep victim quiet and maintain normal body temperature.

    G. Effects may be delayed; keep victim under observation.

HAZARDOUS MATERIALS DEFINITIONS

The following definitions have been abstracted from the Code of Federal Regulations, title 49-Transportation, parts 100 to 199. Refer to the referenced sections for complete details. NOTE: Rule-making proposals are outstanding or are contemplated concerning some of these definitions.

Hazardous material A substance or material determined by the Secretary of Transportation to be capable of posing an unreasonable risk to health, safety, and property when transported in commerce, and which has been so designated. See sec. 1718.

Multiple hazards A material meeting the definitions of more than one hazard class is classed according to the sequence given in sec. 1732.

An explosive Any chemical compound, mixture, or device, the primary or common purpose of which is to function by explosion, i.e., with substantially instantaneous release of gas and heat, unless such compound, mixture, or device is otherwise specifically classified in parts 170–189 (sec. 173.50).

Class A of explosive Detonating or otherwise of maximum hazard. The nine types of class A explosives are defined in sec. 173.53.

Class B explosive In general, function by rapid combustion rather than detonation and include some explosive devices such as special fireworks, flash powders, etc. FLAMMABLE HAZARD (sec. 173.88).

Class C explosive Certain types of manufactured articles containing class A or class B explosives, or both, as components but in restricted quantities and certain types of fireworks. MINIMUM HAZARD (sec. 173.100).

Blasting agents A material designed for blasting which has been tested in accordance with sec. 173.114a(b) and found to be so insensitive that there is very little probability of accidental initiation to explosion or of transition from deflagration to detonation (sec. 173.114a[a].

Combustible liquid Any liquid having a flash point above 100°F, and below 200°F, as determined by tests listed in sec. 173.115(d). Exceptions to this are found in sec. 173.115(b).

Corrosive material Any liquid or solid that causes visible destruction of human skin tissue or a liquid that has a severe corrosion rate on steel (see sec. 173.240 [a] and [b] for details).

Flammable liquid Any liquid having a flash point below 100°F as determined by tests listed in sec. 173.115 (d). Exceptions are listed in sec. 173.115(a).

Pyroforic liquid is any liquid that ignites spontaneously in dry or moist air at or below 130°F (sec. 173.115 [c]).

Compressed gas is any material or mixture having in the container a pressure EXCEEDING 40 psia at 70°F, or a pressure exceeding 104 psi at 100°F (sec. 173.300 [a]).

Flammable gas Any compressed gas meeting the requirements for lower flammability limit, flammability limit range, flame projection, or flame propagation criteria as specified in sec. 173.300(b).

Nonflammable gas Any compressed gas other than a flammable compressed gas.

Flammable solid Any solid material, other than an explosive, which is liable to cause fires through friction, retained heat from manufacturing or processing, or which can be ignited readily and when ignited burns so vigorously and persistently as to create a serious transportation hazard (sec. 173.150).

Organic Peroxide An organic compound containing the bivalent –0–0 structure and which may be considered a derivative of hydrogen peroxide where one or more of the hydrogen atoms have been replaced by organic radicals must be classed as an organic peroxide unless: (see sec. 173.151 [a] for details).

Oxidizer A substance such as chlorate, permanganate, inorganic peroxide, or a nitrate that yields oxygen readily to stimulate the combustion of organic matter (see sec. 173.151).

Poison A EXTREMELY DANGEROUS POISONS: poisonous gases or liquids of such nature that a very small amount of the gas, or vapor of the liquid, mixed with air is DANGEROUS TO LIFE (sec. 173.326).

Poison B LESS DANGEROUS POISONS: substances, liquids, or solids (including pastes and semisolids), other than class A or irritating materials, which are known to be so toxic to humans as to afford a hazard to health during transportation; or which, in the absence of adequate data on human toxicity, are presumed to be TOXIC TO HUMANS (sec. 173.343).

Irritating material A liquid or solid substance which upon contact with fire or when exposed to air gives off dangerous or intensely irritating fumes, but NOT INCLUDING ANY POISONOUS MATERIAL, CLASS A (sec. 173.381).

Etiologic agent A viable microorganism, or its toxin which causes or may cause human disease (sec. 173.386) (refer to the Department of Health, Education and Welfare Regulations, title 42, CFR, sec. 72.25 [c] for details).

Radioactive material Any material, or combination of materials, that spontaneously emits ionizing radiation, and having a specific activity greater than 0.002 microcuries per gram (sec. 173.389). NOTE: See Sec. 173.389(a) through (1) for details.

   ORM-A, B, C, D, or E (OTHER REGULATED MATERIALS): any material that does not meet the definition of a hazardous material, other than a combustible liquid in packagings having a capacity of 110 gallons or less, and is specified in sec. 172.101 as an ORM material or that possesses one or more of the characteristics described in ORM-A through D below (sec. 173.500).

NOTE: An ORM with a FLASH POINT OF 100°F, when transported with more than 110 gallons in one container, SHALL BE CLASSED AS A COMBUSTIBLE LIQUID.

ORM-A A material with an anesthetic, irritating, noxious, toxic, or other similar property and which can cause extreme annoyance or discomfort to passengers and crew in the event of leakage during transportation (sec. 173.500 [a] [1]).

ORM-B A material (including a solid when wet with water) capable of causing significant damage to a transport vehicle or vessel from leakage during transportation. Materials meeting one or both of the following criteria are ORM-B materials: (1) A liquid substance that has a corrosion rate exceeding 0.250 inch per year (IPYO on aluminum (nonclad 7075-T6) at a test temperature of 130°F. An acceptable test is described in NACE Standard TM-01-69, and specifically designated by name in sec. 172.101 (Sec. 173.500 [a] [2]).

ORM-C A material with other inherent characteristics not described as an ORM-A or ORM-B, but which make it unsuitable for shipment unless properly identified and prepared for transportation. Each ORM-C material is specifically named in sec. 172.101 (sec. 173.500 [a] [4]).

ORM-D A material such as a consumer commodity which, though otherwise subject to the regulations of this subchapter, presents a limited hazard during transportation due to its form, quantity, and packaging. They must be materials for which exceptions are provided in sec. 172.101. A shipping description applicable to each ORM-D material or category of ORM-D materials is found in sec. 172.101 (sec. 173.500 [a] [4]).

The systems theft/fraud Exposure is highest; little is known about it. It appears to be the most evident future point of vulnerability. Current prevention systems are few.

11. Cargo Theft and Organized Crime

YOUR OPPONENTS AND HOW THEY ARE ORGANIZED

Just as a manager or law enforcement official may underrate the overall impact of cargo theft by considering only the initial, direct financial losses involved, executives may also underestimate the number of people, and the interplay between them, necessary to make cargo theft the successful and serious enterprise that it is. If management ill perceives those who are stealing, subsequent preventive action is little more than a shot in the dark.

For example, policies aimed at the lone, independent pilferer usually are inadequate to cope with thefts resultant from collusion among a company's employees. When the problem broadens to include collusion among employees in two or more firms, the managerial response must increase accordingly. At this point, the problem and requisite controls become intercompany, intermodal, and interindustry. A final dimension is added when external criminal elements are involved either in the execution of thefts or in the supply of services necessary for profitable theft. When this factor is present, the various affected private sector companies and industries must not only cooperate among themselves but also establish effective working relationships with appropriate governmental units, particularly law enforcement.

This chapter is adapted from U.S. Department of Transportation *Cargo Theft and Organized Crime*, P 5200.6. Washington, D.C.: U.S. Government Printing Office, October, 1972.

Overt Indicators of Collusion

One need only glance at some of the obvious characteristics of many cargo thefts to realize (1) the extent to which collusion must be present and (2) the different sets of individuals who may be necessary to assure the success of such crimes. Even a cursory examination of where cargo thefts occur yields conspicuous conclusions. For instance, a security group at a large air cargo complex analyzed 76 reports of cargo loss, theft, or pilferage and found that in over 48% of the cases, the cargo has been checked into the terminal but could not be found for delivery. On the basis of this and other evidence, the security group concluded that "the majority of thefts are committed within the terminals . . . and must result from collusion between employees and outsiders," the latter including truck drivers, brokers' runners, transients, or employees from other airlines. This assessment agrees with the observations of a number of supervisory customs inspectors at various airports: ". . . of the total losses during 'customs custody,' . . . 65% to 80% occur through collusion between truckers and the carriers' cargo handlers in delivering goods at the warehouse dock. We would expect roughly similar ratios on the waterfront."

According to the experience of one transportation executive, thefts "primarily occur away from the origin terminal." They occur at terminals "where cargo is being turned over to another carrier, or at destination terminals, where cargo is being moved across the dock to go on to the delivery truck." Similarly, 83% of the 1100 respondents (distributors) to a 1980 survey noted "a direct relationship between the number of carriers involved in a single shipment and the extent of loss and damage." Asserted one respondent, "100% of our losses and damages result from shipments transferred in transit. . ."

Perhaps truck hijackings represent the most visible and sensational evidence indicating who is involved in cargo theft and the degree of organization and collusion required. When goods are stolen "on the road," logic dictates that external criminal elements must be involved and frequently, if not usually, must have received advance information from an employee of the carrier. Some truck hijackings have occurred despite measures that turned vehicles "into almost armored cars, with radio control and extra helpers," as one investigator remarked. To execute such a hijack not only required skilled manpower but also facilities and contacts that will assure quick disposal of the goods. Although accounting for the minority of cargo theft losses for motor carrier, there were an estimated 750 truck hijackings during 1979. (Hijacking involves the threat or application of force or injury to an individual, in contrast to truck larcenies, where potential personal harm is not present, as in the theft of an unattended rig and its contents.)

Another overt indicator of the necessity for collusion is the sheer physical size of some of the loads that are stolen. When as many as 50 containers can disappear from a single port during a 12-month period, the only explanation is extensive collusion among longshoremen, checkers, operators of hi-lo equipment, truck drivers, and pier guards.

Still another indication of the cooperation required for the success of many cargo thefts is the nature of the goods stolen. For example, stolen uncut woolens must be preshrunk and pilfered raw furs processed before they are fit for garment manufacture. And not everyone has a need for silver, tin, or copper ingots. The point is, of course, that those who steal such items usually require access to others who are able to do, or arrange for, the necessary processing.

Another type of processing is necessary when the targets of cargo thieves are such items as credit cards, travelers checks, and nonnegotiable securities. Forgers, for example, may be required in the fraudulent negotiation of bonds. And counterfeiters may be tapped to supply false identification documents, such as drivers' license, social security cards, voter registration cards, etc. Like hijacking, this aspect of cargo theft points to the existence of criminal elements other than the ones who may be on a shipper's, carrier's, or warehouseman's payroll.

One of the most significant signs of collusion is the large quantity of merchandise often involved in cargo thefts. The implications of this are twofold. First, when a large quantity of goods is stolen, a well-planned and well-manned effort is usually required. For example, after noting in one city, during a two-month period in 1979, that gangs of marauders attacked freight trains, and 14 boxcars had been emptied of from 50% to 100% of their contents, a carrier's security director told a congressional committee, "Clearly these incidents indicate they are not spur-of-the moment or single-handed, isolated occurrences. They are well-planned, vicious and meticulously executed in a minimum of time at minimal risk to the perpetrator. The situation, if I may draw a comparison, is unfortunately very similar to that faced by America's pioneers as they crossed the Great Plains."

Second, when a theft involves a large quantity of goods—such as a container load of whiskey or $400,000 worth of flash bulbs—common sense dictates the existence of a distribution channel by which to dispose of such merchandise. As an insurance investigator advised, "Put yourself in the position of a hijacker. What would you do with a trailer load of tin, copper, nickel, . . . stainless steel, . . . men's and women's ready-to-wear, TVs, recorders, . . . registered drugs, golf balls, electronic equipment, . . . $250,000 of watch movements . . .? You most certainly would need some criminal channels through which this merchandise could be disposed. And, just as certainly, unless one is to stand on the very shaky assumption that the criminal element is the ultimate consumer of all that is stolen, many if not most of these criminal channels of distribution return stolen goods to the marketplace through innocent and not-so-innocent outlets, which are often in direct competition with businesses that suffered the original loss.

Thus, even a casual observer of the cargo theft problem can surmise the following: (1) some employees in many companies involved in hauling, storing, or otherwise handling cargo while in the transportation system act in collusion with one another to steal goods entrusted to their care; (2) such employees may cooperate with external criminal groups in the execution of a theft or depend on these groups to dispose of what is stolen; (3) these external criminal elements may commit cargo thefts without the assistance of company employees; and (4) a considerable amount of stolen cargo finds its way back to the legitimate marketplace.

Given all this, the term *collusion* becomes an overly conservative assessment of what is going on. On balance, the problem is more accurately characterized by the phrase *organized criminal activity*, which may be defined as an on-going conspiracy wherein each participant or set of participants has a specific role and is dependent upon others for a profitable outcome of the crime. On the one hand, this is not to deny the existence of many independents who work alone; on the other, characterization of cargo theft as a form of organized criminal activity does not imply that there is a mastermind behind whom an army of cargo thieves marches in lockstep fashion. Indeed, as will be shown, contact and working relationships among participants can range from erratic and informal to consistent and highly structured. What is meant is that were it not for the presence of an informal or formal interplay within the between certain employee groups and/or outside criminal elements, the cargo theft problem would not begin to approach its current dimensions.

Such conclusions are hardly news to most of those directly or indirectly involved in the transportation industry. However, those conclusions bear repeating because they call for an industry strategy that is only now beginning to make a significant appearance. When an even loosely organized criminal effort is directed against an industry with as many fragmented components as in the transportation field, there really is no contest unless each component assumes its share of responsibility and dovetails its countermeasures with those of others. In the words of a transportation executive, "The amount of honest cunning we develop must be commensurate with the size of the (cargo theft) challenge." Unfortunately, as indicated below, that part of the challenge represented by the presence of relatively well-organized criminal elements is frequently underestimated.

THE EMPLOYEE-THIEF

The extent and nature of employee involvement in cargo theft as deduced from the circumstantial evidence above is fully supported in reality. Speaking on behalf of freight forwarders, an executive noted that the theft problems of rail carriers are also those of forwarders, "who are no different to the extent that they have dock employees and drivers who steal, pilfer, and work in collusion with outside dishonest elements."

According to one report, the security officer of a large motor carrier "stated flatly that most cargo crimes were perpetrated by one or two trucking employees working in concert with one another and an outside buying source—in some cases the very retailers being serviced by the victim's trucking firm." In analyzing a series of thefts of loaded, unattended trucks, a police department concluded that 60% involved collusion of the driver. If this is a reasonably accurate estimate, the full impact of such collusion is quite apparent when one realizes that during a recent 12-month period, 2,324 loaded but unattended trucks were reported as stolen to this same police department. As the head of a state investigation unit noted, "These were simply trucks where the driver or the people on it left to go somewhere and somebody else got behind the wheel and took them—2,324, a rather interesting figure." The goods on these trucks were valued at approximately $12.6 million. During the same period, 318 trucks were reported as hijacked and carried loads valued at $4.9 million. (About $7.5 million of the $17.5 million total was recovered). And, as a federal investigator asked during an interview, how many of the apparent hijackings are, in reality, give-aways by the driver?

A survey of 25 cargo facilities at a major airport resulted in a list of common problems relating to the vulnerability of air cargo to loss, theft, and pilferage. Topping the list were two items: (1) employees who, in collusion with others, arrange for unlawful removal of cargo from terminals; and (2) employees who remove documents from terminals or relay information contained in the documents to others as a prelude to fraudulent delivery.

According to arrest statistics that were presented by Greater New York's Airport Security Council (comprised of airline and airfreight forwarder members), airline employees accounted for 38% of those arrested for "crimes against air cargo" during 1978 and 1979 at JFK, La Guardia, and Newark airports. In 1979, the council's executive director reported that an in-depth examination of the arrest data "shows a fairly constant correlation between employee and non-employee apprehensions, thus supporting the thesis that our cargo thefts are essentially collusive acts which require employee assistance to achieve success."

The situation on the piers is much the same. Stated a waterfront commission: "Experience has shown that all significant pier thefts are accomplished through the collusion of truck drivers and pier personnel." A particularly startling arrest statistic was cited when the commission reported that during a four-year period, "more port watchmen were apprehended for stealing cargo . . . than they—the port watchman force—apprehended." Not only do they steal for themselves, "They also act in collusion with some truck drivers, checkers and hi-lo drivers to strip the piers."

Beyond rational dispute, therefore, is the conclusion that employee theft and pilferage constitutes a significant part of the cargo theft problem. But how much is a "significant part?" The prevailing consensus among law enforcement and industry sources is that, in terms of the resultant direct dollar losses, employees are participants in a substantial majority—perhaps 80% or more—of all cargo thefts. The following statement by the executive director of the Trucking Industry Committee on Theft and Hijacking accurately reflects this consensus: "Over 80% of the dollar losses sustained by the trucking industry from cargo theft results from pilferage or theft of one or several cartons stolen each time, and repeated thousands of times annually. Cartons are stolen by those who have easy access to shipments and include employees of the shipper, the motor carrier, the consignee, and by persons outside these three industries."

What is not so generally realized or accepted is that although employees may account for 80% of the cargo theft figure, they are motivated to do so, in most cases, by the existence and services of external elements. This is indicated by the flow of stolen cargo beyond the employee-thief's closet, liquor cabinet, or garage. The bulk of this merchandise is poured over the rim of a large funnel supplied by outside criminals who channel stolen goods to the ultimate buyers. In return, the employee receives cash for items for which he has neither the inclination or need to keep nor the facilities, time, or know-how to market on an independent basis.

Informed sources interviewed for this book estimate that, in terms of dollar losses, 70% to 80% of the cargo stolen as the result of employee theft and pilferage is converted into cash through the use of fences. Some sources on the East Coast would adjust that percentage upward, while some of the West Coast would make a significant downward revision. This reflects the reported tendency toward a do-it-yourself approach to fencing by company thieves in the western states. As a federal enforcement official commented, east of the Mississippi the thief and fence are likely to have an ongoing working relationship, whereas in the western areas, the thief is more likely to look for a fence only after the theft.

Overall, therefore, employees who steal cargo do it not so much for the merchandise but for the cash such goods will bring them. Fences, in effect, vastly expand the range and volume of cargo that is both practical and profitable for employees to steal when given the opportunity. And therein lies the true explanation behind the bulk of cargo thefts.

Operational Pattern of Fences

Fences often supply the major link between thieves on the company payroll and outside criminal elements, who can be highly resourceful and well organized. For the purposes of this book a *fence* is one of many types of receivers of stolen goods. A *receiver* is one who knowingly buys, sells, or otherwise trafficks in stolen merchandise better known on the street as *swag*. A fence is a professional receiver, one who derives the bulk of his livelihood by performing a middleman function in the disposition of stolen goods—in contrast to other types of receivers, who regard dealing in such items more as a profitable opportunity and who are principally engaged in other pursuits that are not especially dependent on stolen articles for their success. For example, a restaurant owner who occasionally accepts hijacked loads of meat is a receiver but not a fence according to our definition.

The crucial role played by fences, as well as their efficiency, is attested to by many. An executive of a maritime association asserted, "We believe that it is axiomatic that as long as we have these 'fences'— ready, willing, and able to buy and dispose of stolen cargo—cargo thievery will persist." A Justice Department official observed that because of the "amazing efficiency of hijackers' organized distribution systems, they are able to dispose of hijacked truckloads of goods in a few hours or less."

After indicating the types of merchants, ranging from legitimate to shady, who sell goods originally stolen from interstate and foreign commerce shipments, the chairman of the Senate's Select Committee on Small Business stated, "It is charged that these merchants buy goods from middlemen fences who in turn buy directly or control the operations of thieves preying on cargo shipments from all modes of transport." In referring to the theft of a particular type of cargo, an assistant district attorney concluded that heretofore "the potential thief was deterred from taking something he knew he could not dispose of. However, thanks to fences who developed methods of disposition, they become the major market and reason for the theft."

Fences may be categorized by the geographic scope of their operations. Some are strictly neighborhood hustlers. Others operate on a citywide and intercity basis. Still others have both interstate and international capabilities; for example, a fence operating out of a Gulf Coast port sold bagged coffee to sources in Chicago and disposed of metals to buyers in New Jersey and Canada. Major fences have operated throughout the Boston-Washington corridor, and major fences on the Pacific Coast reportedly have connections in Nevada and Illinois, among other places.

Fences may handle just about anything that comes along, or they may specialize in such items as apparel, watches, cameras, and securities. There are fences in the Midwest who specialize in jewelry, liquor, television sets, or cigarettes. Many of these place orders or have standing orders with "crews" that, similarly, specialize in stealing certain kinds of cargo. Fences may also be pushers and deal with addict-thieves. In any event, junkies are a good source of supply for many fences. For example, in a series of 22 arrests for cargo theft on the waterfront of a Gulf Coast port, all 22 longshoremen were on narcotics.

In contrast to the neighborhood hustler, major fences do not, as a rule, come into physical possession of the goods they handle. Rather, they are brokers or arrangers. The thief or his drop will retain physical possession of the goods until his fence locates a willing purchaser. When large quantities are involved, such arrangements are usually made prior to the actual theft. In one case, a wiretap revealed that a search was on for buyers of merchandise still at sea.

Fences who come into physical possession of stolen cargo may store and dispose of it at their homes, operate out of rented warehouses, or conduct business at a legitimate-appearing outlet in which hot goods may or may not be commingled with legally acquired merchandise. The possibilities are vast.

There is considerable communication and dealings between fences—both vertically and horizontally. For example, one intercity fence may contact another in order to locate an out-of-stock or unstocked item for which there is a customer. Similarly, there may be up-and-down dealings when a small fence requires the expertise or contacts of a large-scale operator to dispose of items. Or a major fence may use neighborhood operators as secondary distributors.

Fences and thieves make initial contact generally through informal means. The previously described fencing operation established by the Waterfront Commission of New York Harbor was "patronized" by longshoremen who simply heard about it through word of mouth. One cargo thief commented that if one is in the business of stealing, fences "just seem to come by naturally." Information of this type may come from a friend of a friend or through tactful inquiries at certain taverns or other well-known hangouts. Depending on the nature of the goods, fences may offer thieves anything from one-third of the retail value to 10 cents on the wholesale dollar or less.

RECEIVERS OTHER THAN FENCES

Fences, and thieves who choose to bypass such middlemen, have dealt with many types of receivers. Among them may be those who hawk their wares on the street, sell from the back of their station wagons, peddle at union halls, rent a booth at a flea market, operate out of bars, or conduct business in private garages, as was the case in Fresno and Phoenix with respect to television sets stolen from a West Coast port.

At a recently visited flea market, for example, first-line sporting goods were selling at 30% of retail price, a motor oil additive at 55%, wigs at 25%, and cosmetics and wearing apparel at equally low prices. Address labels from some shipping cartons had been removed by razor blades. Reinforcing such evidence was a previous conversation between a trucking company's security officer and a booth attendant: "Tell me how you can sell at such discounts?" "We have connections," replied the attendant. "What do you mean, 'connections'?" "You know—connections," he repeated. "I don't understand." "You know, the stuff is hot." Though hot, each item could be backed by a bill of sale, however dubious it might appear. Without doubt, much of the bargain-hungry public there also knew about the origin of much of the merchandise and, to that extent, they became the ultimate receivers.

Receivers may hold various types of sales to move stolen goods, which may be mixed with legitimately obtained merchandise. Salvage, fire, clearance, and going-out-of-business sales have been used for this purpose. Some sales of this type may be handled by auctioneers or liquidation outfits.

Among the many types of businesses and outlets that have been used as receivers for stolen cargo are discount stores, salvage companies, restaurants, building supply companies (one had to return 92 tons of stolen steel), beauty salons, taverns, drug stores (one group had standing orders for aspirin, film, and razor blades), scrap metal yards, catering houses, grocery stores, jewelry stores, electronic equipment outlets, processors of semifinished goods or raw materials (gold and silver have been sent to receivers both in and outside of the country), office equipment dealers, stationers, dealers in secondhand merchandise, and vending machine companies. There are so many others that this listing cannot even be called a sample.

316 Cargo Security: A Nuts and Bolts Approach

Through various forms of collusion, consignees themselves have been the receivers of the very merchandise they claimed was looted and for which they received insurance money. Securities stolen while in the custody of carriers have found their way into the hands of a variety of receivers, notably businessmen who either rented or bought them to shore up sagging balance sheets, to serve as collateral for needed bank loans, or to provide the basis for letters of credit. Marginal insurers have used such securities to beef up otherwise inadequate assets in order to meet the requirements of state regulatory agencies.

Once merchandise leaves the hands of the thief and the fence, it may be involved in several transactions, including industrial processing, and thereby lose any semblance to stolen cargo. For example, $10,000 worth of leather goods stolen from the piers passed through ten buyers in less than two months. The merchandise was finally sold, in good faith, to the original consignee. Authorities believe that the top four buyers had no reason to suspect they were handling stolen goods and thus were not receivers in the criminal sense of the word.

Such multiple handlings of stolen cargo are quite common, but there can be little doubt that in the vast majority of distributions, the merchandise cannot initially enter a legitimate channel without the supposedly reputable employee, proprietor, manager, or official knowing full well the nature of what he is receiving. He may know this through direct knowledge or deduce it because the price he paid was absurdly low or because the source he purchased from was far removed from the distribution system through which the goods would normally flow. Unfortunately, the situation too frequently parallels the reported conversation between a cargo theft victim and an investigator. "How many of your competitors would steal from you?" "None of them," replied the victim. "How many competitors would buy the stolen goods?" "All of them."

Tending to support such a pessimistic view of human nature is the general consensus among informed sources that most of the cargo diverted from legitimate channels through cargo theft eventually reenters those channels for ultimate disposition. So the dreary picture that this paints is one of some businesses growing fat by feeding on the cargo losses of others—and in the process, a conglomerate of criminal interests is enriched.

THE NATURE OF ORGANIZED CRIME

The collusive activities of employees, fences, and other receivers represent organized criminal activity, but this activity may or may not constitute organized crime. Before an unlawful act, however well executed, can be described as committed by organized crime, the activity must be that of a member—in fact or in effect—of a highly organized and disciplined association engaged in supplying illegal goods and services.

If those who commit crimes through collusion or as the result of an ongoing conspiracy are members of such an association, then their organized criminal activity is indeed organized crime, whose implications are a quantum cut above those of similar crimes committed by nonmember individuals. One is not engaging in academic hairsplitting when emphasizing that while organized crime is a form of organized criminal activity, not all organized criminal activity is organized crime. The importance and reality of this distinction is evident from even a brief description of the largest of the many criminal associations, which are usually referred to collectively as simply "organized crime."

Despite an impressive array of indictments, arrests, and convictions resulting from the work of Federal Strike Force personnel and others, the predominant group and inner core of organized crime is still as described in 1967 by a task force of the President's Commission on Law Enforcement and Administration of Justice—namely a nation-wide group divided into 24 to 26 operating units or "families" whose membership is exclusively men of one ethnic group and who number 5000 or more. The task force quoted the FBI's director, who evaluated this core group as "the largest organization of the criminal underworld in this country, very closely organized and disciplined . . . it has been found to control major racket activities in many of our larger metro-politan areas, often working in concert with criminals representing other ethnic backgrounds."

Heading each operating unit, or family, is the boss, whose autho-rity is subject only to the rulings of a national advisory commission, which has the final word on organizational and jurisdictional disputes and is comprised of the more powerful bosses. Beneath each boss, in chain-of-command fashion, is an underboss, several captains (*caporegime*), who supervise lower-echelon soldiers, who in turn oversee large numbers of nonmember street personnel. One such family is said to number 1000—half members, half nonmember street-level workers—with 27 captains and stretching from Connecticut to Philadelphia. Bosses have access to a variety of "staff men," includ-ing attorneys, accountants, business experts, enforcers, and corrupters. Many individuals, while not family members in a formal sense, work closely with these inner-core groups and may be called associates (to distinguish them from mere street workers) and, as is the case with street personnel, should be considered an integral part of organized crime. Some associates are highly respected by family members and are very powerful in their own right.

Through interceptions of phone conversations and other oral communications at different times and places between members and associates of this large criminal nucleus of the organized underworld, its existence, structure, activities, personnel, and such terminology as "boss," "captain," "family," "soldier," "commission" have been confirmed and reconfirmed beyond rational dispute.

Loosely allied with this large criminal nucleus are several other organized crime syndicates or groups, whose members can also be distributed along ethnic lines—just as most neighborhoods can, and probably for much the same sociologic reasons. The various organized crime groups call upon the services and special skills of one another frequently enough for them to be characterized as a loose confederation, a designation reflecting the absence of a boss of bosses at the top. Sometimes these groups are referred to individually or collectively as the "outfit," "mob," or "syndicate."

Taking into account the political organizations, unions, businesses, and other groups directly or indirectly under the thumb of organized crime, the manpower available to the confederation could conceivably run into the hundreds of thousands. Because they are relatively well organized and disciplined and because they possess the demonstrated superior ability to protect themselves from prosecution through corruption and other means, organized crime groups have a strength and permanency beyond the reach of conventional partners in crime.

The difference to management between cargo theft committed under the direction of organized crime and cargo theft executed under the direction of nonmember employees is analogous to the difference between a company's market share being challenged by a multibillion conglomerate and being challenged by a three- or four-man partnership. Both the conglomerate and partnership are engaged in business, just as organized crime groups and other nonmember criminal elements are engaged in organized criminal activity. But there is a world of difference between a conglomerate and a partnership, just as there is between organized crime and less organized and disciplined individuals who may cooperate in crime.

All this is certainly not to say that the absence of crime-family members or those of other organized crime units from a group of employee-thieves necessarily means the latter will never call upon organized crime for such services as fencing. When such services are used on a arm's-length basis, these employees should not and normally do not want to be equated with organized crime. (In this regard, see the end of Charles Roberts's testimony in the case studies examined later in this chapter.

As noted later, there is always the possibility that employees may be coerced into, for example, fingering or stealing cargo for the organized underworld. Although they are the victims of organized crime and are not members of it in any sense, a company experiencing cargo losses under such circumstances certainly is facing a problem initiated by organized crime.

Finally, should one or more employees be so foolish as to abandon arm's-length dealing with an organized crime group and, through entering into an exclusive arrangement with such a group, assume a status comparable to that of the nonmember street-level personnel of crime families, these employees should be considered as de facto members of organized crime. However, most employees guilty of cargo theft do not possess this status.

In sum, organized crime constitutes an ongoing and relatively well-organized and disciplined conspiracy to commit substantive crimes, particularly those supporting the prime objective of supplying illegal goods and services in order to obtain money and power. The list of organized crime's activities would include gambling, usury, bribery, perjury, fraud, extortion, kidnapping, murder, labor racketeering, forgery, counterfeiting, and tax evasion, among many others. And, as President Nixon observed, organized crime "is increasing its enormous holdings and influence in the world of legitimate business." Organized crime's involvement in cargo theft is an excellent case in point.

Organized Crime and Cargo Theft

Recognizing the fragmented nature of the transportation industry and of those who are dependent on it, a member of the House Interstate and Foreign Commerce Committee addressed a conference on cargo theft by saying, only half facetiously, "I acknowledge the real 'pros' who called us together—gentlemen, I refer to organized crime." Organized crime has a direct hand in the execution of cargo thefts, in the distribution of this cargo to various "markets," and in the actual consumption of the stolen goods through the businesses it owns or otherwise controls.

A recent study of organized crime in Illinois ranks truck hijackings and dock thefts as third on the list of key activities of organized crime. Fencing of stolen property and penetration of legitimate businesses follow close behind. Although some Illinois law enforcement officials would rank cargo theft no higher than sixth, the study's observation that "cartage thefts and receiving stolen merchandise are currently favored and lucrative sources of income for the racketeers" should be taken to heart by traffic managers and other transportation executives as well as by law enforcement personnel.

Of course, over the years, there has been ample testimony confirming organized crime's interest in executing cargo thefts and/or distributing the goods so obtained. An executive of a maritime under-writers group is quoted as believing that "organized crime is what is growing in our cargo thefts." An executive in close touch with air freight forwarders stated in an interview that "what would help alleviate the cargo theft problem is to break up organized crime."

A ranking Justice Department official has affirmed, "Of course, large scale thefts require the reliance on well-placed contacts and a sophisticated network of connections and technique which generally can only be provided by organized crime." Accordingly, he stated that a successful attack on organized crime by law enforcement will also be a successful attack on "one of the major sources of the problem of cargo thefts."

Organized Crime: The Thief

Current estimates indicate that thefts representing 15% to 20% of the value of all stolen cargo are committed by organized crime. Police officials in New York City, for example, estimate that of the 378 truck hijackings there were planned and committed by, or at the direction of, syndicate figures. And regarding those responsible for the other 25%, many of them must deal with organized crime to get rid of the load.

According to a police official who specialized in organized crime cases, when the syndicate engineers a hijacking, all of the following details are normally ironed out in advance: who will finger the job, who will actually execute the hijack, where the transfer will be made (the drop, a location where the goods are transferred from the stolen truck to another vehicle), how and where the load will be disposed of (including temporary storage if needed), and who will get what percentage of the proceeds.

Reviewing the cartage theft activity in Chicago, a study notes that "very few of the upper echelon outfit people in the Chicago metropolitan area take part in actual thefts or hijacking, but impressions are that they control the overall operation, using criminal specialists." Echoing this is the conclusion of a New York law enforcement task force: "Although the actual hijacking may be committed by the younger fringe type individual, who is not a 'made man' (formal member of a crime "family"), it is the organized crime syndicate which has planned and directed the operation and has made the profit-able arrangements to dispose of the merchandise."

Interestingly, during a 12-month period in an eastern city, of the 72 who were convicted of truck thefts (hijacked or stolen while unattended) under the Theft from Interstate Shipment Statute, 22 were members of, or associated with, crime families. And in one federal judicial district in the Midwest, organized crime cases pertaining to thefts from interstate shipments (all modes) accounted for 7.3% of the year's total case load and represented 21.9% of those cases relating to organized crime.

Thefts of containers or trailers from marine and rail facilities involve operational patterns similar to those described for truck thefts. And, as indicated by a Treasury Department official, organized crime also has its hand in many of the less publicized thefts, which may occur "during unloading and delivery to the storage area, while cargo is in the terminal awaiting release, and especially during delivery to the pick-up trucker. . ."

The indirect influence of the organized underworld in the execution phase of cargo thefts may be felt when an independent fence has lined up a theft beyond his financial means to distribute, in which case organized crime has been known to finance the deal and receive a cut. (In some areas, trouble ensues for those independents who commit major thefts without permission from, and cuts to, organized crime.) Or when transportation employees have been unable to raise the necessary cash to pay off gambling or loan shark debts to organized criminals, the latter will occasionally accept other forms of payment: an open warehouse door, theft of certain cargo, transport of stolen goods, etc. Or racketeer-dominated locals may pressure employers to hire certain employees, who in turn will finger or steal merchandise. Reflecting such indirect strategies of organized crime, a federal report describing strike force observations in New Jersey states, "The team discovered large-scale gambling and shylocking operations coupled with organized hijacking and other types of thefts. Labor unions were infiltrated or controlled by organized crime. . . ."

Whether because of such indirect involvement by organized crime in cargo theft or because of public-image reasons, or both, there is the temptation to downgrade or deny the presence of organized crime at facilities where cargo is transported or otherwise handled. For example, at a southern location, a shipping executive did not believe organized crime was connected to pier thefts. However, other sources in the area revealed the following information: (1) the local crime family boss held meetings with warehousemen, grocers, truckers, etc; (2) this boss offered his assistance in establishing another local of a waterfront union; (3) a shylock has solicited loans at 5 for 4 (25% weekly interest) from longshoremen and has been in collusion with a local waterfront union, which permitted the presence of the loan shark on payday and held back the wages of those indebted to him;

(4) a syndicate-connected gambler is quoted as saying he expects to get "a lot of action off longshoremen"; (5) the president of a local dock workers union wrote a federal judge about the fine character of the area's mob boss, who was about to receive a sentence from the jurist; and (6) the same union president at one time used the services of a syndicated-connected bodyguard.

Those who doubt the involvement of organized crime in the planning and execution of thefts accounting for 15% to 20% of the total dollar value of cargo stolen by all sources should begin to ask, "Has anyone taken an honest look lately?"

Organized Crime: The Fence

The operation of, and participation in, the fencing of stolen cargo, by organized crime has been alluded to several times on previous pages. The bulk, quantity, specialized nature, or other characteristics of much stolen cargo presents incontrovertible evidence—circumstantial as it is—of facilities, contacts, and know-how of a coordinated underworld. Referring to a series of sizable cargo thefts, the head of a state investigation unit asserted that "the merchandise involved must be disposed of by the thieves and it is equally obvious that it can only be disposed of through organized crime channels." Impressive evidence of organized crime's fencing network is indicated by a police department's chart festooned with colorful symbols indicating the many locations of syndicate drops and fences.

In commenting on an aspect of cargo theft, an assistant district attorney asserted that "Organized crime is both stealing and controlling the disposition. But they don't have the sole market in stealing. The amateurs and organized crime are stealing. Everybody is stealing. ORGANIZED CRIME IS HANDLING THE DISPOSITION." The criminals would agree, as in this exchange between Senator McClellan and a major cargo thief who operated nationwide:

> *Chairman McClellan*   How important were these organized crime connected fences to your operation? In other words, if you did not have them to fence the stolen goods for you and take them off your hands and pay you something for them could your operation have been successful? Would it have been very profitable?
>
> *Witness*   No, not without a fence.
>
> *Chairman McClellan*   You would have to have a fence?
>
> *Witness*   Yes, sir.

Chairman McClellan	And you found that requirement fulfilled in the ranks of the syndicate or organized crime?
Witness	Yes, sir.
Chairman McClellan	Do you feel that was true in each instance?
Witness	Yes, sir.

Organized Crime: The Consumer

According to informed observers, in dollar terms the bulk of stolen cargo passes through the hands of organized crime and most of that amount returns to legitimate channels—that is, to businesses neither owned nor otherwise controlled by organized crime. Nonetheless, a significant amount, perhaps 25% according to one crime expert, is consumed by outlets under the operational control of criminal syndicates. To justify this estimate, one need only look at the extent of organized crime's business interests.

One federal official, who is a respected authority on organized crime, estimates that the organized underworld "owns hundreds of businesses in each metropolitan area." A federally financed study indicates that there are as many as 500 outfit-owned businesses in a certain metropolitan area. An Internal Revenue Service study showed that leading racketeers in one midwestern city were involved in 89 businesses, with total assets of more than $800 million and annual receipts exceeding $900 million. In another IRS survey, 98 of 113 major organized crime figures were identified as involved in 159 businesses, two-thirds of which fell into the categories of casinos, night clubs, hotels, real estate, machine vending, restaurants, trucking, manufacturing, sports, entertainment, and food wholesaling. Intelligence available to a state law enforcement unit indicates that a major organized crime figure has established two large conglomerates, multinational in scope, with representatives in every major city in the United States.

A recent study indicates that there may be 15,000 companies owned by members of the organized underworld and cites an estimate that syndicate personnel may have decision-making influence in 35,000 other firms. This same study focused on the participation in business firms by 200 individuals identified as "principals and associates of major crime 'families'" operating in an eastern state. These individuals were linked to 407 businesses, and there were strong indications that the true total, if known, would be close to 600. Not surprisingly, a healthy 47 of the 200 underworld figures also engaged in hijacking and other theft. The study emphasizes that the "larger the size and number of businesses operated by organized crime, the greater are the outlets for hijackings, auto theft, pilferage, stolen securities, and so on."

Obviously, organized crime is a "full line" outfit, possessing the facilities, manpower, and know-how to steal, market, and consume large quantities of cargo. If a moral is in order, perhaps it should be along the lines of this congressional testimony by an insurance association investigator:

> Why give in to a group ... who have chosen to practice crime in our city and reap the benefits and profits of their crime by selling to unscrupulous businessmen. It is high time we gathered our resources. . . . The problem is to get human interest, dynamic drive and coordination. If everyone concerned would sincerely contribute his best efforts, many of the problems would evaporate.

THE OPPOSITION AT WORK: CASE STUDIES

In 1969 a congressional committee indicated that "the technique used by cargo thieves can only be guessed at; all we can say at this time is that they are successfully practiced, at a rapidly increasing rate." Today, these techniques for theft and disposition of cargo are still unfamiliar to many top and middle managers, upon whose policies and support the success or failure of cargo theft countermeasures usually depends. Although executives can hardly be expected to become criminologists, something more than vague awareness is required because, as the congressional committee observed, "To devise strategies of crime prevention, it is necessary to ascertain in detail the techniques used by the thieves and the circumstances surrounding the theft."

Thus the cases that follow are not merely interesting "war stories" but are valuable clues to the type and scope of the required managerial (and law enforcement) response, particularly as some of these details come from the lips of thieves themselves or from informers. (To protect certain sources, the names, dates, products, locations, and so forth mentioned below have been changed.)

Following a look at various kinds of employee thieves, from the loner to those working nationwide, this section examines theft and fencing operations of organized crime. And, in so doing, the previously described interplay between thief, fence, and ultimate consumers of stolen cargo will be reconfirmed, as will the distinction between organized crime and other forms of organized criminal activity.

The Operations of a Loner

Although most cargo thefts involve varying degrees of collusion, substantial losses can be inflicted by independents, as is illustrated in the case of Tony Musco, who, during his six months as a carloader at a midwestern rail terminal, stole shipments of raw furs valued at $150,000. At the time, this was described as "probably the largest single-handed theft of raw furs on record."

Musco's method was as simple as it was effective: remove the shipping tags from the cargo and substitute new waybills and new incoming tags with the consignee's address changed so that the furs would be delivered to Trade Brokers Inc., a phony company located at Musco's residence. There he repacked and readdressed the shipments, which he sent to legitimate furdealers in Illinois, Missouri, and New York, among other places. Musco had read the trade journal advertisements of these dealers, who were requesting collectors of raw fur pelts to forward them for sale.

A Conspiracy to Steal

As revealed by informants and other sources, the cast of characters in this case were five employees of Major Airlines (MA) and a forwarder employee. They had been on their employers' payrolls from 6 to 13 years. As charged by law enforcement officials, the employees participated in a loose and general conspiracy to steal items from the export section of MA's cargo division.

Operating for several months as an independent thief, Alione, an export supervisor, stole a .38 revolver ($100) from the dock of a cargo building and sold the weapon six months later to an MA driver. Alione then stole two shipments of pearls ($9,000) destined for the Orient. He stored them in his garage. In many of these and subsequent thefts, Alione or others destroyed the shipping documents, thus making it impossible for either law enforcement or MA to confirm that the cargo had ever been in the custody or control of the carrier.

Shortly after the pearl thefts, Alione became aware that a large amount of cargo was being stolen by other MA employees and decided to try to join the group in order to dispose of stolen merchandise more easily. Alione befriended a fellow employee who conceded he also stole and indicated that others did so too. Alione was accepted by the other employees. He was told that an MA driver could assist in "removing almost anything from the airport."

When Alione told one of the group about the stolen pearls, the latter referred him to an air freight forwarder employee, who said he would be able to sell any merchandise taken from MA. Alione received $500 for the pearls.

Alione noted a bale of fur skins ($10,000) and a box whose label indicated it contained an antique silver cat ($2000). The MA driver took the cargo from the airport. The cargo's documentation was altered to reflect that the articles were transferred from MA to an airline serving the Orient. In another fur theft, Alione put the furs aside and another employee removed them to his car. He gave the pelts to a contact downtown, who sold them.

After spotting several 200-pound cartons of police revolvers ($8,000) en route to Europe, Alione reported this to another member of the theft ring, who said he knew a contact who could dispose of them. The cartons were moved to a bin on the MA dock. In a few hours, the outside contact arrived with a friend, and the cartons were transferred to the contact's car. The weapons were eventually sold out of a bar on Seacoast Freeway.

A more complex theft involved $25,000 worth of pharmaceuticals that Alione had "pushed aside." He informed another employee, who recommended that an owner of a pharmaceutical laboratory be contacted. Once convicted of conspiring to purchase unlicensed blood plasma, the owner of the lab referred Alione to a self-employed financial adviser, who acted as a courier for the pharmaceutical executive. The upshot was that the executive drove to the airport, picked up the pharmaceuticals, and went to the financial adviser's residence. He, in turn, shipped the drugs overseas to a European, whose previous record included an arrest for smuggling pharmaceuticals into the United States. Alione received $6,000.

Theft on the Freight Dock

Despite extensive physical security measures, cargo continued to disappear from the freight dock of a trucking company at the rate of $20,000 a year. (One trucker interviewed for this book indicated he had been losing $300,000 yearly from one dock; another reported the apprehension of employees who stole cargo at the rate of $700 daily for six months.) Responsible for the thefts was a close-knit group of seven employees—four checkers and three hi-lo drivers, who specialized in stealing small television and radio parts.

One of the checkers would receive advance notice of when incoming shipments were scheduled to arrive. With the aid of a price list, the employees would decide whether a given shipment was worth stealing.

To execute the theft, a checker would record the desired carton as short from the incoming truck, thereby casting suspicion on the driver. Or the carton would be noted as received, in which case a hi-lo operator would hide it in a pile of other freight. The carton might then be recorded as having been loaded on an outgoing truck to throw suspicion on the driver, who of course never received it.

To remove the goods from company property, they were secreted in lunch boxes, pant legs, pockets, or taped to the body.

Subsequent investigations revealed that, as a sideline, one of the checkers had gone into the TV and radio repair business and had used this business, located six blocks from the terminal, as an outlet for many of the parts he stole. Additional parts were sold to a local TV sales and service firm.

Collusion on the Piers

A port security organization received information that large numbers of television sets were available in the area at giveaway prices. Investigation disclosed that the sets were of the type imported at the port by a certain company. Additional probing revealed that several containers of this merchandise were in the port aboard a dockside vessel, which was awaiting the outcome of a longshoremen's strike. Locks and seals of containers stowed on the afterdeck had been broken and 530 television sets ($53,000) were stolen. They had been off-loaded at night to a vessel brought alongside. Of the six people ultimately convicted, one was a security guard.

In another port, many thefts occur by overloading trucks. For example, a driver and a checker both know that 200 cartons were put on a truck but acknowledge only 175. Although realizing that the full shipment of 200 was delivered, the consignee signs for 175 and files a claim for the "missing" 25. Should someone question the discrepancy, all parties have ready answers: the checker miscounted, the driver relied on the checker, and the consignee counted skids of cartons, not pieces.

Other Theft Techniques of Employees

In addition to the cargo theft techniques illustrated above, many other methods are used, some of which are capsuled here.

1. An importer had prelogged (filed in advance) papers at the piers indicating that ABC Trucking Co. would pick up two recently arrived containers of his merchandise. A driver pulls in with a rented truck and presents the rental agreement, which is in the name of ABC Trucking. He is permitted to take a container in the morning and another in the afternoon, thereby stealing two containers. A variation on this theme occurred when a rental truck arrived bearing the identification placards of the trucking company that was supposed to pick up the goods.

2. Bills of lading, which are frequently all but illegible, are doctored by drivers to cover up, for example, a theft of cashew nuts dropped off at a grocery store a few blocks from the pier.
3. Cartons in the bottom two layers of a seven-tier pallet are filled with bricks instead of appliances.
4. Shipper and consignee collusion occurred when a COD shipment was unloaded so fast that the truck driver lost count, resulting in a "shortage."
5. At the "$500 coffee stop," drivers are asked to take a walk for $500 to $1000.
6. Two operators of a meat store agreed to purchase a couple of trailer loads of meat from two rail employees, who merely entered a rail facility where trailers were stored, hooked up, and pulled out two loads. The theft occurred on a Sunday, the one day of the week when watchmen are not scheduled for duty.
7. Port checkers declare less than the full quantity of goods actually landed. The "shortage" is hidden, then sold at the end of the year in a salvage sale along with damaged imports.
8. Cargo documentation was forced to cover thefts of antibiotics, which were being replaced with powdered milk.
9. A terminal supervisor adds a loaded trailer to a row of empties parked outside the fence, where another employee later completes the theft. Or a driver fakes a breakdown, goes for help, and returns to find his rig either gone or empty.
10. According to one report, when a certain driver is short on cash he contacts a bartender who spreads the word that a load is available. The driver proceeds to an overnight spot where he and the thief have agreed the theft will take place. The driver is quoted as saying, "After my eight in the sack, I pick up the rig and drive on. Next stop. I go to sleep again. When I get up, that's when I report the load missing. Cops don't know where the load was lifted. I know it was Chicago, driven somewhere, unloaded and returned."
11. A driver diverts a load directly to a fence's warehouse, instead of delivering it to the consignee, when he services two or three times daily. On the next trip he gives the documentation for both loads to an accomplice at the consignee's receiving dock, who assures that the records reflect delivery of both loads.
12. After a truck is overloaded, an employee of the shipper gives the driver a seal that is noted on the bill of lading

and puts another one on the door. After removing the overage somewhere en route, the driver places the bill-of-lading seal on the trailer and proceeds to the consignee.

13. "Hard to get into but easy to swipe." This definition of a container was presented by an executive of a customs brokers association in his congressional testimony. "All you do is switch a number, and one container looks very much like another, and you can take delivery of one for the other." Or, "If they got into a container, these thieves, you do not know that they have been inside. The doors are opened; they take what they want; the doors are closed; and no one discovers the theft. The container passes from hand to hand. . . . Anywhere along that voyage someone might have gotten into that container and taken out part or all the contents, switched the contents . . . but you do not know until you finally receive it and open the doors, and then how do you assess the blame?"

Organized Crime at Work

In 1967, a W.S. District Court Judge gave 12 defendants sentences ranging from 10 to 20 years. The syndicate-connected defendants were charged with four truck hijackings, three involving the theft of silver bars and one of cameras, film, and photographic equipment. Total value: $1 million.

In one hijacking, a trailer containing 50 boxes of cameras and 125 cartons of photographic equipment and film was en route to an Illinois terminal. Driver Buck of Freight Lines, Inc. noticed two cars following closely behind. One pulled ahead of the truck, forcing it to stop. The left door of the tractor was yanked open by a gunman who said, "Get out or I'll blow your head off." Buck was forced into one of the two cars following him, and a white cloth bag was placed over his head. "Be quiet and nothing will happen," he was warned. After considerable driving, one of the men said to Buck, "Here's a big bill. You don't know nothing. You didn't see nothing and you heard nothing." Buck was let out of the car and ordered to kneel and stay down for two minutes.

Meanwhile, the stolen rig had been taken to Fast Motor Repair, located in a nearby town. The truck was unloaded, the contents being transferred to another vehicle later. Some of the film was accepted by a Chicago fence, who paid $15,000 for it. The balance of the stolen cargo was sent to New York.

In other hijackings, a similar procedure was followed. Sometimes the cab of the stolen truck had been repainted or the trailer sprayed with a fine dust to obscure identification markings. The hijacked silver was marketed by a former scrap iron dealer who now handles precious silver. An employee with Freight Lines, Inc. for 25 years fingered all the hijackings by alerting the gang to the contents of trailers and when they would be shipped

A recent mob-engineered hijacking of a load of coffee in the New York area illustrates the speed with which ultimate disposition can be accomplished. The hijack occurred at 4:30 p.m. By 5:15 p.m. the coffee was being sold in a supermarket at $1.34 for a 2-pound can. The normal price was about $1.89.

Commenting on the ability of organized crime to hijack and bootleg and then dispose of truckloads of cigarettes in New York City, a police intelligence officer compared activites of organized crime to the operations of a well-integrated company: "In other words, (organized crime is) complete from one end to the other. The driver, the warehouse facilities, the salesmen, the office help, the territory, and everything else. . . . We think probably they are responsible for about 20% of all cigarettes sold in the City of New York."

One means by which the organized underworld markets certain types of stolen cargo, including cigarettes, is through the organized underworld's machine-vending operations. In New York City, the syndicate will funnel loans to grills, bars, restaurants, etc., so that they can renovate their premises. In return, such establishments permit the installation of organized crime's vending machines. As the intelligence officer concluded, "They put the machines in here, and organized crime . . . would get a monopoly of this type."

Illustrating one of the more unusual outlets for mob-stolen cargo is a report stating that once "the family" that owned a string of meat shops discovered it was losing patronage to nonracket shops that gave trading stamps, the racketeers countered by going into the trading stamp business themselves. "And to supply the merchandise or the redemption center, they organized regular thefts from nearby waterfront piers!"

Organized Crime's Fencing Network

The syndicate has demonstrated many times its ability to market stolen cargo on a nationwide basis. One of the best examples involves a theft of a registered airmail pouch at JFK International Airport by a member of Roberts' team. Among other items, the pouch contained a conservatively estimated $21 million in common stocks, bonds, bills, notes, and traveler's checks. The estimate represented only 16 of a possible 68 claims by the mailers. The traveler's checks were cashed by members of the team or wholesaled to a fence, while the securities, principally in nonnegotiable form, were turned over to a mob fence. After the June 13, 1968, theft, the following events were noted by postal authorities:

Within 48 hours, travelers checks from the pouch surfaced in New York City, Las Vegas, and in several towns in New Jersey. During the ensuing months, other travelers checks from the pouch were cashed in cities stretching from coast to coast.

Within two months, $50,000 in Treasury bonds were negotiated at a bank in Le Moyne, Pennsylvania. On December 6, someone tried to use $136,000 in securities as the basis for a collateral loan in Miami. He was a major securities fence and had received part of the June 13 theft from a Massachusetts source, who, in turn, received the securities from a fence in New York City. Over the course of the next year and a half, securities appeared in Coral Gables, Miami, San Diego, Houston, Oklahoma City, Phoenix, Los Angeles, Boston, Mexico City, Chicago, and Toronto.

12. Management Controls and Procedures

A FRAMEWORK FOR COMPANY ACTION

Because usually it is far easier and cheaper to prevent a cargo theft than to catch the thief, business has both an economic stake and a social responsibility to evaluate its policies and procedures from a crime prevention standpoint as well as from other perspectives. Contrary to some sentiment, cargo theft is not purely a matter for the police. Rather, the crime often reflects a failure by executives to understand that law enforcement begins with management. As someone wryly commented, "Law enforcement is not a game of cops and robbers in which the citizens play the trees."

In October, 1982, a spokesman for a carrier security organization correctly told a congressional committee that crime "actually rises or falls with the quality of deterrence built into the flow of cargo." He also indicated that these deterrents are, on balance, more important and effective than primary reliance on guard forces, police response, and other peripheral elements of security, although the latter are "extremely important." In short, as the security official noted on another occasion, "the elements of real and lasting security must be tied into the framework of an efficient operation."

Such a stance is similar to that of a federal report: "Most of the transportation operations affected by crime . . . require a significant managerial actions in addition to the development of technical means of detecting and preventing crime. Our experience indicates that top

---

This chapter is adapted from U.S. Department of Transportation *Cargo Theft and Organized Crime*, P 5200.6. Washington, D.C.: U.S. Government Printing Office, October, 1972.

management should, in many companies, first take a look at its security functions in the scheme of management, and then develop new concepts and new programs that would be based on loss prevention and audit rather than emergency police responses. On the whole, suppliers and users of transportation are not well equipped from a managerial standpoint to deal with this problem, and because of this they cannot effectively coordinate their own management controls with law enforcement agencies.

"As illustrated by several of the case studies, many times management does not realize that a theft has occurred and/or where it took place and how much of what cargo was stolen. This puts law enforcement agencies behind the proverbial eight ball.

"Not infrequently, when management attempts to tackle the problem, results may be as described in another federal study: "Despite the intensity of the campaign and the amount of executive talent expended, the activity resembles more the community chest drive than a conscious management effort to solve purely management problem. There appears to be no management control reform. . . ."

This emphasis on the role of management policies and procedures is not meant to downgrade physical security measures—guards, locks, fencing, lighting, seals, etc. What is meant is that management controls and physical security controls must dovetail and that, in too many cases, there has been precious little of the former. The interrelationship of these two types of controls is clearly described by two well-known experts on industrial security:

"The sequence of control development should start with the management controls to set broad guidelines. Procedural controls follow as a detailed implementation of the policies. Specific physical controls generally come as subsets or aspects of the procedures controls. In the ideal situation physical controls are the last to be selected and are dictated by the earlier management and procedure controls. In too many enterprises, the physical controls are considered first and often are not related at all to overall planning. The lack of control that results in theft losses can exist despite apparent physical countermeasures."

OBJECTIVES OF EFFECTIVE MANAGEMENT CONTROLS AND PROCEDURES

Specific managerial steps by which to reduce company exposure to cargo theft must, of course, be tailored to conditions both within and outside of a given firm; so a gleaming set of handy, universally applicable countermeasures is unavailable. To whatever extent preventive steps may, and should, differ from firm to firm, they nonetheless share several common objectives:

1. Minimize company exposure to those individuals with a predisposition or motive to steal. Illustrative countermeasures: screen prospective employees; eliminate in-plant gambling, which can stimulate organized crime's interest in the employees and through them, in cargo; revise personnel policies that can only cultivate a "get even" attitude among employees.
2. Reduce exposure of cargo to theft and pilferage. Illustrative countermeasures: package shipments properly, keep shipping and receiving docks free from congestion, route shipments so to minimize interline transfers.
3. Reduce the available opportunities and methods for theft and pilferage. Illustrative countermeasures; verify with consignee or carrier pick-up orders, and the drivers who present them before releasing cargo for loading into rented vehicles; restrict access to cargo documentation; arrange work flows or divide duties so that, without duplication, the work of one person acts as a check on the work of another (a load is picked by one employee, taken to the loading dock by another, and checked onto a carrier by a third—all of whose tallies should agree).
4. Increase the probability of detection when thefts do occur. Illustrative countermeasures: institute a system whereby management receives timely reports on the what, when, and where of thefts; establish performance standards and fix responsibility and accountability so that results or lack thereof can be linked to identifiable personnel (this not only provides an audit trail by which to narrow the list of suspects but also acts as a deterrent in that potential cargo thieves must exercise considerably more ingenuity than would otherwise be required).
5. Discipline those apprehended for theft or pilferage. For example, adopt a consistent pro-prosecution policy.
6. Obtain feedback to determine whether promulgated cargo theft countermeasures have, indeed, been (1) implemented and (2) are being properly followed by operating personnel. The failure by top management to conduct such follow-up efforts is reported as widespread and is a serious deficiency. Spot checks, operational audits, deliberate injection of errors into operations to see if they are detected represent common feedback procedures.

The effective implementation of policies and procedures necessary to achieve these six goals requires the support and cooperation not only of all levels of management but also of managers in all major departments: personnel, marketing, finance, legal, purchasing, packaging, traffic, labor relations, etc. Obviously, many, if not most, companies that are users or suppliers of cargo transportation will be either too small to warrant such an array of departments or too understaffed to implement countermeasures to the nth degree. In such cases, some of the procedures that follow must be scaled down accordingly. And, in any event, the cargo theft countermeasures noted below are not unalterable perscriptions but merely represent a framework or approach that must be molded to fit the requirements and characteristics of each individual company, be it shipper, carrier, consignee, etc. Basically, these measures constitute nothing more than good management per se, as opposed to procedures whose applicability is limited to the prevention of cargo theft.

The Critical Role of Personnel Policies

Although this would be a mere truism were it not so honored in the breach, the best way to deny theft opportunities to the employee-thief is not to hire him in the first place. Adequate screening of prospective employees is one of the most important and underutilized measures available to control cargo theft. This procedure gives a company a fair chance of weeding out not only those with unacceptable records of dishonesty but also those with personal habits (such as gambling or living beyond one's means) that could supply the motivation to steal. Yet, as one person noted, "Some companies won't even invest 10 cents to call an applicant's previous employer."

The employment application form is the point at which the screening process begins, not ends. The significance of questions aimed at disclosing gaps in employment continuity, frequent job shifts, bonding history, and type of military discharge is obvious. Reasons behind other information required by the application form are equally obvious, but such information is either not asked to the extent necessary or not used effectively. For example, where the employment form requests the applicant's name, all the names he or she has used in the past should also be required. Of course this should not be asked in the context of seeking information about the applicant's nationality or ethnic background but in terms of permitting the employer to make inquiries about past activities (schooling, prior employment, etc.) during periods when other names were used.

Space for the applicant's social security number is a common item on the employment forms. But is its value fully exploited? One interviewed security officer notes whether the applicant's background includes residency in the region where the social security card was issued. If an applicant states he has always lived in the Midwest but has a social security card issued in California, additional investigation is warranted.

If there is even a remote chance that the applicant may be called upon to drive a vehicle for business purposes, he should be required to provide appropriate information about his driver's license and driving record. Additionally, the employer should request driving record information from the state licensing authority.

Although it is a delicate area to probe, many employers request the applicant to supply information regarding his financial condition and/or to permit a credit check. (If a credit check is run, be sure to conform to the applicable provisions of the Consumer Credit Protection Act.) Should financial pressures exceed the salary or wages and other income at the applicant's disposal, this may indicate that the candidate is marginally employable.

To the extent permitted by law, the applicant should be requested to answer questions pertinent to his criminal history, if any, and his permission should be sought for background investigations of this type. When permitted by law, indictment, arrest, and conviction data should be obtained. Bear in mind that indictments and arrests, in the absence of convictions, do not necessarily mean the applicant actually committed the offenses charged. On the other hand, conviction on a misdemeanor charge does not preclude that the applicant really committed a felony and the charge was reduced through plea bargaining.

Even felony convictions should not necessarily bar applicants from employment, however, and this should be so stated on the employment form. First, this will encourage applicants with criminal histories to tell the truth. Second, one of the leading causes of recidivism among exoffenders is the arbitrary denial of legitimate avenues of employment. Granted, not all exoffenders should or deserve to be hired. What is required is a balanced, and often difficult, judgment by employers.

Some police departments supply criminal records to employers on request or for a nominal fee. Most, however, do not; however, insurers, private investigation firms, or various credit-checking companies may have such data in their files. All should note the opinion of a federal court, which stated that "information concerning a prospective employee's record of arrests without convictions is irrelevant to his suitability or qualifications for employment." Prevailing opinion seems to hold that criminal records showing arrests but not final dispositions are misleading and violate the rights of those involved.

Two other aspects of the preemployment process are described by a West Coast forwarder: "In these times few employers may insist upon fingerprinting, identification photos, etc., as a prerequisite to employment, yet one may always ask for them, and if they are withheld, then the job can also be withheld. It is as simple as that. The employer still has some rights, and he can obtain benefits by exercising them." The company's employment manual states: "The advantage of a simple photographing procedure is that it discourages undesirables and deters thieves or wanted persons from applying under assumed names. Photos are of extreme help in the event of any later necessary investigative activities."

A similar statement appears with reference to the value of fingerprinting, along with this caution and advice: "They can be good insurance both before and after the fact. They must be voluntary, but who, after all, should wholly trust the prospective employee who will not volunteer them?" The deterrent value of fingerprinting has been demonstrated on a number of occasions, even though requests for fingerprint checks to local authorities often cannot be accommodated and similar requests to federal agencies must be refused (because of a 1971 decision of a United States District Court, which prohibited federal dissemination of identification records in response to fingerprints submitted in connection with non-law enforcement purposes). As one West Coast security official put it, "You'd be amazed to see how many, after fingerprinting, don't show up for work."

Directly above the line where the applicant is to sign the employment form, the following conditions, to which he agrees by signing, should be noted: misrepresentations on the form shall be considered acts of dishonesty; permission is granted to the employer or his agent to investigate the applicant's background and he releases all persons from liability with regard to disclosure they may make regarding his background; the application for employment in no way obligates the employer to hire the applicant; if hired, the employee may be on probation for a period during which he may be discharged without recourse.

As noted above, the information developed by the application form may have to be supplemented by outside credit checks, criminal record searches, and so forth. Reinforcing advocates of such investigations are the reported results of a major, manufacturer-sponsored study of over 6000 employment applicants. Information resulting from investigation of applicants, and which could have not been developed from application data, disclosed such serious "unfavorable background characteristics as to warrant rejection" of one of every ten prospective employees. Interestingly, the application forms and questionnaires were so designed that the "omit or disguise the real data required a conscious effort to deceive."

In the absence of a security department, personnel managers may wish to retain a private investigation service to check out applicants. A nationwide detective agency charges about $70 for what is described as a thorough background check. Such screening can also be conducted on a per-lead basis, whereby each lead to be investigated (credit, criminal record, last job, etc.) would cost $12.

As part of its personnel policy, a New England carrier requires each new employee to sign a form entitled "Integrity in Employment." At the top of the form, company policy is stated: "The great majority of our people are of high moral character. When we uncover the dishonest individual who sometimes enters our company, we deal with him quickly and severely. For our company to be known for its integrity, every one of us must himself meet high standards." Consequences of dishonesty are tersely noted: "Proven dishonesty can result in immediate dismissal and criminal prosecution to the full extent of the law. Since much of the cargo you handle moves interstate, thefts of these shipments is a violation investigated by the FBI. Conviction brings a maximum penalty of 10 years imprisonment and/or a fine of $5000."

After cataloging a number of civil rights that felons forfeit, the form declares "There are several infractions which unions define as indefensible—proven dishonesty is on the list." Finally, "We request all employees to report acts of dishonesty. We will grant a reward of $1100 for information leading to the arrest and conviction of any person who has stolen merchandise or other valuables from the company. Our primary intention is to prevent thefts, not catch thieves after losses have occurred."

At meetings and through the house organ, the thrust of this message is repeated periodically to keep employees aware of the problem and of the company's policy. The following points are emphasized regarding the $1100 reward: all information received will be held in confidence, those furnishing information need not testify in court, the reward money can be paid in cash, and identities will not be revealed if this is requested.

While the above personnel policies can help keep cargo thieves off the payroll, management should periodically assess whether other policies generate unnecessary employee frustrations that breed hostility toward the company. Questioned by a reporter at a truck stop about what he would do if he found his rig missing, a driver replied, "Driving for this outfit, I'd go back in and have a couple more cups of coffee and give whoever took the thing all the time he could." Said another,

"I work for a good outfit. They don't cheat the drivers and we don't cheat the company."

Implications of Collective Bargaining Agreements

Just as with all other aspects of a company's operation, the impact on cargo theft of proposed collective bargaining provisions should be carefully considered, as illustrated by the congressional testimony of a waterfront security executive:

> Cases of cargo are lost when truckers working alone or with swampers or with a cooperative marine checker unlawfully place other cargo aboard trucks at crowded busy terminals. In other instance, truckers take advantage of inexperienced parttime checkers. . . Current labor agreements prohibit or restrict management a clear choice of any marine checker he wishes. . . . The checker then acts as a representative of management and actually has in many instances free access to several million dollars' worth of cargo which he could and sometimes does release unlawfully to suspect truckers."

And, as a federal official testified,

> The concept of containerization to start with was designed to keep down this pilferage and stealing on the waterfronts. Unfortunately, the movement of containerization is not going along as it had been initially programmed because the longshoremen negotiated . . . that much of this stuffing of containers should be done at the piers themselves. So what is happening is that the containers are coming in, and they may be fully loaded, and they are unpacked and restuffed again to provide man-hours. This also provides the possibility of pilferage of small items in that area. But it is a serious one. . . .

An agreement between a union and carrier on the East Coast provides that all parties will be bound by the determination of an arbitrator regarding whether an employee is guilty of theft and thus should be dismissed. Such a determination holds even though a prosecutor may not accept the case. In other pacts, the parties are bound by the outcome of court action—with the employer liable for back pay of a suspended employee if a verdict of not guilty is reached or if the prosecutor belatedly decides not to pursue a previously accepted case (this reportedly cost one employer $25,000). Whether management should push for one approach or the other requires balancing a number of factors, including court backlogs, willingness of prosecutors to accept cargo theft cases, etc.

The Financial Executive and Cargo Theft

Often working in close cooperation with the claims and/or security manager, the financial officer can make a particularly valuable contribution to the deterrence and detection of cargo thefts, as well as conduct analyses that form the basis for countermeasures.

This is illustrated by a recently cited case of a distributor who was losing tons of metal at the rate of $160,000 yearly. For two years, management attributed the shortage to accounting errors. Finally, an investigation pinpointed driver/loader collusion in the shipping department. As a result, the firm now watches its accounting records more closely—and acts promptly and accordingly.

Management might have reacted sooner and identified the department where losses were occurring more quickly if that firm's budgeting and accounting structure were not only oriented along traditional lines (chart of accounts, type of expenditures) but also were geared to the responsibilities and performance standards of key personnel at each organizational level, from loading dock supervisor to president. This approach frequently is called responsibility reporting: it identifies responsibility for all controllable costs by the individuals accountable and meshes standard cost reporting with the company's budgetary controls.

Responsibility reporting, which a knowledgeable accountant should be able to implement, need not be a complicated or cumbersome procedure. With such pinpointing by individuals of dollars and cents accountability, employee dishonesty is deterred, or at least more readily detected.

At a minimum, shippers, carriers, warehouse operators, and consignees should have a cost accounting system capable of assessing cost and revenue trends by commodity or product. Out of a sizeable group of carriers, however, only five were described as capable of reporting their revenue, and thus their costs, by commodity. But, as a spokesman for a carrier security group observed, experience elsewhere "has taught the value of cost accounting data in controlling and improving the organization and conduct of business." He also referred to "the importance of clearer and more detailed studies of cargo costs."

First, cost studies can lead to cargo-handling procedures that at first blush might not seem profitable to adopt. For example, a cargo security organization noted that one of the more significant factors why a theft-promoting and otherwise uneconomical practice was still being followed by a group of carriers was that "cost accounting enjoys little vogue."

Second, cost accounting can highlight those commodities most susceptible to theft, both in absolute terms and in relation to the revenues they produce. The security group just referred to concluded that although all cargo may be considered equal and is entitled to equal attention, "this does not result in equal profitability in transporting all commodities." Financial analyses of carrier claims figures, for example, indicated that certain commodities cost "much more than is justified—actually destroying profitability."

The cargo security implications of the following loss ratios developed by these analyses is obvious: 55.26% for jewelry, gold, silver coins; 35.19% for watches, clocks and parts; 34.24% for fur skins and pelts; 13.75% for wearing apparel with fur (but without fur, 6.51%). As a group, valuables cost in claims 39.1% of its revenue, while wearing apparel cost 5.5%. Carrying the analysis further, it was found that wearing apparel produced 8.3% of total revenue and 25.5% of total claims; valuables generated 0.4% of revenues while amounting to 13.2% of the total claim bill. One security official interviewed for this report indicated that cargo loss records could be related to drivers and to routes traveled. As a result, subsequent analysis could highlight certain patterns that can be nipped in the bud.

But before such analyses are possible, a method must exist for obtaining the raw data in sufficient detail that trends or patterns will not be lost in grand totals. Among the types of information that may be valuable to financial, claims, security, and other personnel are the following: the person or carrier reporting the loss; origin and destination of the shipment; type of loss (theft, pilferage, undetermined); shipping document number and date (bill of lading, airbill, manifest, etc.); value of loss; date and time loss discovered; where loss occurred (on ramp or loading dock from a truck or warehouse, while enroute, etc.); description of missing commodities or articles, including serial numbers or other special identification, such as type of packaging (pallet, carton, container, etc., and markings thereon); accountability audit (identification of carriers and individuals handling the shipment between the time it was last accounted for and time of loss); enforcement agencies contacted to date (FBI), customs, local police, etc.). As users and suppliers of transportation well know, acquisition of such an array of data borders on the utopian, depending as it does on an intercompany, interindustry cooperation and on a degree of management expertise that is too often absent. Nonetheless, the goal is worth aiming for.

A CRITICAL FACTOR: THE PACKAGING DECISION

As with other management decisions that improve cargo security, the ones pertaining to packaging, in the vast majority of instances, do not require breakthroughs in equipment or expertise. What is needed is merely the intelligent application of existing knowledge. In this regard whatever information shippers do not have, but would like, is often more than willingly supplied by carriers upon request. Obviously improperly packaged goods leads to damaged or ruptured cartons or containers. Damage invites entry by thieves; burst packaging virtually gives the contents to pilferers.

Principal factors to evaluate when selecting exterior containers or cartons are their ability to resist (1) compression, (2) puncture, and, in the case of fiberboard cartons, (3) the strength of score lines and (4) humidity.

Even when a carton or other type of exterior packaging meets freight classification requirements, improper stacking may result in crushed cartons or burst seams; too tight strapping or netting results in a bulged or dented carton; inadequate interior packing results in punctured containers from shifting contents or crumbled cartons caused by insufficient support to carton walls; overstuffing causes bulged packing.

According to the advice of one security organization, the proper response by carriers to poor packaging should be as follows: "Shipping packages should not be accepted if in the judgement of the receiving carrier, the packing is inadequate, requires coopering or has other deficiencies. Bad order cases in possession of carrier, upon discovery, must be immediately placed in a safe location and recoopered. Under no circumstance release a bad order package against an exception without determining the quantity and condition of its contents."

Many interviewed carrier spokesmen cautioned against the use of affixing computer-prepared address labels to cartons. Because the printing is so small, misrouting often results. When this occurs, both the clever and not-so-clever thief realize that the audit trail or accountability chain has been broken and that the shipment is ripe for the taking. Carriers also advise that misrouting also may result when shippers reuse cartons and fail to remove all of the old address labels. (Freight may also be misdirected because of a ship to/bill to mix up, whereby the shipment is mistakenly sent to the billing address. And when delivering merchandise to several local branches of the same store chain, cartons for one location may be erroneously dropped off at another. If there is a dishonest employee at the consignee's receiving dock, such a misrouted package is a tempting target).

The question of carton advertising or other markings that identify contents is another packaging-related invitation to theft. Although experienced thieves frequently can determine the contents of a package by its shape, feel (as in the identification of registered air mail pouches), and/or name of consignee and shipper, there are numerous instances where removal of such identification has resulted in a marked decrease in cargo theft.

Obviously, greater security results from unitized, containerized, or similarly assembled loads that reduce or eliminate manual handling.

PREVENTIVE STEPS FOR MARKETING AND PURCHASING

Not only to preserve a reputation for quality but also to help prevent first-line merchandise from being peddled by thieves or fences in "salvage" sales or from being touted as seconds, one firm insists on the return of all damaged goods even though the company may be liable for the freight charges. The goods are then destroyed. For similar reasons, some marketing executives insist that the company's label be removed from goods that are released as seconds.

Marketing management, in cooperation with the manufacturing and shipping departments, can also be instrumental by (1) devising methods by which identification numbers or other unique markings can be stamped or otherwise affixed to merchandise and (2) by implementing procedures by which these identification markings can be related to shipments so that if the goods are stolen and then recovered by police, management will be able to identify the goods as those manufactured by the company and tendered to a certain carrier on June 6, 1982. Prosecution of fences or others can hardly proceed if the companies from which the cargo is stolen cannot distinguish between merchandise legitimately marketed and those items marketed as the result of theft.

Admittedly, such an identification procedure usually would present significant problems and costs. But could not at least the cartons, if not the merchandise, be coded in some unique way during process? Or could not 5% or 10% of the serial numbers involved in a shipment of appliances be recorded? On certain products, could serial numbers be located so that removal of the number would entail damaging or otherwise rendering the product unmarketable?

In addition, each company's sales and service force should be instructed to be alert for company products being sold at abnormal discounts or distributed through unusual channels or outlets. They could also be given serial numbers of stolen products. In one case, a repairman for an office equipment manufacturer noted that the serial numbers on the equipment he was servicing were on his employer's hot list. This was reported and the equipment was recovered from a public accountant who had purchased it from a legitimate outlet. In another instance, however, a shortsighted view prevailed. After receiving reports from its salesmen that cigarette purchases through the company's vending machines at some locations had suddenly dropped from 260 packs a week to 40 when a competitor's machines were installed, management did not report this obvious signal of hijacked or bootleg cigarettes to police out of concern that if the taverns and restaurants were closed by authorities, there would be one less outlet for even 40 packs of cigarettes.

Finally, marketing executives should carefully check out new sources of business. Several years ago, the sales manager of a well-known Chicago area company received an order for a large quantity of goods to be shipped to South America. Having long wanted to penetrate that market, he permitted a substantial discount. A container load of goods was shipped to New Orleans for export. Although documentation indicated that a certain ship took the goods to South America, later information revealed that there was no such ship in existence and that the container had been taken from New Orleans to Detroit where the goods were depressing the market because of their low price.

Buyers and purchasing managers should also carefully screen those with whom they do business. Extraordinarily good bargains should be carefully studied before acceptance, especially if the items to be purchased are being offered by those operating outside typical distribution channels for the product. And top management, while insisting on good performance, should be careful not to exert so much pressure on buyers that they become ready and willing to deal with cut-rate criminal sources.

When subcontracting, a company should know with whom it is dealing. For example, a forwarder once subcontracted a load to a gypsy operator, who conveniently left it in a parking lot for the weekend. When he returned to check his rig, it and its cargo of $25,000 worth of coffee were missing.

Both purchasing and marketing personnel should endeavor to specify direct routing of shipments to minimize multiple handling and interline transfers. When at all practical, incoming and outgoing goods should be shipped in such quantities that permit unitization, containerization, or other forms of consolidation. Purchasing agents may find that overly restrictive inventory control policies are responsible for aggravating the problems associated with small orders.

A special word of caution is in order for those in the financial world who, on several occasions, have been flimflammed or otherwise induced into accepting stolen securities for loans or for sale. Know your customers and know your merchandise. According to many sources, existing technology and methods by which to establish the identity of such customers and the status of such securities are either underutilized or ignored.

WHAT LEGAL COUNSEL CAN CONTRIBUTE

A number of questions related to combatting cargo theft should be asked of corporate counsel—and this should be done before, not after, a theft. For example, who should be authorized to sign a complaint or warrant? (Do not forget to alert appropriate personnel about company policy in this regard.) What elements of proof should the company assemble before accusing someone of cargo theft? What procedures should be followed to preclude a successful false-arrest suit? How should statements or confessions by the accused be taken—written, recorded, witnessed, advisement of rights, signed, etc.?

Should restitution by the accused be accepted? According to one source, although an employer is under no legal obligation to report or prosecute those guilty of cargo theft, "neither does the employer have the statutory right to grant immunity from prosecution—even if restitution is made by the employee. Thus a promise to refrain from prosecuting or from reporting the crime to authorities should not be made. Actually, such a promise could be regarded as compounding a crime, whereby the injured party now commits his own offense by explicitly agreeing with the criminal not to press charges. Also, "acceptance of repayment could jeopardize a company's recourse to third parties—such as banks that cashed forged checks or outlets that received stolen merchandise." A final caveat: if an employer accepts restitution from someone covered by a blanket bond, the insurer may have grounds to deny future claims occasioned by this individual.

Counsel can also advise about the most advantageous court in which to bring theft cases. Federal? State? Local? What about a trial before a U.S. magistrate? Under certain conditions, the latter may try cases involving misdemeanors punishable under the laws of the United States. While a magistrate may not impose sentences as severe as could be levied by a federal district court, cases usually reach a magistrate court much more quickly and the trials often require less time than at the district court level. This advantage of swift justice may be particularly significant when collective bargaining packs condition the dismissal (and/or deregistration of waterfront employers in some areas) of employees upon a court conviction.

Other areas to explore in advance with counsel are (1) the conditions under which recovery from a receiver of stolen goods is possible through civil action and (2) the conditions under which such civil recovery will not jeopardize subsequent criminal action.

Obviously, these and other similar questions warrant study and resolution before a company is faced with a theft. If they are not, management's response to cargo theft may be so sluggish as to jeopardize fast police response in the future, so ill-prepared as to expose the company to suit, or so disorganized as to permit the retention of a thief on the payroll.

MANAGEMENT CHECKLIST FOR THE MOVEMENT OF CARGO

There are hundreds of management-oriented theft-prevention methods that can be built into the processes by which cargo is shipped, transported, received, stored, and documented. Of necessity, therefore, the several dozen preventive steps that follow do not represent an all-embracing checklist but are important as illustrations of the type of thinking that executives can and should bring to bear on the cargo theft problem. The suggestions below are hardly revolutionary nor are they revealed here for the first time. Procedural in nature, they do not require hardware to implement, just the will to do so. Though presented in piecemeal fashion here, such measures should not be applied on an ad hoc basis but molded to fit local conditions and fielded as a well-coordinated team. To facilitate future reference, the numbers preceding those measures or approaches considered particularly applicable might be circled.

1. Consignee management should instruct its receiving department to notify purchasing when incoming items arrive. This will help prevent fraudulent purchase orders originated by someone outside of purchasing from getting into the flow and will force receiving to make a careful count.
2. To help assure timely detection of thefts occurring before goods get into the consignee's record system, request purchasing personnel to contact the supplier directly when an order is not filled within a reasonable time.
3. To prevent spurious purchase orders and subsequent thefts, prohibit purchasing department from receiving ordered merchandise and from having access to such merchandise. Likewise, assure that receiving personnel do not perform purchasing duties.
4. Only specified individuals should be authorized to check in merchandise received. Unless responsibility is fixed, shortages can be blamed on others easily.
5. Consignee employees who check incoming goods should reconcile such goods with a purchase order and remove goods

to the storage area immediately thereafter. Absence of a purchase order could mean the merchandise was ordered fraudulently with the intention of removing it before it got into the record flow. Prompt transfer of goods to storage not only gets them into the record flow but also removes them from a traditionally high-theft area.

6. Receiving personnel should use a prenumbered form on which to record delivered merchandise and copies should be sent to purchasing and accounts payable. This will help deter destruction of receiving records and theft of merchandise. Failure to furnish purchasing with a record will spur an investigation, and failure to advise accounts payable will result in a complaint by the supplier.

7. Regarding outbound shipments, freight bills are totaled and compared to the number recorded on the manifest. Discrepancies are promptly corrected. The same holds for incoming shipments except that discrepancies are immediately reported to the terminal manager and/or security director for investigation.

8. Freight received without accompanying documentation should be stored in a secure place.

9. Record the number of shipping documents given to strippers or loaders. When the documents are returned, count them again and compare totals.

10. When returned by the local driver, delivery receipts should be compared with terminal control copies and all bills accounted for.

11. Consignees should not delay taking delivery of goods. Anticipate difficulties regarding import license, exchange control, or other regulations. Those who have taken advantage of free time in customs and of free storage time at carrier terminals often find that the practice is penny-wise but pound foolish. For example, an importer of canned goods took prompt delivery and suffered only limited pilferage in contrast to the heavy losses of his procrastinating competitors.

12. Require positive identification from pickup drivers to insure they are the legal representatives of the carrier. Record license numbers, especially on rental vehicles.

13. Prepare legible bills of lading and other shipping documents, which are manufactured from a paper stock that will hold up under multiple handlings. Try to use classification descriptions instead of trade names and avoid listing values.

14. Periodically rotate drivers among runs. Otherwise, there is too great a chance that they might develop contacts for collusion. Beware of drivers who request certain routes despite lower wages associated with those routes.
15. Change truck stops frequently.
16. Develop incentive plans to control losses—payments to employees being based on reductions in insurance premiums and/or actual losses.
17. On multipiece shipments, shippers should label each package. As the driver instruction manual of one carrier reads, "The driver must check all shipments to determine that each piece is legibly, durably, and properly marked. The name and address of the shipper must be shown on each piece of freight in any shipment. The marking on each article should be checked to determine if the consignee's name and address is the same as shown on the airbill. Drivers must be certain that the marking will not tear off when the shipment is in transit."
18. Exposure to loss often increases with higher turnover of personnel on shipping and receiving docks.
19. Advertise your security efforts in high-theft locations.
20. Know employees on all shifts.
21. Do not use advertisements on trucks, such as "Smoke Brand X—Distributed by. . . ."
22. Run radio and TV spots indicating the convenience and other advantage (such as service) of buying through regular channels.
23. Request truck rental companies to post signs warning users that the rental agent is cooperating in theft prevention.
24. Conceal or seal in a pouch the papers covering a load.
25. Provide cargo checkers with self-inking identification stamps. When receipting for cargo, in addition to affixing his signature on the receipt, the checker stamps the document, thereby clearly identifying himself.
26. Utilize color-coded vehicle passes (keyed to specific areas in the terminal) and time-stamp them.
27. Establish advance-notice procedures whereby consignee is notified at least 24 hours prior to the arrival of sensitive shipments. Alert intermediate points as well.
28. Negotiate with carriers for what one large shipper calls "signature security service" for certain kinds of shipments, whereby a signature and tally are required from each person handling the shipment at each stage of its transit, from point of origin to destination.

29. Analyze claims to determine type of cargo most subject to thefts and where its being lost.

30. Periodically review carrier performance to identify those having a high incidence of loss or damage.

31. Receiving stations should assign a trusted employee to review advance manifests or, if none, the documents arriving with the cargo to identify and segregate for special attention theft-prone cargo. Such "paper alerts" should also be supplemented by actual examination of the cargo. For example, a manifest described one shipment as "electrical equipment," but the carton identified the goods as calculators. Relying on the manifest, a cargo handler treated the shipment as general cargo; one of the calculators was later stolen.

32. Security rooms for valuable cargo should have adequate inventory control procedures. In one case, a bale of furs was lost for two weeks because of a lack of such controls.

33. Maintain a tally as cargo is transferred from vessel to terminal. This is frequently, if not usually, omitted, with the result that (1) detection of thefts are delayed until consignee complains, and (2) buck-passing is promoted inasmuch as no one knows whether the goods were stolen before or after the ship was unladen.

34. Remove loose or broached cargo to cooperage shops as soon as possible.

35. Use shipper's initials rather than full name on labels if the full name would tip off thieves to the nature of the carton's contents.

36. Seal cartons with a tape having a special design and color. If a carton is opened and resealed, this would be evident.

37. Indicate lot numbers on each carton and on the bill of lading in order to highlight a short carton.

38. Whenever practicable, insist on piece counts when cargo is moved to and from vehicles and in and out of storage areas, vessels, railcars, aircraft, etc. Insist on clear identification of those who conduct such counts—driver, checker, receiving personnel, terminal cargo handler, or any others. The two parties involved in a cargo transfer should not take each other's word regarding the count. Accountability then becomes blurred. As a carrier executive advised, employees who check cargo must be told, "You are individually responsible. You must know. You must count." Among his instructions to drivers are: (1) "If the bill calls for 'CS. No. 1234,' don't accept a case marked '4567' for it." (2) "A driver should

never accept a shipment described as 'one bundle tires.' The airbill should indicate how many articles are in the bundle. For example: 'one bundle (3) tires,' " (3) If a shortage exists in a shipment, determine the exact piece short. "If it is shoes, the exception should be '1 cs. shoes short.' A general statement such as '1 cs short' is not sufficient. . . ."

39. Load each delivery vehicle in conformance with its routing so that unloading delays—with concomitant unnecessary exposure to theft—will be minimized.

40. Segregate shipping from receiving areas, inbound from outbound cargo.

41. Require company name of carriers to be shown on all equipment. Do not accept temporary placards or cardboard signs as proper identification; Nor should lease agreements for rented vehicles be considered as sufficient identification. Independent verification is necessary.

42. Release cargo only to the carrier specified in the delivery order unless a release authorizing delivery to another carrier, signed by the original carrier is presented and verified. Accept only original copies of the delivery or pickup orders.

43. Prelodged delivery or pickup order should be safeguarded from theft or unauthorized observation. Verify identity of carrier and carrier employee before releasing a prelodged pickup order. An operator of large terminals noted the potential advantages of prelodging: "We encourage truckers to bring their documentation to the terminal the day before they deliver cargo. We prepare our receiving documents from the trucker's papers and when trucks arrive, give priority in handling to the loads for which we were furnished advanced documentation. Cargo handling is expedited, checking is more precise, the documents themselves are more accurate. Our cargo accounting has improved significantly. . . ." This confirms the observation in a carrier task force report: "Reforms in paperwork to eliminate bottlenecks and to raise accuracy also may make it less easy to smudge the responsibility for cargo and cargo records."

44. Restrict access to cargo documentation to a need-to-know basis. Systems assuring strict accountability for documentation are as important as those designed for the cargo itself. For example, after several thefts in a terminal involved stolen documentation as well as its cargo, an internal release order was devised. The cargo handler who is to retrieve a shipment in the terminal is given the release order, which

describes the cargo and its location. Source documents remain in the custody of the clerk preparing the release order. The clerk retains a copy of the release, on which he records time of preparation and the name of the cargo handler, who brings the shipment to his control supervisor, who in turn verifies the identity of the cargo handler and the description and quantity of cargo to be delivered. The supervisor requests the signature of the trucker after recording date and time of release. Finally, the release order is returned to the clerk who prepared it.

45. Release seals to as few people as possible. Require all persons handling seals to maintain tight control over them.

46. Log movements of containers into or out of a holding area. Indicate date, time, seal number, truckman and company making pickup, and registration number of equipment used.

47. Accept only legible documentation.

48. Obtain clearly written signatures—not blurred initials—on cargo documentation.

49. Neither accept nor prepare penciled documentation.

50. Cargo entering a terminal from shippers or other stations should be thoroughly inspected, accurately counted, properly classified, and immediately stored. Paperwork should reflect all decisions and actions taken.

51. The employee withdrawing goods from storage should be different from the one actually releasing the merchandise.

52. An integral part of terminal security is a workable, accurate cargo location system. Delays in, or confusion over, removing cargo from storage increases the risk of theft or pilferage. Among other things, a good locator system does not give cargo handlers the excuse to wander all over the terminal when looking for a shipment.

53. Devise procedures to minimize terminal congestion and poor housekeeping, which result in obstructed visibility of cargo, misplaced cargo, less efficient checking and handling, and other situations promoting theft and pilferage. Stated a highly knowledgeable source interviewed for this segment, "The real enemy of security is congestion. When goods pile up, you lose control, no matter what procedures are in effect." Many carriers try to combat this by discouraging consignees from delaying pickup or acceptance of cargo. In the event that strikes hit other modes or carriers, some carrier terminals have readied emergency plans by which to handle in an orderly fashion the anticipated extra flow

of cargo, such as through a pickup and delivery appointment system for shippers and consignees.

54. Establish space standards, which fix the quantity of cargo that can be safely stored in a given area or terminal.

55. High-value air freight should be the last to be loaded at origin and the first to be unloaded (and piece-counted) at destination. If practicable during surface transport, bury high-value shipments in the other cargo so that an unauthorized opening of trailer or container doors will not immediately expose the valuable articles.

56. To facilitate timely detection of theft, among other reasons, a weekly or twice-weekly telephone conference should be arranged between a carrier's various terminals (or a consignee's various branch stores) to reconcile cargo overages and shortages experienced at different locations.

57. Shippers should await the arrival of the carrier before loads staged for shipment are final-counted. Otherwise, between the time of the count and the arrival of the carrier, pieces could be added surreptiously and than hauled away through collusion between an inside employee and the carrier's driver.

58. Shippers should not permit customers to dictate routing. If every customer were permitted to route his orders, dock congestion (which breeds theft) would be inevitable because of the sheet number of different carriers that would be required each day to satisfy customer requests.

59. In areas where the rate of truck hijacking is high, suggested a police official, at each delivery point drivers should note the indicated mileage, leaving a record at the dock and in their log. If the truck is hijacked, the difference between the mileage recorded at the last delivery and the indicated mileage at the point of recovery, combined with other driversupplied information, will assist police in pinpointing the drop or fence.

60. Rather than ship a fully assembled product, some companies ship the components and, in so doing, have reduced cargo theft. For example, an encyclopedia publisher is said to ship odd-numbered volumes in one carton, even-numbered in another.

As indicated earlier, neither the above nor the many other possible procedures will achieve full potential unless they are implemented as a well-coordinated series of measures. That is, they should function as a system —not as unrelated, ad hoc controls.

A good illustration of such an integrated approach is the Military Traffic Management and Terminal Service (MTMTS) card packet system. (MTMTS is a Department of Defense agency that centralizes and coordinates the procurement and operation of transportation services for the movement of military freight and personnel.) The computerized card packet system, Cardpac, was designed to operate at six high-volume marine terminals, through which about 85% of the MTMTS surface export cargo flows.

When a DOD shipper alerts the computer at an MTMTS area command that a shipment is destined for overseas is in the transportation pipeline, this information is relayed by the area command to the computer at the water terminal scheduled to receive the shipment for export. The terminal's computer automatically generates a set of punched cards containing all the data necessary for terminal personnel to process the incoming shipment. These cards are the basis for management printouts for controlling the cargo as it moves through the terminal and are the means by which to update the area command master file.

When the shipment is received, one of the advance-prepared cards is used as a receipt document. The checker at the gate records the date of receipt and the location within the terminal where the cargo is stored. The card is used to update the system's file. If the shipment is transferred within the terminal, this is recorded on another card, which updates the system's computers. When the shipment is loaded aboard ship, the date, ship number, and storage location is entered on still another card, which is entered into the system to complete the cycle.

Thus, management is able to receive cargo inventory and location printouts, which assist terminal personnel in selecting shipments for loading. Management also receives a load list, which is used to plan the storage of the ship. After loading, print-outs list the on-board cargo for the benefit of the ship's master.

By incorporating a coordinated series of measures—improved documentation, tightened inventory control, greater accountability, etc.—the Cardpac system serves to speed the orderly flow of cargo and thus promotes superior security.

The point, of course, is not that a computer is necessary to deter cargo theft, but that to combat cargo theft involves the application of various preventive measures that must dovetail, one with the other. If there are significant gaps, however, cargo will most likely drop through them and into the hands of thieves and fences.

THE STRATEGY OF JOINT ACTION

Although there are many measures an individual firm can implement to combat cargo theft, certain desirable courses of action inevitably will not be taken, and of the measures that are implemented, several will not be exploited to their fullest. A number of excellent reasons account for this.

First, there is just so much time that can be devoted to the cargo theft problem. Second, manpower and financial constraints limit the range of the possible. Third, needed expertise may not be available. Fourth, because a firm must be preoccupied with its problems and its requirements, valuable insights derived from a full perspective are not obtained. Fifth, fear or apprehension may limit, or preclude entirely, the application of certain necessary measures. However, these and other obstacles can be substantially overcome if the efforts of individual companies are reinforced by an organization to which all belong and support, from which all benefit, and by which what cannot be accomplished individually can be implemented jointly.

This organization, the association, may be local, regional, or national in membership and structured along either intraindustry lines (airline members only, for example) or interindustry lines (e.g., comprised of importers, terminal operators, and marine carriers). The association may be independent or an adjunct to an existing organization. It may concentrate on a specific facet of cargo theft or concern itself with a range of activities, including liaison with such outside sources of assistance as law enforcement agencies. In any event, the association can compensate for the previously mentioned weaknesses of its members because of the following factors:

1. It has a sufficiently large and professional staff to devote the required time, manpower, and expertise to cargo theft problems.
2. It is supported on an equitable basis by all and thus is unduly expensive to none.
3. It studies each member's problems and thereby gains a broad perspective.
4. It is the vehicle for unified action and as such can effectively shield its individual members from adverse consequences that perhaps would result if, in the absence of the association, this action were taken by a few firms but not by others. Such consequences might include retaliation by criminal elements, operating costs out of line with those of competitors that did not implement measures, and loss of business because customers do not want to extend the cooperation required by certain theft-prevention measures, such as agreeing to piece counts. However, if through the vehicle of an association various measures were implemented on an across-the-board basis by all members, no one member could be singled out as out-of-line and therefore subjected to various pressures.

How these factors come into play and how working through an association often results in a "2 + 2 = 5" effect are obvious from a review of what these associations are doing or could do.

Centralized Screening of Personnel

If, for example, only a few carriers and terminal operators located at a large cargo facility adequately screen employees, cargo theft may be reduced in such companies but is not likely to decrease on a facility-wide basis. Employees rejected or dismissed from alert companies merely walk across the street, as it were, and are accepted for employment next door. Enlightened association action could require adherence to uniform standards of preemployment screening and authorize the creation of an association-maintained clearinghouse whereby the job histories of facility employees are available for inspection, thus minimizing the chance of an employer unwittingly hiring someone who was recently discharged by another.

One association revised its members' employment applications in order to elicit information from prospective employees "concerning previous records or activities which bear upon his eligibility for a position of trust." Each applicant fills out a short biographical summary, which along with a color photograph, is furnished to the association. "Upon receipt of the biographical and identifying data, we submit that information to the law enforcement agencies. . . . We also run him through our own individual indices for past employments. . . ."

A requirement for which a maritime association has gained union acceptance is the registration of waterfront workers. On any given day, the vast majority of longshoremen, working for member companies are registered with the association. Under most situations, a man cannot work anywhere on the waterfront unless he submits a card indicating that he is registered. The labor contracts state that registered workers convicted of theft on the waterfront will have their registration cards suspended or revoked. Applicants for employment on the piers must complete a preregistration form and physical examination. A screening procedure is then conducted by the association. From time to time, the association may register those with criminal offenses in their background. "These attempts at rehabilitation are carefully weighed, however, in terms of their effect on cargo security."

A Uniform Central Reporting System

An association can persuade its members not only to maintain meaningful cargo theft records but also to relay those reports to the association.

Only by so doing can the overall theft trend at an airport, rail center, or warehouse complex be discerned. Also, the perspective afforded by an analysis of overall data can reveal patterns not evident from the records of any given member company. For example, analysis of members' loss data may reveal shortages at four different terminals involving trailers originating from a common terminal. As one association notes, it "maintains loss records to determine pattern, areas, and cause of loss and recommends deterrents in connection therewith."

Some associations have designed uniform loss report forms, copies of which are forwarded to the appropriate law enforcement agencies as well as to the association. According to an account by one association the following system is in effect:

> A system for reporting missing cargo, "Missing Cargo Report," has been adopted. Through these reports, customs, the FBI, the harbor police department, the association, and the private investigators engaged by the association are informed of cargo that is stolen or otherwise missing. It is felt that prompt notification to those agencies which generally come in contact with all forms of missing cargo will increase their ability to recover the stolen cargo and prosecute the thieves. The missing cargo procedures require prompt telephone notification to all agencies at the time the disappearance is discovered and follow-up documentation. While we are aware that missing cargo reports are still not filed in every instance where cargo has disappeared, we feel that this can be solved through continually impressing our membership with the need for these reports. We have seen a great increase in the security consciousness of our members and feel this will cause more complete reporting in the future.

Should law enforcement agencies complain to this association about an uncooperative member, an association executive will contact the top management of the company involved.

Development and Enforcement of Performance Standards

To help overcome an "I don't want to be the first to do this" attitude among members, associations may develop and/or enforce standards of performance relating to theft prevention efforts. Among the tasks of one cargo protection council are designing, and recommending improvements in, procedures for cargo handling and supervision, methods for packaging and storing high-risk commodities, and methods related to such physical security measures as lighting and fencing.

Possessing the power to fine members if certain procedures are not followed, one association has done considerable spade work in devising and implementing procedural and other standards relating to such areas as space use, planning procedures, terminal layout plans, performance controls, cargo document control uniform cargo, release form, physical and record accountability for delivered cargo, cargo locator systems, and a variety of physical security measures.

To help members live up to these standards, training may also be among an association's activities. One group helps to train guards, watchmen, and other personnel. Others prepare procedure or physical security manuals. Or, as one association does, frequent training conferences may be held "where small groups of cargo and security personnel exchange ideas, individual problems and solutions. . . ."

As a means by which to obtain information on which to base standards, one association has organized meetings of "small groups of executives from allied industries, such as jewelers, truckers and others for intensified consideration of specific problems and exchange of perinent data affecting each area of operation and responsibility."

Assisting Law Enforcement

Associations can offer considerable help to law enforcement through permitting access to their centralized personnel files and assuring that members promptly report losses to the appropriate agencies. Frequently, associations will conduct their own investigations of thefts—not in competition with law enforcement agencies but in cooperation with them. This may be done by the association's own investigative staff or subcontracted.

This staff may administer a reward system, facilitate coordination among law enforcement agencies, and maintain a network of informants, who are of critical importance according to numerous sources interviewed for this book. Over a seven-year span, one investigation-oriented cargo protection association conducted 943 investigations resulting in 408 apprehensions and arrests, 241 convictions, and over $1 million in recovered merchandise and equipment.

As a further means of cooperating with law enforcement and of assisting its members, the association could request reports from members concerning signs of organized crime or other racketeer influences that come to their attention, such as in-plant gambling, loan sharking, illegal labor tactics, suspected fences or other receivers of stolen goods, etc. The association, in so doing, would remove the onus of reporting from the backs of the actual sources of information. What law enforcement needs, and what business so often can give, is information pertinent to criminal presence in legitimate business. As one observer commented:

It is precisely in this realm that the gulf between information normally available to business and that normally accessible to law enforcement agencies has been the most apparent. The business community possesses intimate knowledge of industrial and commercial operations but is lacking in ability to identify the associates and functionaries of organized crime. Law enforcement officials, on the other hand, have voluminous information identifying these individuals but have not normally carried on sustained and detailed investigations of their activities in the sphere of legitimate business. . . .

Enhancing the Changes for Successful Prosecution

The frustration reported by law enforcement officers over the unwillingness of many companies to prosecute cargo thieves is at times more than matched by the frustration experienced by many other companies over the failure of prosecutors to accept solid cases. A security officer of a motor carrier stated in testimony before a congressional committee:

> . . . we are the victims of a conflict between the unions on the one hand and the law enforcement agencies on the other. The inability to prosecute (because prosecutors did not accept the case) means the inability to discharge a dishonest employee and it usually ends up that we pay the employee for the time he didn't work while he was awaiting the prosecution that didn't occur. This in turn means we end up with the thief back in our truck or back on our dock to steal again.

In this regard, there are, of course, many crimes that are prosecutable only through United States attorneys. In one jurisdiction, such crimes represented over 50% of the federal prosecutor's case load. So he has his priorities, and unless a cargo theft is of unusual significance in terms of the value or the criminals involved, cargo thefts do not make his list. Similarly, local and state prosecutors are frequently swamped, too. And, as a former district attorney remarked, "No one likes to prosecute a petty cargo theft case, involving as it often does the husband of a sick wife with five kids."

To solve this apparent dilemma, one source proposed that federal funds be given to local prosecutors for the exclusive purpose of getting more cargo theft cases to court. Another proposal, offered by an association executive, would have associations "actively solicit the support of all law enforcement, prosecutive, and judicial groups—to invite them into terminals to acquaint them with freight operations—to get their advice and learn of their needs, with respect to prosecution for theft."

A third proposal, which could dovetail with the other two, takes note that prosecutors at all levels often have problems with cargo documentation: "They can't get it, can't read it, or can't interpret it," declared a former district attorney. This was confirmed by a transportation security officer: "They (prosecutors) do not understand our procedure. It is difficult to present a piece of paper in evidence when you do not understand what all these markings are on there (bill of lading), where three lines on there mean a lot to me and mean nothing to them." As a result, at least two associations devote considerable time facilitating prosecution by making the process easier for complainants and less time-consuming for prosecutors.

To overcome a long-entrenched fear and hesitancy among members to initiate criminal prosecutions, one association has issued bulletins explaining the steps taken in prosecution and the operations of the various criminal courts. A summary of laws pertaining to larceny, false arrest, false imprisonment, malicious prosecution and slander was also distributed to members. "A decided improvement in the industry's attitude toward prosecution resulted."

When an arrest is made or contemplated and a member is requested to sign a complaint, the association's legal staff is consulted. If the evidence warrants the signing of a criminal complaint, the staff determines who the proper complainant should be. "The form of the complaint, the charge, and the need for corroborating affidavits from the arresting officers are all matters to be considered." No member company that has consulted with the association has ever been subjected to any lawsuit arising out of signing a criminal complaint, reports the association.

After the complaint is signed, the association works closely with the prosecutor to produce witnesses and interpret cargo documentation. In some instance, a member of the association's staff will present all witnesses and documents to the prosecutor and rapidly explains, "This first witness will testify to this fact; the second witness will substantiate. . . ." In five minutes the case is laid out for a decision by the prosecutor.

During the trial stage, an association representative is present in court to determine if the case will be called or continued or have some other disposition. If it appears that the case will proceed and previously alerted witnesses will be needed in court, a phone call summons them from work. In this way their time is not wasted and they and the complainant do not become discouraged by repeated continuances, which frequently are engineered by defense attorneys to wear down the opposition. Because of the association's strategy, however, such an attorney quickly realizes that the only person's time and money being wasted by delaying tactics are his own.

Summing up, the executive vice president of the association commented, "The importance of these efforts cannot be overemphasized.

They have eliminated the hesitancy and anxiety once typical of the industry when a company was called upon to sign a complaint." In an average year, the association's legal staff makes more than 300 appearances in various criminal courts and before administrative agencies.

Other Roles for the Association

Some have suggested that associations could play more active roles in connection with federal funds allocated to each state for law enforcement purposes. Not only could such funds be used as seed money to get new associations off the ground, but money could be channeled into law enforcement agencies for the purpose of combatting cargo theft. This is not likely to result unless associations do their part at the state and local levels by urging allocation of these funds for such purposes. A nationwide association established to combat cargo theft has requested that its local units do the following:

1. Request State legislatures to pass measures that would permit employers legal access to criminal records of applicants.
2. Develop regional seminars on transportation security.
3. Promote state legislation permitting those victimized by cargo theft to bring civil action against thieves, fences, and buyers of stolen merchandise to recover actual and punitive damages.

And, of course, associations are in a good position to explain to members the significance of such pending federal legislation as the Customs Port Security Act, the stated purpose of which is "to increase the security and protection of imported merchandise and merchandise of export at ports of entry in the United States from loss or damage as a result of criminal and corrupt practice"; the Cargo Commission Act, which would create a two-year federal commission to study various aspects of cargo security and safety; amendments to a proposed bill providing compensation to innocent victims of crime, which would alter the theft from interstate shipment statute in significant respects, including a provision whereby civil action would be authorized so that cargo theft victims could recover the value of triple damages from the responsible parties that are in violation of the statute.

Although other appropriate areas for association action could be listed, the undeniable rationale for joint action is the same and is described by a proverb about everyone hanging together or hanging separately. The opposition is organized; why not the intended victims?

ASSISTANCE FROM LAW ENFORCEMENT
AND OTHER ORGANIZATIONS

As emphasized throughout this book, the extent to which law enforcement agencies or other organizations can cope with cargo theft depends to a great degree on the quality of management's policies and procedures. If management cannot identify recovered cargo as that stolen, or has no idea where or when the theft or pilferage occurred, or has an ambivalent attitude toward prosecution, the effectiveness of outside sources of assistance is immensely reduced.

One of the most extreme examples of how management can shackle such assistance occurred when a special agent of a waterfront commission asked a terminal manager to sign a complaint against a man caught in the act of stealing 100 pounds of sugar from a terminal. The manager replied, "It is my company's policy under no circumstances will we ever sign a criminal complaint against anyone who commits a criminal act against persons or property in our care."

On the other hand, those companies that are taking appropriate preventive steps to combat cargo theft have the right to expect effective cooperation from law enforcement and other agencies. If, for example, a carrier heeds admonitions to prosecute cargo thieves, the company deserves better than to watch a solid case bounce from one prosecutor to another and ultimately be declined. Nor, as happened in one instance, should complainants have to appear in court eight times before proceedings finally get under way.

Assistance from State and Local Police

To doublecheck its own observations, management may want to seek the opinion of local law enforcement personnel about what they regard as the currently favored targets of cargo thieves. Studies indicate that on a nationwide basis, clothing and textiles, electrical machinery (including appliances), transportation equipment, jewelry and coins, food products, and metal products and hardware are at the top of the cargo theft list. Obviously, this varies according to location and mode of transport. For example, at a West Coast port the following goods, ranked according to frequency of loss, are among the favored targets: electronic equipment (radios, televisions, tape recorders), liquor, wearing apparel (knitwear, sweaters, shirts, suits), tires, bicycles, toys, shoes, sporting goods, auto parts, and food products (frozen meat, lobsters, cheese, tuna).

When a particular form of cargo theft, such as hijacking, is wide-spread in the area, local police can be expected to develop special procedures to deal with the problem—certainly something better than indicated in the following account of a trucking executive who described state and local police response to a reported hijacking.

> ... we had great evidence that the man was hijacked and we called the state police immediately and asked them to at least put a wire out, stop traffic as they go through tolls ... They stated they couldn't put a wire out, but to call the local police, which we did. And the local police wouldn't put a wire out until they had a detective come down to the office. And by the time the detective would come down and make out a report and then go back and put a wire out ... It is something to be in a booth with a communicator and know you are losing $60,000 and know you have absolutely no cooperation.

Fortunately, there are also highly effective police responses to hijack reports, including a special number for carriers to call in the event of a suspected hijack, a special detail ready to swing into action, a helicopter by which to spot the truck through identification numbers painted on the top of the trailer, and a collection of color photographs of local trucks that frequently haul especially theft-prone products. In addition, one department maintains a special file on everyone known to operate in, or on the fringes of, the truck-theft area. Finally, the department encourages carriers to take advantage of certain procedural and physical security measures.

In some cities, police are initiating special task forces comprised of officers from many different specialties who will be concerned with "thefts from airports, piers, loading platforms, delivery entrance, and ... the resale of stolen property through criminal receivers," as one chief of intelligence expressed it. Because cargo thieves and fences often engage in one or more illegal sidelines, such a task force will try to make a case against a fence on a gambling, forgery, narcotics, or even a traffic charge if court-worthy evidence relating to his fencing is unavailable.

At this writing, plans are being readied for one such task force to concentrate on identified individuals, representing 13 criminal groups, who are actively engaged in cargo theft in an eastern region. Obviously, extensive intelligence gathering forms the foundation of task force action. (And, unfortunately, because so much cargo theft is reported to no one, police intelligence often must determine whether there is a significant problem in the first place.)

Alert patrolmen can provide substantial assistance if they notice and report the following events:

1. Unusual activity at an unusual time occurs in a warehouse area.
2. A warehouse that is usually empty is now full.
3. Goods are transferred from the truck of a well-known company to an unmarked truck or vehicle; or goods are transferred from a rental vehicle to another unit.
4. Merchandise is transferred from a truck to the garage of a residence.
5. A truck is loaded at a location other than a depot or shipping dock.
6. A neighborhood outlet opens for business and then closes after a few weeks or months.
7. An outlet receives deliveries of goods that appear inconsistent with the nature of the business—e.g., bulky packages delivered to a coin shop.
8. Local merchants complain about a competitor's unbeatable prices.
9. A store seems to receive many deliveries but few customers.
10. A retailer's racks and shelves always seem sparsely stocked.
11. A truck appears abandoned.
12. Canvas covers the top of a truck, as if to conceal a painted identification number.
13. At certain hours, there is a consistent marked increase in "visitors" to a residence.
14. Packing cartons, left outside a store for refuse collection, bear labels with an address inconsistent with the store's displayed merchandise.
15. Goods delivered to an outlet are unloaded from the trunk of a car.
16. A retailer seems to have a perpetual sale, or a store remains in operation after a "going-out-of-business sale."
17. A pedestrian looks over the contents of a truck parked for a delivery. He returns to a car down the block.
18. A car circles a block where a truck is making a delivery.
19. Stopped for a traffic violation, a truck driver hesitates when asked about the nature of his load. He cannot produce appropriate cargo documentation.
20. An unusual number of patrons emerge from a tavern with packages.

In one city, the police are charged with enforcing comprehensive regulations directed at over 50 different types of businesses considered to be likely outlets for fencing or other forms of criminal or undesirable activity. Some kinds of businesses are prohibited entirely, such as flea markets. Both the premises and records of regulated businesses are subject to police inspection. Proprietors may be fingerprinted. Other regulations pertain to the location and hours of business, the maintenance of records and submission of reports, advertising, recovery of stolen property found on the premises, etc. Typifying the enforcement philosophy, a police official commented, "When an outlet advertises a going-out-of-business sale, it goes out of business."

Police units usually are more than willing to assist companies exposed to cargo theft by recommending various controls and security devices. Some units have conducted security surveys on request.

Sources of Other Local Help

In addition to the type of associations described in the previous section, one of the most useful private-sector organizations that may be available is a citizens' crime commission. It may be able to supply valuable intelligence and recommend practical countermeasures. Also, it may provide detailed information on the operation and weaknesses of the local criminal justice system (types of courts, their procedures, police effectiveness, attitude of prosecutors and judges toward cargo theft cases, etc.). The crime prevention unit of the local chamber of commerce also may be of substantial assistance in this regard.

In many areas, authorities or commissions may be charged with law enforcement responsibilities at local airports or piers. Obviously, an effective working relationship with such organizations will be beneficial.

DEPARTMENT OF JUSTICE

Under modern legal definitions, rare is the shipment that is not of an interstate character and the theft of which would not fall within the investigative jurisdiction of the FBI. During fiscal 1981 FBI investigations of such thefts resulted in 1106 convictions and savings and recoveries of about $14.5 million as explained by a publication of the FBI, its investigative jurisdiction over thefts of property and valuables involved in interstate or foreign commerce related to the following offenses:

1. Obtaining by theft or embezzlement or by fraud or deception any goods or chattels which are moving as, or constitute a part of, an interstate or foreign shipment.

2. Buying, receiving, or possessing such goods, or chattels, knowing that they were stolen, embezzled, or obtained by fraud or description.
3. Embezzling of certain monies of any corporation engaged in interstate or foreign commerce as a common carrier by employees or officers of that corporation.
4. Unlawfully breaking the seal or lock of, or entering with intent to commit larcency, any railroad car, truck, aircraft, vessel, or other vehicle containing interstate or foreign shipments.

The FBI has authority to investigate the above offenses no matter what the value of the stolen property. The maximum penalty for thefts from interstate shipments is imprisonment for 10 years and/or a $5000 fine for each offense. If the amount stolen does not exceed $100, the offender may be fined not more than $1000 and/or imprisoned for not more than one year. Interestingly, thefts of goods in intrastate commerce may also fall within FBI investigative jurisdiction if, during the course of the theft, the following occurs: a truck or airplane containing an intrastate shipment is stolen and driven across state lines; stolen property worth at least $5000 is transported across state lines by persons who know the goods were stolen; an intrastate shipment containing federal property is stolen.

According to the FBI, when there is doubt as to whether a cargo theft is or may become a violation of federal law, "the best policy is to call the nearest FBI office promptly and give a full account of the facts." Not only should the crime be reported but also any serial numbers that might be on the stolen goods. These numbers can be entered into the FBI's National Crime Information Center, a large computerized data bank of criminal and stolen property records through which much stolen cargo has been identified and recovered.

Caution: Do not assume that a Federal Prosecution will result because the FBI is investigating. This is a decision for United States attorneys, who may well decline prosecution for reasons previously noted.

If there are reasonable grounds to believe that organized crime is involved, a federal strike force might also be alerted, assuming one is operating in the area. Strike forces are operative in many cities and are staffed by Justice Department personnel as well as those of many other federal units, including the Bureau of Customs, Securities and Exchange Commission, Internal Revenue Service, Postal Service, Secret Service, and Department of Labor. The purpose of the strike forces is to bring the full weight of federal law enforcement to bear on certain organized criminals and to examine their activities from every possible angle to determine if prosecution is possible. Though hardly a certainty, a cargo theft incident reported to a strike force may involve organized criminals in whom the force has a current interest. If a strike force is not active in an area, cargo theft incidents clearly involving the organized underworld could be reported to the Organized Crime and Racketeering Section of the Department of Justice, Washington, D.C. In any event, however, the FBI primary unit to contact.

DEPARTMENT OF THE TREASURY

Through its Bureau of Customs, the treasury department has implemented a cargo security program at all 291 ports of entry. The rationale for this, of course, is that any theft or pilferage of merchandise occurring between the time it is landed from airplane or vessel and its release by customs for entry into United States commerce threatens the proper execution of two major responsibilities of customs: collection of duty and prevention of smuggling.

The treasury program is a three-part package. The first part seeks to establish closer accountability for imported cargo, from the time of unloading until delivery to the consignee or his agent. For example, customs inspectors have been directed to identify high-risk merchandise and shipments and to the extent possible, personally supervise its discharge. Also, at least 10% of the bills of lading are verified upon delivery to the onward carrier or importer. Through such procedures, the treasury department also hopes to accumulate statistics whereby it can pinpoint where losses are occurring and how much of what merchandise is being stolen.

The second part of the program focuses especially on secure storage and handling of cargo with a high value-to-weight ratio and on cargo with broken packaging. This aspect of the program strives to promote improved physical and procedural security through establishing elementary standards for the handling and storage of international cargo and providing for better authentication of pick-up orders and verification of delivered quantities.

At present, the final phase of the treasury program is pending before Congress. If passed, the legislation would give the Secretary of the Treasury authority to establish nationwide standards for physical and procedural security at seaports and airports of entry. These standards are considered minimal. Should these minimum standards not suffice in certain instances, the bill provides for the establishment of customs security areas, wherein more stringent measures would be authorized. According to a ranking treasury official, within six months to a year after passage of the legislation, cargo theft would be reduced to a minimum at all United States airports of entry, and would be reduced substantially at all seaports of entry within one year.

In January, 1972, the Treasury released a set of voluntary guidelines (Standards for Cargo Security), which "experts in industrial security believe should be implemented at cargo handling facilities to provide a minimum level of security."

There are many who maintain that the most effective deterrent to cargo theft at airports and seaports of entry is a customs presence. They declare that the biggest existing hole through which stolen cargo is pushed is the one represented by the lack of adequate stop-and-search authority by port security officers, who "no matter how well trained, are hesitant to stop a person even though they see him take a case of cargo and put it in a car—they are afraid of false arrest or false detention." However, customs personnel—inspectors, agents, and enforcement officers—are vested with unique powers of search and seizure in that they are not required to produce a warrant to show probable cause. No one pretends that customs presence will supplant private security guards or local police, simply that it will supply a very important link, heretofore often missing or too weak, in the chain of cargo security methods.

DEPARTMENT OF TRANSPORTATION

A basic reason for the Department of Transportation's increasing concern about, and reaction to, the cargo theft problem is evident from congressional testimony of a ranking transportation official:". . . one of the department's primary missions is to coordinate federal transportation policies and programs and relate these to the operations of the transportation industries. To the extent these programs and the transportation industries are adversely affected by criminal activities, our mission is accordingly affected."

Thus in 1971 the department established an Office of Transportation Security (OTS), which now is the department's focal point for providing leadership in all phases of cargo security. Not conflicting with the law enforcement or other activities of any other agency or department, OTS is concerned with the deterrence of cargo theft through various "preventive maintenance" measures and seeks to accomplish this not only by initiating its own programs and recommendations but also by stimulating coordination and cooperation among those federal agencies whose responsibilities can be brought to bear on the cargo theft problem.

To facilitate such coordination, the Department of Transportation sponsored the establishment of an Interagency Committee on Transportation Security to identify interagency responsibilities. Having held its first meeting in June, 1971, the committee approved a 12-point cargo security program in October, 1971. Various reports, recommendations, and publications will be issued for the benefit of users and suppliers of cargo transportation, among others. (The Committee is comprised of representatives from the Department of Transportation, State, Treasury, Commerce, Defense, Justice, and Labor; and from the Civil Aeronautics Board, Interstate Commerce Commission, Federal Maritime Commission, United States Postal Service, General Services Administration, Small Business Administration, and Atomic Energy Commission.)

The activities of other units within the Department of Transportation also relate to the cargo theft problem. For example, the Federal Aviation Administration supplies intelligence assistance to the Organized Crime and Racketeering Section of the Department of Justice by, among other things, determining whether known criminals are among currently certified pilots and owners of aircraft. The Coast Guard has intelligence operations in the areas of port security, smuggling, and other criminal activities involving vessels of the use of ports. More recently, the Coast Guard initiated a pilot program in which a number of reservist experts in security surveys on the waterfront and to advise on appropriate theft-prevention measures.

THE REGULATORY AGENCIES

The Civil Aeronautics Board, Federal Maritime Commission, and Interstate Commerce Commission also have roles to play in the overall effort to combat cargo theft. All, for example, are involved in designing a uniform loss-reporting system by which to put the cargo-theft problem into better focus. All periodically review claims-processing methods and liability limits of carriers. All can encourage carriers to engage in joint discussions leading to the establishment of better security practices. All can be receptive to carrier proposals to organize joint action associations along the lines discussed in a preceding section. All can review their regulations to determine if they cause undue delays and thereby increase the exposure of cargo to theft. All could be attuned to theft-prevention suggestions and determine the extent to which regulatory authority permits across-the-board implementation by agency action. For example, some truckers interviewed for this book expressed the desire for a regulation that would require shippers to forward a duplicate bill of lading to carrier management as a control by which to determine if the driver had altered his copy. Others would like a more standardized bill of lading, with requirements pertaining to dimensions, paper grade, legibility, common elements in common locations, etc., the point being that this would reduce confusion, increase accuracy, better fix accountability, and thereby improve the cargo theft picture.

Finally, in view of the current impact of cargo theft on carriers and on the shipping public, all could review whether their existing regulatory authority could, by logical interpretation, be extended in some cases into the cargo security area.

Index

WALK TWO MOONS
BY SHARON CREECH

HarperTrophy®
An Imprint of HarperCollins*Publishers*

For my sister and brothers:
Sandy, Dennis, Doug, Tom
with love
from
The Favorite

Harper Trophy® is a registered trademark of HarperCollins Publishers Inc.

Walk Two Moons
Copyright © 1994 by Sharon Creech
Printed in the United States of America. For information address
HarperCollins Children's Books, a division of HarperCollins Publishers,
1350 Avenue of the Americas, New York, NY 10019.

Library of Congress Cataloging-in-Publication Data
Creech, Sharon.
   Walk two moons / by Sharon Creech.
      p.   cm.
   Summary: After her mother leaves home suddenly, thirteen-year-old Sal
and her grandparents take a car trip retracing her mother's route. Along
the way, Sal recounts the story of her friend Phoebe, whose mother also
left.
   ISBN 0-06-023334-6. — ISBN 0-06-023337-0 (lib. bdg.)
   ISBN 0-06-440517-6 (pbk.) — ISBN 0-06-056013-4 (rack)
   ISBN 0-06-073949-5 (special ed. pbk.)
   [1. Death—Fiction. 2. Grandparents—Fiction. 3. Family life—Fiction.
4. Friendship—Fiction.] I. Title.
PZ7.C8615Wal 1994   93-31277
[Fic]—dc20   CIP
                                                                    AC

Typography by Alicia Mikles
❖
First Harper Trophy edition, 1996

Visit us on the World Wide Web!
www.harperchildrens.com

DON'T JUDGE A MAN UNTIL YOU'VE WALKED
TWO MOONS IN HIS MOCCASINS.

CONTENTS

1
A FACE AT THE WINDOW

GRAMPS SAYS THAT I AM A COUNTRY GIRL AT HEART, and that is true. I have lived most of my thirteen years in Bybanks, Kentucky, which is not much more than a caboodle of houses roosting in a green spot alongside the Ohio River. Just over a year ago, my father plucked me up like a weed and took me and all our belongings (no, that is not true—he did not bring the chestnut tree, the willow, the maple, the hayloft, or the swimming hole, which all belonged to me) and we drove three hundred miles straight north and stopped in front of a house in Euclid, Ohio.

"No trees?" I said. "This is where we're going to live?"

"No," my father said. "This is Margaret's house."

The front door of the house opened and a lady with wild red hair stood there. I looked up and

down the street. The houses were all jammed together like a row of birdhouses. In front of each
house was a tiny square of grass, and in front of
that was a thin gray sidewalk running alongside a
gray road.

"Where's the barn?" I asked. "The river? The
swimming hole?"

"Oh, Sal," my father said. "Come on. There's
Margaret." He waved to the lady at the door.

"We have to go back. I forgot something."

The lady with the wild red hair opened the
door and came out onto the porch.

"In the back of my closet," I said, "under the
floorboards. I put something there, and I've got to
have it."

"Don't be a goose. Come and see Margaret."

I did not want to see Margaret. I stood there,
looking around, and that's when I saw the face
pressed up against an upstairs window next door. It
was a round girl's face, and it looked afraid. I didn't
know it then, but that face belonged to Phoebe
Winterbottom, a girl who had a powerful imagination, who would become my friend, and who
would have many peculiar things happen to her.

Not long ago, when I was locked in a car with
my grandparents for six days, I told them the story

of Phoebe, and when I finished telling them—or maybe even as I was telling them—I realized that the story of Phoebe was like the plaster wall in our old house in Bybanks, Kentucky.

My father started chipping away at a plaster wall in the living room of our house in Bybanks shortly after my mother left us one April morning. Our house was an old farmhouse that my parents had been restoring, room by room. Each night as he waited to hear from my mother, he chipped away at that wall.

On the night that we got the bad news—that she was not returning—he pounded and pounded on that wall with a chisel and a hammer. At two o'clock in the morning, he came up to my room. I was not asleep. He led me downstairs and showed me what he had found. Hidden behind the wall was a brick fireplace.

The reason that Phoebe's story reminds me of that plaster wall and the hidden fireplace is that beneath Phoebe's story was another one. Mine.

2
THE CHICKABIDDY
STARTS A STORY

IT WAS AFTER ALL THE ADVENTURES OF PHOEBE that my grandparents came up with a plan to drive from Kentucky to Ohio, where they would pick me up, and then the three of us would drive two thousand miles west to Lewiston, Idaho. This is how I came to be locked in a car with them for nearly a week. It was not a trip that I was eager to take, but it was one I had to take.

Gramps had said, "We'll see the whole ding-dong country!"

Gram squeezed my cheeks and said, "This trip will give me a chance to be with my favorite chickabiddy again." I am, by the way, their *only* chickabiddy.

My father said that Gram couldn't read maps worth a hill of beans, and that he was grateful that I had agreed to go along and help them find their

4

way. I was only thirteen, and although I did have a way with maps, it was not really because of that skill that I was going, nor was it to see the "whole ding-dong country" that Gram and Gramps were going. The real reasons were buried beneath piles and piles of unsaid things.

Some of the real reasons were:

1. Gram and Gramps wanted to see Momma, who was resting peacefully in Lewiston, Idaho.

2. Gram and Gramps knew that I wanted to see Momma, but that I was afraid to.

3. Dad wanted to be alone with the red-headed Margaret Cadaver. He had already seen Momma, and he had not taken me.

Also—although this wasn't as important—Dad did not trust Gram and Gramps to behave themselves along the way unless they had me with them. Dad said that if they tried to go on their own, he would save everyone a lot of time and embarrassment by calling the police and having them arrested before they even left the driveway. It might sound a bit extreme for a man to call the police on his own tottery old parents, but when my grandparents got in a car, trouble just naturally followed them like a filly trailing behind a mare.

My grandparents Hiddle were my father's parents, full up to the tops of their heads with goodness and sweetness, and mixed in with all that goodness and sweetness was a large dash of peculiarity. This combination made them interesting to know, but you could never predict what they would do or say.

Once it was settled that the three of us would go, the journey took on an alarming, expanding need to hurry that was like a walloping great thundercloud assembling around me. During the week before we left, the sound of the wind was *hurry, hurry, hurry*, and at night even the silent darkness whispered *rush, rush, rush.* I did not think we would ever leave, and yet I did not want to leave. I did not really expect to survive the trip.

But I had decided to go and I would go, and I had to be there by my mother's birthday. This was extremely important. I believed that if there was any chance to bring my mother back home it would happen on her birthday. If I had said this aloud to my father or to my grandparents, they would have said that I might as well try to catch a fish in the air, so I did not say it aloud. But I believed it. Sometimes I am as ornery and stubborn as an old donkey. My father says I lean on broken reeds and will get a face full of swamp mud one day.

When at last Gram and Gramps Hiddle and I set out that first day of the trip, I prayed for the first thirty minutes solid. I prayed that we would not be in an accident (I was terrified of cars and buses) and that we would get there by my mother's birthday—seven days away—and that we would bring her home. Over and over, I prayed the same thing. I prayed to trees. This was easier than praying directly to God. There was nearly always a tree nearby.

As we pulled onto the Ohio Turnpike, which is the flattest, straightest piece of road in God's whole creation, Gram interrupted my prayers. "Salamanca—"

I should explain right off that my real name is Salamanca Tree Hiddle. Salamanca, my parents thought, was the name of the Indian tribe to which my great-great-grandmother belonged. My parents were mistaken. The name of the tribe was Seneca, but since my parents did not discover their error until after I was born and they were, by then, used to my name, it remained Salamanca.

My middle name, Tree, comes from your basic

tree, a thing of such beauty to my mother that she made it part of my name. She wanted to be more specific and use Sugar Maple Tree, her very favorite, but Salamanca Sugar Maple Tree Hiddle was a bit much even for her.

My mother used to call me Salamanca, but after she left, only my grandparents Hiddle called me Salamanca (when they were not calling me chickabiddy). To most other people, I was Sal, and to a few boys who thought they were especially amusing, I was Salamander.

In the car, as we started our long journey to Lewiston, Idaho, my grandmother Hiddle said, "Salamanca, why don't you entertain us?"

"What sort of thing did you have in mind?"

Gramps said, "How about a story? Spin us a yarn."

I certainly do know heaps of stories, but I learned most of them from Gramps. Gram suggested I tell one about my mother. That I could not do. I had just reached the point where I could stop thinking about her every minute of every day.

Gramps said, "Well then, what about your friends? You got any tales to tell about them?"

Instantly, Phoebe Winterbottom came to mind. There was certainly a hog's belly full of things to tell about her. "I could tell you an extensively strange story," I warned.

"Oh, good!" Gram said. "Delicious!"

And that is how I happened to suspend my tree prayers and tell them about Phoebe Winterbottom, her disappearing mother, and the lunatic.

3
BRAVERY

BECAUSE I FIRST SAW PHOEBE ON THE DAY MY father and I moved to Euclid, I began my story of Phoebe with the visit to the red-headed Margaret Cadaver's, where I also met Mrs. Partridge, her elderly mother. Margaret nearly fell over herself being nice to me. "What lovely hair," she said, and "Aren't you sweet!" I was *not* sweet that day. I was being particularly ornery. I wouldn't sit down and I wouldn't look at Margaret.

As we were leaving, Margaret whispered to my father, "John, have you told her yet—how we met?"

My father looked uncomfortable. "No," he said. "I tried—but she doesn't want to know."

Now that was the truth, absolutely. Who cares? I thought. Who cares how he met Margaret Cadaver?

When at last we left Mrs. Cadaver and Mrs.

Partridge, we drove for approximately three minutes. Two blocks from Margaret Cadaver's was the
place where my father and I were now going to
live.

Tiny, squirt trees. Little birdhouses in a row—
and one of those birdhouses was ours. No swimming hole, no barn, no cows, no chickens, no pigs.
Instead, a little white house with a miniature patch
of green grass in front of it. It wasn't enough grass
to keep a cow alive for five minutes.

"Let's take a tour," my father said, rather too
heartily.

We walked through the tiny living room into
the miniature kitchen and upstairs into my father's
pint-sized bedroom and on into my pocket-sized
bedroom and into the wee bathroom. I looked out
the upstairs window down into the backyard. Half
of the tiny yard was a cement patio and the other
half was another patch of grass that our imaginary
cow would devour in two bites. There was a tall
wooden fence all around the yard, and to the left
and right of our yard were other, identical fenced
plots.

After the moving van arrived and two men
crammed our Bybanks furniture into our bird-
house, my father and I inched into the living room,

crawling over sofas and chairs and tables and boxes, boxes, boxes. "Mm," my father said. "It looks as if we tried to squeeze all the animals into the chicken coop."

Three days later, I started school and saw Phoebe again. She was in my class. Most of the kids in my new school spoke in quick, sharp bursts and dressed in stiff, new clothes and wore braces on their teeth. Most girls wore their hair in exactly the same way: in a shoulder-length "bob" (that's what they called it) with long bangs that they repeatedly shook out of their eyes. We once had a horse who did that.

Everybody kept touching my hair. "Don't you ever cut it?" they said. "Can you sit on it? How do you wash it? Is it naturally black like that? Do you use conditioner?" I couldn't tell if they liked my hair or if they thought I looked like a whangdoodle.

One girl, Mary Lou Finney, said the most peculiar things, like out of the blue she would say, "Omnipotent!" or "Beef brain!" I couldn't make any sense of it. There were Megan and Christy, who jumped up and down like parched peas, moody Beth Ann, and pink-cheeked Alex. There was Ben, who drew cartoons all day long, and a peculiar

English teacher named Mr. Birkway.

And then there was Phoebe Winterbottom. Ben called her "Free Bee Ice Bottom" and drew a picture of a bumblebee with an ice cube on its bottom. Phoebe tore it up.

Phoebe was a quiet girl who stayed mostly by herself. She had a pleasant round face and huge, enormous sky-blue eyes. Around this pleasant round face, her hair—as yellow as a crow's foot—curled in short ringlets.

During that first week, when my father and I were at Margaret's (we ate dinner there three times that week), I saw Phoebe's face twice more at her window. Once I waved at her, but she didn't seem to notice, and at school she never mentioned that she had seen me.

Then one day at lunch, she slid into the seat next to me and said, "Sal, you're so courageous. You're ever so brave."

To tell you the truth, I was surprised. You could have knocked me over with a chicken feather. "Me? I'm not brave," I said.

"You are. You are brave."

I was not. I, Salamanca Tree Hiddle, was afraid of lots and lots of things. For example, I was terrified of car accidents, death, cancer, brain tumors, nuclear war, pregnant women, loud noises, strict teachers, elevators, and scads of other things. But I was not afraid of spiders, snakes, and wasps. Phoebe, and nearly everyone else in my new class, did not have much fondness for these creatures.

But on that day, when a dignified black spider was investigating my desk, I cupped my hands around it, carried it to the open window, and set it outside on the ledge. Mary Lou Finney said, "Alpha and Omega, will you look at that!" Beth Ann was as white as milk. All around the room, people were acting as if I had singlehandedly taken on a fire-breathing dragon.

What I have since realized is that if people expect you to be brave, sometimes you pretend that you are, even when you are frightened down to your very bones. But this was later, during the whole thing with Phoebe's lunatic, that I realized this.

At this point in my story, Gram interrupted me to say, "Why, Salamanca, of course you're brave. All the Hiddles are brave. It's a family trait. Look at your daddy—your momma—"

"Momma's not a real Hiddle," I said.

"She practically is," Gram said. "You can't be married to a Hiddle that long and not *become* a Hiddle."

That is not what my mother used to say. She would tell my father, "You Hiddles are a mystery to me. I'll never be a true Hiddle." She did not say this proudly. She said it as if she were sorry about it, as if it were some sort of failing in her.

My mother's parents—my other set of grandparents—are Pickfords, and they are as unlike my grandparents Hiddle as a donkey is unlike a pickle. Grandmother and Grandfather Pickford stand straight up, as if sturdy, steel poles ran down their backs. They wear starched, ironed clothing, and when they are shocked or surprised (which is often), they say, "Really? Is that so?" and their eyes open wide and their mouths turn down at the corners.

Once I asked my mother why Grandmother and Grandfather Pickford never laughed. My mother said, "They're just so busy being respectable. It takes a lot of concentration to be that respectable." And then my mother laughed and laughed, in a gentle way, and you could tell her own spine was not made of steel because she bent in half, laughing and laughing.

My mother said that Grandmother Pickford's one act of defiance in her whole life as a Pickford was in naming her. Grandmother Pickford, whose own name is Gayfeather, named my mother Chanhassen. It's an Indian name, meaning "tree sweet juice," or—in other words—maple sugar. Only Grandmother Pickford ever called my mother by her Indian name, though. Everyone else called my mother Sugar.

Most of the time, my mother seemed nothing like her parents at all, and it was hard for me to imagine that she had come from them. But occasionally, in small, unexpected moments, the corners of my mother's mouth would turn down and she'd say, "Really? Is that so?" and sound exactly like a Pickford.

4
THAT'S WHAT I'M TELLING YOU

ON THE DAY THAT PHOEBE SAT NEXT TO ME AT lunch and told me I was brave, she invited me to her house for dinner. To be honest, I was relieved that I would not have to eat at Margaret's again. I did not want to see Dad and Margaret smiling at each other.

I wanted everything to be like it *was*. I wanted to be back in Bybanks, Kentucky, in the hills and the trees, near the cows and chickens and pigs. I wanted to run down the hill from the barn and through the kitchen door that banged behind me and see my mother and my father sitting at the table peeling apples.

Phoebe and I walked home from school together. We stopped briefly at my house so that I could call my father at work. Margaret had helped him find a job selling farm machinery. He said it made him happy as a clam at high water to know I had a new friend. Maybe this is really why he was happy, I thought, or maybe it was because he could be alone with Margaret Cadaver.

Phoebe and I then walked to her house. As we passed Margaret Cadaver's house, a voice called out. "Sal? Sal? Is that you?"

In the shadows on the porch, Margaret's mother, Mrs. Partridge, sat in a wicker rocker. A thick, gnarled cane with a handle carved in the shape of a cobra's head lay across her knees. Her purple dress had slipped up over her bony knees, which were spread apart, and I hate to say it, but you could see right up her skirt. Around her neck was a yellow feather scarf. ("My boa," she once told me, "my most favoritest boa.")

As I started up the walk, Phoebe pulled on my arm. "Don't go up there," she said.

"It's only Mrs. Partridge," I said. "Come on."

"Who's that with you?" Mrs. Partridge said. "What's that on her face?" I knew what she was going to do. She did this with me the first time I met her.

Phoebe placed her hands on her own round face and felt about.

"Come here," Mrs. Partridge said. She wriggled

her crooked little fingers at Phoebe.

Mrs. Partridge put her fingers up to Phoebe's face and mashed around gently over her eyelids and down her cheeks. "Just as I thought. It's two eyes, a nose, and a mouth." Mrs. Partridge laughed a wicked laugh that sounded as if it were bouncing off jagged rocks. "You're thirteen years old."

"Yes," Phoebe said.

"I knew it," Mrs. Partridge said. "I just knew it." She patted her yellow feather boa.

"This is Phoebe Winterbottom," I said. "She lives right next door to you."

When we left, Phoebe whispered, "I wish you hadn't done that. I wish you hadn't told her I lived next door."

"Why not? You don't seem to know Mrs. Cadaver and Mrs. Partridge very well—"

"They haven't lived there very long. Only a month or so."

"Don't you think it's remarkable that she guessed your age?"

"I don't see what is so remarkable about it." Before I could explain, Phoebe started telling me about the time that she and her mother, father, and sister, Prudence, had gone to the State Fair. At one booth, a crowd was gathered around a tall, thin man.

"So what was he doing?" I asked.

"That's what I'm telling you," Phoebe said. Phoebe had a way of sounding like a grown-up sometimes. When she said, "That's what I'm telling you," she sounded like a grown-up talking to a child. "What he was doing was guessing people's ages. All around, people were saying, 'Oh!' and 'Amazing!' and 'How does he do that?' He had to guess your correct age within one year or else you won a teddy bear."

"How did he do it?" I asked.

"That's what I'm telling you," Phoebe said. "The thin man would look someone over carefully, close his eyes, and then he would point his finger at the person and shout, 'Seventy-two!'"

"At everyone? He guessed everyone to be seventy-two?"

"Sal," she said. "That's what I am trying to tell you. I was just giving an example. He might have said 'ten' or 'thirty' or—'seventy-two.' It just depended on the person. He was astounding."

I really thought it was more astounding that Mrs. Partridge could do this, but I didn't say anything.

Phoebe's father wanted the thin man to guess his age. "My father thinks he looks very young, and he was certain he could fool the man. After study-ing my father, the thin man closed his eyes, pointed his finger at my father and shouted, 'Fifty-two!' My father gave a little yelp, and all around people were automatically saying, 'Oh!' and 'Amazing' and all that. But my father stopped them."

"Why?"

Phoebe pulled on one of her yellow curls. I think she wished she hadn't started this story in the first place. "Because he wasn't anywhere near fifty-two. He was only thirty-eight."

"Oh."

"And all day long, my father followed us through the fair, carrying his prize, a large, green teddy bear. He was miserable. He kept saying, 'Fifty-two? *Fifty-two?* Do I look fifty-two?'"

"Does he?" I said.

Phoebe pulled harder on her hair. "No, he does not look fifty-two. He looks thirty-eight." She was very defensive about her father.

Phoebe's mother was in the kitchen. "I'm making blackberry pie," Mrs. Winterbottom said. "I hope you like blackberries—is there something wrong? Really, if you don't like blackberries, I could—"

"No," I said. "I like blackberries very much. I

just have some allergies, I think."

"To blackberries?" Mrs. Winterbottom said.

"No, not to blackberries." The truth is, I do not have allergies, but I could not admit that blackberries reminded me of my mother.

Mrs. Winterbottom made me and Phoebe sit down at the kitchen table and tell her about our day. Phoebe told her about Mrs. Partridge guessing her age.

"She's really remarkable," I said.

Phoebe said, "It's not *that* remarkable, Sal. I wouldn't exactly use the word *remarkable*."

"But Phoebe," I said. "Mrs. Partridge is blind."

Both Phoebe and her mother said, *"Blind?"*

Later, Phoebe said to me, "Don't you think it's odd that Mrs. Partridge, who is blind, could see something about me—but I, who can see, was blind about her? And speaking of odd, there's something very odd about that Mrs. Cadaver."

"Margaret?" I said.

"She scares me half to death," Phoebe said.

"Why?"

"That's what I'm telling you," she said. "First, there is that name: *Cadaver*. You know what cadaver means?"

Actually, I did not.

"It means *dead body*."

"Are you sure?" I said.

"Of course I'm sure, Sal. You can check the dictionary if you want. Do you know what she does for a living—what her job is?"

"Yes," I was pleased to say. I was pleased to know *something*. "She's a nurse."

"Exactly," Phoebe said. "Would you want a nurse whose name meant *dead body*? And that hair—don't you think all that sticking-out red hair is *spooky*? And that voice—it reminds me of dead leaves all blowing around on the ground."

This was Phoebe's power. In her world, no one was ordinary. People were either perfect—like her father—or, more often, they were lunatics or axe murderers. She could convince me of just about anything—especially about Margaret Cadaver. From that day on, Margaret Cadaver's hair did look spooky and her voice did sound exactly like dead leaves. Somehow it was easier to deal with Margaret if there were *reasons* not to like her, and I definitely did not want to like her.

"Do you want to know an absolute secret?" Phoebe said. (I did.) "Promise not to tell." (I promised.) "Maybe I shouldn't," she said. "Your father goes over there all the time. He likes her, doesn't he?" She twirled her finger through her curly hair and let those big blue eyes roam over the ceiling. "Her name is *Mrs.* Cadaver, right? Have you ever wondered what happened to *Mr.* Cadaver?"

"I never really thought about—"

"Well, I think I know," Phoebe said, "and it is awful, purely awful."

5

A Damsel in Distress

At this point in my story about Phoebe, Gram said, "I knew somebody like Peeby once."

"*Phoebe,*" I said.

"Yes, that's right. I knew someone just like Peeby, only her name was Gloria. Gloria lived in the wildest, most pepped-up world—a scary one, but oh!—scads more exciting than my own."

Gramps said, "Gloria? Is she the one who told you not to marry me? Is she the one who said I would be your ruination?"

"Shoosh," Gram said. "Gloria was right about that at least." She elbowed Gramps. "Besides, Gloria only said that because she wanted you for herself."

"Gol-dang!" Gramps said, pulling into a rest stop along the Ohio Turnpike. "I'm tired."

I did not want to stop. *Rush, rush, rush* whispered the wind, the sky, the clouds, the trees. *Rush, rush, rush.*

If all he wanted to do was take a rest, that seemed a safe enough and quick enough thing for him to do. My grandparents can get into trouble as easily as a fly can land on a watermelon.

Two years ago when they drove to Washington, D.C., they were arrested for stealing the back tires off a senator's car. "We had two flat, sprunkled tires," my grandfather explained. "We were only *borrowing* the senator's tires. We were going to return them." In Bybanks, Kentucky, you could do this. You could borrow someone's back tires and return them later, but you could not do this in Washington, D.C., and you could especially not do this to a senator's car.

Last year when Gram and Gramps drove to Philadelphia, they were stopped by the police for irresponsible driving. "You were driving on the shoulder," a policeman told Gramps. Gramps said, "Shoulder? I thought it was an extra lane. That's a mighty fine shoulder."

So here we were, just a few hours into our trip out to Lewiston, Idaho, and we were safely stopped in a rest area. Then Gramps noticed a woman leaning over the fender of her car. The woman was peering at her engine and dabbing a white handkerchief at various greasy items inside.

"Excuse me," Gramps said gallantly. "I believe I see a damsel in some distress," and off he marched to her rescue.

Gram sat there patting her knees and singing, "Oh meet me, in the tulips, when the tulips do bloooom—"

The woman's white handkerchief, now spotted with black grease, dangled from her fingertips as she smiled down on the back of Gramps, who had taken her place leaning over the engine.

"Might be the car-bust-er-ator," he said, "or maybe not." He tapped a few hoses. "Might be these dang snakes," he said.

"Oh my," the woman said. "Snakes? In my engine?"

Gramps waggled a hose. "This here is what I call a snake," he said.

"Oh, I see," the woman said. "And you think those—those snakes might be the problem?"

"Maybe so." Gramps pulled on one and it came loose. "See there?" he said. "It's off."

"Well, yes, but you—"

"Dang snakes," Gramps said, pulling at another one. It came loose. "Lookee there, another one."

The woman smiled a thin, little, worried smile. "But—"

Two hours later, there was not a single "snake" still attached to anything to which it was supposed to be attached. The "car-bust-erator" lay dismantled on the ground. Various other pieces of the woman's engine were scattered here and there.

The woman called a mechanic, and once Gramps was satisfied that the mechanic was an honest man who might actually be able to repair her car, we started on our trip again.

"Salamanca," Gram said, "tell us more about Peeby."

"Phoebe," I said. "Phoebe Winterbottom."

"Yes, that's right," Gram said. "Peeby."

6
BLACKBERRIES

"WHAT WAS THE DIABOLIC THING THAT HAPPENED to Mr. Cadaver?" Gramps asked. "You didn't tell us that yet."

I explained that just as Phoebe was going to divulge the purely awful thing that had happened to Mr. Cadaver, her father came home from work and we all sat down to dinner: me, Phoebe, Mr. and Mrs. Winterbottom, and Phoebe's sister, Prudence.

Phoebe's parents reminded me a lot of my other grandparents—the Pickfords. Like the Pickfords, Mr. and Mrs. Winterbottom spoke quietly, in short sentences, and sat straight up as they ate their food. They were extremely polite to each other, saying "Yes, Norma," and "Yes, George," and "Would you please pass the potatoes, Phoebe?" and "Wouldn't your guest like another helping?"

They were picky about their food. Everything they ate was what my father would call "side dishes": potatoes, zucchini, bean salad, and a mystery casserole that I could not identify. They didn't eat meat, and they didn't use butter. They were very much concerned with cholesterol.

From what I could gather, Mr. Winterbottom worked in an office, creating road maps. Mrs. Winterbottom baked and cleaned and did laundry and grocery shopping. I had a funny feeling that Mrs. Winterbottom did not actually like all this baking and cleaning and laundry and shopping, and I'm not quite sure why I had that feeling because if you just listened to the *words* she said, it sounded as if she was Mrs. Supreme Housewife.

For example, at one point Mrs. Winterbottom said, "I believe I've made more pies in the past week than I can count." She said this in a cheery voice, but afterward, in the small silence, when no one commented on her pies, she gave a soft sigh and looked down at her plate. I thought it was odd that she baked all those pies when she seemed so concerned about cholesterol.

A little later, she said, "I couldn't find exactly that brand of muesli you like so much, George, but I bought something similar." Mr. Winterbottom kept eating, and again, in that silence, Mrs. Winterbottom sighed and examined her plate.

I was happy for her when she announced that since Phoebe and Prudence were back in school, she thought she would return to work. Apparently, during the school terms she worked part-time at Rocky's Rubber as a receptionist. When no one commented on her going back to work, she sighed again and poked her potatoes.

A few times, Mrs. Winterbottom called her husband "sweetie pie" and "honey bun." She said, "Would you like more zucchini, sweetie pie?" and "Did I make enough potatoes, honey bun?"

For some reason that surprised me, those little names she used. She was dressed in a plain brown skirt and white blouse. On her feet were sensible, wide, flat shoes. She did not wear makeup. Even though she had a pleasant, round face and long, curly yellow hair, the main impression I got was that she was used to being plain and ordinary, that she was not supposed to do anything too shocking.

And Mr. Winterbottom was playing the role of Father, with a capital *F*. He sat at the head of the table with his white shirt cuffs rolled back neatly. He still wore his red-and-blue–striped tie. His expression was serious, his voice was deep, and his words were clear. "Yes, Norma," he said, deeply and clearly. "No, Norma." He looked more like fifty-two than thirty-eight, but this was not something I would ever call to his—or Phoebe's—attention.

Phoebe's sister, Prudence, was seventeen years old, but she acted like her mother. She ate primly, she nodded politely, she smiled after everything she said.

It all seemed peculiar. They acted so thumpingly *tidy* and *respectable*.

After dinner, Phoebe walked me home. She said, "You wouldn't think it to look at her, but Mrs. Cadaver is as strong as an ox." Phoebe looked behind her, as if she expected someone to be following us. "I have seen her chop down trees and lug the remains clear across her backyard. Do you know what I think? I think maybe she killed Mr. Cadaver and chopped him up and buried him in the backyard."

"Phoebe!" I said.

"Well, I'm just telling you what I think, that's all."

That night, as I lay in bed, I thought about Mrs. Cadaver, and I wanted to believe that she was capable of killing her husband and chopping him into pieces and burying him in the backyard.

And then I started thinking about the blackberries, and I remembered a time my mother and I walked around the rims of the fields and pastures in Bybanks, picking blackberries. We did not pick from the bottom of the vine or from the top. The ones at the bottom were for the rabbits, my mother said, and the ones at the top were for the birds. The ones at people-height were for people.

Lying in bed, remembering those blackberries, made me think of something else too. It was something that happened a couple years ago, on a morning when my mother slept late. It was that time she was pregnant. My father had already eaten breakfast, and he was out in the fields. On the table, my father had left a single flower in each of two juice glasses—a black-eyed susan in front of my place, and a white petunia in front of my mother's.

When my mother came into the kitchen that day, she said, "Glory!" She bent her face toward each flower. "Let's go find him."

We climbed the hill to the barn, crawled between the fence wires, and crossed the field. My father was standing at the far end of the field, his back to us, hands on his hips, looking at a section of fence.

My mother slowed down when she saw him. I was right behind her. It looked as if she wanted to creep up and surprise him, so I was quiet too and cautious in my steps. I could hardly keep from giggling. It seemed so daring to be sneaking up on my father, and I was sure my mother was going to throw her arms around him and kiss him and hug him and tell him how much she loved the flower on the kitchen table. My mother always loved anything that normally grows or lives out of doors—*anything*—lizards, trees, cows, caterpillars, birds, flowers, crickets, toads, ants, pigs.

Just before we reached my father, he turned around. This startled my mother and threw her off guard. She stopped.

"Sugar—" he said.

My mother opened her mouth, and I was thinking, "Come on! Throw your arms around him! Tell him!" But before she could speak, my father pointed to the fence and said, "Look at that. A morning's work." He indicated a new length of wire strung between two new posts. There was sweat on his face and arms.

And then I saw that my mother was crying. My father saw it too. "What—" he said.

"Oh, you're too *good*, John," she said. "You're too *good*. All you Hiddles are too good. I'll never be so good. I'll never be able to think of all the things—"

My father looked down at me. "The flowers," I said.

"Oh." He put his sweaty arms around her, but she was still crying and it wasn't what I had imagined it would be. It was all sad instead of happy.

The next morning when I went into the kitchen, my father was standing beside the table looking at two small dishes of blackberries—still shiny and wet with dew—one dish at his place and one at mine. "Thanks," I said.

"No, it wasn't me," he said. "It was your mother."

Just then, she came in from the back porch. My father put his arms around her and they smooched and it was all tremendously romantic, and I started to turn away, but my mother caught my arm. She pulled me to her and said to me—though it was meant for my father, I think—"See? I'm *almost* as good as your father!" She said it in a shy way, laughing a little. I felt betrayed, but I didn't know why.

It is surprising all the things you remember just by eating a blackberry pie.

7
ILL-AH-NO-WAY

"WELL, LOOKEE HERE!" GRAMPS SHOUTED. "THE Illinois state line!" He pronounced Illinois "Ill-ah-no-way," exactly the way everyone in Bybanks, Kentucky, pronounced it, and hearing that "Ill-ah-no-way" made me suddenly homesick for Bybanks.

"What happened to Indiana?" Gram said.

"Why, you gooseberry," Gramps said. "That's where we've been the past three hours, barreling through Indiana. You've been listening to the story of Peeby and plumb missed Indiana. Don't you remember Elkhart? We ate lunch in Elkhart. Don't you remember South Bend? You took a pee in South Bend. Why, you missed the entire Hoosier state! You gooseberry." He thought this was very funny.

Just then, the road curved (it actually *curved*—this was a shock), and off to the right was a huge jing-bang mass of water. It was as blue as the blue-

36

bells that grow behind the barn in Bybanks, and that water just went on and on—it was all you could see. It looked like a huge blue pasture of water.

"Are we at the ocean?" Gram asked. "We're not supposed to be passing the ocean, are we?"

"You gooseberry, that's Lake Michigan." Gramps kissed his finger and put it against Gram's cheek.

"I sure would like to put my feet in that water," Gram said.

Gramps swerved across two lanes of traffic and onto the exit ramp, and faster than you could milk a cow we were standing barefoot in the cool water of Lake Michigan. The waves splashed up on our clothes, and the sea gulls flew in circles overhead, calling in one great chorus, as if they were glad to see us.

"Huzza, huzza!" Gram said, wriggling her heels into the sand. "Huzza, huzza!"

We stopped that night on the outskirts of Chicago. I looked around at what I could see of Ill-ah-no-way from the Howard Johnson Motel, and it might as well have been seven thousand miles from the lake. It all looked precisely like northern Ohio to me, with its flat land and long, straight roads, and I thought what a very long journey this was going to be. With the dark came the whispers: *rush, hurry, rush*.

That night I lay there trying to imagine Lewiston, Idaho, but my mind would not go forward to a place I had never been. Instead, I kept drifting back to Bybanks.

When my mother left for Lewiston, Idaho, that April, my first thoughts were, "How could she do that? How could she leave me?"

As the days went on, many things were harder and sadder, but some things were strangely easier. When my mother had been there, I was like a mirror. If she was happy, I was happy. If she was sad, I was sad. For the first few days after she left, I felt numb, non-feeling. I didn't know how to feel. I would find myself looking around for her, to see what I might want to feel.

One day, about two weeks after she had left, I was standing against the fence watching a newborn calf wobble on its thin legs. It tripped and wobbled and swung its big head in my direction and gave me a sweet, loving look. "Oh!" I thought. "I am happy at this moment in time." I was surprised that I knew this all by myself, without my mother there. And that night in bed, I did not cry. I said to myself, "Salamanca Tree Hiddle, you can be happy without her." It seemed a mean thought and I was sorry for it, but it *felt* true.

In the motel, as I was remembering these things, Gram came and sat on the edge of my bed. She said, "Do you miss your daddy? Do you want to call him?"

I did miss him, and I did want to call him, but I said, "No, I'm fine, really." He might think I was a goose if I had to call him already.

"Okay, then, chickabiddy," Gram said, and when she leaned over to kiss me, I could smell the baby powder she always used. That smell made me feel sad, but I didn't know why.

The next morning, when we got lost leaving Chicago, I prayed: "Please don't let us get in an accident, please get us there in time—"

Gramps said, "At least it's a mighty fine day for a drive." When we finally found a road heading west, we took it. Our plan was to curve across the lower part of Wisconsin, veer into Minnesota, and then barrel straight on through Minnesota, South Dakota, and Wyoming, sweep up into Montana, and cross the Rocky Mountains into Idaho. Gramps figured it would take us about a day in each state. He didn't intend to stop too much until we reached South Dakota, and he was really looking forward to South Dakota. "We're gonna see the Badlands," he said. "We're gonna see the Black Hills."

I didn't like the sound of either of those places, but I knew why we were going there. My mother had been there. The bus that she took out to Lewiston stopped in all the tourist spots. We were following along in her footsteps.

8
THE LUNATIC

ONCE WE WERE WELL ON THE ROAD OUT OF ILL-ah-no-way, Gram said, "Go on with Peeby. What happened next?"

"Do you want to hear about the lunatic?"

"Goodness!" Gram said, "as long as it's not too bloody. That Peeby is just like Gloria, I swear. A 'lunatic.' Imagine."

Gramps said, "Did Gloria really have a hankering for me?"

"Maybe she did, and maybe she didn't," Gram said.

"Well, gol-dang, I was only asking—"

"Seems to me," Gram said, "you've got enough to worry about, concentrating on these roads, without worrying about Gloria—"

Gramps winked at me in the rear-view mirror. "I think our gooseberry is jealous," he said.

"I am not," Gram said. "Tell about Peeby, chickabiddy."

I didn't want Gram and Gramps to get in a fight over Gloria, so I was happy to continue telling Phoebe's story.

I was at Phoebe's one Saturday morning when Mary Lou Finney called and invited us over to her house. Phoebe's parents were out, and Phoebe went all around the house checking to make sure that the doors and windows were locked. Her mother had already done this, but she made Phoebe promise to do it as well. "Just in case," Mrs. Winterbottom had said. I was not sure "just in case" of what—maybe in case someone had snuck in and opened all the windows and doors in the fifteen minutes between the time she left and the time we did. "You can never be *too* careful," Mrs. Winterbottom had said.

The doorbell rang. Phoebe and I looked out the window. Standing on the porch was a young man who looked about seventeen or eighteen, although I am not as good at guessing people's ages as blind Mrs. Partridge is. The young man was wearing a black T-shirt and blue jeans, and his hands were stuffed into his pockets. He seemed nervous.

"My mother hates it when strangers come to the door," Phoebe said. "She is convinced that any day one of them will burst into the house with a gun and turn out to be an escaped lunatic."

"Oh, honestly, Phoebe," I said. "Do you want me to answer the door?"

Phoebe took a deep breath. "We'll do it together." She opened the door and said hello in a cool voice.

"Is this 49 Gray Street?" the young man said.

"Yes," Phoebe said.

"So the Winterbottoms live here?"

After Phoebe admitted that yes, it was the Winterbottom residence, she said, "Excuse me a moment, please," and she closed the door. "Sal, do you detect any signs of lunacy? There doesn't appear to be any place he could be hiding a gun. His jeans are really tight. Maybe he has a knife tucked into his socks."

Phoebe could really be dramatic. "He isn't wearing any socks," I said. Phoebe opened the door again.

The young man said, "I want to see Mrs. Winterbottom. Is she here or what?"

"Yes," Phoebe lied.

The young man looked up and down the street. His hair was curly and mussed, and there were bright pink circles on his cheeks.

He wouldn't look us straight in the eye, but instead kept glancing to left and right. "I want to talk to her," he said.

"She can't come to the door right now," Phoebe said.

I thought he might actually cry when Phoebe said that. He chewed on his lip and blinked three or four times quickly. "I'll wait," he said.

"Just a minute," Phoebe said, closing the door. She pretended to look for her mother. "Mom!" she called. "Yoo-hoo!" She went upstairs, thumping loudly on the steps. "Mother!"

Phoebe and I returned to the door. He was still standing there with his hands in his pockets staring mournfully at Phoebe's house. "That's strange," Phoebe said to him. "I *thought* she was here, but she must have gone out. There's a whole lot of other people here though," she added quickly. "Scads and scads of people, but no Mrs. Winterbottom."

"Is Mrs. Winterbottom your mother?" he asked.

"Yes," Phoebe said. "Would you like me to leave a message?"

The little pink circles on his cheeks became even pinker. "No!" he said. "No. I don't think so. No." He looked up and down the street and then up at the number above the door. "What's your name?"

"Phoebe."

He repeated her name. "Phoebe Winterbottom." I thought he was going to make a joke about her name, but he didn't. He glanced at me. "Are you a Winterbottom too?" he asked.

"No," I said. "I'm a visitor."

And then he left. He just turned around, walked slowly down the porch steps and on down the street. We waited until he had turned the corner before we left. We ran all the way to Mary Lou's. Phoebe was certain that the young man was going to ambush us. Honestly. Like I said, she has a vivid imagination.

9
THE MESSAGE

ON THE WAY TO MARY LOU'S, PHOEBE SAID, "MARY Lou's family is not nearly as civilized as ours."

"In what way?" I asked.

"Oh, you'll see," Phoebe said.

Mary Lou Finney and Ben Finney were both in our class at school. At first I thought they were sister and brother, but Phoebe told me they were cousins, and that Ben was living with Mary Lou's family temporarily. Apparently there was always at least one stray relative living at the Finneys' temporarily.

It was complete pandemonium at the Finneys'. Mary Lou had an older sister and three brothers. In addition, there were her parents and Ben. There were footballs and basketballs lying all over the place, and boys sliding down the banister and leaping over tables and talking with their mouths full and interrupting everyone with endless questions. Phoebe took one look around and whispered to me, "Mary Lou's parents do not seem to have much control over things." Phoebe could sound a bit prissy sometimes.

Mr. Finney was lying in the bathtub, with all his clothes on, reading a book. From Mary Lou's bedroom window, I saw Mrs. Finney lying on top of the garage with a pillow under her head. "What's she doing?" I asked.

Mary Lou peered out the window. "King of kings! She's taking a nap."

When Mr. Finney got out of the bathtub, he went out in the backyard and tossed a football around with Dennis and Dougie, two of Mary Lou's brothers. Mr. Finney shouted, "Over here!" and "Thataway!" and "Way to go!"

The previous weekend, we had had a school sports day. Parents were watching their children show off, and there were even some events for the parents too, such as the three-legged race and pass-the-grapefruit. My father could not come, but Mary Lou's parents were there and so were Phoebe's.

Phoebe had said, "The games are a little childish sometimes, which is why my parents don't usually participate." Her parents stood on the sidelines while Mr. and Mrs. Finney ran around shouting "Over here!" and "Way-ta-go!" In the three-legged race, the Finneys kept falling over. Phoebe said, "I wonder if Mary Lou is embarrassed because of the way her parents are acting."

I didn't think it was embarrassing. I thought it was nice, but I didn't say so to Phoebe. I think that deep down Phoebe thought it was nice too, and she wished her own parents would act more like the Finneys. She couldn't admit this, though, and in a way, I liked this about Phoebe—that she tried to defend her family.

On the day that Phoebe and I met the potential lunatic and then went over to Mary Lou's, a couple other peculiar things happened. We were sitting on the floor of Mary Lou's room, and Phoebe was telling Mary Lou about the mysterious potential lunatic. Mary Lou's brothers, Dennis, Doug, and Tommy, kept dashing in and out of the room, leaping on the bed and squirting us with squirt guns.

Mary Lou's cousin Ben was lying on her bed, staring at me with his black, black eyes. They looked like two sparkly black discs set into big, round sockets. His dark eyelashes were long and feathery, casting shadows on his cheeks.

"I like your hair," he said to me. "Can you sit on it?"

"Yes, if I want."

Ben picked up a piece of paper from Mary Lou's desk, lay back down on the bed and drew a picture of a lizardlike creature with long black hair that, as it ran down the lizard's back and under its bottom, became a chair with legs. Underneath this, Ben had written, "Salamander sitting on her hair."

"Very amusing," Phoebe said. She left the room, and Mary Lou followed her.

I turned around to hand the drawing back to Ben, just as he leaned forward and mashed his lips into my collarbone. His lips rested there a moment. My nose was pressed into his hair, which smelled like grapefruit. Then he rolled off the bed, grabbed the drawing, and dashed out of the room.

Did he actually *kiss* my collarbone? And if he did, why did he do that? Was the kiss supposed to land somewhere else, like on my mouth, for example? That was a chilling thought. Had I imagined it? Maybe he merely brushed against me as he was rolling off the bed.

On the way home from Mary Lou's that day, Phoebe said, "Wasn't it, well, *loud* there?"

"I didn't mind," I said. I was thinking of something my father once said to my mother, "We'll fill the house up with children! We'll fill it right up to the brim!" But they hadn't filled it up. It was just me and them, and then it was just me and my father.

When we got back to Phoebe's house, her mother was lying on the couch, dabbing at her eyes with a tissue. "Is something wrong?" Phoebe asked.

"Oh no," Mrs. Winterbottom said. "Nothing's wrong."

Then Phoebe told her mother about the potential lunatic who had come to the house earlier. This news upset Mrs. Winterbottom. She wanted to know exactly what he had said and what Phoebe said and what he looked like and how he acted and how Phoebe acted, on and on. At last Mrs. Winterbottom said, "I think we had better not mention this to your father." She reached forward as if to hug Phoebe, but Phoebe pulled away.

Later Phoebe said, "That's odd. Usually my mother tells my father absolutely everything."

"Maybe she's just trying to save you from getting into trouble for talking with a stranger."

"I still don't like keeping it secret from him," Phoebe said.

We walked out onto her porch and there, lying on the top step was a white envelope. There was no name or anything on the outside. I thought it was one of those advertisements for painting your house or cleaning your carpets. Phoebe opened it. "Gosh," she said. Inside was a small piece of blue paper and on it was printed this message: *Don't judge a man until you've walked two moons in his moccasins.*

"What an odd thing," Phoebe said.

When Phoebe showed the message to her mother, Mrs. Winterbottom clutched at her collar. "Who could it be for?" Mrs. Winterbottom asked.

Mr. Winterbottom came in the back door, carrying his golf clubs. "Look, George," Mrs. Winterbottom said. "Who could this be for?"

"I couldn't say, really," Mr. Winterbottom said.

"But George, why would someone send us that message?"

"I couldn't say, Norma. Maybe it isn't for us."

"Not for us?" Mrs. Winterbottom said. "But it was on our steps."

"Really, Norma. It could be for anyone. Maybe it's for Prudence. Or Phoebe."

"Phoebe?" Mrs. Winterbottom asked. "Is it for you?"

"For me?" Phoebe said. "I don't think so."

"Well, who is it *for*?" Mrs. Winterbottom said. She was awfully worried. I believe she thought it came from the potential lunatic.

10
HUZZA, HUZZA

I HAD JUST FINISHED TELLING GRAM AND GRAMPS about the mysterious message when Gramps pulled off the freeway. He said he was tired of chewing up the road, and the white lines down the middle of the highway were starting to wiggle. As he drove into Madison, Wisconsin, Gram said, "I feel a little sorry for Mrs. Winterbottom. She doesn't sound very happy."

"They all sound screwy, if you ask me," Gramps said.

"Being a mother is like trying to hold a wolf by the ears," Gram said. "If you have three or four—or more—chickabiddies, you're dancing on a hot griddle all the time. You don't have time to think about anything else. And if you've only got one or two, it's almost harder. You have room left over—empty spaces that you think you've got to fill up."

"Well, it sure ain't a cinch being a father, either," Gramps said.

Gram touched his arm. "Horsefeathers," she said.

Round and round we drove until Gramps saw a parking space. Another car saw it too, but Gramps was fast and pulled in, and when the man in the other car waved his fist, Gramps said, "I'm a veteran. See this leg? Shrapnel from German guns. I saved our country!"

We did not have the correct change for the parking meter, so Gramps wrote a long note about how he was a visitor from Bybanks, Kentucky, and he was a World War II veteran with German shrapnel in his leg, and he kindly appreciated the members of the fair city of Madison allowing him to park in this space even though he did not have the correct change for the meter. He put this note on the dashboard.

"Do you really have German shrapnel in your leg?" I asked.

Gramps looked up at the sky. "Mighty nice day," he said.

The shrapnel was imaginary. Sometimes I am a little slow to figure these things out. My father once said I was as gullible as a fish. I thought he said *edible*. I thought he meant I was tasty.

The city of Madison sprawls between two lakes, Lake Mendota and Lake Monona, and dribbling out of these are other piddly lakes. It seemed as if the whole city was on vacation, with people riding around on their bikes and walking along the lakes and feeding the ducks and eating and canoeing and windsurfing. I'd never seen anything like it. Gram kept saying, "Huzza, huzza!"

There's a part of the city where no cars can go, and thousands of people stroll around eating ice cream. We went into Ella's Kosher Deli and Ice Cream Parlor and ate pastrami sandwiches and kosher dill pickles, followed by raspberry ice cream. After we walked around some more, we were hungry again, and so we had lemon tea and blueberry muffins at the Steep and Brew.

All the while, I heard the whispers: *rush, hurry, rush*. Gram and Gramps moved so slowly. "Shouldn't we go now?" I kept asking, but Gram would say, "Huzza, huzza!" and Gramps would say, "We'll go soon, chickabiddy, soon."

"Don't you want to send any postcards?" Gram asked.

"No, I do not."

"Not even to your daddy?"

"No." There was a good reason for this. All along her trip, my mother had sent me postcards. She wrote, "Here I am in the Badlands, missing you terribly," and "This is Mount Rushmore, but I don't see any Presidents' faces, I only see yours." The last postcard arrived two days after we found out she wasn't coming back. It was from Coeur d'Alene, Idaho. On the front was a picture of a beautiful blue lake surrounded by tall evergreens. On the back she had written, "Tomorrow I'll be in Lewiston. I love you, my Salamanca Tree."

At last, Gramps said, "I sure hate to get back on the road, but time's a-wastin'!"

Yes, I thought, yes, yes, yes!

Gram settled back for a nap while I said a few thousand more prayers. The next thing I knew, Gramps was pulling off the road again. "Lookee here," he said. "The Wisconsin Dells." He drove into a vast parking area and said, "Why don't you two go look around? I'm going to get a little shut-eye."

Gram and I poked our noses into an old fort, and then sat on the grass watching a group of Native Americans dance and beat drums. My mother had not liked the term *Native Americans*. She thought it sounded primitive and stiff. She said, "My great-grandmother was a Seneca Indian, and

I'm proud of it. She wasn't a Seneca Native American. *Indian* sounds much more brave and elegant." In school, our teacher told us we had to say Native American, but I agreed with my mother. *Indian* sounded much better. My mother and I liked this Indian-ness in our background. She said it made us appreciate the gifts of nature; it made us closer to the land.

I lay back and closed my eyes, listening to the drums beat *rush-rush-rush* and the dancers chant *hurry-hurry-hurry*. Someone was jingling bells, too, and for a moment I thought of Christmas and sleigh bells. When I opened my eyes again, Gram was gone.

I glanced around, trying to remember where we had parked the car. I looked through the crowd, back at the trees, over at the concession stand. "They've gone," I thought. "They've left me." I pushed through the people.

The crowd was clapping, the drums were beating. I was all turned around and could not remember which way we had come. There were three signs indicating different parking areas. The drums thundered. I pushed further into the crowd of people, who were now clapping louder, in time with the drums.

The Indians had formed two circles, one inside
the other, and were hopping up and down. The
men danced in the outer circle and wore feather
headdresses and short leather aprons. On their
feet were moccasins, and I thought again about
Phoebe's message: *Don't judge a man until you've*
walked two moons in his moccasins.

Inside the circle of men, the women in long
dresses and ropes of beads had joined arms and
were dancing around one older woman who was
wearing a regular cotton dress. On her head was an
enormous headdress, which had slipped down
over her forehead.

I looked closer. The woman in the center was
hopping up and down. On her feet were flat, white
shoes. In the space between drum beats, I heard
her say, "Huzza, huzza."

11
FLINCHING

EARLY THE NEXT MORNING, WE LEFT WISCONSIN and drove on, eating up the road through the lower rim of Minnesota. The land here was hilly and green, forests tucked in close beside the road, and the air smelled of pine.

"At last," Gramps said, "some scenery! I love a place that has scenery, don't you, chickabiddy?"

I had not said anything about what had happened the day before—about being scared down to my very bones when I thought they had left me. I don't know what came over me. Ever since my mother left us that April day, I suspected that everyone was going to leave, one by one.

I was glad to be able to go on with Phoebe's story, because when I was talking about Phoebe, I wasn't thinking about much else.

"Did Peeby get any more messages?" Gram asked.

cc

She did. The following Saturday, Phoebe and I were going to Mary Lou's again. As we left Phoebe's house, there on the front steps was another white envelope with a blue sheet of paper inside. The message was: *Everyone has his own agenda*.

Phoebe and I looked up and down the street. There was no sign of the message-leaver. Mary Lou thought the messages (this one and the other one) were intriguing. "How exciting!" she said. "I wish someone would leave *me* messages!"

Phoebe thought the messages were spooky. It was not the words that bothered her—nothing too frightening there—it was the idea that someone was sneaking around and leaving them on her porch. She worried that someone was watching their house, waiting for the right moment to leave the message. Phoebe was a champion worrier.

We tried to figure out what the message meant. "Okay," Phoebe said, "an agenda is a list of things to be discussed at a meeting—"

"So maybe it's for your dad," I suggested. "Does he go to meetings?"

"Well, I guess," Phoebe said. "He's ever so busy all day long."

"Maybe it's from his boss," Mary Lou said. "Maybe your father hasn't been conducting his meetings very well."

"My father is very organized," Phoebe said.

"What about the other message?" Mary Lou said. "Don't judge a man until you've walked two moons in his moccasins."

"I know what it means," I said. "I've heard my father use it lots of times. I used to imagine that there were two moons sitting in a pair of Indian shoes, but my father said it means that you shouldn't judge someone until you've walked in their moccasins. Until you've been in their shoes. In their place."

"And your father says this often?" Phoebe said.

"I know what you're thinking," I said, "but my father isn't creeping around leaving those messages. It isn't his handwriting."

When Ben came into Mary Lou's room, she asked him what he thought it meant. He took a sheet of paper from her desk and quickly drew a cartoon. It was a little spooky, because what he drew was identical to what I used to imagine: a pair of Indian moccasins with two moons in them.

"Maybe," Mary Lou said to Phoebe, "your father is being too quick to judge people at work. He needs to walk in their moccasins first."

"My father does *not* judge too quickly," Phoebe said.

"You don't have to get defensive," Ben said.

"I am not getting defensive. I'm just telling you that my father does not judge too quickly."

Later, we went to the drugstore. I thought it was going to be only me and Phoebe and Mary Lou going, but by the time we left the house, we had accumulated Tommy and Dougie as well. At the last minute, Ben said he was coming too.

"I don't know how you can stand it," Phoebe said to Mary Lou.

"Stand what?"

Phoebe pointed to Tommy and Dougie, who were running around like wound-up toys, making airplane noises and train noises and zooming in between us and then running up ahead and falling over each other and crying and then leaping back up again and socking each other and chasing after bumblebees.

"I'm used to it," Mary Lou said. "My brothers are always doing beef-brained things."

Ben walked right behind me all the way, which made me nervous. I kept turning around to see what he was doing back there, but he was just strolling along smiling.

Tommy bashed into me, and when I started to fall backward, Ben caught me. He put his arms around my waist and held on to me, even after it was obvious that I was not going to fall. I could smell that funny grapefruit smell again and feel his face pressed up against my hair. "Let go," I said, but he didn't let go. I had an odd sensation, as if a little creature was crawling up my spine. It wasn't a horrible sensation, more light and tickly. I thought maybe he dropped something down my shirt. "Let *go!*" I said, and finally he did.

It was at the drugstore that I got a little scared. Maybe I had been listening to Phoebe's tales of lunatics and axe murderers too much. Phoebe and I were looking at the magazines when I felt as if someone was watching us. I looked over to where Ben was standing, but he and Mary Lou were busy rummaging around in the chocolate bars. The feeling did not go away. I turned the other way around, and there on the far side of the store was the nervous young man who had come to Phoebe's house. He was at the cash register, paying for something, but he was staring at us while he was handing his money to the clerk. I nudged Phoebe. "Oh no," she said, "the lunatic." Phoebe hustled over to Ben and Mary Lou. "Look, quick, it's the lunatic."

"Where?"

"At the cash register."

"There's nobody there," Mary Lou said.

"Honest, he was there," Phoebe said. "I swear he was. Ask Sal."

"He was there," I said.

Later, when we had left Mary Lou and were on our way to Phoebe's house, we heard someone running up behind us. Phoebe thought we were doomed. "If we get our heads bashed in and that lunatic leaves us here on the sidewalk—" she said.

I felt a hand on my shoulder, and I opened my mouth to scream, but nothing came out. My brain was saying, "Scream! Scream!" but my voice was completely shut off.

It was Ben. He said, "Did I scare you?"

"That wasn't very funny," Phoebe said.

"I'll walk home with you," he said. "Just in case there are any—any—lunatics around." He had difficulty saying *lunatic*. On the way to Phoebe's house Ben said some odd things. First, he said, "Maybe you shouldn't call him a lunatic."

"And why not?" Phoebe said.

"Because a lunatic is—it means—it sounds like—oh, never mind." He would not explain, and he seemed embarrassed to have mentioned this in the first place. Then he said to me, "Don't people touch each other at your house?"

"What's that supposed to mean?"

"I just wondered," he said. "You flinch every time someone touches you."

"I do not."

"You do." He touched my arm. I have to admit, my instinct was to flinch but I caught myself. I pretended not to notice that his hand was resting there on my arm. That creature tickling my spine was back. "Hmm," he said, like a doctor examining a patient. "Hmm." He removed his hand. "Where's your mother?"

I had not mentioned my mother to anyone, not even Phoebe, except for the one time Phoebe had asked about her and I had only said she didn't live with us.

Ben said, "I saw your father once, but I've never seen your mother. Where is she?"

"She's in Idaho. Lewiston, Idaho."

"What's she doing there?" Ben said.

"I don't really feel like saying." It didn't occur to me to ask him where *his* mother was.

He touched my arm again. When I flinched, he said, "Ha! Gotcha!"

It bothered me, what he had said. It occurred to me that my father didn't hug me as much anymore, and that maybe I *was* starting to flinch whenever anyone touched me. I wasn't always like that. We used to be a hugging family. As I walked along with Ben and Phoebe, I remembered a time when I was nine or ten. My mother crawled into bed with me and snuggled close and said, "Let's build a raft and float away down a river." I used to think about that raft a lot, and I actually believed that one day we might build a raft and float away down a river together. But when she went to Lewiston, Idaho, she went alone.

Ben touched Phoebe's arm. She flinched. "Ha," he said. "Gotcha. You're jumpy, too, Free Bee."

And that, too, bothered me. I had already noticed how tense Phoebe's whole family seemed, how tidy, how respectable, how thumpingly *stiff*. Was I becoming like that? Why were they like that? A couple times I had seen Phoebe's mother try to touch Phoebe or Prudence or Mr. Winterbottom, but they all drew back from her. It was as if they had outgrown her.

Had I been drawing away from my own

mother? Did she have empty spaces left over? Was that why she left?

When we reached Phoebe's driveway, Ben said, "I guess you're safe now. I guess I'll go."

"Go ahead," Phoebe said.

Mrs. Cadaver came screeching up to the curb in her yellow Volkswagen, with her wild red witch hair flying all over the place. She waved at us and started pulling things out of the car and plopping them on the sidewalk.

"Who's that?" Ben asked.

"Mrs. Cadaver."

"Cadaver? Like dead body?"

"That's right."

"Hi, Sal," Mrs. Cadaver called. She dumped a pile of lumpy bags on the sidewalk. Ben asked if she wanted any help. "My, you're very polite," Mrs. Cadaver said, flashing her wild gray eyes.

"She scares me half to death," Phoebe said. "Don't go inside," she whispered to Ben.

"Why not?" he said, too loudly, because Mrs. Cadaver looked up and said, "What?"

"Oh nothing," Phoebe said.

Mrs. Cadaver said, "Sal, do you want to come in?"

"I was just going to Phoebe's," I said, glad for an excuse.

Phoebe's mother came to her front door. "Phoebe? What are you doing? Are you coming in?"

We left Ben. As we were going in Phoebe's house, we saw Ben lift something off the sidewalk. It was a shiny new axe.

Phoebe's mother said, "Is that Mary Lou's brother? Was he walking you home? Where's Mary Lou?"

"I hate it when you ask me three questions in a row," Phoebe said. Through the window, we could see Ben lugging the axe up the front steps of Mrs. Cadaver's house. Phoebe called out, "Don't go in!" but when Mrs. Cadaver held the front door open, Ben disappeared inside.

"Phoebe, what *are* you doing?" her mother asked.

Then Phoebe pulled the envelope out of her pocket, the envelope containing the newest message. "I found this outside," Phoebe said.

Mrs. Winterbottom opened the envelope carefully, as if it might contain a miniature bomb. "Oh sweetie," she said. "Who is it from? Who is it for? What does it mean?" Phoebe explained what an agenda was. "I know what an agenda is, Phoebe. I don't like this at all. I want to know who is sending these."

I was waiting for Phoebe to tell her about seeing the nervous young man at the drugstore, but Phoebe didn't mention it. A little later we saw Ben leave Mrs. Cadaver's house. He appeared to be all in one piece.

That day when I got home, my father was in the garage, tinkering with the car. He was leaning over the engine, and I couldn't see his face at first. "Dad—what do you think it means if someone touches someone else and the person being touched flinches? Do you think it means that the person being touched is getting too stiff?"

Dad turned slowly around. His eyes were red and puffy. I think he had been crying. His hands and shirt were greasy, but when he hugged me, I didn't flinch.

12
THE MARRIAGE BED

WHEN I HAD FIRST STARTED TELLING PHOEBE'S story, Gram and Gramps sat quietly and listened. Gramps concentrated on the road, and Gram gazed out the window. Occasionally, they interjected a "Gol-dang!" or a "No kidding?" But as I got farther into the story, they began to interrupt more and more.

When I told about the message *Everyone has his own agenda*, Gram thumped on the dashboard and said, "Isn't that the truth! Lordy! Isn't that what it is all about?"

I said, "How do you mean?"

"Everybody is just walking along concerned with his own problems, his own life, his own worries. And we're all expecting other people to tune into our own agenda. 'Look at my worry. Worry with me. Step into my life. Care about my problems. Care about me.'" Gram sighed.

Gramps scratched his head. "You turning into a philosopher or something?"

"Mind your own agenda," she said.

When I mentioned about Ben asking where my mother was and my saying that she was in Lewiston, but that I didn't want to elaborate, Gram and Gramps looked at each other. Gramps said, "One time my father took off for six months and didn't tell a soul where he was going. When my best friend asked me where my father was, I hauled off and punched him in the jaw. My best friend. I punched him dang in the jaw."

"You never told me that," Gram said. "I hope he socked you back."

Gramps pointed to a gap in his teeth. "See that? He knocked my tooth dang out."

And when I told Gram and Gramps about flinching when Ben touched me and about how I went home and found Dad in the garage, Gram unbuckled her seat belt, turned all the way around and leaned over the back of her seat. She took my hand and kissed it. Gramps said, "Give her one for me, too," and so Gram kissed my hand again.

Several times when I described Phoebe's world of lunatics and axe murderers, Gram said, "Just like Gloria, I swear to goodness. Just exactly like

Gloria." Once, after she said this, Gramps got a dreamy look on his face and Gram said, "Quit that mooning over Gloria. I know what you're thinking."

Gramps said, "Hear that, chickabiddy? This here gooseberry knows everything that runs through my head. Isn't she something?"

Just before we reached the South Dakota border, Gramps took a detour north because he had seen a sign advertising the Pipestone National Monument in Pipestone, Minnesota. On the sign was a picture of an Indian smoking a pipe.

"What do you want to go see an old Indian smoking a pipe for?" Gram asked. She didn't like the term *Native American* any more than my mother did.

"I just do," Gramps said. "We might not ever get the chance again."

"To see an Indian smoking a pipe?" Gram said.

"Will it take very long?" I asked as the air screamed, *hurry, hurry, hurry.*

"Not too long, chickabiddy. We've got to cool off our car-bust-er-ators. These roads are taking the poop out of me."

The detour to Pipestone wound through a cool, dark forest and if you closed your eyes and smelled the air, you could smell Bybanks, Kentucky.

Pipestone was a small town. Everywhere we went, people were talking to each other: standing there talking, or sitting on a bench talking, or walking along the street talking. When we passed by, they looked up at us, right into our faces and said "Hi" or "Howdy," and although it sounds corny to say it, we felt right at home there. It was so like Bybanks, where everyone you see stops to say something because they know you and have known you their whole lives.

We went to the Pipestone National Monument and saw Indians thunking away at the stone in the quarry. I asked one if he was a Native American, but he said, "No. I'm a person." I said, "But are you a Native American person?" He said, "No, I'm an American Indian person." I said, "So am I. In my blood."

We watched other American Indian persons making pipes out of the stone. In the Pipe Museum, we learned more about pipes than any human being ought to know. In a little clearing outside the museum, an American Indian person was sitting on a tree stump smoking a long peace pipe. After watching him for about five minutes, Gramps asked if he could try it.

The man passed Gramps the pipe, and Gramps

sat down on the grass, took two puffs and passed it to Gram. She didn't even blink. She took two puffs and passed it to me. There was a sweet, sticky taste on the end of the pipe. With the stem in my mouth, I gave it two little kisses, which is what it looked like Gram and Gramps had done. The smoke came into my mouth, and I held it there while I passed the pipe back.

I held that smoke in my mouth while Gram and Gramps puffed some more. I was feeling slightly whang-doodled. I opened my mouth a wee bit, and a tiny stream of smoke curled out into the air, and when I saw that, for some reason I was reminded of my mother. It didn't make any sense, but my brain was saying, "There goes your mother," and I watched the trail of smoke disappear into the air.

In the shop attached to the pipe museum, Gramps bought two peace pipes. One was for him and one was for me. "It's not for smoking with," he said. "It's for remembering with."

That night we stayed in Injun Joe's Peace Palace Motel. On a sign in the lobby, someone had crossed out "Injun" and written "Native American" so the whole sign read: "Native American Joe's Peace Palace Motel." In our room, the "Injun Joe's" embroidered on the towels had been changed with black marker to "Indian Joe's." I wished everybody would just make up their minds.

By now I was used to staying in a room with Gram and Gramps. Every night when they climbed into bed, they lay right beside each other on their backs and Gramps said, every single night, "Well, this ain't our marriage bed, but it will do."

Probably the most precious thing in the whole world to Gramps—besides Gram—was their marriage bed. This is what he called their bed back home in Bybanks, Kentucky. One of the stories that Gramps liked to tell was about how he and all his brothers had been born in that bed, and all Gram and Gramps's own children had been born in that same bed.

When Gramps tells this story, he starts with when he was seventeen years old and living with his parents in Bybanks. That's when he met Gram. She was visiting her aunt who lived over the meadow from where Gramps lived. "I was a wild thing then," Gramps said, "and I didn't stand still for any girl, I can tell you that." They had to try to catch Gramps on the run. But when he saw Gram running in the meadow, with her long hair as silky as a filly's, he was the one who was trying to do the catching. "Talk about wild things! Your grandmother was the wildest, most untamed, most ornery and beautiful creature ever to grace this earth."

Gramps said he followed her like a sick, old dog for twenty-two days, and on the twenty-third day, he marched up to her father and asked if he could marry her. Her father said, "If you can get her to stand still long enough and if she'll have you, I guess you can."

When Gramps asked Gram to marry him, she said, "Do you have a dog?" Gramps said that yes, as a matter of fact, he had a fat old beagle named Sadie. Gram said, "And where does she sleep?"

Gramps stumbled around a bit and said, "To tell you the truth, she sleeps right next to me, but if we was to get married, I—"

"And when you come in the door at night," Gram said, "what does that dog do?"

Gramps couldn't figure what she was getting at, so he just told the truth. "She jumps all over me, a-lickin' and a-howlin'."

"And then what do *you* do?" Gram said.

"Well, gosh—" Gramps said. He did not like to admit it, but he said, "I take her in my lap and pet her till she calms down, and sometimes I sing her a song. You're making me feel foolish."

"I don't mean to," she said. "You've told me all I

need to know. I figure if you treat a dog that good, you'll treat me better. I figure if that old beagle Sadie loves you so much, I'll probably love you better. Yes, I'll marry you."

They were married three months later. During that time between his proposal and their wedding day, Gramps and his father and brothers built a small house in the clearing behind the first meadow. "We didn't have time," Gramps said, "to completely finish it, and there wasn't a single stick of furniture in it yet, but that didn't matter. We were going to sleep there on our wedding night all the same."

They were married in an aspen grove on a clear July day, and afterward they and all their friends and relatives had a wedding supper on the banks of the river. During the supper, Gramps noticed that his father and two of his brothers were absent. He thought maybe they were planning a wet cheer, which is when the men kidnap the groom for an hour or so and they all go out to the woods and share a bottle of whiskey. Before the end of the supper his father and brothers came back, but they did not kidnap him for a wet cheer. Gramps was just as glad, he said, because he needed his wits about him that evening.

At the end of the supper, Gramps picked up Gram in his arms and carried her across the meadow. Behind them, everyone was singing, "Oh meet me, in the tulips, when the tulips do blooom—" This is what they always sing at weddings when the married couple leaves. It is supposed to be a joke, as if Gram and Gramps were going away by themselves and might not reappear until the following spring when the tulips were in bloom.

Gramps carried Gram all the way across the meadow and through the trees and into the clearing where their little house stood. He carried her in through the door, and took one look around and started to cry.

The reason Gramps cried when he carried Gram into the house was that there, in the center of the bedroom, stood his own parents' bed—the bed that Gramps and each of his brothers had been born in, the bed his parents had always slept in. This was where his father and brothers had disappeared to during the wedding supper. They had been moving the bed into Gram and Gramps's new house. At the foot of the bed, wiggling and slurping, was Sadie, Gramps's old beagle dog.

Gramps always ends this story by saying, "That

bed has been around my whole entire life, and I'm going to die in that bed, and then that bed will know everything there is to know about me."

So each night on our trip out to Idaho, Gramps patted the bed in the motel and said, "Well, this ain't our marriage bed, but it will do," while I lay in the next bed wondering if I would ever have a marriage bed like theirs.

13
BOUNCING BIRKWAY

IT WAS TIME TO TELL GRAM AND GRAMPS ABOUT
Mr. Birkway.

Mr. Birkway was mighty strange. I didn't know
what to make of him. I thought he might have a
few squirrels in the attic of his brain. He was one
of those energetic teachers who loved his subject
half to death and leaped about the room dramatically, waving his arms and clutching his chest and
whomping people on the back.

He said, "Brilliant!" and "Wonderful!" and "Terrific!" He was tall and slim, and his bushy black hair
made him look wild, but he had enormous deep
brown cowlike eyes that sparkled all over the place,
and when he turned these eyes on you, you felt as if
his whole purpose in life was to stand there and listen to you, and you alone.

Midway through the first class, Mr. Birkway
asked for everyone's summer journals. He flung

himself up and down the aisles, receiving the journals as if they were manna from heaven. "Wonderful!" he said to each journal-giver.

I was worried. I had no journal.

On top of Mary Lou Finney's desk were six journals. *Six.* Mr. Birkway said, "Heavens. Mercy. Is it—can it be—Shakespeare?" He counted the journals. "Six! Brilliant! Magnificent!"

Christy and Megan, two girls who had their own club called the GGP (whatever that meant), were whispering over on the other side of the room and casting malevolent looks in Mary Lou's direction. Mary Lou kept her hand on top of the journals as Mr. Birkway reached for them. In a low voice she said, "I don't want you to read them."

"What?" Mr. Birkway boomed. "Not *read* them?" The whole room was silent. Mr. Birkway scooped up Mary Lou's journals before she could even blink. He said, "Don't be silly. Brilliant! Thank you!"

Another girl, Beth Ann, looked as if she might cry. Phoebe was sending me messages with her eyebrows that indicated that she was not too pleased either. I think they were all hoping that Mr. Birkway was not actually going to read these journals.

Mr. Birkway went around the whole room snatching journals. Alex Cheevey's journal was covered with basketball stickers. Christy's and Megan's were slathered over with pictures of male models. The cover of Ben's was a cartoon of a boy with a normal boy's head, but the arms and legs were pencils, and out of the tips of the hands and feet were dribbles of words.

When he got to Phoebe's desk, Mr. Birkway lifted up her plain journal and peeked inside. Phoebe was trying to slide down in her chair. "I didn't write much," Phoebe said. "In fact, I can hardly remember what I wrote about at all."

By the time Mr. Birkway got to me, my heart was clobbering around so hard I thought it might leap straight out of my chest. "Deprived child," he said. "You didn't have a chance to write a journal."

"I'm new—"

"New? How blessed," he said. "There's nothing in this whole wide world that is better than a new person!"

"So I didn't know about the journals—"

"Not to worry!" Mr. Birkway said. "I'll think of something."

I wasn't sure what that meant. I thought maybe he would give me a whole lot of extra homework or something. For the rest of the day, you could see little groups of people asking each other, "Did you write about me?" I was very glad I hadn't written anything.

For a while, we didn't hear any more about the journals. We had absolutely no idea all the trouble they were going to cause.

14

THE RHODODENDRON

ONE SATURDAY, I WAS AT PHOEBE'S AGAIN. HER FA-
ther was golfing, and her mother was running errands. Mrs. Winterbottom had read out a long list
to us of where she would be in case we needed her.
If we heard any noises at all, we were supposed to
call the police immediately. "After you call the police," Mrs. Winterbottom said, "call Mrs. Cadaver.
I think she's home today. I'm sure she would come
right over."

"Oh *sure*," Phoebe whispered to me. "That's
about the last person I would call." Phoebe imagined that every noise was the lunatic sneaking in or
the message-leaver creeping up to drop off another anonymous note. She was so jumpy that I
began to feel uneasy too.

After her mother left, Phoebe said, "Mrs.
Cadaver works odd hours, doesn't she? Sometimes
she works every night for a week, straggling home

when most people are waking up, but sometimes she works during the day."

"She's a nurse, so I guess she works different shifts," I said.

That day Mrs. Cadaver was home, puttering around her garden. We saw her from Phoebe's bedroom window. Actually, puttering is not the best word. What she was doing was more like slogging and slashing. Mrs. Cadaver hacked branches off of trees and hauled these to the back of her lot where she lumped them into a pile of branches that she had hacked off last week.

"I told you she was as strong as an ox," Phoebe said.

Next, Mrs. Cadaver slashed and sliced at a pitiful rosebush that had been trying to creep up the side of her house. Then she sheared off the tops of the hedge that borders Phoebe's yard. She moved on to a rhododendron bush, which she was poking and prodding when a car pulled into her driveway. A tall man with bushy black hair leaped out and, seeing her, he practically skipped back to where she was. They hugged each other.

"Oh no," Phoebe said. The man with the bushy black hair was Mr. Birkway, our English teacher.

Mrs. Cadaver pointed to the rhododendron

bush and then at the axe, but Mr. Birkway shook his head. He disappeared into the garage and returned with two shovels. Then he and Mrs. Cadaver gouged and prodded and tunneled around in the dirt until the poor old rhododendron flopped onto its side. They lugged the bush to the opposite side of the yard where there was a mound of dirt, and they replanted the bush.

"Maybe there's something hidden under the bush," Phoebe said.

"Like what?"

"Like Mr. Cadaver—as I told you before. Maybe Mr. Birkway helped her chop up her husband and bury him and maybe they were getting worried and decided to disguise the spot with a rhododendron bush." I must have looked skeptical. Phoebe said, "Sal, you never can tell. And Sal, I don't think you or your father should go over there anymore."

I certainly agreed with her on that one. Dad and I had been there two nights earlier, and I had hardly been able to sit still. I started noticing all these frightening things in Margaret's house: creepy masks, old swords, books with titles like *The Murders in the Rue Morgue* and *The Skull and the Hatchet*. Margaret cornered me in the kitchen and said, "So what has your father told you about me?"

"Nothing," I said.

"Oh." She seemed disappointed.

My father's behavior was always different at Margaret's. At home, I would sometimes find him sitting on his bed staring at the floor, or reading through old letters, or gazing at the photo album. He looked sad and lonely. But at Margaret's, he would smile, and sometimes even laugh, and once she touched his hand, and he let her hand rest there on top of his. I didn't like it. I didn't want my father to be sad, but at least when he was sad, I knew he was remembering my mother. So when Phoebe suggested that my father and I should not go to Margaret's, I was quite willing to agree with that notion.

When Phoebe's mother came home from running all her errands, she looked terrible. She was sniffling and blowing her nose.

Phoebe said that we were going to do our homework. Upstairs, I said, "Maybe we should have helped her put away the groceries."

"She likes to do all that by herself," Phoebe said.

"Are you sure?"

"Of course I'm sure," Phoebe said. "I've lived here my whole life, haven't I?"

"She looked as if she'd been crying. Maybe something is wrong. Maybe something is bothering her."

"Don't you think she would say so then?"

"Maybe she's afraid to," I said. I wondered why it was so easy for me to see that Phoebe's mother was worried and miserable, but Phoebe couldn't see it—or if she could, she was ignoring it. Maybe she didn't *want* to notice. Maybe it was too frightening a thing. I wondered if this was how it had been with my mother. Were there things I didn't notice?

Later that afternoon, when Phoebe and I went downstairs, Mrs. Winterbottom was talking with Prudence. "Do you think I lead a tiny life?" she asked.

"How do you mean?" Prudence said, as she filed her nails. "Do we have any nail polish remover?"

Phoebe's mother retrieved a bottle of nail polish remover from the bathroom.

"Oh!" Prudence said. "Before I forget—do you think you could sew up the hem on my brown skirt so I could wear it tomorrow? Oh, please?"

Prudence tilted her head to the side, tugged at her hair in exactly the same way Phoebe does, and smooshed up her mouth into a little pout.

"Doesn't Prudence know how to sew?" I asked.

"Of course she does," Phoebe said. "Why?"

"I was just wondering why she doesn't sew her own skirt."

"Sal, you're becoming very critical."

Before I left Phoebe's that day, Mrs. Winterbottom handed Prudence her brown skirt with the newly sewn hem, and all the way home I wondered about Mrs. Winterbottom and what she meant about living a tiny life. If she didn't like all that baking and cleaning and jumping up to get bottles of nail polish remover and sewing hems, why did she do it? Why didn't she tell them to do some of these things themselves? Maybe she was afraid there would be nothing left for her to do. There would be no need for her and she would become invisible and no one would notice.

When I got home that day, my father handed me a package. "It's from Margaret," he said.

"What is it?"

"I don't know. Why don't you open it?"

Inside was a blue sweater. I put it back in the box and went upstairs. My father followed me.

"Sal—? Sal—do you like it?"

"I don't want it," I said.

"She was just trying to—she likes you—"

"I don't care if she likes me or not," I said.

My father stood there looking around the room. "I want to tell you something about Margaret," he said.

"Well, I don't want to hear it." I was feeling so completely ornery. When my father left the room, I could still hear my own voice saying, "I don't want to hear it." I sounded exactly like Phoebe.

15
A SNAKE HAS A SNACK

It was hotter than blazes in South Dakota. In Sioux Falls, Gramps took off his shirt. Passing Mitchell, Gram unbuttoned her dress down to her waist. Just beyond Chamberlain, Gramps took a detour to the Missouri River. He parked the car beneath a tree overlooking a sandy bank.

Gram and Gramps kicked off their shoes. It was quiet and hot, hot, hot. All you could hear was a crow calling somewhere up river and the distant sound of cars along the highway. The hot air pressed against my face, and my hair was like a hot, heavy blanket draped on my neck and back. It was so hot you could smell the heat baking the stones and dirt along the bank.

Gram pulled her dress up over her head, and Gramps undid his buckle and let his pants slide to the ground. They started kicking water at each other and scooping it up and letting it run down their faces. They walked in to where it was knee deep and sat down.

"Come on, chickabiddy," Gramps called.

Gram said, "It's delicious!"

I gazed up and down the river. Not a soul in sight. The water looked cool and clear. Gram and Gramps sat there in the river, grinning away. I waded in and sat down. It was nearly heaven, with that cool water rippling and a high, clear sky all around us, and trees waving along the banks.

My hair floated all around me. My mother's hair had been long and black, like mine, but a week before she left, she cut it. My father said to me, "Don't cut yours, Sal. Please don't cut yours."

My mother said, "I knew you wouldn't like it if I cut mine."

My father said, "I didn't say anything about yours."

"But I know what you're thinking," she said.

"I loved your hair, Sugar," he said.

I saved her hair. I swept it up from the kitchen floor and wrapped it in a plastic bag and hid it beneath the floorboards of my room. It was still there, along with the postcards she sent.

As Gram, Gramps, and I sat in the Missouri River, I tried not to think of the postcards. I tried to concentrate on the high sky and the cool water. It would have been perfect except for that ornery crow calling away: *car-car-car*. "Will we be here long?" I asked.

The boy came out of nowhere. Gramps saw him first and whispered, "Get behind me, chick-abiddy. You too," he said to Gram. The boy was about fifteen or sixteen, with shaggy dark hair. He wore blue jeans and no shirt, and his chest was brown and muscular. In his hand he held a long bowie knife, its sheath fastened to his belt. He stood next to Gramps's pants on the bank.

I thought of Phoebe and knew that if she were here, she would be warning us that the boy was a lunatic who would hack us all to pieces. I was wishing we had never stopped at the river, and that my grandparents would be more cautious, maybe even a little more like Phoebe, who saw danger everywhere.

As the boy stared at us, Gramps said, "Howdy."

The boy said, "This here's private property."

Gramps looked all around. "Is it? I didn't see any signs."

"It's private property."

"Why heck," Gramps said, "this here's a river. I never heard of no river being private property."

The boy picked up Gramps's pants and slid his hand into a pocket. "This land where I'm standing is private property."

I was frightened of the boy and wanted Gramps to do something, but Gramps looked cool and calm. He sounded as if he hadn't a care in the world, but I knew that he was worried by the way he kept inching in front of me and Gram.

I felt around the riverbed, pulled up a flat stone, and skimmed it across the water. The boy watched the stone, counting the skips.

A snake flickered along the bank and slid into the water.

"See that tree?" Gramps said. He pointed to an old willow leaning into the water near where the boy stood.

"I see it," the boy said, sliding his hand into another of Gramps's pockets.

Gramps said, "See that knothole? Watch what this here chickabiddy can do to a knothole." Gramps winked at me. The veins in his neck were standing out. You could practically see the blood rushing through them.

I felt around the riverbed and pulled up another flat, jagged rock. I had done this a million times in the swimming hole in Bybanks. I pulled my arm back and tossed the rock straight at the tree. One edge embedded itself in the knothole. The boy stopped rummaging through Gramps's pockets and eyed me.

Gram said, "Oh!" and flailed at the water. She reached down, pulled up a snake, and gave Gramps a puzzled look. "It's a water moccasin, isn't it?" she said. "It's a poisonous one, isn't it?" The snake slithered and wriggled, straining toward the water. "I do believe it has had a snack out of my leg." She stared hard at Gramps.

The boy stood on the bank holding Gramps's wallet. Gramps scooped up Gram and carried her out of the water. "Would you mind dropping that thing?" he said to Gram, who was still clutching the snake. To me he said, "Get on out of there, chickabiddy."

As Gramps put Gram on the riverbank, the boy came and knelt beside her. "I'm sure glad you have that knife," Gramps said, reaching for it. As he made a slit in Gram's leg across the snake bite, blood trickled down her ankle. I grabbed Gram's hand as she stared up at the sky. Gramps knelt to suck out the wound, but the boy said, "Here, I'll do it." The boy placed his mouth against Gram's bloody leg. He sucked and spit, sucked and spit.

Gram's eyelids fluttered.

"Can you point us to a hospital?" Gramps said.

The boy nodded as he spit. Gramps and the boy carried Gram to the car and settled her in the back seat while I snatched their clothes from the river-bank. We placed Gram's head on my lap and her feet on the boy's lap, and all the while the boy continued sucking and spitting. In between, he gave directions to the hospital. Gram held onto my hand.

Gramps, still in his boxer shorts, and dripping wet, carried Gram into the hospital. The boy's mouth hovered over her leg the whole time, sucking and spitting.

Gram spent the night in the hospital. In the waiting room, the boy from the riverbank sprawled in a chair. I offered him a paper towel. "You've got blood on your mouth," I said. I handed him a fifty-dollar bill. "My grandfather said to give you this. That's all the cash he has right now. He said to tell you thanks. He'd come out himself, but he doesn't want to leave her."

He looked at the fifty-dollar bill in my hand. "I don't need it."

"You don't have to stay," I said.

He glanced around the waiting room. "I know

it." He looked away and then said, "I like your hair."

"I was thinking of cutting it."

"Don't."

I sat down beside him.

He said, "It wasn't really private property."

"I didn't think so."

Later, when I went in to see Gram, she was all tucked up in bed, pale and sleepy. Next to her on the narrow bed, Gramps was lying on top of the covers, stroking her hair. A nurse came in and made him get off the bed. He had, by now, put his pants on, but he looked a wreck.

I asked Gram how she was feeling. She blinked her eyes a few times and said, "Piddles."

Gramps said, "They must've given her something. She doesn't know what she's saying."

I leaned down and whispered in her ear. "Gram, don't leave us."

"Piddles," Gram said.

When the nurse left the room, Gramps climbed back on top of the bed and lay down next to Gram. He patted the bed. "Well," he said, "this ain't our marriage bed, but it will do."

16
THE SINGING TREE

GRAM WAS RELEASED FROM THE HOSPITAL THE NEXT morning mainly because she was so ornery. Gramps wanted her to stay another day, but Gram climbed out of bed and said, "Where's my underwear?"

"I guess this cantankerous woman is getting out of here," Gramps said.

I think fear had made us all a little cantankerous. I had spent the night in the waiting room. Gramps offered to get me a motel room, but I was afraid that if I left the hospital, I would never see Gram again. The boy we had met at the river curled up in an armchair, but I don't think he slept either. Once he used the telephone. I heard him say, "Yeah, I'll be home in the morning. I'm with some friends."

The boy woke me up at six o'clock and said Gram was much better. He handed me a piece of paper. "It's my address, in case you ever want to write or anything, but I'd understand if you didn't—"

I opened the paper. "What's your name?"

He smiled. "Oh yeah, right." He took the paper and added his name: Tom Fleet. "See ya," he said.

As we were checking out of the hospital, I asked if we should call my father. Gramps said, "Well, now, chickabiddy, I thought about that, but it's only going to make him worry. Do you think we could wait to call him when we get to Idaho?"

Gramps was right, but I was disappointed. I was ready to call my father. I wanted very much to hear his voice, but I was also afraid that I might ask him to come and get me.

Outside the hospital, I heard the warbling of a bird, and it was such a familiar warble that I stopped and listened for its source. Bordering the parking lot was a rim of poplars. The sound was coming from somewhere in the top of one of those trees, and I thought, instantly, of the singing tree in Bybanks.

Next to my favorite sugar maple tree beside the barn is a tall aspen. When I was younger, I heard the most beautiful birdsong coming from the top of that tree. It was not a call; it was a true birdsong, with trills and warbles. I stood beneath that tree for the longest time, hoping to catch sight of the bird who was singing such a song. I saw no bird— only leaves waving in the breeze. The longer I stared up at the leaves, the more it seemed that it was the tree itself that was singing. Every time I passed that tree, I listened. Sometimes it sang, sometimes it did not, but from then on I always called it the singing tree.

The morning after my father learned that my mother was not coming back, he left for Lewiston, Idaho. Gram and Gramps came to stay with me. I had pleaded to go along, but my father said he didn't think I should have to go through that. That day I climbed up into the maple and watched the singing tree, waiting for it to sing. I stayed there all day and on into the early evening. It did not sing.

At dusk, Gramps placed three sleeping bags at the foot of the tree, and he, Gram, and I slept there all night. The tree did not sing.

In the hospital parking lot, Gram heard the song, too. "Oh Salamanca," she said. "A singing tree!" She pulled at Gramps's sleeve.

"Oh, it's a good sign, don't you think?"

As we swept on across South Dakota toward

the Badlands, the whispers no longer said, *hurry, hurry* or *rush, rush*. They now said, *slow down, slow down*. I could not figure this out. It seemed some sort of warning, but I did not have too much time to think about it, as I was busy telling about Phoebe.

17
IN THE COURSE OF A LIFETIME

A FEW DAYS AFTER PHOEBE AND I HAD SEEN MR. Birkway and Mrs. Cadaver whacking away at the rhododendron, I walked home with Phoebe after school. She was as crotchety and sullen as a three-legged mule, and I was not quite sure why. She had been asking me why I had not said anything to my father about Mrs. Cadaver and Mr. Birkway, and I told her that I was waiting for the right time.

"Your father was over there yesterday," Phoebe said. "I saw him. He'd better watch out. What would you do if Mrs. Cadaver chopped up your father? Would you go live with your mother?"

It surprised me when she said that, reminding me that I had told Phoebe nothing about my mother. "Yes, I suppose I would go live with her." That was impossible and I knew it, but for some reason I could not tell Phoebe that, so I lied.

Phoebe's mother was sitting at the kitchen table

when we walked in. In front of her was a pan of burned brownies. She blew her nose. "Oh sweetie," she said, "you startled me. How was it?"

"How was what?" Phoebe said.

"Why, sweetie, school of course. How was it? How were your classes?"

"Okay."

"Just okay?" Mrs. Winterbottom suddenly leaned over and kissed Phoebe's cheek.

"I'm not a baby, you know," Phoebe said, wiping off the kiss.

Mrs. Winterbottom stabbed the brownies with a knife. "Want one?" she asked.

"They're burned," Phoebe said. "Besides, I'm too fat."

"Oh sweetie, you're not fat," Mrs. Winterbottom said.

"I am."

"No, you're not."

"I am, I am, I am!" Phoebe shouted at her mother. "You don't have to bake things for me. I'm too fat. And you don't have to wait here for me to come home. I'm thirteen now."

Phoebe marched upstairs. Mrs. Winterbottom offered me a brownie, so I sat down at the table. What I started doing was remembering the day before my mother left. I did not know it was to be her last day home. Several times that day, my mother asked me if I wanted to walk up in the fields with her. It was drizzling outside, and I was cleaning out my desk, and I just did not feel like going. "Maybe later," I kept saying. When she asked me for about the tenth time, I said, "No! I don't want to go. Why do you keep asking me?" I don't know why I did that. I didn't mean anything by it, but that was one of the last memories she had of me, and I wished I could take it back.

Phoebe's sister, Prudence, stormed into the house, slamming the door behind her. "I blew it, I just know it!" she wailed.

"Oh sweetie," her mother said.

"I did!" Prudence said. "I did, I did, I did."

Mrs. Winterbottom half-heartedly chipped away at the burned brownies and asked Prudence if she would have another chance at cheerleading tryouts.

"Yes, tomorrow. But I know I'm going to blow it!"

Her mother said, "Maybe I'll come along and watch." I could tell that Mrs. Winterbottom was trying to rise above some awful sadness she was feeling, but Prudence couldn't see that. Prudence had her own agenda, just as I had had my own agenda that day my mother wanted me to walk with her. I couldn't see my own mother's sadness.

"What?" Prudence said. "Come along and *watch*?"

"Yes, wouldn't that be nice?"

"No!" Prudence said. "No, no, no. You can't. It would be awful."

I heard the front door open and shut and Phoebe came in the kitchen waving a white envelope. "Guess what was on the steps?" she said.

Mrs. Winterbottom took the envelope and turned it over and over before she slowly unsealed it and slipped out the message.

"Oh," she said. "Who is doing this?" She held out the piece of paper: *In the course of a lifetime, what does it matter?*

Prudence said, "Well, I have more important things to worry about, I can assure you. I know I'm going to blow those cheerleading tryouts. I just know it."

On and on she went, until Phoebe said, "Cripes, Prudence, in the course of a lifetime, what does it matter?"

At that moment, it was as if a switch went off in Mrs. Winterbottom's brain. She put her hand to her mouth and stared out the window. She was invisible to Prudence and Phoebe, though. They did not notice.

Phoebe said, "Are these cheerleading tryouts such a big deal? Will you even remember them in five years?"

"Yes!" Prudence said. "Yes, I most certainly will."

"How about ten years? Will you remember them in ten?"

"Yes!" Prudence said.

As I walked home, I thought about the message. *In the course of a lifetime, what does it matter?* I said it over and over. I wondered about the mysterious messenger, and I wondered about all the things in the course of a lifetime that would not matter. I did not think cheerleading tryouts would matter, but I was not so sure about yelling at your mother. I was certain, however, that if your mother left, it would be something that mattered in the whole long course of your lifetime.

18
THE GOOD MAN

I SHOULD MENTION MY FATHER.

When I was telling Phoebe's story to Gram and Gramps, I did not say much about my father. He was their son, and not only did they know him better than I, but as Gram often said, he was the light of their lives. They had three other sons at one time, but one son died when a tractor flipped over on him, one was killed when he skied into a tree, and the third died when he jumped into the freezing cold Ohio River to save his best friend (the best friend survived but my uncle did not).

My father was the only son left, but even if their other sons were still alive, my father might still be their light because he is also a kind, honest, simple, and good man. I do not mean simple as in simple-minded—I mean he likes plain and simple things. His favorite clothes are the flannel shirts and blue jeans that he has had for twenty years. It nearly killed him to buy white shirts and a suit for his new job in Euclid.

He loved the farm because he could be out in the real air, and he wouldn't wear work gloves because he liked to touch the earth and the wood and the animals. It was painful for him to go to work in an office when we moved. He did not like being sealed up inside with nothing real to touch.

We'd had the same car, a blue Chevy, for fifteen years. He couldn't bear to part with it because he had touched—and repaired—every inch of it. I also think he couldn't bear the thought that if he sold it, someone might take it to the junkyard. My father hated the whole idea of putting cars out to pasture. He often prowled through junkyards touching old cars and buying old alternators and carburetors just for the joy of cleaning them up and making them work again. My grandfather had never quite gotten the hang of car mechanics, and so he thought my father was a genius.

My mother was right when she said my father was good. He was always thinking of little things to cheer up someone else. This nearly drove my mother crazy because I think she wanted to keep up with him, but it was not her natural gift like it was with my father. He would be out in the field and see a flowering bush that my grandmother might like, and he would dig the whole thing up and take it straight over to Gram's garden and re-plant it. If it snowed, he would be up at dawn to trek over to his parents' house and shovel out their driveway.

If he went into town to buy supplies for the farm, he would come back with something for my mother and something for me. They were small things—a cotton scarf, a book, a glass paper-weight—but whatever he brought, it was exactly what you would have picked out for yourself.

I had never seen him angry. "Sometimes I don't think you're human," my mother told him. It was the sort of thing she said just before she left, and it bothered me, because it seemed as if she wanted him to be meaner, less good.

Two days before she left, when I first heard her raise the subject of leaving, she said, "I feel so rotten in comparison."

"Sugar, you're not rotten," he said.

"See?" she said. "See? Why couldn't you at least believe I am rotten?"

"Because you're not," he said.

She said she had to leave in order to clear her head, and to clear her heart of all the bad things.

She needed to learn about what she was.

"You can do that here, Sugar," he said.

"I need to do it on my own," she said. "I can't think. All I see here is what I am not. I am not brave. I am not good. And I wish someone would call me by my real name. My name isn't Sugar. It's Chanhassen."

She had not been well. She had had some terrible shocks, it is true, but I did not understand why she could not get better with us. I begged her to take me with her, but she said I could not miss school and my father needed me and besides, she had to go alone. She *had* to.

I thought she might change her mind, or at least tell me when she was leaving. But she did neither of those things. She left me a letter which explained that if she said good-bye, it would be too terribly painful and it would sound too permanent. She wanted me to know that she would think of me every minute and that she would be back before the tulips bloomed.

But, of course, she was not back before the tulips bloomed.

It nearly killed my father after she left, I know it, but he continued on doing everything just as before, whistling and humming and finding little gifts for people. He kept bringing home gifts for my mother and stacking them in a pile in their bedroom.

On the day after he found out she wasn't returning, he flew to Lewiston, Idaho, and when he came back, he spent three days chipping away at the fireplace hidden behind the plaster wall. Some of the cement grouting between the bricks had to be replaced, and he wrote her name in the new cement. He wrote *Chanhassen*, not *Sugar*.

Three weeks later he put the farm up for sale. By this time he was receiving letters from Mrs. Cadaver, and I knew that he was answering her letters. Then he drove up to see Mrs. Cadaver while I stayed with Gram and Gramps. When he came back, he said we were moving to Euclid. Mrs. Cadaver had helped him find a job.

I didn't even wonder how he had met Mrs. Cadaver or how long he had known her. I ignored her whole existence. Besides, I was too busy throwing the most colossal temper tantrums. I refused to move. I would not leave our farm, our maple tree, our swimming hole, our pigs, our chickens, our hayloft. I would not leave the place that belonged to me. I would not leave the place to which, I was convinced, my mother might return.

At first my father did not argue with me. He let me behave like a wild boar. At last, he took down the For Sale sign and put up a For Rent sign. He said he would rent out the farm, hire someone to care for the animals and the crops, and rent a house for us in Euclid. The farm would still belong to us and one day we could return to it. "But for now," he said, "we have to leave because your mother is haunting me day and night. She's in the fields, the air, the barn, the walls, the trees." He said we were making this move to learn about bravery and courage. That sounded awfully familiar.

In the end, I think I merely ran out of steam. I stopped throwing tantrums. I didn't help pack, but when the time came, I climbed in the car and joined my father for our move to Euclid. I did not feel brave, and I did not feel courageous.

When I told my story of Phoebe to Gram and Gramps, I mentioned none of this. They knew it already. They knew my father was a good man, they knew I did not want to leave the farm, they knew my father felt we had to leave. They also knew that my father had tried, many times, to explain to me about Margaret, but that I wouldn't hear it.

On that long day that my father and I left the

farm behind and drove to Euclid, I wished that my father was not such a good man, so there would be someone to blame for my mother's leaving. I didn't want to blame her. She was my mother, and she was part of me.

19
FISH IN THE AIR

GRAM SAID, "WHERE DID WE LEAVE OFF WITH Peeby? What was happening?"

"What's the matter, gooseberry?" Gramps said. "Did that snake bite your brains?"

"No," she said. "It did not bite my brains. I was just trying to refresh my memory."

"Let's see," Gramps said, "didn't Peeby want you to tell your daddy about Mrs. Cadaver and Mr. Birkway hacking up her husband?"

Yes, that is what Phoebe wanted, and it is what I tried to do. One Sunday, when my father was looking through the photo albums, I asked him if he knew much about Mrs. Cadaver. He looked up quickly. "You're ready to talk about Margaret?" he said.

"Well—there were a few things I wanted to mention—"

"I've been wanting to explain—" he said.

I plunged on. I didn't want him to explain. I wanted to warn him. "Phoebe and I saw her slashing and hacking away at the bushes in her backyard."

"Is there something wrong with that?" he asked.

I tried another approach. "Her voice is like dead leaves blowing around, and her hair is spooky."

"I see," he said.

"And there is a man who visits her—"

"Sal, that sounds like spying."

"And I don't think we should go over there anymore."

Dad took off his glasses and rubbed them on his shirt for about five minutes. Then he said, "Sal, you're trying to catch fish in the air. Your mother is not coming back."

It looked like I was merely jealous of Mrs. Cadaver. There in the calm light of my father, all those things that Phoebe had said about Mrs. Cadaver seemed foolish.

"I'd like to explain about her," my father said.

"Oh, never mind. Just forget I mentioned her. I don't need any explanations."

Later, when I was doing my homework, I found myself doodling in the margin of my English book. I had drawn a figure of a woman with wild hair and evil eyes and a rope around her neck. I drew a tree, fastened the rope to it, and hung her.

The next day at school, I studied Mr. Birkway as he leaped and cavorted about the classroom. If he was a murderer, he certainly was a lively one. I had always pictured murderers as being mopey and sullen. I hoped Mr. Birkway was in love with Margaret Cadaver and would marry her and take her away so that my father and I could go back to Bybanks.

What I found most surprising about Mr. Birkway was that he increasingly reminded me of my mother—or at least of my mother *before* the sadness set in. There was a liveliness to both Mr. Birkway and my mother, and an excitement—a passion—for words and for stories.

That day, as Mr. Birkway talked about Greek mythology, I started daydreaming about my mother, who loved books almost as much as she loved all her outdoor treasures. She liked to carry little books in her pocket and sometimes when we were out in the fields, she would flop down in the grass and start reading aloud.

My mother especially liked Indian stories. She knew about thunder gods, earth-makers, wise crows, sly coyotes, and shadow souls. Her favorite stories were those about people who came back, after death, as a bird or a river or a horse. She even knew one story about an old warrior who came back as a potato.

The next thing I knew, Mr. Birkway was saying, "Right, Phoebe? Are you awake? You have the second report."

"Report?" Phoebe said.

Mr. Birkway clutched his heart. "Ben is doing an oral report on Prometheus this Friday. You're doing one on Pandora next Monday."

"Lucky me," Phoebe muttered.

Mr. Birkway asked me to stay after class for a minute. Phoebe sent me warning messages with her eyebrows. As everyone else was leaving the room, Phoebe said, "I'll stay with you if you want."

"Why?"

"Because of him hacking up Mr. Cadaver, that's what. I don't think you should be alone with him."

He did not hack me up. Instead, he gave me a special assignment, a "mini journal." "I don't know what that is," I said. Phoebe was breathing on my shoulder. Mr. Birkway said I should write about something that interested me. "Like what?" I said.

"Oh, a place, a room, a person—don't worry about it too much. Just write whatever comes to mind."

Phoebe and I walked home with Mary Lou and Ben. My brain was a mess, what with trying not to flinch whenever Ben brushed against me. When we left Ben and Mary Lou and turned the corner onto Phoebe's street, I wasn't paying much attention. I suppose I was aware that someone was coming along the sidewalk in our direction, but it wasn't until the person was about three feet away that I really took notice.

It was Phoebe's lunatic, coming toward us, staring right at us. He stopped directly in front of us, blocking our way.

"Phoebe Winterbottom, right?" he said to Phoebe.

Her voice was a little squeak. The only sound that came out was a tiny "Erp—"

"What's the matter?" he said. He slid one hand into his pocket.

Phoebe pushed him, yanked my arm, and started running. "Oh-my-god!" she said. "Oh-my-god!"

I was grateful that we were nearly at Phoebe's

house, so if he stabbed us in broad daylight, maybe one of her neighbors would discover our bodies and take us to the hospital before we bled entirely to death. I was beginning to believe he was a lunatic.

Phoebe tugged at her doorknob, but the door was locked. Phoebe beat on the door, and her mother suddenly pulled it open. She looked rather pale and shaken herself.

"It was locked!" Phoebe said. "Why was the door locked?"

"Oh sweetie," Mrs. Winterbottom said. "It's just that—I thought that—" She peered around us and looked up and down the street. "Did you see someone—did someone frighten you—"

"It was the lunatic," Phoebe said. "We saw him just now." She could hardly catch her breath. "Maybe we should call the police—or tell Dad."

I took a good long look at Phoebe's mother. She did not seem capable of phoning the police or Mr. Winterbottom. I think she was more scared than we were. She went around locking all the doors.

Nothing more happened that evening, and by the time I went home, the lunatic did not seem quite so threatening. No one called the police, and to my knowledge, Mrs. Winterbottom had not yet told Mr. Winterbottom, but right before I left Phoebe's house, Phoebe said to me, "If I see the lunatic once more, I'll phone the police myself."

20
THE BLACKBERRY KISS

THAT NIGHT I TRIED TO WRITE THE MINI JOURNAL for Mr. Birkway. First I made a list of all the things I liked, and they were all things from Bybanks— the trees, the cows, the chickens, the pigs, the fields, the swimming hole. It was a complete jumble of things, and when I tried to write about any one of those things, I ended up writing about my mother, because everything was connected to her. At last, I wrote about the blackberry kiss.

One morning when I awoke very early, I saw my mother walking up the hill to the barn. Mist hung about the ground, finches were singing in the oak tree beside the house, and there was my mother, her pregnant belly sticking out in front of her. She was strolling up the hill, swinging her arms and singing:

Oh, don't fall in love with a sailor boy,

A sailor boy, a sailor boy—
Oh, don't fall in love with a sailor boy,
'Cause he'll take your heart to sea—

As she approached the corner of the barn where the sugar maple stands, she plucked a few blackberries from a stray bush and popped them into her mouth. She looked all around her—back at the house, across the fields, and· up into the canopy of branches overhead. She took several quick steps up to the trunk of the maple, threw her arms around it, and kissed that tree soundly.

Later that day, I examined this tree trunk. I tried to wrap my arms about it, but the trunk was much bigger than it had seemed from my window. I looked up at where her mouth must have touched the trunk. I probably imagined this, but I thought I could detect a small dark stain, as from a blackberry kiss.

I put my ear against the trunk and listened. I faced that tree squarely and kissed it firmly. To this day, I can smell the smell of the bark—a sweet, woody smell—and feel the ridges in the bark, and taste that distinctive taste on my lips.

In my mini journal, I confessed that I had since kissed all different kinds of trees, and each family of trees—oaks, maples, elms, birches—had a special flavor all its own. Mixed in with each tree's own taste was the slight taste of blackberries, and why this was so, I could not explain.

The next day, I turned in this story to Mr. Birkway. He didn't read it or even look at it, but he said, "Marvelous! Brilliant!" as he slipped it into his briefcase. "I'll put it with the other journals."

Phoebe said, "Did you write about me?"

Ben said, "Did you write about me?"

Mr. Birkway bounded around the room as if the opportunity to teach us was his notion of paradise. He read a poem by e. e. cummings titled "the little horse is newlY" and the reason why the only capital letter in the title is the Y at the end of *newlY* is because Mr. Cummings liked to do it that way.

"He probably never took English," Phoebe said.

To me that Y looked like the newly born horse standing up on his thin legs.

The poem was about a newlY born horse who doesn't know anything but feels everything. He lives in a "smoothbeautifully folded" world. I liked that. I was not sure what it was, but I liked it. Everything sounded soft and safe.

That day, Phoebe left school early for a dentist

appointment. I started walking home alone, but Ben joined me. I was completely unprepared for what happened on the way home, and for what would happen later. Ben and I were simply walking along and he said, "Did anyone ever read your palm?"

"No."

"I know how to do it," he said. "Want me to read yours?" He took my hand and stared at it for the longest time. His own hand was soft and warm. Mine was sweating like crazy. He was saying, "Hm" and tracing the lines of my palm with his finger. It gave me the shivers, but not in an entirely unpleasant way. The sun was beating down on us, and I thought it might be nice to stay there forever with him just running his finger along my palm like that. I thought about the newly born horse who knows nothing and feels everything. I thought about the smoothbeautifully folded world. Finally, Ben said, "Do you want the good news first or the bad news?"

"The bad news. It isn't real bad, is it?"

He coughed. "The bad news is that I can't really read palms." (I snatched my hand away.) "Don't you want to know the good news?" he asked. (I started walking.) "The good news is that you let me hold your hand for almost five minutes and you didn't flinch once."

I didn't know what to make of him. He walked me all the way to my house, even though I refused to speak to him. He waited on the porch until I was ready to go to Phoebe's, and then he walked me to her house.

When I knocked at Phoebe's door, Ben said, "I'll be going now." I took a quick look at him and turned back to the door, but in that instant that I was turning my head, he leaned forward, and I do believe his lips kissed my ear. I was not sure this was what he intended. In fact, I was not sure it happened at all, because before I knew it, he had hopped down the steps and was walking away.

The door inched open and there was Phoebe's round face, as white and frightened as ever you could imagine. "Quick," she said. "Come in." She led me into the kitchen. On the kitchen table was an apple pie, and beside it were three envelopes: one for Phoebe, one for Prudence, and one for their father.

"I opened my note," Phoebe said, showing it to me. It said, *Keep all the doors locked and call your father if you need anything. I love you, Phoebe.* It was signed, *Mom.*

I didn't think too much of it. "Phoebe—" I said.

"I know, I know. It doesn't sound terrible or anything. In fact, my first thought was, 'Well, good. She knows I am old enough to be here by myself.' I figured she was out shopping or maybe she even decided to return to work, even though she wasn't supposed to go back to Rocky's Rubber until next week. But then Prudence came home and opened her note."

Phoebe showed me the note left for Prudence. It said, *Please heat up the spaghetti sauce and boil the spaghetti. I love you, Prudence.* It was signed, *Mom.*

I still didn't think too much of it, but Phoebe was suspicious. Prudence made the spaghetti, while I helped Phoebe set the table. Phoebe and I even made a salad. "I do feel sort of independent," Phoebe said.

When Phoebe's father came home, Phoebe showed him his note. He opened it and sat down, staring at the piece of paper. Phoebe looked over his shoulder and read his note aloud: *I had to go away. I can't explain. I'll call you in a few days.*

I had a sinking, sinking feeling.

Prudence started asking a million questions. "What does she mean? Go away where? Why can't she explain? Why didn't she tell you? Did she mention this? A few *days*? Where did she go?"

"Maybe we should call the police," Phoebe said. "I think she was kidnapped or something."

"Oh, Phoebe," Mr. Winterbottom said.

"I'm serious," she said. "Maybe a lunatic came in the house and dragged her off—"

"Phoebe, that is not funny."

"I'm not being funny. I mean it. It could happen."

Prudence was still asking her questions. "Where did she go? Why didn't she mention this? Didn't she tell you? Where did she go?"

"Prudence, I honestly cannot say," her father said.

"I think we should call the police," Phoebe repeated.

"Phoebe, if she was kidnapped, would the lunatic—as you say—allow her to sit down and write these notes? Mm?"

He stood up, removed his coat, and said, "Let's eat."

As I left, Phoebe said, "My mother has disappeared. Sal, don't tell anyone. Don't tell a soul."

At home, my father was slumped over the photo album. He used to close the album quickly when I came in the room, as if he were embarrassed to be caught with it. Lately, however, he didn't bother to close it. It was as if he didn't have the strength to do that.

On the opened page was a photo of my father and mother sitting in the grass beneath the sugar maple. His arms were around her and she was sort of folded into him. His face was pressed up next to hers and their hair blended together. They looked like they were connected.

"Phoebe's mother went away," I said.

He looked up at me.

"She left some notes. She says she's coming back, but I don't believe it."

I went upstairs and tried to work on my mythology report. My father came to the doorway and said, "People usually come back."

Now I can see that he was just talking in general, just trying to be comforting, but then—that night—what I heard in what he said was the tiniest reassurance of something I had been thinking and hoping. I had been praying that a miracle would happen and my mother would come back and we would return to Bybanks and everything would be exactly as it used to be.

21
SOULS

AT SCHOOL THE NEXT DAY, PHOEBE WORE A FIXED expression: a sealed, thin smile. It must have been hard for her to maintain that smile, because by the time English class came around, her chin was quivering from the strain. She was extremely quiet all day. She didn't speak to anyone but me, and the only thing she said to me was, "Stay at my house tomorrow night." It wasn't a question; it was a command.

Mr. Birkway gave us a fifteen-second exercise. As fast as we could, without thinking, we were to draw something. He would tell us what we were to draw when everyone was ready. "Remember," he said. *"Don't think.* Just draw. Fifteen seconds. Ready? Draw your *soul*. Go."

We all wasted five seconds staring blankly back at him. When we saw that he was serious and was watching the clock, our pencils hit the paper. I wasn't thinking. There wasn't time to think.

When Mr. Birkway called "Stop!" everyone looked up, dazed. Then we looked down at our papers, and a buzz went around the room. We were surprised at what had come out of our pencils.

Mr. Birkway zipped around, scooping up the papers. He shuffled them and tacked them up on the bulletin board. He said, "We now have everyone's soul captured." We all crowded around.

The first thing I noticed was that every single person had drawn a central shape—a heart, circle, square, or triangle. I thought that was unusual. I mean, no one drew a bus or a spaceship or a cow— they all drew these same shapes. Next, I noticed that inside each figure was a distinct design. At first it seemed that every one was different. There was a cross, a dark scribble, an eye, a mouth, a window.

There was one with a teardrop inside that I thought must be Phoebe's.

Then Mary Lou said, "Look at that—two are exactly the same." People were saying, "Geez" and "Wow" and "Whose are those?"

The duplicate designs were: a circle with a large maple leaf in the center, the tips of the leaf touching the sides of the circle. One of the maple leaf circles was mine. The other was Ben's.

22
EVIDENCE

I SPENT THE NEXT NIGHT AT PHOEBE'S HOUSE, BUT I could hardly sleep. Phoebe kept saying, "Hear that noise?" and she would jump up to peer out the window in case it was the lunatic returning for the rest of us. Once she saw Mrs. Cadaver in her garden with a flashlight.

I must have fallen asleep after that, because I awoke to the sound of Phoebe crying in her sleep. When I woke her, she denied it. "I was not crying. I most certainly was not."

In the morning, Phoebe refused to get up. Her father rushed into the room with two ties slung around his neck and his shoes in his hand. "Phoebe, you're late."

"I'm sick," she said. "I have a fever and a stomachache."

Her father placed his hand on her forehead, looked deep into her eyes and said, "I'm afraid you have to go to school."

"I'm sick. Honest," she said. "It might be cancer."

"Phoebe, I know you're worried, but there's nothing we can do but wait. We have to go on with things. We can't malinger."

"We can't what?" Phoebe said.

"Malinger. Here. Look it up." He tossed her the dictionary from her desk and tore down the hall.

"My mother is missing, and my father hands me a dictionary," Phoebe said. She looked up *malinger* and read the definition: "'To pretend to be ill in order to escape duty or work.'" She slammed the book shut. "I am *not* malingering."

Prudence was in a frenzy. "Where is my white blouse? Phoebe, have you seen—? I could have sworn—!" She pulled things out of her closet and flung them on the bed.

Phoebe reluctantly got dressed, pulling a wrinkled blouse and skirt from the closet. Downstairs, the kitchen table was bare. "No bowls of muesli," Phoebe said. "No glasses of orange juice or whole wheat toast." She touched a white sweater hanging on the back of a chair. "My mother's favorite white cardigan," she said. She snatched the sweater and waved it in front of her father. "Look at this! Would she leave this behind? Would she?"

He reached forward and touched its sleeve, rubbing the fabric between his fingers for a moment. "Phoebe, it's an old sweater." Phoebe put it on over her wrinkled blouse.

I was uneasy because everything that happened at Phoebe's that morning reminded me of when my mother left. For weeks, my father and I fumbled around like ducks in a fit. Nothing was where it was supposed to be. The house took on a life of its own, hatching piles of dishes and laundry and newspapers and dust. My father must have said "I'll be jiggered" three thousand times. The chickens were fidgety, the cows were skittish, and the pigs were sullen and glum. Our dog, Moody Blue, whimpered for hours on end.

When my father said that my mother was not coming back, I refused to believe it. I brought all her postcards down from my room and said, "She wrote me all these, she must be coming back." And just like Phoebe, who had waved her mother's sweater in front of her father, I had brought a chicken in from the coop: "Would Mom leave her favorite chicken?" I demanded. "She loves this chicken."

What I really meant was, "How can she not come back to *me*? She loves me."

At school, Phoebe slammed her books on her desk. Beth Ann said, "Hey, Phoebe, your blouse is a little wrinkled—"

"My mother's away," Phoebe said.

"I iron my own clothes now," Beth Ann said. "I even iron—"

To me, Phoebe whispered, "I think I'm having a genuine heart attack."

I thought about a baby rabbit that our dog, Moody Blue, caught and carried around—she was not actually lunching on the rabbit, just playing. I finally coaxed Moody Blue to drop it, and when I picked up the rabbit, its heart was beating faster than anything. Faster and faster it went, and then all of a sudden its heart stopped.

I took the rabbit to my mother. She said, "It's dead, Salamanca."

"It can't be dead," I said. "It was alive just a minute ago."

I wondered what would happen if all of a sudden Phoebe's heart beat itself out like the rabbit's, and she fell down and died right there at school. Her mother would not even know Phoebe was dead.

After homeroom, Mary Lou said to Phoebe, "Did I hear you say your mother is away—?"

Christy and Megan gathered around. "Is your mother on a business trip?" Christy said. "My mother's always going to Paris on business trips. So where is your mother? On a business trip?"

Phoebe nodded.

"Where did she go?" Megan said. "Tokyo? Saudi Arabia?"

Phoebe said, "London."

"Oh, London," Christy said. "My mother's been there."

Phoebe turned to me with a puzzled expression on her face. I think that she was surprised at what she had said, but I knew exactly why she had lied. It was easier sometimes. I had done this myself when people asked about my mother. "Don't worry, Phoebe," I said.

She snapped, "I am *not* worried."

I had done that too. Whenever anyone tried to console me about my mother, I had nearly chomped their heads off. I was a complete ornery old donkey. When my father would say, "You must feel terrible," I denied it. "I don't," I told him. "I don't feel anything at all." But I did feel terrible. I didn't want to wake up in the morning, and I was afraid to go to sleep at night.

By lunchtime, people were coming at Phoebe from all directions. "How long will your mother be in London?" Mary Lou asked. "Is she having tea with the queen?"

"Tell her to go to Convent Garden," Christy said. "My mother just loves Convent Garden."

"It's *Cov*ent Garden, cabbage-head," Mary Lou said.

"It isn't," Christy said. "I'm sure it's *Con*vent Garden."

After school, we walked home with Ben and Mary Lou. Phoebe wouldn't say a word. "Whatsa matter, Free Bee?" Ben asked. "Talk."

Out of the blue, I said, "Everyone has his own agenda." Ben tripped over the curb, and Mary Lou gave me a peculiar look. I kept hoping that Phoebe's mother would be home. Even though the door was locked, I kept hoping. "Are you sure you want me to come in?" I said. "Maybe you want to be alone."

Phoebe said, "I *don't* want to be alone. Call your dad and see if you can stay for dinner again."

Inside, Phoebe called, "Mom?" She walked through the house, looking in each room. "That's it," Phoebe said. "I'm going to search for clues, for evidence that the lunatic has been here and dragged my mother off." I wanted to tell her that she was just fishing in the air and that probably her mother had not been kidnapped, but I knew that Phoebe didn't want to hear it.

When my mother did not return, I imagined all sorts of things. Maybe she had cancer and didn't want to tell us and was hiding in Idaho. Maybe she got knocked on the head and had amnesia and was wandering around Lewiston, not knowing who she really was, or thinking she was someone else. My father said, "She does not have cancer, Sal. She does not have amnesia. Those are fishes in the air." But I didn't believe him. Maybe he was trying to protect her—or me.

Phoebe prowled through the house, examining the walls and carpet, searching for bloodstains. She found several suspicious spots and unidentifiable hair strands. Phoebe marked the spots with pieces of adhesive tape and collected the hairs in an envelope.

Prudence was in a lather when she came home. "I made it!" she said. "I made it!" She was jumping all about. "I made cheerleading!" When Phoebe reminded her that their mother had been kidnapped, Prudence said, "Oh Phoebe, Mom wasn't kidnapped." She stopped jumping and looked around the kitchen. "So what are we supposed to have for dinner?"

Phoebe rummaged around in the cupboards. Prudence opened the freezer compartment and said, "Look at this." For a terrible moment, I thought she had found some chopped-up body parts in there. Maybe, just maybe, Phoebe was right. Maybe a lunatic *had* done away with her mother. I couldn't look. I could hear Prudence moving things in the freezer. At least she wasn't screaming.

There were no body parts in the freezer. Instead, stacked neatly, were plastic containers, each with a note attached. "Broc-Len Cas, 350, 1 hr," Prudence read, and "Mac Che, 325, 45 min," on and on and on.

"What's Broc-Len Cas?" I said.

Phoebe pried open the lid. Inside was a green and yellow hardened mass. "Broccoli and lentil casserole," she said.

When their father came home and was surprised to see dinner on the table, Prudence showed him the freezer contents. "Hm," he said. At dinner, we all ate quietly.

"I don't suppose you've heard anything—from Mom?" Prudence asked her father.

"Not yet," he said.

"I think we should call the police," Phoebe said.

"Phoebe."

"I'm *serious*. I found some suspicious spots." Phoebe pointed toward two adhesive-taped areas beneath the dining room table.

"What's that tape doing down there?" he asked.

Phoebe explained about the potential blood spots.

"Blood?" Prudence said. She stopped eating.

Phoebe pulled out the envelope and emptied the hair strands on the table. "Strange hairs," Phoebe explained.

Prudence said, "Uck."

Mr. Winterbottom tapped his fork against his knife. Then he stood up, took Phoebe's arm, and said, "Follow me." He went to the refrigerator, opened the freezer compartment, and indicated the plastic containers. "If your mother had been kidnapped by a lunatic, would she have had time to prepare all these meals? Would she have been able to say, 'Excuse me, Mr. Lunatic, while I prepare ten or twenty meals for my family to eat while I am kidnapped?'"

"You don't care," Phoebe said. "Nobody cares. Everyone has his own idiot agenda."

I left shortly after dinner. Mr. Winterbottom was in his study, phoning his wife's friends to see if they had any idea of where she might have gone.

"At least," Phoebe said to me, "he's doing something, but I still think we should call the police."

As I left Phoebe's, the dead-leaf crackly voice of Margaret Cadaver called to me from her house next door. "Sal? Do you want to come in? Your father's here—we're having dessert. Join us."

My father appeared behind her. "Come on, Sal," he said. "Don't be a goose."

"I am not a goose," I said. "I already had dessert, and I'm going home to work on my English report."

My father turned to Margaret. "I'd better go with her. Sorry—"

Margaret didn't say anything. She just stood there as my father retrieved his jacket and joined me. I knew it was mean, but I felt as if I had won a little victory over Margaret Cadaver.

On the way home, when Dad asked if Phoebe's mother had come back yet, I said, "No. Phoebe thinks a lunatic has carried her off."

"A lunatic? Isn't that a bit farfetched?"

"That's what I thought at first, but you never

know, do you? I mean it *could* happen. There could actually be a lunatic who—"

"Sal."

I was going to explain about the nervous young man and the mysterious messages, but my father would call me a goose. Instead, I said, "How do you know that someone—not exactly a lunatic, but just someone—didn't make Mom go to Idaho? Maybe it was blackmail—"

"Sal. Your mother went because she wanted to go."

"We should have stopped her."

"A person isn't a bird. You can't cage a person."

"She shouldn't have gone. If she hadn't gone—"

"Sal, I'm sure she intended to come back." We had reached our house, but we didn't go in. We sat on the porch steps. Dad said, "You can't predict—a person can't foresee—you never know—"

He looked away, and I felt miserable right along with him. I apologized for being ornery and for upsetting him. He put his arm around me and we sat there together on the porch, two people being completely pitiful and lost.

23
THE BADLANDS

Gramps said, "How's your snake leg, Gooseberry?" He was worried about Gram, but less about her leg than her raspy breathing. "We'll stop in the Badlands, okay?" Gram merely nodded.

The closer we got to the Badlands, the more wicked were the whispers in the air: *Slow down, slow, slow, slow.* "Maybe we shouldn't go to the Badlands," I suggested.

"What? Not go? Of course we should go," Gramps said. "We're almost there. It's a national treasure."

My mother must have traveled on this road. What was she thinking about when she saw that sign? Or that one? When she reached this spot in the road?

My mother did not drive. She was terrified of cars. "I don't like all that speed," she said. "I like to be in control of where I'm going and how fast I'm going." When she said she was going all the way to Lewiston, Idaho, on a bus, my father and I were astonished.

I could not imagine why she had chosen Idaho. I thought perhaps she had opened an atlas and pointed a finger at any old spot, but later I learned that she had a cousin in Lewiston, Idaho. "I haven't seen her for fifteen years," my mother said, "and that's good because she'll tell me what I'm really like."

"I could tell you that, Sugar," my father said.

"No, I mean before I was a wife and a mother. I mean *underneath*, where I am Chanhassen."

After driving for so long through the flat South Dakota prairie, it was a shock to come upon the Badlands. It was as if someone had ironed out all the rest of South Dakota and smooshed all the hills and valleys and rocks into this spot. Right smack in the middle of flat plains were jagged peaks and steep gorges. Above was the high blue sky and below were the pink and purple and black rocks. You can stand right on the edge of the gorges and see down, down into the most treacherous ravines, lined with sharp, rough outcroppings. You expect to see human skeletons dangling here and there.

Gram tried to say, "Huzza, huzza," but she

could not breathe well. "Huz—huz—" she rasped. Gramps placed a blanket on the ground so that she could sit and look.

My mother sent two postcards from the Badlands. One of them said, "Salamanca is my left arm. I miss my left arm."

I told Gram and Gramps a story that my mother had told me about the high sky, which looked higher here than anywhere else I had been. Long ago, the sky was so low that you might bump your head on it if you were not careful, and so low that people sometimes disappeared right up into it. People got a little fed up with this, so they made long poles, and one day they all raised their poles and pushed. They pushed the sky as high as they could.

"And lookee there," Gramps said. "They pushed so good, the sky stayed put."

While I was telling this story, a pregnant woman stood nearby, dabbing at her face with a tissue. "That woman looks world-weary," Gramps said. He asked her if she would like to rest on our blanket.

"I'll go look around," I said. Pregnant women frightened me.

When my mother first told me she was pregnant, she added, "At last! We really are going to fill this house up with children." At first I didn't like the idea. What was wrong with having just me? My mother, father, and I were our own little unit.

As the baby grew inside her, my mother let me listen to its heartbeat and feel it kicking against her, and I started looking forward to seeing this baby. I hoped it would be a girl, and I would have a sister. Together, my father, my mother, and I decorated the nursery. We painted it sparkling white and hung yellow curtains. My father stripped an old dresser and repainted it. People gave us the tiniest baby clothes. We washed and folded each shirt, each jumpsuit, each sleeper. We bought fresh new cloth diapers because my mother liked to see diapers hanging on the line outside.

The one thing we could not do was settle on a name. Nothing seemed quite right. Nothing was perfect enough for this baby. My father seemed more worried about this than my mother. "Something will come to us," my mother said. "The perfect name will arrive in the air one day."

Three weeks before the baby was due, I was out in the woods beyond the farthest field. My father was in town on errands; my mother was scrubbing the floors. She said that scrubbing the floors made her back feel better. My father didn't like her to do this, but she insisted. My mother was not a fragile, sickly woman. It was normal for her to do this sort of thing.

In the woods, I climbed an oak, singing my mother's song: *Oh, don't fall in love with a sailor boy, a sailor boy, a sailor boy*—I climbed higher and higher. *Don't fall in love with a sailor boy*—

Then the branch I stepped on snapped, and I grabbed out at another, but it was dead and came away in my hands. I fell down, down, as if I were in slow motion. I saw leaves. I knew I was falling.

When I came to, I was on the ground with my face pressed into the dirt. My right leg was twisted beneath me and when I tried to move, it felt as if sharp needles were shooting all up and down my leg. I tried to drag myself across the ground, but the needles shot up to my brain and made everything black. There was a walloping buzzing in my head.

I must have passed out again, because the next time I opened my eyes, the woods were darker and the air was cooler. I heard my mother calling. Her voice was distant and faint, coming, I thought, from near the barn. I answered, but my voice was caught in my chest.

My mother found me and carried me back through the woods, across the fields, and down the long hill to the house. She called my grandparents to come take us to the hospital. It took forever just to get a cast, and by the time we got home we were all exhausted. My father felt awful that he had been away and fussed over both of us constantly.

The baby came that night. I heard my father telephoning the doctor. "She won't make it," he said. "It's happening now, right now."

On my new crutches, I tottered down the hall. My mother was sunk into the pillow, sweating and groaning. "Something's wrong," she said to my father. She saw me standing there and said, "You shouldn't watch. I don't think I'm very good at this."

In the hallway outside her room, I lowered myself to the floor. The doctor came. My mother screamed just once, one long, mournful wail, and then it was quiet.

When the doctor carried the baby out of the room, I asked to see it. It had a pale, bluish tinge and there were marks on its neck where the umbilical chord had strangled it. "It might have been dead for hours," the doctor told my father. "I just can't say exactly."

"Was it a boy or a girl?" I asked.

The doctor whispered his answer, "A girl."

I asked if I could touch her. She was still a little warm from being inside my mother. She looked so sweet and peaceful, all curled up, and I wanted to hold her, but the doctor said that was not a good idea. I thought maybe if I held her she would wake up.

My father looked shaken, but he didn't seem concerned about the baby anymore. He kept going in and touching my mother. He said to me, "It wasn't your fault, Sal—it wasn't because she carried you. You mustn't think that."

I didn't believe him. I hobbled into my mother's room and crawled up on the bed beside her. She was staring at the ceiling.

"Let me hold it," she said.

"Hold what?"

"The baby," she said. Her voice was odd and silly.

My father came in and she asked him for the baby. He leaned down and said, "I wish—I wish—"

"The baby," she said.

"It didn't make it," he said.

"I'll hold the baby," she said.

"It didn't make it," he repeated.

"It can't be dead," she said in that same singsong voice. "It was alive just a minute ago."

I slept beside her until I heard her calling my father. When he turned on the light, I saw the blood spread out all across the bed. It had soaked the sheets and the blanket; it had soaked into the white plaster of my cast.

An ambulance came and took her and my father away. Gram and Gramps came to stay with me. Gram took all the sheets and boiled them. She scrubbed the blood from my cast as best she could, but a dark pink stain remained.

My father came home from the hospital briefly the next day. "We should name the baby anyway," he said. "Do you have any suggestions?"

The name came to me from the air. "Tulip," I said.

My father smiled. "Your mother will like that. We'll bury the baby in the little cemetery near the aspen grove—where the tulips come up every spring."

My mother had two operations in the next two days. She wouldn't stop bleeding. Later, my mother said, "They took out all my equipment." She would not have any more babies.

CC

I sat on the edge of a gorge in the Badlands, looking back at Gram and Gramps and the pregnant woman on the blanket. I pretended that it was my mother sitting there and she would still have the baby and everything would be the way it was supposed to be. And then I tried to imagine my mother sitting here on her trip out to Lewiston, Idaho. Did all the people on the bus get out and walk around with her or did she sit by herself, like I was doing? Did she sit here in this spot and did she see that pink spire? Was she thinking about me?

I picked up a flat stone and sailed it across the gorge where it hit the far wall and plummeted down, down, careening off the jagged outcroppings. My mother once told me the Blackfoot story of Napi, the Old Man who created men and women. To decide if these new people should live forever or die, Napi selected a stone. "If the stone floats," he said, "you will live forever. If it sinks, you will die." Napi dropped the stone into the water. It sank. People die.

"Why did Napi use a stone?" I asked. "Why not a leaf?"

My mother shrugged. "If you had been there, you could have made the rock float," she said. She was referring to my habit of skipping stones across the water.

I picked up another rock and sailed it across the gorge, and this one, too, hit the opposite wall and fell down and down and down. It was not a river. It was a hole. What did I expect?

24
BIRDS OF SADNESS

As we were leaving the Badlands, Gramps swore at a driver who cut us off. Usually when Gramps cussed like this, Gram threatened to go back to the egg man. I don't know that whole story, just that one time when Gramps was cussing up a storm, Gram ran off with the man who regularly bought eggs from Gramps. Gram stayed with the egg man for three days and three nights until Gramps came to get her and promised he wouldn't swear anymore.

I once asked Gram if she would really go back to the egg man if Gramps cussed too much. She said, "Don't tell your grandfather, but I don't mind a few hells and damns. Besides, that egg man snored to beat the band."

"So you didn't leave Gramps just because of the cussing?"

"Salamanca, I don't even remember why I did

that. Sometimes you know in your heart you love someone, but you have to go away before your head can figure it out."

That night we stayed at a motel outside of Wall, South Dakota. They had one room left, with only one bed in it, but Gramps was tired, so he said it would do. The bed was a king-size water bed. "Gol-dang," Gramps said. "Lookee there." When he pressed his hand on it, it gurgled. "Looks like we'll all have to float on this raft together tonight."

Gram flopped down on the bed and giggled. "Huz-huz," she said, in her raspy voice. She rolled into the middle. "Huz-huz." I lay down next to her, and Gramps tentatively sat down on the other side. "Whoa," he said. "I do believe this thing's alive." The three of us lay there sloshing around as Gramps turned this way and that. "Gol-darn," he said. Tears were streaming down Gram's face she was giggling so hard.

Gramps said, "Well, this ain't our marriage bed—"

That night I dreamed that I was floating down a river on a raft with my mother. We were lying on our backs looking up at the high sky. The sky moved closer and closer to us. There was a sudden popping sound and then we were up in the sky. Momma looked all around and said, "We can't be dead. We were alive just a minute ago."

In the morning, we set out for the Black Hills and Mt. Rushmore, hoping to be there by lunchtime. No sooner were we in the car than Gramps said, "So what happened to Peeby's mother and did Peeby get any more of those messages?"

"I hope everything turned out all right," Gram said. "I'm a little worried about Peeby."

On the day after Phoebe showed her father the suspicious spots and the unidentifiable hair strands, another message appeared: *You can't keep the birds of sadness from flying over your head, but you can keep them from nesting in your hair.* Phoebe brought the message to school to show me. "The lunatic again," she said.

"If he has already kidnapped your mother, why would he still be leaving messages?"

"They're clues," she said.

At school, people kept asking Phoebe about her mother's business trip to London. She tried to ignore them, but it wasn't always possible. She had to answer some of the time.

When Megan asked Phoebe what sights her mother had seen, Phoebe said, "Buckingham Palace—"

"Of course," Megan nodded knowingly.

"And Big Ben, and—" Phoebe was struggling. "Shakespeare's birthplace."

"But that's in Stratford-on-Avon," Megan said. "I thought your mother was in London. Stratford is miles away. Did she go on a day trip or something?"

"Yes, that's what she did. She went on a day trip."

Phoebe couldn't help it. She looked as if a whole family of the birds of sadness were nesting in her hair.

In English class, Ben had to give his mythology report. He was nervous. He explained that Prometheus stole fire from the sun and gave it to man. Zeus, the chief god, was angry at man and at Prometheus for taking some of his precious sun. As punishment, Zeus sent Pandora (a woman) to man. Then Zeus chained Prometheus to a rock and sent vultures down to eat Prometheus's liver. In Ben's nervousness, he mispronounced Prometheus, so what he actually said was that Zeus sent vultures down to eat porpoise's liver.

Mary Lou invited both me and Phoebe to dinner that night. When I phoned my father, he did not seem to mind, and I knew he wouldn't. All he said was, "That will be nice for you, Sal. Maybe I'll go eat over at Margaret's."

25
CHOLESTEROL

DINNER AT THE FINNEYS' WAS AN EXPERIENCE. When we arrived, Mary Lou's brothers were running around like crazed animals, jumping over the furniture and tossing footballs. Mary Lou's older sister, Maggie, was talking on the telephone and plucking her eyebrows at the same time. Mr. Finney was cooking something in the kitchen, with the help of four-year-old Tommy. Phoebe whispered, "I am not too optimistic about the possibilities of this meal."

When Mrs. Finney straggled in the door at six o'clock, Tommy and Dougie and Dennis tugged at various parts of her, all of them talking at once. "Look at this," and "Mom, Mom, Mom," and "Me first!" She made her way into the kitchen, trailing all three of them like a fishhook that has snagged a tangle of old tires and boots and other miscellaneous rubbish. She gave Mr. Finney a sloppy kiss on the lips, and he slipped a piece of cucumber into her mouth.

Mary Lou and I set the table, although I think it was largely a wasted effort. Everyone descended on the table in a chaotic flurry, knocking over glasses and sending forks onto the floor and picking up plates (which did not match, Phoebe pointed out to me) and saying, "That's my plate. I want the daisy plate," and "Give me the blue one! It's my turn for the blue plate."

Phoebe and I sat between Mary Lou and Ben. In the center of the table was a whomping platter of fried chicken. Phoebe said, "Chicken? Fried? I can't eat fried foods. I have a sensitive stomach." She glanced at the three pieces of chicken on Ben's plate. "You really shouldn't eat that, Ben. Fried foods aren't good for you. First of all, there's the cholesterol—"

Phoebe removed two pieces of chicken from Ben's plate and put them back on the serving platter. Mr. Finney coughed. Mrs. Finney said, "You're not going to eat the chicken then, Phoebe?"

Phoebe smiled. "Oh no, Mrs. Finney. I couldn't possibly. Actually, Mr. Finney shouldn't be eating it either. I don't know if you're aware of this, but men should really be careful about their cholesterol."

Mr. Finney stared down at his chicken. Mrs. Finney was rolling her lips around peculiarly. By this time, the beans had been passed to Phoebe. "Did you put butter on these beans, Mrs. Finney?"

"Yes, I did. Is there something wrong with butter?"

"*Cholesterol*," Phoebe said. "Cho-les-ter-ol. In the butter."

"Ah," Mrs. Finney said. "Cholesterol." She looked at her husband. "Be careful, dear. There's cholesterol on the beans."

I stared at Phoebe. I am sure I was not the only one in the room who wanted to strangle her.

Ben pushed his beans to one side of his plate. Maggie picked up a bean and examined it. When the potatoes came around, Phoebe explained that she was on a diet and could not eat starch. The rest of us looked glumly down at our plates. There was nothing at all on Phoebe's plate. Mrs. Finney said, "So what do you eat, Phoebe?"

"My mother makes special vegetarian meals. Low-calorie and no cholesterol. We eat a lot of salads and vegetables. My mother's an excellent cook."

She never mentioned the cholesterol in all those pies and brownies her mother made. I wanted to jump up and say, "Phoebe's mother has disappeared and that is why Phoebe is acting like a complete donkey," but I didn't.

Phoebe repeated, "A truly excellent cook."

"Marvelous," Mrs. Finney said. "And what do you propose to eat tonight?"

"I don't suppose you have any unadulterated vegetables?"

"Unadulterated?" Mrs. Finney said.

"It means unspoiled, without any butter or stuff added—"

"I know what it means, Phoebe," Mrs. Finney said.

"I can eat unadulterated vegetables. Or if you have any red bean salad handy—or stuffed cabbage leaves? Broccoli and lentil casserole? Macaroni and cheese? Vegetarian spaghetti?"

One by one, everyone at the table turned to stare at Phoebe. Mrs. Finney got up from the table and went into the kitchen. We heard her opening and closing cupboards. She returned to the doorway. "Muesli?" she asked Phoebe. "Can you eat muesli?"

Phoebe said, "Oh yes, I eat muesli. For breakfast."

Mrs. Finney disappeared again and returned

with a bowl of dried-up muesli and a bottle of milk.

"For dinner?" Phoebe asked. She gazed down at the bowl. "I usually eat it with yogurt on it—not milk," she said.

Mrs. Finney turned to Mr. Finney. "Dear, did you buy yogurt this week?"

"Blast it! How could I forget the yogurt?"

Phoebe ate her dried-up muesli without milk. All through dinner, I kept thinking of Bybanks, and what it was like when we went to my grandparents' house for dinner. There were always tons of people—relatives and neighbors—and lots of confusion. It was a friendly sort of confusion, and it was like that at the Finneys'. Tommy spilled two glasses of milk, Dennis punched Dougie, and Dougie punched him back. Maggie socked Mary Lou, and Mary Lou flipped a bean at her. Maybe this is what my mother had wanted, I thought. A house full of children and confusion.

On the way home, I said, "Didn't everyone seem unusually quiet after dinner?"

Phoebe said, "It was probably because of all that cholesterol sitting heavily on their stomachs."

I asked Phoebe if she wanted to spend the weekend at my house. I'm not sure why I did this.

It was an impulse. I had not yet invited anyone to my house. She said, "I guess. That is, if my mother is still—" She coughed. "Let's go ask my dad."

In the kitchen, her father was washing the dishes. He was wearing a frilly apron over his white shirt and tie. "You're supposed to rinse the soap off," Phoebe said. "And is that cold water you're using? You're supposed to use really, really hot water. To kill the germs."

He didn't look at Phoebe. I thought maybe he was embarrassed to be caught doing the dishes.

"You've probably washed that plate enough," Phoebe said. He had been rubbing it around and around with the dishcloth. He stopped and stared down at the plate. I could practically see the birds of sadness pecking at his head, but Phoebe was busy swatting at her own birds.

"Did you call all of Mom's friends?" Phoebe asked.

"Phoebe," he said. "I'm looking into it. I'm a little tired. Do you mind if we don't discuss this now?"

"But don't you think we should call the police?"

"Phoebe—"

"Sal wants to know if I can spend the weekend at her house."

"Of course," he said.

"But what if Mom comes back while I'm at Sal's? Will you call me? Will you let me know?"

"Of course."

"Or what if she telephones? Maybe I should stay home. I think I should be here if she calls."

"If she telephones, I'll have her call you at Sal's," he said.

"But if we don't have any news by tomorrow," Phoebe said, "we should definitely call the police. We've waited too long already. What if she's tied up somewhere and waiting for us to rescue her?"

At home that night, I was working on my mythology report when Phoebe called. She was whispering. When she went downstairs to say good night to her father, he was sitting in his favorite chair staring at the television, but the television wasn't on. If she did not know her father better, she would have thought he had been crying. "But my father never cries," she said.

26
SACRIFICES

THE WEEKEND WAS UNBELIEVABLY LONG. PHOEBE arrived with her suitcase on Saturday morning. I said, "Golly, Phoebe, are you planning to spend a month here?" When I took her up to my room, she asked if she was going to be sharing the room with me. "Why no, Phoebe," I said. "We built a whole new extension just for you."

"You don't have to be sarcastic," she said.

"I was only teasing, Phoebe."

"But there's only one bed."

"Good powers of observation, Phoebe."

"I thought you might sleep downstairs on the couch. People usually try to make their guests comfortable." She looked around my room. "We're going to be a little crowded in here, aren't we?"

I did not answer. I did not bash her over the head. I knew why she was acting this way. She sat down on my bed and bounced on it a couple times.

"I guess I'll have to get used to your lumpy mattress, Sal. Mine is very firm. A firm mattress is much better for your back. That's why I have such good posture. The reason you slouch is probably because of this mattress."

"Slouch?" I said.

"Well, you do slouch, Sal. Look in the mirror sometime." She mashed on my mattress. "Don't you know anything about having guests? You're supposed to give your guests the *best* that you have. You're supposed to make some sacrifices, Sal. That's what my mother always says. She says, 'In life, you have to make some sacrifices.'"

"I suppose your mother made a great sacrifice when she took off," I said. I couldn't help it. She was really getting on my nerves.

"My mother didn't 'take off.' Someone kidnapped her. She is undergoing tremendous sacrifice at this very moment in time." She started unpacking. "Where shall I put my things?" When I opened up the closet, she said, "What a mess! Do you have some extra hangers? Am I supposed to leave my clothes jammed up in the suitcase all weekend? A guest is supposed to have the best. It is only courtesy, Sal. My mother says—"

"I know, I know—sacrifice."

Ten minutes later, Phoebe mentioned that she was getting a headache. "It might even be a migraine. My aunt's foot doctor used to get migraines, only they turned out not to be migraines at all. Do you know what they were?"

"What?" I said.

"A brain tumor."

"Really?" I said.

"Yes," Phoebe said. "In her brain."

"Well, of course it would be in her brain, Phoebe. I figured that out when you said it was a brain tumor."

"I don't think that's a particularly sympathetic way to speak to someone with a migraine or potential brain tumor."

In my book was a picture of a tree. I drew a round head with curly hair, put a rope around the neck, and attached it to that tree.

It went on and on like that. I hated her that day. I didn't care how upset she was about her mother, I really hated her, and I wanted her to leave. I wondered if this was how my father felt when I threw all those temper tantrums. Maybe he hated me for a while.

After dinner, we walked over to Mary Lou's. Mr. and Mrs. Finney were rolling around on the front lawn in a pile of leaves with Tommy and Dougie, and Ben was sitting on the porch. I sat down beside him while Phoebe went looking for Mary Lou.

Ben said, "Phoebe's driving you crazy, isn't she?" I liked the way he looked right in your eyes when he talked to you.

"Extensively," I said.

"I bet Phoebe is lonely."

I don't know what came over me, but I almost reached up and touched his face. My heart was thumping so loudly that I thought he would be able to hear it. I went into the house. From the back window, I watched Mrs. Finney climb a ladder placed against the garage. On the roof, she took off her jacket and spread it out. A few minutes later, Mr. Finney came around the back of the house and climbed up the ladder. He took off his jacket and spread it out next to her. He lay down on the roof and put his arm around her. He kissed her.

On the roof, in the wide open air, they lay there kissing each other. It made me feel peculiar. They reminded me of my parents, before the stillborn baby, before the operation.

Ben came into the kitchen. As he reached into

the cupboard for a glass, he stopped and looked at me. Again I had that odd sensation that I wanted to touch his face, right there on his cheek, in that soft spot. I was afraid my hand might just lift up and drift over to him if I was not careful. It was most peculiar.

"Guess where Mary Lou is?" Phoebe said when she came in. "She's with *Alex*. On a *date*."

I had never been on a date. Neither, I assumed, had Phoebe.

That night at my house, I pulled the sleeping bag out of the closet and spread it on the floor. Phoebe looked at it as if it were a spider. "Don't worry," I said, "I'll sleep in it." I crawled in and pretended to fall asleep immediately. I heard Phoebe get into bed.

A little later, my father came into the room. "Phoebe?" he said. "Is something the matter?"

."No," she said.

"I thought I heard someone crying. Are you okay?"

"Yes," she said.

"Are you sure?"

"Yes."

I felt bad for Phoebe. I knew I should get up and try to be nice, but I remembered when I had felt like that, and I knew that sometimes you just wanted to be alone with the birds of sadness. Sometimes you had to cry by yourself.

That night I dreamed that I was sitting on the grass peering through a pair of binoculars. Far off in the distance, my mother was climbing up a ladder. She kept climbing and climbing. It was a thumpingly tall ladder. She couldn't see me, and she never came down. She just kept on going.

27
PANDORA'S BOX

THE NEXT DAY, AS I WAS HELPING PHOEBE LUG HER suitcase home, I said, "Phoebe, I know you've been upset lately—"

"I have not been upset lately," she said.

"Sometimes, Phoebe, I like you a lot—"

"Why, thank you."

"—but sometimes, Phoebe, I feel like dumping your cholesterol-free body out the window."

She did not have a chance to respond, because we were at her house, and she was more interested in besieging her father with questions. "Any news? Did Mom come back? Did she call?"

"Sort of," he said. "She phoned Mrs. Cadaver—"

"Mrs. Cadaver? Whatever for? Why would she—"

"Phoebe, calm down. I don't know why she phoned Mrs. Cadaver. I haven't been able to speak to Mrs. Cadaver myself yet. She isn't home. She left a note here." He showed it to Phoebe: *Norma called to say she is okay*. Beneath Mrs. Cadaver's signature was a P.S. saying that Mrs. Cadaver would be away until Monday.

"I don't believe that Mom called Mrs. Cadaver. Mrs. Cadaver is making it up. Mrs. Cadaver probably killed her and chopped her up. I'm calling the police."

They had a huge argument, but at last Phoebe fizzled out. Her father said he had been calling everyone he could think of, to see if her mother had indicated where she might be going. He would continue calling tomorrow, he promised, and he would speak with Mrs. Cadaver. If he did not receive a letter—or a direct phone call—from her mother by Wednesday, he would call the police.

Phoebe came out on the porch with me as I was leaving. She said, "I've made a decision. I'm going to call the police. I might even go to the police station. I don't have to wait until Wednesday. I can go whenever I want."

That night she phoned me. She was whispering again. "It seems so quiet here. I don't know what is the matter with me. I was lying on my bed and I can't sleep. My bed's too hard."

On Monday, Phoebe gave her oral report on

Pandora. She began in a quivering voice. "For some reason, Ben already talked about my topic, Pandora, when he did his report on Prometheus. However, Ben made a few little mistakes about Pandora."

Everyone turned around to stare at Ben. "I did not," he said.

"Yes, you did." Phoebe's lip trembled. "Pandora was *not* sent to man as a *punishment*, but as a *reward*—"

"Was not," Ben said.

"Was too," Phoebe said. "Zeus decided to give man a present, since man seemed lonely down there on Earth, with only the animals to keep him company. So Zeus made a sweet and beautiful woman, and then Zeus invited all the gods to dinner. It was a very civilized dinner, with *matching plates*."

Mary Lou and Ben exchanged an eyebrow message.

"Zeus asked the gods to give the woman presents—to make her feel like a *welcome guest*." Phoebe glanced at me. "They gave her wonderful things: a fancy shawl, a silver dress, beauty—"

Ben interrupted. "I thought you said she was already beautiful."

"They gave her *more* beauty. Are you satisfied?" Her lip was no longer trembling, but she was blushing. "The gods also gave her the ability to sing, the power of persuasion, a gold crown, flowers, and many truly wonderful things such as that. Because of all these gifts, Zeus named her Pandora, which means 'the gift of all.'"

Phoebe was getting into it. "There were two other gifts that I have not mentioned yet. One of them was curiosity. That is why all women are curious, by the way, because it was a gift given to the very first woman."

Ben said, "I wish she had been given the gift of silence."

"Last, there was a beautiful box, covered in gold and jewels, and this is very important—she was forbidden to open the box."

Ben said, "Then why did they give it to her?"

He was beginning to irritate Phoebe, you could tell. She said, "That's what I'm telling you. It was a *present.*"

"But why did they give her a present that she couldn't open?"

"I-do-not-know. It's just in the story. As I was *saying*, Pandora was not supposed to open the box, but because she had been given so much curiosity, she really, really, really wanted to know what was inside, so one day she opened the box."

"I knew it," Ben said. "I knew she was going to open the box the minute that you said she was not supposed to open it."

"Inside the box were all the evils in the world, such as hatred, envy, plagues, sickness, and cholesterol. There were brain tumors and sadness, lunatics and kidnapping and murders"—she glanced at Mr. Birkway before rushing on—"and all that kind of thing. Pandora tried to close the lid when she saw all the horrible things that were coming out of it, but she could not get it closed, and that is why there are all these evils in the world. There was only one good thing in the box."

"What was it?" Ben asked.

"As I was *about* to explain, the only good thing in the box was Hope, and that is why, even though there are many evils in the world, there is still a little hope." She held up a picture of Pandora opening up the box and a whole shebang of gremlins floating out. Pandora looked frightened.

That night I kept thinking about Pandora's box. I wondered why someone would put a good thing such as Hope in a box with sickness and kidnapping and murder. It was fortunate that it was there, though. If not, people would have the birds of sadness nesting in their hair all the time, because of nuclear war and the greenhouse effect and bombs and stabbings and lunatics.

There must have been another box with all the good things in it, like sunshine and love and trees and all that. Who had the good fortune to open that one, and was there one bad thing down there in the bottom of the good box? Maybe it was Worry. Even when everything seems fine and good, I worry that something will go wrong and change everything.

My mother, my father, and I all seemed fine and happy at our house until the baby died. Could you actually say that the baby died, since it had never breathed? Did its birth and death occur at the same moment? Could you die *before* you were born?

Phoebe's family had *not* seemed fine, even before the arrival of the lunatic and the messages, and the disappearance of Mrs. Winterbottom. I knew that Phoebe was convinced that her mother was kidnapped because it was impossible for Phoebe to imagine that her mother could leave for any other reason. I wanted to call Phoebe and say that maybe her mother had gone looking for something, maybe her mother was unhappy, maybe there was nothing Phoebe could do about it.

When I told this part to Gram and Gramps, Gramps said, "You mean it had nothing to do with Peeby?" They looked at each other. They didn't say anything, but there was something in that look that suggested I had just said something important. For the first time, it occurred to me that maybe my mother's leaving had nothing whatsoever to do with me. It was separate and apart. We couldn't own our mothers.

On that night after Phoebe had given her Pandora report, I thought about the Hope in Pandora's box. Maybe when everything seemed sad and miserable, Phoebe and I could both hope that something might start to go right.

28
THE BLACK HILLS

When we saw the first sign for the Black Hills, the whispers changed and once again commanded, *rush, hurry, rush*. We had spent too long in South Dakota. There were only two days left and a long way to go.

"Maybe we should skip the Black Hills," I said.

"What?" Gramps said. "Skip the Black Hills? Skip Mount Rushmore? We can't do that."

"But today's the eighteenth. It's the fifth day."

"Do we have a deadline someone didn't tell me about?" Gramps asked. "Heck, we've got all the time in the—" Gram gave him a look. "I've just gotta see these Black Hills," Gramps said. "We'll be quick about it, chickabiddy."

The whispers walloped me: *rush, rush, rush*. I knew we wouldn't make it to Idaho in time. I thought about sneaking off while Gram and Gramps were looking at the Black Hills. Maybe I could hitch a ride with someone who drove fast, but the thought of someone speeding, careening around curves—especially the snaking curves down into Lewiston, Idaho, which I had heard so much about—when I thought about that, it made me dizzy and sick.

"Heck," Gramps said, "I oughta turn this wheel over to you, chickabiddy. All this driving is making me crazy as a loon."

He was only joking, but he knew I could drive. He had taught me to drive his old pickup truck when I was eleven. We used to ride around on the dirt roads on their farm. I drove, and he smoked his pipe and told stories. He said, "You're a helluva driver, chickabiddy, but don't you tell your Momma I taught you. She'd thrash me half to death."

I used to love to drive that old green pickup truck. I dreamed about turning sixteen and getting my license, but then when Momma left, something happened to me. I became afraid of things I had never been afraid of before, and driving was one of these things. I didn't even like to *ride* in cars, let alone drive the truck.

The Black Hills were not really black. Pines covered the hills, and maybe at dusk they looked black, but when we saw them at midday, they were dark green. It was an eerie sight, all those rolling dark hills. A cool wind blew down through the pines, and the trees swished secrets among them.

My mother had always wanted to see the Black Hills. It was one of the sights she was most looking forward to on her trip. She used to tell me about the Black Hills, which were sacred to the Sioux Indians. It was their Holy Land, but white settlers took it as their own. The Sioux are still fighting for their land. I half expected a Sioux to stop our car from entering, and the thing is, I would have been on his side. I would have said, "Take it. It's yours."

We drove through the Black Hills to Mt. Rushmore. At first we didn't think we were in the right place, but then, jing-bang, it was right before us. There, high up on a cliff face, were the sixty-foot-tall faces of Washington, Jefferson, Lincoln, and Teddy Roosevelt, carved right into the rock, staring somberly down on us.

It was fine seeing the presidents, I've got nothing against the presidents, but you'd think the Sioux would be mighty sad to have those white faces carved into their sacred hill. I bet my mother was upset. I wondered why whoever carved them couldn't have put a couple Indians up there too.

Gram and Gramps seemed disappointed as

well. Gram didn't even want to get out of the car, so we didn't stay long. Gramps said, "I've had enough of South Dakota, how about you, chick-abiddy? How about you, gooseberry? Let's get a move on."

By late afternoon, we were well into Wyoming, and I added up the miles left to go. Maybe we could make it, just maybe. Then Gramps said, "I hope nobody minds if we stop at Yellowstone. It would be a sin to miss Yellowstone."

Gram said, "Is that where Old Faithful is? Oh, I would love to see Old Faithful." She looked back at me. "We'll hurry. Why, I bet we'll be in Idaho by the twentieth without any problem at all."

29
THE TIDE RISES

"DID PEEBY'S MOTHER CALL?" GRAM SAID. "DID she come home? Did Peeby phone the police? Oh, I hope this isn't a sad story."

Phoebe did go to the police. It was on the day that Mr. Birkway read us the poem about the tide and the traveler—a poem that upset both me and Phoebe, and I think it is what convinced her, finally, that she had to tell the police about her mother.

Mr. Birkway read a poem by Longfellow: "The Tide Rises, The Tide Falls." The way Mr. Birkway read this poem, you could hear the tide rising and falling, rising and falling. In the poem, a traveler is hurrying toward a town, and it is getting darker and darker, and the sea calls to the traveler. Then the waves "with their soft, white hands" wash out the traveler's footprints. The next morning,

The day returns, but nevermore
Returns the traveller to the shore,
And the tide rises, the tide falls.

Mr. Birkway asked for reactions to this poem. Megan said that it sounded soft and gentle, and it almost made her go to sleep.

"Gentle?" I said. "It's terrifying." My voice was shaking. "Someone is walking along the beach, and the night is getting black, and the person keeps looking behind him to see if someone is following, and a jing-bang wave comes up and pulls him into the sea."

"A murder," Phoebe said.

I went barreling on as if it was my poem and I was an expert. "The waves, with their 'soft, white hands' grab the traveler. They drown him. They kill him. He's gone."

Ben said, "Maybe he didn't drown. Maybe he just died, like normal people die."

Phoebe said, "He drowned."

I said, "It isn't normal to die. It isn't normal. It's terrible."

Megan said, "What about heaven? What about God?"

Mary Lou said, "God? Is He in this poem?"

Ben said, "Maybe dying could be normal *and* terrible."

When the bell rang, I raced out of the room. Phoebe grabbed me. "Come on," she said. From her locker, she took the evidence she had brought from home, and we both ran the six blocks to the police station. I am not exactly sure why I went along with Phoebe. Maybe it was because of that poem about the traveler, or maybe it was because I had begun to believe in the lunatic, or maybe it was because Phoebe was taking some action, and I admired her for it. I wished I had taken some action when my mother left. I was not sure what I could have done, but I wished I had done *something*.

Phoebe and I stood for five minutes outside the police station, trying to make our hearts slow down, and then we went inside and stood at the counter. On the other side of it, a thin man with big ears was writing in a black book.

"Excuse me," Phoebe said.

"I'll be right with you," he said.

"This is absolutely urgent. I need to speak to someone about a murder," Phoebe said.

He looked up quickly. "A murder?"

"Yes," Phoebe said. "Or possibly a kidnapping.

But the kidnapping might turn into a murder."

"Is this a joke?"

"No, it is not a joke," Phoebe said.

"Just a minute." He whispered to a plump woman in a dark blue uniform. She wore glasses with thick lenses. "Is this something you girls have read about in a book?" she asked.

"No, it is not," I said. That was a turning point, I think, when I came to Phoebe's defense. I didn't like the way the woman was looking at us—as if we were two fools. I wanted that woman to understand why Phoebe was so upset. I wanted her to believe Phoebe.

"May I ask who it is who has been kidnapped or possibly murdered?" the woman said.

Phoebe said, "My mother."

"Oh, your mother. Come along, then." Her voice was sugary and sweet, as if she was speaking to tiny children. We followed her to a room with glass partitions. An enormous man with a huge head and neck, and massive shoulders, sat behind the desk. His hair was bright red, and his face was covered in freckles. He did not smile when we entered. After the woman repeated what we had told her, he stared at us for a long time.

His name was Sergeant Bickle, and Phoebe

told him everything. She explained about her mother disappearing, and the note from Mrs. Cadaver, and Mrs. Cadaver's missing husband, and the rhododendron, and finally about the lunatic and the mysterious messages. At this point, Sergeant Bickle said, "What sort of messages?"

Phoebe was prepared. She pulled them out of her book bag and laid them on the desk in the order in which they had arrived. He read each one aloud.

Don't judge a man until you've walked two moons in his moccasins.

Everyone has his own agenda.

In the course of a lifetime, what does it matter?

You can't keep the birds of sadness from flying over your head, but you can keep them from nesting in your hair.

Sergeant Bickle looked up at the woman seated next to us, and the corners of his mouth twitched slightly. To Phoebe, he said, "And how do you think these are related to your mother's disappearance?"

"I don't know," she said. "That's what I want you to find out."

Sergeant Bickle asked Phoebe to spell Mrs. Cadaver's name. "It means corpse," Phoebe said. "Dead body."

"I know. Is there anything else?"

Phoebe pulled out the envelope with the unidentifiable hair strands. "Perhaps you could have these analyzed," she suggested.

Sergeant Bickle looked at the woman, and again the corners of his mouth twitched slightly. The woman removed her glasses and wiped the lenses.

They were not taking us seriously, and I felt my ornery donkey self waking up. I mentioned the potential blood spots that Phoebe had marked with adhesive tape.

"But my father removed the tape," Phoebe said.

Sergeant Bickle said, "I wonder if you would excuse me a few minutes?" He asked the woman to stay with us, and he left the room.

The woman asked Phoebe about school and

about her family. She had an awful lot of questions. I kept wondering where Sergeant Bickle had gone and when he was coming back. He was gone for over an hour. There were three framed pictures on Sergeant Bickle's desk, and I tried to lean forward to see them, but I couldn't. I was afraid the woman would think I was nosy.

Sergeant Bickle finally returned. Behind him was Phoebe's father. Phoebe looked extensively relieved, but I knew it was not a coincidence that her father was there.

"Miss Winterbottom," Sergeant Bickle said, "your father is going to take you and your friend home now."

"But—" Phoebe said.

"Mr. Winterbottom, we'll be in touch. And if you would like me to speak with Mrs. Cadaver—"

"Oh no," Mr. Winterbottom said. He looked embarrassed. "Really, that won't be necessary. I do apologize—"

We followed Mr. Winterbottom outside. In the car, he said nothing. I thought he might drop me off at my house, but he didn't. When we got to their house, the only thing he said was, "Phoebe, I'm going to go talk with Mrs. Cadaver. You and Sal wait here."

Mrs. Cadaver was unable to give him any more information about Phoebe's mother's call. All Mrs. Winterbottom had said was that she would phone soon.

"That's all?" Phoebe asked.

"Your mother also asked Mrs. Cadaver how you and Prudence were. Mrs. Cadaver told her that you and Prudence were fine."

"Well, I am *not* fine," Phoebe said, "and what does Mrs. Cadaver know anyway, and besides, Mrs. Cadaver is making the whole thing up. You should let the police talk to her. You should ask her about the rhododendron. You should find out who this lunatic is. Mrs. Cadaver probably hired him. You should—"

"Phoebe, your imagination is running away with you."

"It is not. Mom loves me, and she would not leave me without any explanation."

And then her father began to cry.

30
BREAKING IN

"GOL-DANG!" GRAMPS SAID. "WHAT A LOT OF BIRDS of sadness wing-dinging their way around Peeby's family."

Gram said, "You liked Peeby, didn't you, Salamanca?"

I did like Phoebe. In spite of all her wild tales and her cholesterol-madness and her annoying comments, there was something about Phoebe that was like a magnet. I was drawn to her. I was pretty sure that underneath all that odd behavior was someone who was frightened. And, in a strange way, she was like another version of me— she acted out the way I sometimes felt.

I do not think that Phoebe actually planned to break into Mrs. Cadaver's house, but as Phoebe was going to bed, she saw Mrs. Cadaver, in her nurse's uniform, get into her car and leave. Phoebe waited until her father was asleep, and then she phoned me. "You've got to come over," she said. "It's urgent."

"But Phoebe, it's late. It's dark."

"It's urgent, Sal."

Phoebe was waiting in front of Mrs. Cadaver's house. There were no lights on at Mrs. Cadaver's. Phoebe said, "Come on," and she started up the walk. I admit that I was reluctant. "I just want to take a quick look," she said. She crept up onto the porch and stood by the door. She listened, tapped twice, and turned the doorknob. The door was unlocked.

I don't think Phoebe intended to go inside, but she did, and I followed. We stood in the dark hallway. In the room to the right, a shaft of light from the streetlamp came in through the window. We went into that room. We both nearly leaped through the window when someone said, "Sal?" I started backing toward the door.

"It's a ghost," Phoebe said.

"Come here," the voice said.

As my eyes adjusted to the dim light, I could see someone huddled in a chair in the far corner. When I saw the cane, I was relieved. "Mrs. Partridge?"

"Come over here," she said. "Who's that with you? Is that Phoebe?"

Phoebe said, "Yes." Her voice was high and quivery.

"I was just sitting here reading," Mrs. Partridge said.

"Isn't it awfully dark in here?" I said, bumping a table.

Mrs. Partridge laughed her wicked laugh. "It's always dark in here. I don't need lights, but you can turn some on if you want to."

As I stumbled around looking for a lamp, Phoebe stood, frozen, near the doorway. "There," I said. "That's much better." Mrs. Partridge was sitting in a big, overstuffed chair. She was wearing a purple bathrobe and pink slippers with floppy bunny ears at the toes. On her lap was a book, her fingers resting on the page. "Is it Braille?" I asked, waving at Phoebe to come into the room. I was afraid she was going to run out and leave me.

Mrs. Partridge handed me the book, and I slid my fingers over the raised bumps. "How did you know it was us?" I asked.

"I just knew," she said. "Your shoes make a particular sound and you have a particular smell."

"What's the name of this book? What's it about?"

Mrs. Partridge said, "*Murder at Midnight*. It's a mystery."

Phoebe said, "Erp," and looked around the room.

Each time I went into that house I noticed new things. It was a scary place. The walls were lined with shelves crammed with old musty books. On the floor were three rugs with dark, swirly patterns of wild beasts in forests. Two chairs were covered in similar ghastly designs. A sofa was draped in a bear skin.

On the wall behind the couch were two thumpingly grim African masks. The mouths on the masks were wide open, as if in the midst of a scream. Everywhere you looked there was something startling: a stuffed squirrel, a kite in the shape of a dragon, a wooden cow with a spear piercing its side.

"Goodness," Phoebe said. "What a lot of—of—unusual things." She knelt to examine a spot on the floor.

"What's the matter?" Mrs. Partridge said.

Phoebe jumped up. "Nothing. Nothing whatsoever."

"Did I drop something on the floor?" Mrs. Partridge asked.

"No. Nothing whatsoever on the floor," Phoebe

said. Leaning against the back of the sofa was an enormous sword. Phoebe examined the blade.

"Careful you don't cut yourself," Mrs. Partridge said.

Phoebe stepped back. Even I found this unsettling, that Mrs. Partridge could see what Phoebe was doing even though she couldn't actually *see* her.

Mrs. Partridge said, "Isn't this a grandiful room? Grandiful—and a little peculible, too, I suppose."

"Phoebe and I have to be going—" We backed toward the door.

"By the way," Mrs. Partridge said as we reached the doorway, "what was it you wanted?"

Phoebe looked at me and I looked at Phoebe. "We were just passing by," I said, "and we thought we would see how you were doing."

"That's nice," Mrs. Partridge said, patting her knees. "Oh, Phoebe, I think I met your brother."

Phoebe said, "I don't have a brother."

"Oh?" Mrs. Partridge tapped her head. "I guess this old noggin isn't as sharp as it used to be." As we left, she said, "Goodness, you girls stay up late."

Outside, Phoebe said, "I'll make a list of items which the police will want to investigate further: the sword, the suspicious spot on the floor, and several hair strands which I picked up."

"Phoebe, you know when you said that your mother would never leave without an explanation? Well, she might. A person—a mother—might do that."

Phoebe said, "*My* mother wouldn't. *My* mother loves me."

"But she might love you and still not have been *able* to explain." I was thinking about the letter my mother left me. "Maybe it would be too painful for her to explain. Maybe it would seem too permanent."

"I don't know what in the world you are talking about."

"She might not come back, Phoebe—"

"Shut up, Sal."

"She might not. I just think you should be prepared—"

"She is too coming back. You don't know what you're talking about. You're being horrid." Phoebe ran into the house.

When I got home and had crept up to my room, I remembered how Phoebe had shown me some things in her room that reminded her of her mother: a handmade birthday card, a photograph of Phoebe and her mother, and a bar of lavender soap. When Phoebe pulled a blouse out of the closet, she said she could see her mother standing at the ironing board smoothing the blouse with her hand. The wall opposite Phoebe's bed was painted violet. She said, "My mother painted it last summer while I painted the trim at the bottom."

And I knew exactly what Phoebe was doing and exactly why. I had done the same things when my mother left. My father was right: my mother did haunt our house in Bybanks, and the fields and the barn. She was everywhere. You couldn't look at a single thing without being reminded of her.

When we moved to Euclid, one of the first things I did was to unpack gifts my mother had given me. On the wall, I tacked the poster of the red hen which my mother had given me for my fifth birthday, and the drawing of the barn she had given me for my last birthday. On my desk were pictures of her and cards from her. On the bookshelf, the wooden animals and books were presents from her.

Sometimes, I would walk around the room and look at each of these things and try to remember exactly the day she had given them to me. I tried to picture what the weather was like and what room we were in and what she was wearing and what precisely she had said. This was not a game. It was a necessary, crucial thing to do. If I did not have these things and remember these occasions, then she might disappear forever. She might never have been.

In my bureau were three things of hers that I had taken from her closet after she left: a red, fringed shawl; a blue sweater; and a yellow-flowered cotton dress that was always my favorite. These things had her smell on them.

Once, before she left, my mother said that if you visualize something happening, you can make it happen. For example, if you are about to run a race, you visualize yourself running the race and crossing the finish line first, and presto! When the time comes, it really happens. The only thing I did not understand was what if *everyone* visualized himself winning the race?

Still, when she left, this is what I did. I visualized her reaching for the phone. Then I visualized her dialing the phone. I visualized our phone number clicking through the wires. I visualized the phone ringing.

It did not ring.

I visualized her riding the bus back to Bybanks. I visualized her walking up the driveway. I visualized her opening the door.

It did not happen.

While I was thinking about all of this that night after Phoebe and I crept into Mrs. Cadaver's house, I also thought about Ben. I had the sudden urge to run over to the Finneys and ask him where his own mother was, but it was too late. The Finneys would be asleep.

Instead, I lay there thinking of the poem about the traveler, and I could see the tide rising and falling, and those horrid white hands snatching the traveler. How could it be normal, that traveler dying? And how could such a thing be normal *and* terrible both at the same time?

I stayed awake the whole night. I knew that if I closed my eyes, I would see the tide and the white hands. I thought about Mr. Winterbottom crying. That was the saddest thing. It was sadder than seeing my own father cry, because my father is the sort of person you expect might cry if he was terribly upset. But I had never, ever, expected Mr. Winterbottom—stiff Mr. Winterbottom—to cry. It was the first time I realized that he actually *cared* about Mrs. Winterbottom.

As soon as it was daylight, I phoned Phoebe. "Phoebe, we've got to find her."

"That's what I've been telling you," she said.

31
THE PHOTOGRAPH

THE NEXT DAY WAS MOST *PECULIBLE*, AS MRS. PAR-tridge would say.

Phoebe arrived at school with another message, which she had found on her porch that morning: *We never know the worth of water until the well is dry.* "It's a clue," Phoebe said. "Maybe my mother is hidden in a well."

I walked straight into Ben when I went to my locker. That grapefruit aroma was in the air. "You've got something on your face," he said. With soft, warm fingers he rubbed the side of my face. "It's probably your breakfast."

I don't know what came over me. I was going to kiss him. I leaned forward just as he turned around and slammed the door of his locker. My lips ended up pressed against the cold, metal locker.

"You're weird, Sal," he said.

Kissing was thumpingly complicated. Both people had to be in the same place at the same time, and both people had to remain still so that the kiss ended up in the right place. But I was relieved that my lips ended up on the cold metal locker. I could not imagine what had come over me, or what might have happened if the kiss had landed on Ben's mouth. It was a shivery thing to consider.

I made it through the rest of my classes without losing control of my lips.

Mr. Birkway sailed into class carrying our journals. I had forgotten all about them. He was leaping all over the place exclaiming, "Dynamite! Unbelievable! Incredible!" He said he couldn't wait to share the journals with the class.

Mary Lou Finney said, "*Share* with the *class*?"

Mr. Birkway said, "Not to worry! Everyone has something magnificent to say. I haven't read through every page yet, but I wanted to share some of these passages with you right away."

People were squirming all over the room. I was trying to remember what I had written. Mary Lou leaned over to me and said, "Well, I'm not worried. I wrote a special note in the front of mine distinctly asking him not to read it. Mine was private."

Mr. Birkway smiled at each nervous face. "You

needn't worry," he said. "I'll change any names that you've used, and I'll fold this piece of yellow paper over the cover of whichever journal I'm reading, so that you won't know whose it is."

Ben asked if he could go to the bathroom. Christy said she felt sick and begged to see the nurse. Phoebe asked me to touch her forehead because she was pretty sure she had a fever. Usually Mr. Birkway would let people go to the bathroom or to the nurse, but this time he said, "Let's not malinger!" He picked up a journal, slipping the yellow paper over it before anyone had a chance to examine the cover for clues as to its author's identity. Everyone took a deep breath. You could see people poised nervously, waiting as tensely as if Mr. Birkway was going to announce someone's execution. Mr. Birkway read:

> *I think that Betty* [he changed the
> name, you could tell, because there
> was no Betty in our school] *will go
> to hell because she always takes the
> Lord's name in vain. She says
> "God!" every five seconds.*

Mary Lou Finney was turning purple. "Who

wrote that?" she said. "Did you, Christy? I'll bet you did."

Christy stared down at her desk.

"I do not say 'God!' every five seconds. I do not. And I am not going to hell. Omnipotent—that's what I say now. I say, *Omnipotent*! And *Alpha and Omega!*"

Mr. Birkway was desperately trying to explain what he had enjoyed about that passage. He said that most of us are not aware that we might be using words—such as God!—that offend other people. Mary Lou leaned over to me and said, "Is he *serious*? Does he actually, really and truly believe that beef-brained Christy is troubled by my saying God?—which I do not, by the way, say anymore anyway."

Christy wore a pious look, as if God Himself had just come down from heaven to sit on her desk.

Mr. Birkway quickly selected another journal. He read:

> *Linda* [there was no Linda in our class either] *is my best friend. I tell her just about everything and she tells me EVERYTHING, even things*

*I do not want to know. Like what she
ate for breakfast and what her father
wears to bed and how much her
new sweater cost. Sometimes things
like that are just not interesting.*

Mr. Birkway liked this passage because it
showed that even though someone might be our
best friend, he or she could still drive us crazy.
Beth Ann turned all the way around in her seat
and sent wicked eyebrow-messages to Mary Lou.

Mr. Birkway flipped ahead in the same journal
to another passage. He read:

*I think Jeremiah is pig-headed. His
skin is always pink and his hair is
always clean and shiny . . . but he is
really a jerk.*

I thought Mary Lou Finney was going to fall
out of her chair. Alex was bright, bright pink. He
looked at Mary Lou as if she had recently plunged
a red hot stake into his heart. Mary Lou said,
"No—I—no, it isn't what you think—I—"

Mr. Birkway liked this passage because it
showed conflicting feelings about someone.

"I'll say it does," Alex said.

The bell rang. First, you could hear sighs of relief from the people whose journals had not been read, and then people started talking a mile a minute. "Hey, Mary Lou, look at Alex's pink skin," and "Hey Mary Lou, what *does* Beth Ann's father wear to bed?"

Beth Ann was standing one inch away from Mary Lou's face. "I do not talk on and on," Beth Ann said, "and that wasn't very nice of you to mention that, and I do not tell you everything, and the only reason I ever mentioned what my father wore to bed was because we were talking, if you will recall, about men's bathing suits being more comfortable than women's and—" On and on she went.

Mary Lou was trying to get across the room to Alex, who was standing there as pink as can be. "Alex!" she called. "Wait! I wrote that *before*— wait—"

It was a jing-bang of a mess. I was glad I had to get out of there. Phoebe and I were going to the police again.

We got in to see Sergeant Bickle right away. Phoebe slapped the newest message about the water in the well onto his desk, dumped the hairs which she had collected at Mrs. Cadaver's house on top of the message, and then placed her list of "Further Items to Investigate" on top of that.

Sergeant Bickle frowned. "I don't think you girls understand."

Phoebe went into a rage. "You idiot," she said. She scooped up the message, the hairs, and her list and stormed out of the office.

Sergeant Bickle followed her while I waited, thinking he would bring Phoebe back and calm her down. I looked at the photographs on his desk, the ones I had not been able to see the day before. In one was Sergeant Bickle and a friendly-looking woman—his wife, I supposed. The second picture was of a shiny black car. The third picture was of Sergeant Bickle, the woman, and a young man— their son, I figured. I looked closer.

I recognized the son. It was the lunatic.

32
CHICKEN AND BLACKBERRY KISSES

GRAMPS BARRELED THROUGH WYOMING LIKE A house afire. We snaked through winding roads where the trees leaned close, rustling *rush, rush, rush, rush, rush*. The road curved alongside rivers that rolled and gabbled *hurry, hurry, hurry*.

It was late when we arrived at Yellowstone. All we got to see that evening was a hot spring. We walked on boardwalks placed across the bubbling mud ("Huzza, huzza!" Gram said), and we stayed at the Old Faithful Inn in a Frontier Cabin. I'd never seen Gram so excited. She could not wait for the next morning. "We're gonna see Old Faithful," she said, over and over.

"It won't take too very long, will it?" I said, and I felt like a mule saying it, because Gram was so looking forward to it.

"Don't you worry, Salamanca," Gram said.

"We'll just watch that old geyser blow and then we'll hit the road."

I prayed all night long to the elm tree outside. I prayed that we would not get in an accident, that we would get to Lewiston, Idaho, in time for my mother's birthday, and that we would bring her home. Later I would realize that I had prayed for the wrong things.

That night, Gram was so excited that she could not sleep. She rambled on about all sorts of things. She said to Gramps, "Remember that letter from the egg man that you found under the mattress?"

"Of course I remember. We had a wing-ding of an argument over it. You told me you had no dang idea how it got there. You said the egg man must've slipped into the bedroom and put it there."

"Well, I want you to know that I put it there."

"I know that," Gramps said. "I'm not a complete noodle."

"It's the only love letter anybody ever wrote me," Gram said. "You never wrote me any love letters."

"You never told me you wanted one."

To me, Gram said, "Your grandfather nearly killed the egg man over that letter."

"Hell's bells," Gramps said. "He wasn't worth killing."

"Maybe not, but Gloria was."

"Ah yes," Gramps said, placing his hand on his heart and pretending to swoon, "Gloria!"

"Cut that out," Gram said, rolling over on her side. "Tell me about Peeby. Tell me that story, but don't make it too awfully sad." She folded her hands on her chest. "Tell me what happened with the lunatic."

When I saw the picture of the lunatic on Sergeant Bickle's desk, I tore out of that office faster than lightning. I ran past Sergeant Bickle standing in the parking lot. No sign of Phoebe. I ran all the way to her house. As I passed Mrs. Cadaver's house, Mrs. Partridge called to me from her porch.

"You're all dressed up," I said. "Going somewhere?"

"Oh yes," she said. "I'm redible." She tottered down the steps, swinging her cobra cane in front of her.

"Are you walking?" I asked.

She reached down and touched her legs. "Isn't that what you call it when you move your legs like I'm doing?"

"No, I meant are you walking to wherever you're going?"

"Oh no, it's much too far for these legs. Jimmy's coming. He'll be here any minute." A car pulled up in front of the house. "There he is," she said. She called out to the driver, "I'm redible. I said I would be, and here I am."

The driver leaped out of the car. "Sal?" he said. "I had no idea you two were neighbors." It was Mr. Birkway.

"We're not," I said. "It's Phoebe who is the neighbor—."

"Is that right?" he said, opening the car door for Mrs. Partridge. "Come on, Mom. Let's get a move on."

"Mom?" I said. I looked at Mrs. Partridge. "This is your son?"

"Why, of course," Mrs. Partridge said. "This is my little Jimmy."

"But he's a Birkway—?"

Mrs. Partridge said, "I was a Birkway once. Then I was a Partridge. I'm still a Partridge."

"Then who is Mrs. Cadaver?" I said.

"My little Margie," she said. "She was a Birkway too. Now she's a Cadaver."

I said to Mr. Birkway, "Mrs. Cadaver is your sister?"

"We're twins," Mr. Birkway said.

When they had driven away, I knocked at Phoebe's door, but there was no answer. At home, I dialed Phoebe's number over and over. No answer.

The next day at school, I was relieved to see Phoebe. "Where were you?" I said. "I have something to tell you—"

She turned away. "I don't want to talk about it," she said. "I do not wish to discuss it."

I couldn't figure out what was the matter with her. It was a terrible day. We had tests in math and science. At lunch, Phoebe ignored me. Then came English.

Mr. Birkway skipped into the room. People were gnawing on their fingers and tapping their feet and wriggling around and generally getting ulcers, wondering if Mr. Birkway was going to read from the journals. I stared at him. He and Margaret Cadaver were twins? Was that possible? The most disappointing part of that piece of knowledge was that he was not going to fall in love with Mrs. Cadaver and marry her and take her away.

Mr. Birkway opened a cupboard, pulled out the journals, slipped the yellow paper over the cover of one and read:

*This is what I like about Jane. She is
smart, but doesn't act like she knows
everything. She is cute. She smells
good. She is cute. She makes me
laugh. She is cute.*

I got a prickly feeling up and down my arms. I
wondered if Ben had written this about me, but
then I realized that Ben didn't even know me
when he wrote his journal. A little buzz was going
around the room as people shifted in their seats.
Christy was smiling, Megan was smiling, Beth Ann
was smiling, Mary Lou was smiling. Every girl in
the room was smiling. Each girl thought that this
had been written about her.

I looked carefully at each of the boys. Alex was
gazing nonchalantly at Mr. Birkway. Then I saw
Ben. He was sitting with his hands over his ears,
staring down at his desk. The prickly feeling traveled all the way up to my neck and then went skipping down my spine. He did write that, but he did
not write it about me.

Mr. Birkway exclaimed, "Ah love, ah life!" Sigh-
ing, he pulled out another journal and read:

Jane doesn't know the first thing

about boys. She once asked me what kisses taste like, so you could tell she hadn't ever kissed anyone. I told her that they taste like chicken, and she believed me. She is so dumb sometimes.

Mary Lou Finney jumped out of her chair. "You cabbage-head," she said to Beth Ann. "You beef brain." Beth Ann wound a strand of hair around her finger. Mary Lou said, "I did *not* believe you, and I do know what they taste like, and it isn't chicken."

Ben drew a cartoon of two stick-figures kissing. In the air over their heads was a cartoon bubble with a chicken saying, "Bawk, bawwwk, bawwwk."

Mr. Birkway turned a few pages in the same journal and read:

I hate doing this. I hate to write. I hate to read. I hate journals. I especially hate English where teachers only talk about idiot symbols. I hate that idiot poem about the snowy woods, and I hate it when people say the woods symbolize death or

beauty or sex or any old thing you
want. I hate that. Maybe the woods
are just woods.

Beth Ann stood up. "Mr. Birkway," she said, "I do hate school, I do hate books, I do hate English, I do hate symbols, and I most especially hate these idiot journals."

There was a hush in the room. Mr. Birkway stared at Beth Ann for a minute, and in that minute, I was reminded of Mrs. Cadaver. For that brief time, his eyes looked just like hers. I was afraid he was going to strangle Beth Ann, but then he smiled and his eyes became friendly enormous cow eyes once again. I think he hypnotized her, because Beth Ann sat down slowly. Mr. Birkway said, "Beth Ann, I know exactly how you feel. Exactly. I love this passage."

"You do?" she said.

"It's so honest."

I had to admit, you couldn't get more honest than Beth Ann telling her English teacher that she hated symbols and English and idiot journals.

Mr. Birkway said, "I used to feel exactly like this. I could not understand what all the fuss was about symbols." He rummaged around in his desk.

"I want to show you something." He was pulling papers out and flinging them around. Finally, he held up a picture. "Ah, here it is. Dynamite! What is this?" he asked Ben.

Ben said, "It's a vase. Obviously."

Mr. Birkway held the drawing in front of Beth Ann, who looked as if she might cry. Mr. Birkway said, "Beth Ann, what do you see?" A little tear dropped down on her cheek. "It's okay, Beth Ann, what do *you* see?"

"I don't see any idiot vase," she said. "I see two people. They're looking at each other."

"Right," Mr. Birkway said. "Bravo!"

"I'm right? Bravo?"

Ben said, "Huh? Two people?" I was thinking the same thing myself. What two people?

Mr. Birkway said to Ben, "And you were right, too. Bravo!" He asked everyone else, "How many see a vase?" About half the class raised their hands. "And how many see two faces?" The rest of the class raised their hands.

Then Mr. Birkway pointed out how you could see both. If you looked only at the white part in the center, you could clearly see the vase. If you looked only at the dark parts on the side, you could see two profiles. The curvy sides of the vase became the outline of the two heads facing each other.

Mr. Birkway said that the drawing was a bit like symbols. Maybe the artist only intended to draw a vase, and maybe some people look at this picture and see only that vase. That is fine, but if some people look at it and see faces, what is wrong with that? It *is* faces to that person who is looking at it. And, what is even more magnificent, you might see *both*.

Beth Ann said, "Two for your money?"

"Isn't it interesting," Mr. Birkway said, "to find both? Isn't it interesting to discover that snowy woods could be death *and* beauty *and* even, I suppose, *sex*? Wow! Literature!"

"Did he say *sex*?" Ben said, copying the drawing.

I thought Mr. Birkway was finished with the journals for that day, but he made a great show of closing his eyes and pulling something from near the bottom of the stack.

> *She popped the blackberries into her mouth. Then she looked all around—*

It was mine. I could hardly bear it.

She took two steps up to the maple
tree and threw her arms around it,
and kissed it.

People were giggling.

. . . I thought I could detect a small
dark stain, as from a blackberry
kiss.

Ben looked at me from across the room. After Mr.
Birkway read about my mother's blackberry kiss,
he read about how I kissed the tree and how I have
kissed all different kinds of trees since then and
how each tree has a special taste all its own, and
mixed in with that taste is the taste of blackberries.

By now, because both Ben and Phoebe were
staring at me, everyone else stared too. "She kisses
trees?" Megan said. I might have died right then
and there, if Mr. Birkway had not immediately
picked up another journal. He stabbed his finger
into the middle of the page and read:

I am very concerned about Mrs.——

Mr. Birkway stared down at the page. It looked

as if he couldn't read the handwriting. He started again.

>*I am very concerned about Mrs., uh,*
>*Mrs. Corpse. Her suspicious behav-*
>*ior suggests that she has murdered*
>*her own husband—*

Phoebe's eyes blinked rapidly.

"Go on," Ben said. "Finish!"

You could tell that Mr. Birkway was regretting that he had ever started this business with the journals, but all around the room people were shouting, "Yes, finish!" and so he reluctantly continued.

>*I believe she has buried him in her*
>*backyard.*

When the bell rang, people went berserk. "Wow! A murder! Who wrote that?" and "Is it real?"

I was out of that room faster than anything, chasing after Phoebe. Megan called out after me, "You kiss *trees*?" I tore out of the building. No Phoebe.

Idiot journals, I thought. Gol-darn idiot journals.

33
THE VISITOR

GRAM AND GRAMPS WERE BOTH STILL AWAKE IN our Frontier Cabin on the edge of Yellowstone National Park. "Aren't you sleepy yet?" I said.

Gram said, "I don't know what's the matter with me. I don't feel like going to sleep at all. I want to know what happened to Peeby."

"I'll tell you about Mr. Birkway's visit. Then I'll stop for tonight."

I went over to Phoebe's after dinner on the day Mr. Birkway had read from my journal about the blackberry kisses and from Phoebe's about Mrs. Cadaver. In Phoebe's bedroom, I said, "I've got two important things to tell you—" The doorbell rang, and we heard a familiar voice.

"That sounds like Mr. Birkway," Phoebe said.

"That's one of the things I want to tell you," I said. "About Mr. Birkway—"

There was a tap on Phoebe's door. Her father

said, "Phoebe? Could you and Sal come downstairs with me?"

I thought Mr. Birkway was going to be mad at Phoebe for what she had written about his sister. The worst thing was that Phoebe didn't even know yet that Mrs. Cadaver was Mr. Birkway's sister. I felt like we were lambs being led to the slaughter. Take us, I thought. Take us and do away with us quickly. We followed Phoebe's father downstairs. There on the sofa was Mr. Birkway, holding Phoebe's journal and looking embarrassed.

"That is my own private journal," Phoebe said. "With my own private thoughts."

"I know," Mr. Birkway said, "and I want to apologize for reading it aloud."

Apologize? That was a relief. It was so quiet in the room that I could hear the leaves being blown off the trees outside.

Mr. Birkway coughed. "I want to explain something," he said. "Mrs. Cadaver is my sister."

"Your sister?" Phoebe said.

"And her husband is dead."

"I thought so," Phoebe said.

"But she didn't murder him," Mr. Birkway said. "Her husband died when a drunk driver rammed into his car. My mother—Mrs. Partridge—was also in the car with Mr. Cadaver. She didn't die, as you know, but she lost her sight."

"Oh—" I said. Phoebe stared at the floor.

"My sister Margaret was the nurse on duty in the emergency room when they brought in her husband and our mother. Margaret's husband died that night."

The whole time Mr. Birkway was talking, Phoebe's father was sitting beside her with his hand resting on her shoulder. It looked like the only thing that was keeping Phoebe from vaporizing into the air and disappearing was his hand resting there.

"I just wanted you to know," Mr. Birkway said, "that Mr. Cadaver is not buried in her backyard. I've also just learned about your mother, Phoebe, and I'm sorry that she's gone, but I assure you that Margaret would not have kidnapped or murdered her."

After Mr. Birkway left, Phoebe and I sat on the front porch. Phoebe said, "If Mrs. Cadaver didn't kidnap or murder my mother, then where *is* she? What can I do? Where should I look?"

"Phoebe," I said. "There's something I've got to tell you."

"Look, Sal, if you're going to tell me she's not

coming back, I don't want to hear it. You might as well go home now."

"I know who the lunatic is. It's Sergeant Bickle's son."

And so we devised a plan.

At home that night, all I could think about was Mrs. Cadaver. I could see her in her white uniform, working in the emergency room. I could see an ambulance pulling up with its blue lights flashing, and her walking briskly to the swinging doors, with her wild hair all around her face. I could see the stretchers being wheeled in, and I could see Mrs. Cadaver looking down at them.

I could feel her heart thumping like mad as she realized it was her own husband and her own mother lying there. I imagined Mrs. Cadaver touching her husband's face. It was as if I was walking in her moccasins, that's how much my own heart was pumping and my own hands were sweating.

I started wondering if the birds of sadness had built their nest in Mrs. Cadaver's hair afterward, and if so, how she got rid of them. Her husband dying and her mother being blinded were events that *would* matter in the course of a lifetime. I saw everyone else going on with their own agendas while Mrs. Cadaver was frantically trying to keep her husband and her mother alive. Did she regret anything? Did she know the worth of water before the well was dry?

All those messages had invaded my brain and affected the way I looked at things.

"Are you sleepy yet, Gram?" I asked. My voice was hoarse from talking so much.

"No, chickabiddy, but you go on to sleep. I'm just going to lie here a while and think about things." She nudged Gramps. "You forgot to say about the marriage bed."

Gramps yawned. "Sorry, gooseberry." He patted the bed and said it.

34
OLD FAITHFUL

THAT NEXT DAY WAS PROBABLY ONE OF THE BEST, and surely the worst, in Gram's and Gramps's lives. The whispers woke me early. It was the sixth day, and the next day was my mother's birthday. We had to get out of Wyoming and through Montana. Gramps was already up, but Gram was lying on the bed, staring at the ceiling. "Did you ever go to sleep?" I asked.

"No," she said, "I didn't feel like sleeping. I can sleep later." She climbed out of bed. "Let's go see that Old Faithful. I've waited my whole entire life to see Old Faithful."

"You've sure got your heart set on that, don't you, you stubborn gooseberry?" said Gramps.

"I sure do," Gram said.

We parked the car and walked up a low hill. I was afraid Gram was going to be disappointed because it didn't look like much at first. There was a rope fence around a mound on the side of the hill. The ground was scrabbly dirt, and in the center of the rope enclosure, about twenty feet away, was a hole.

"Heck," Gram said, "can't we get any closer than this?"

Gramps and I walked over to read a sign about Old Faithful. A park ranger rushed past us yelling, "Ma'am! Ma'am!"

"Gol-dang," Gramps said.

Gram was crawling under the rope. The ranger stopped her. "Ma'am, there's a reason for that rope," he said.

Gram brushed off her dress. "I just wanted a better look."

"Don't worry," the ranger said. "You'll get a good look. Please stay behind the rope."

The sign said that Old Faithful was due to erupt in fifteen minutes. More and more people gathered around the rope. There were people of all ages: little babies crying, grannies sitting on folding stools, teenagers plugged into radio head-sets, couples smooching. There were people speaking languages other than English: next to us was a tour group of Italians; across the way was a group of Germans.

Gram tapped her fingers together, getting more and more excited. "Is it time?" she kept saying. "Is it almost time?"

The crowd became quiet a few minutes before Old Faithful was due to go off. Everyone stared at the hole. Everyone was listening.

"Is it time?" Gram said.

There was a faint noise and a little spit shot out of the hole. The man next to me said, "Aww, is that all—" Another noise, this time a little louder, a grating and crunching sound like walking on gravel. Two fitful spits. "Aww—" the man said.

Then it was like the radiator boiling over or the tea kettle blowing its top. Old Faithful hissed and steamed. A sudden spout of water shot out, maybe three feet high.

"Aww—" the man said. "Is that all—"

More steam, boiling and hissing, and a huge jing-bang spray of water surged out, climbing and climbing, and then more and more, until it looked like a whole river of water was shooting straight up into the air. "It looks like an upsidey-down water-fall!" Gram said. All the while there was a walloping hissing, and I could have sworn the ground rumbled and trembled underneath us. The warm mist blew toward us and people started backing away.

All except Gram. She stood there grinning, tilting her face up to the mist, and staring at that fountain of water. "Oh," she said. "Oh, huzza,

huzza!" She shouted it into the air and noise.

Gramps wasn't watching Old Faithful. He was watching Gram. He put his arms around her and hugged her. "You like this old geyser, don't you?" he said.

"Oh!" Gram said. "Oh yes, I do."

The man next to me was staring open-mouthed at Old Faithful. "Lordy," he said. "Lordy, that's amazing."

Gradually, Old Faithful slowed down. We watched it undo itself and retreat into its hole. We stood there even after everyone else had drifted away. At last Gram sighed and said, "Okay, let's go."

We were inside the car and about to leave when Gram started to cry. "Gol-dang—" Gramps said. "What's the matter?"

Gram sniffled. "Oh nothing. I'm so happy I got to see Old Faithful."

"You old gooseberry," Gramps said, and on we went. "We're gonna eat up Montana," Gramps said. "We're gonna get to the I-dee-ho border tonight. You watch me. I'm putting this pedal to the metal—" He stepped on the gas and peeled out of the parking lot. "I-dee-ho, here we come."

35
THE PLAN

ALL DAY LONG WE ATE UP THE ROAD THROUGH Montana. It hadn't looked so far on the map, but it was all mountains. We started in the foothills of the Rockies as we left Yellowstone, and all day we climbed up and down. Sometimes the road snaked along the side of a cliff, and the only thing between us and the sharp drop was a piddly railing. Often, as we sailed around a bend, we came face to face with a camping trailer swinging its wide body around the curve.

"These roads are a dinger," Gramps said, but he was like a little kid riding a hobby horse. "Gid-yap, let's get a move on," he said, encouraging the car up a hill. "Hee-ya," he said as we swept down the other side.

I felt as if I was torn in two pieces. Half of me was ogling the scenery. I had to admit that it was as pretty as—maybe even prettier than—Bybanks. Trees and rocks and mountains. Rivers and flowers.

Deer and moose and rabbits. It was an amazing country, an enormous country.

But the other half of me was a quivering pile of jelly. I could see our car bursting through the railing and plunging down the cliff. As we approached each curve, I could see us smashing straight on into a truck or a camper. Every time I saw a bus, I watched it sway. I watched its tires spin dangerously close to the gravel at the road's edge. I watched it plunge on, eating up the road, defying those curves.

Gram sat quietly, with her hands folded on her lap. I thought she might sleep, especially after staying awake all night, but she didn't. She wanted to hear about Peeby. So all day long, as I took in the scenery, and as I imagined us in a thousand accidents, and as I prayed underneath it all to any tree whizzing by, I talked about Peeby. I wanted to tell it all today. I wanted to finish it.

On the day after Mr. Birkway appeared at Phoebe's house and told us about Mr. Cadaver, Phoebe and I put our plan in motion. We were going to track down Sergeant Bickle's son and, according to Phoebe, discover the whereabouts of Phoebe's mother. I wasn't positive that Sergeant Bickle's son was a lunatic, and I wasn't convinced he would lead us to Phoebe's mother, but enough of Phoebe's tales had been transplanted into my brain so that I was caught up in the plan. Like Phoebe, I was ready to take some action.

We could hardly sit still all day at school. Phoebe, especially, was fired up. She was worried, too. She was afraid we might not discover her mother alive, and I was beginning to share that fear.

At school, everyone was still buzzing about the journal readings. Everyone wanted to know who had written about the murder. Alex avoided Mary Lou because of what she had said about his being a pink jerk, and Mary Lou avoided Beth Ann because of what Beth Ann had written about the chicken kisses. Megan and Christy taunted Beth Ann with, "Did you really tell Mary Lou that kisses taste like chicken? Did she really believe you?" and they taunted me with, "Do you really kiss *trees*? Didn't you know you're supposed to kiss *boys*?"

In English class, everyone badgered Mr. Birkway to finish reading the journal entry that he had begun yesterday, the one about Mrs. Corpse and the body, but Mr. Birkway did not read any more journals. Instead, he apologized for hurting people's feelings by reading their private thoughts aloud, and he sent us to the library.

There, Ben trailed me. If I looked at the fiction section, he was right beside me. If I moved over to examine the magazines, there he was flipping through one as well. Once, his face made contact with my shoulder. He was definitely trying to plant a kiss on me, I knew he was, but there was nothing I could do about it. I could not help it that whenever he aimed his mouth in my direction, my body was already moving away. I needed a little warning.

I tried remaining completely still for several consecutive minutes, and during those minutes, I detected Ben leaning slightly toward me several times. Each time, however, he drew back, as if someone were controlling him by an invisible thread.

Across the library, Beth Ann called, "Sal, there's a spider—oh, Sal, kill it!"

When the final bell rang, Phoebe and I were out of school like a shot. At Phoebe's house, we examined the telephone directory. "We've got to hurry," Phoebe said, "before Prudence or my father comes home." There were six Bickles listed in the directory. We took turns calling. Each time, we asked for Sergeant Bickle. The first two people said we must have the wrong number. The third number we dialed was busy. The fourth, no answer. The fifth was answered by a crotchety woman who said, "I don't know any sergeants!"

The sixth number was answered by an elderly man who must have been lonely because he talked on and on about once knowing a Sergeant Freeman in the war, but that was back in 1944, and he also knew a Sergeant Bones and a Sergeant Dowdy, but he did not know a Sergeant Bickle.

"What are we going to do?" Phoebe wailed. "Prudence will be home any minute, and we still don't know which is the right Bickle."

The busy number was still busy. The previously unanswered one rang and rang, and just as Phoebe was about to hang up, she heard a voice. "Hello?" she said. "May I speak with Sergeant Bickle, please?" There was a pause as she listened. "He's still at work?" Phoebe was jumping up and down. "Thank you," she said, trying to make her voice serious. "I'll call later. No, no message. Thank you."

"Yes!" she said when she hung up. "Yes, yes, yes!" She was hugging me half to death. "You'll have to do Phase Two. Tonight."

That night, while my father was at Margaret's, I phoned the Bickles. I prayed that Sergeant Bickle wouldn't answer, but I was prepared to disguise my voice in case he did. The phone rang and rang. I hung up. I rehearsed my voice and what I would say. I tried again. On the seventh ring, the phone was answered. It was Sergeant Bickle.

"My name is Susan Longfellow," I said. "I'm a friend of your son's. I was wondering if I might speak with him." I prayed and prayed that he had only one son.

"He isn't here," Sergeant Bickle said. "Would you like to leave a message?"

"Do you know when he'll be home?"

There was a pause. "How did you say you know my son?"

This made me nervous. "How do I know your son? Well, that's a long story—I—basically, the way I know him is—actually, this is a little embarrassing to admit"—my hands were sweating so much I could hardly hang on to the phone—"the library, yes, I know him from the library, and he loaned me a book, but I've lost the book—"

"Maybe you should explain this all to him," Sergeant Bickle said.

"Yes, maybe I should do that."

"I wonder why he gave you this phone number," he said. "I wonder why he didn't give you his number at school."

"At school? Actually, the thing is, I think he did give me that number too, but I've lost it—"

"You sure lose a lot of things," he said. "Would you like his number at school?"

"Yes," I said. "Or better yet, maybe you could give me his address and I'll just send him the book."

"I thought you said you lost the book."

"Actually, yes, but I'm hoping to find it," I said.

"I see," he said. "Just a minute." There was a muffled pause as he put his hand over the receiver and called, "Honey, where's Mike's address?"

Mike! Brilliant! A name! I felt like the Chief Inspector! I felt like I had just discovered the most important clue in the criminal investigation of the century. To top it off, Sergeant Bickle gave me Mike's address. I was sorely tempted to end the conversation by informing Sergeant Bickle that his son was a potential lunatic, but I refrained. I thanked him and immediately phoned Phoebe.

"You're brilliant!" she said. "Tomorrow we'll nail Mike the Lunatic."

36
THE VISIT

THE NEXT DAY, SATURDAY, WHEN PHOEBE AND I reached the bus stop, Ben was standing there. "Oh crud," Phoebe muttered. "Are you waiting for this bus? Are you going to Chanting Falls?"

"Yup," he said.

"To the university?"

"Nope." Ben pushed his hair from his eyes. "There's a hospital there. I'm going to see someone."

"So you're taking this bus," Phoebe said.

"Yes, Free Bee, I am taking this bus. Do you mind?"

The three of us sat on the long bench at the back of the bus. I was in between Phoebe and Ben, and his arm pressed up against mine. Phoebe said we were visiting an old friend, at the university. Each time we rounded a curve, Ben leaned against me or I leaned against him. "Sorry," he said. "Sorry," I said.

At Chanting Falls, we stood on the pavement as the bus roared off. "The university is over there—" Ben pointed down the road. "See ya." And he walked off in the other direction.

"Oh lord," Phoebe said. "Why did Ben have to be on the same bus? It made me very nervous."

It made me nervous too, but for different reasons. Every time I was with him now, my skin tickled and my brain buzzed and my blood romped around as if it were percolating.

The address we had for Mike Bickle was a freshman dormitory. It was a three-story brick building, with hundreds of windows. "Oh no," Phoebe wailed. "I thought it might be a little house or something." Students were coming in and out of the building and walking across the lawn. Some were sitting on the grass or benches studying. In the lobby was a reception desk, with a handsome young man standing behind it. "You do it," Phoebe said. "I just can't."

We stood out like pickles in a pea patch. There were all these grown-up college students and here we were, two puny thirteen-year-old girls. Phoebe said, "I wish I had worn something else." She picked lint off her sweater.

I explained to the man at the desk that I was

looking for my cousin, Mike Bickle. The young man smiled a wide, white smile at me. He checked a roster and said, "You're in the right place. Room 209. You can go on up."

Phoebe nearly choked. "You mean we could go right up to his room?"

"Sure," the young man said. "Through there."

We walked through swinging doors. Phoebe said, "Really, I'm having a heart attack, I know it. I can't do this. Let's get out of here." At the end of the hall, we slipped out the exit. "What if we knocked on his door and he opened it and pulled us inside and slit our throats?"

Students were milling around on the lawn. I looked for an empty bench on which we might sit. On the far side of the lawn I saw the backs of two people, a young man and an older woman. They were holding hands. She turned to him and kissed his cheek.

"Phoebe—" On the bench was Phoebe's mother, and she was kissing the lunatic.

37
A KISS

PHOEBE WAS STUNNED AND ANGRY, BUT SHE WAS braver than I was. She could watch, but I could not. I assumed that Phoebe would follow me, but I didn't look back. Down the street I tore, trying to remember where the bus stop was. It wasn't until I saw the hospital that I realized I must have missed the bus stop. I ducked inside and was surprised that Phoebe was not behind me.

What I did next was an impulse. A hunch. I asked the hospital receptionist if I could see Mrs. Finney. She flipped through a roster. "Are you a family member?" she said.

"No."

"I'm afraid you can't go up then," she said. "Mrs. Finney is on the psychiatric ward. Family only."

"I was looking for her son. He came here to visit her."

"Maybe they went outside. You could look out back."

Behind the hospital was a wide, sloping lawn, bordered by flower gardens. Scattered across the lawn were benches and chairs, most of them occupied with patients and their visitors. It was a scene much like the one I had just left at the university, except here no one was studying, and some of the people wore dressing gowns.

Ben was sitting cross-legged on the ground in front of a woman in a pink robe. She fidgeted with the sash. Ben saw me and stood up as I crossed the lawn. "This is my mother," he said. I said hello, but she didn't look at me. Instead, she stood and drifted off across the lawn as if we were not there. Ben and I followed.

She reminded me so much of my mother after she returned from the hospital. My mother would stop right in the middle of doing something inside the house and walk out the door. Halfway up the hill, she would sit down to catch her breath. She picked at the grass, got up again, and went a little farther. Sometimes my mother went in the barn and filled the pail with chicken feed, but before she reached the chicken coop, she set the pail down and moved off in another direction. When she could walk farther, my mother rambled over the fields and meadows, in a weaving, snaking pattern, as if she could not make up her mind which way to turn.

We followed Ben's mother back and forth across the lawn, but she never seemed to notice our presence. At last I said I had to go, and that's when it happened.

For one quick moment we both had the same agenda. I looked at him and he looked at me. Both of our heads moved forward. It must have been in slow motion, because I had a split second there to be reminded of Mr. Birkway's drawing of the two heads facing each other, with the vase in between. I wondered, just for an instant, if a vase could fit between us.

If there *had* been a vase, we would have squashed it, because our heads moved completely together and our lips landed in the right place, which was on the other person's lips. It was a real kiss, and it did not taste like chicken.

And then our heads moved slowly backward and we stared out across the lawn, and I felt like the newlY born horse who knows nothing but feels everything.

Ben touched his lips. "Did it taste a little like blackberries to you?" he said.

38
SPIT

AT THIS POINT IN MY STORY, GRAM INTERRUPTED. "Oh yes, yes, yes!" she said. "I've been waiting for that kiss for days. I do like a story with some good kisses in it."

"She's such a gooseberry," Gramps said.

We were churning through Montana. I didn't dare check our progress on the map. I didn't want to discover that we couldn't make it in time. I thought that if I kept talking, and praying underneath, and if we kept moving along those mountainous roads, we had a chance.

Gram said, "But what about Peeby? What about her mother kissing the lunatic? I didn't like that kiss very much. It was the other one I liked—the one with Ben."

I found Phoebe at the bus stop, sitting on the bench. "Where were you?" she asked.

I did not tell her about seeing Ben or his mother. I wanted to, but I couldn't. "I was afraid, Phoebe. I couldn't stay there."

"And I thought you were the brave one," she said. "Oh well, it doesn't matter. Nothing matters. I'm sick of it."

"What happened?"

"Nothing. They sat there on the bench having a gay old time. If I could toss rocks like you can toss rocks, I'd have plonked them both in the back of the head. Did you notice her hair? She's cut it. It's short. And do you know what else she did? In the middle of talking, she leaned over and spit on the grass. Spit! It was disgusting. And the lunatic, do you know what he did when she spit? He *laughed*. Then he leaned over and *he* spit."

"Why would they do that?"

"Who knows? I'm sick of it. My mother can stay there for all I care. She doesn't need me. She doesn't need any of us."

Phoebe was like that all the way home on the bus. She was in an extensively black mood. We got to Phoebe's house just as her father pulled in the driveway. Prudence rushed out of the house saying, "She called, she called, she called! Mom called! She's coming home."

"Terrific," Phoebe muttered.

"What was that, Phoebe?" her father said.

"Nothing."

"She's coming tomorrow," Prudence said. "But—"

"What's wrong?" her father said. "What else did she say?"

"She sounded nervous. She wanted to talk with you—"

"Did she leave a number? I'll call her back—"

"No, she didn't leave any number. She said to tell you not to make any prejudgments."

"What is that supposed to mean?" her father said. "Not make any prejudgments about what?"

"I don't know," Prudence said. "And oh! Most, most, important! She said that she was bringing someone with her."

"That's just grand," Phoebe said. "Just grand."

"Phoebe—?" her father said. "Prudence—did she say who she's bringing?"

"I honestly could not say."

"Did she refer to this person at all? Did she mention a name?" He was getting agitated.

"Why no," Prudence said. "She didn't mention a name. She just said that she was bringing him with her—"

"*Him?*"

Phoebe looked at me. "Cripes," she said, and she went into the house, slamming the door behind her.

I couldn't believe it. Wasn't she going to tell her father what she had seen? I was bursting at the seams to tell my own father, but when I got home, he and Margaret were sitting on the porch.

Margaret said, "My brother told me you're in his English class. What a surprise." She must have already told my father this, because he didn't look too surprised. "He's a terrific teacher. Do you like him?"

"I suppose." I didn't want to talk about it. I wanted Margaret to vanish.

I had to wait until she went home to tell my father about Phoebe's mother, and when I did tell him, all he said was, "So Mrs. Winterbottom is coming home. That's good." Then he went over to the window and stared out of it for the longest time, and I knew he was thinking about my mother.

All that night I thought about Phoebe and Prudence and Mr. Winterbottom. It seemed like their whole world was going to fall apart the next day when Mrs. Winterbottom walked in all cuddly with the lunatic.

39
HOMECOMING

THE NEXT MORNING, PHOEBE PHONED, BEGGING me to come over. "I can't stand it," she said. "I want a witness."

"For what?"

"I just want a witness."

"Did you tell your father? About your mother and—"

"Are you kidding?" Phoebe said. "You should see him. He and Prudence spent all last night and this morning cleaning the house. They've scrubbed floors and bathrooms, they dusted like fiends, they did laundry and ironing, and they vacuumed. Then they took a good look around. My father said, 'Maybe it looks too good. Your mother will think we can function without her.' So they messed things up. He's very put out with me that I wouldn't help."

I did not want to be a witness to anything, but I felt guilty for running away the day before, and so

I agreed. When I got to her house, Phoebe, Mr. Winterbottom, and Prudence were sitting there staring at each other.

"Didn't she say what time she was coming?" Mr. Winterbottom asked.

Prudence said, "No she did not, and I wish you would quit acting as if it is my fault that she did not say more than she did."

Mr. Winterbottom was a wreck. He jumped up to straighten a pillow, sat back down, and then he leaped up to mess up the pillow again. He went out in the yard and walked around in circles. He changed his shirt twice.

"I hope you don't mind that I'm here," I said.

"Why would I mind?" Mr. Winterbottom said.

Just as I thought they would all go stark raving mad, a taxi pulled up outside. "I can't look," Mr. Winterbottom said, escaping to the kitchen.

"I can't look either," Phoebe said. She followed her father, and I followed Phoebe.

"Well, *gosh*," Prudence said. "I don't know what has gotten into everybody. Aren't you excited to see her?"

From the kitchen, we heard Prudence open the front door. We heard Mrs. Winterbottom say, "Oh sweetie—" Mr. Winterbottom wiped the kitchen counter. We heard Prudence gasp and her mother say, "I'd like you to meet Mike."

"Mike?" Mr. Winterbottom said. He was quite red in the face. I was glad there was no axe in the house or I am fairly certain he would have picked it up and headed straight for Mike.

Phoebe said, "Now, Dad, don't do anything too rash—"

"Mike?" he repeated.

Mrs. Winterbottom called, "George? Phoebe?" We heard her say to Prudence, "Where are they? Didn't you tell them we were coming?"

Mr. Winterbottom took a deep breath. "Phoebe, I'm not sure you or Sal should be around for this."

"Are you kidding?" Phoebe said.

He took another deep breath. "Okay," he said. "Okay. Here we go." He stood up straight and tall and walked through to the living room. Phoebe and I followed.

Honest and truly, I think Phoebe nearly fainted dead away on the carpet. There were two reasons for this. The first one was that Mrs. Winterbottom looked different. Her hair was not only short but also quite stylish. She was wearing lipstick, mascara, and a little blush on her cheeks, and her clothes were altogether unlike anything I had ever seen her in: a white T-shirt, blue jeans, and flat black shoes. Dangling from her ears were thin silver hoop earrings. She looked magnificent, but she did not look like Phoebe's mother.

The second reason that I think Phoebe nearly fainted dead away was that there was Mike Bickle, Phoebe's potential lunatic, in her own living room. It was one thing to *think* he was coming, and another thing to actually see him standing there.

I didn't know what to think. For a second, I thought maybe Mike *had* kidnapped Mrs. Winterbottom and was bringing her back for some ransom money or maybe he was now going to do away with the rest of us. But I kept thinking of seeing them together the day before, and besides, Mrs. Winterbottom looked too terrific to have been held captive. She did look frightened, but not of Mike. She seemed afraid of her husband.

"Dad," Phoebe whispered, "that's the lunatic."

"Oh Phoebe," her mother said, pressing her fingers to her cheek, and when she made that familiar gesture, Phoebe looked as if her heart was splitting into a thousand pieces. Mrs. Winterbottom hugged Phoebe, but Phoebe did not hug her back.

Mr. Winterbottom said, "Norma, I hope you are going to explain exactly what is going on here." He was trying to make his voice firm, but it trembled.

Prudence stared at Mike. She seemed to find him handsome and was flirting with him. She fluffed her hair away from her neck.

Mrs. Winterbottom tried to put her arms around Mr. Winterbottom, but he pulled away. "I think we deserve an explanation," he said. He, too, stared at Mike.

Was she in love with Mike? He seemed awfully, awfully young—not much older than Prudence.

Mrs. Winterbottom sat down on the sofa and began to cry. It was a terrible, terrible moment. It was hard to make any sense out of what she said at first. She was talking about being respectable and how maybe Mr. Winterbottom would never forgive her, but she was tired of being so respectable. She had tried very, very hard all these years to be perfect, but she had to admit she was quite unperfect. She said there was something that she had never told her husband, and she feared he would not forgive her for it.

Mr. Winterbottom's hands trembled. He did not say anything. Mrs. Winterbottom motioned for Mike to join her on the sofa. Mr. Winterbottom cleared his throat several times, but still he said nothing.

Mrs. Winterbottom said, "Mike is my son."

Mr. Winterbottom, Prudence, Phoebe, and I all said, "Your *son*?"

Mrs. Winterbottom stared at her husband. "George, I know you will think I am not—or was not—respectable, but it was before I met you, and I had to give him up for adoption and I could hardly bear to think of it and—"

Mr. Winterbottom said, "Respectable? Respectable? The hell with respectable!" Mr. Winterbottom did not normally swear.

Mrs. Winterbottom stood up. "Mike found *me*, and at first I was frightened of what that would mean. I've lived such a tiny life—"

Phoebe took her father's hand.

"—and I had to go away and sort things out. I haven't yet met Mike's adoptive parents, but Mike and I have spent a lot of time talking, and I've been thinking—"

Mike looked down at his feet.

"Are you going to leave?" Mr. Winterbottom asked.

Mrs. Winterbottom looked as if he had slapped her. "Leave?"

"Again, I mean," Mr. Winterbottom said.

"Only if you want me to," she said. "Only if you

cannot live with such an unrespectable—"

"I said to hell with respectable!" Mr. Winterbottom said. "What's all this about respectable? It's not respectable I'm concerned about. I'm more concerned that you couldn't—or wouldn't—tell me about any of this."

Mike stood up. "I knew it wouldn't work," he said.

Mr. Winterbottom said, "I have nothing against you, Mike—I just don't know you." He looked at his wife. "I don't think I know you, either."

I was wishing I was invisible. Outside, the leaves were falling to the ground, and I was infinitely sad, sad down to my bones. I was sad for Phoebe and her parents and Prudence and Mike, sad for the leaves that were dying, and sad for myself, for something I had lost.

I saw Mrs. Partridge through the window, standing on Phoebe's front walk.

Mr. Winterbottom said, "I think we all need to sit down and talk. Maybe we can sort something out." Then he did what I think was a noble thing. He went over to Mike and shook his hand and said, "I did always think a son would be a nice addition to this family."

Mrs. Winterbottom looked relieved. Prudence

smiled at Mike. Phoebe stood motionless, off to the side.

"I'd better go," I said.

Everyone turned to me as if I had just dropped through the roof. Mr. Winterbottom said, "Sal, I'm sorry, I truly am." To Mike, he said, "Sal is like another member of the family."

Mrs. Winterbottom said, "You're mad at me, aren't you, Phoebe?"

"Yes," Phoebe said. "I most certainly am." Phoebe took my sleeve and pulled me toward the door. "When you all decide exactly how many people are in this family, let me know."

We stepped out on the porch just as Mrs. Partridge placed a white envelope on the steps.

40
THE GIFTS

IT SEEMED FITTING THAT AT THIS POINT IN MY STORY of Phoebe, Gramps called out, "I-dee-ho!" We were high in the mountains and had just crossed the Montana border into Idaho. For the first time, I believed we were going to make it to Lewiston by the next day, the twentieth of August, my mother's birthday.

Gramps suggested we press on to Coeur d'Alene, about an hour away, where we could spend the night. From there, Lewiston was about a hundred miles due south, an easy morning's journey. "How does that sound to you, gooseberry?" Gram was still, her head pressed against the back of the seat and her hands folded in her lap. "Gooseberry?"

When Gram spoke, you could hear the rattle in her chest. "Oh, that's fine," she said.

"Gooseberry, are you feeling okay?"

"I'm a little tired," she said.

"We'll get you to a bed real soon." Gramps glanced back at me, troubled.

"Gram, if you want to stop now, that would be okay," I said.

"Oh no," she said. "I'd like to sleep in Coeur d'Alene tonight. Your momma sent us a postcard from Coeur d'Alene, and on it was a bountiful blue lake." She coughed a long, rattly cough.

Gramps said, "Okay then, bountiful blue lake, here we come."

Gram said, "I'm so glad Peeby's momma came home. I wish your momma could come home too."

Gramps nodded his head for about five minutes. Then he handed me a tissue and said, "Tell us about Mrs. Partridge. What was she doing leaving a gol-dang envelope on Peeby's porch?"

That's what Phoebe and I wanted to know. "Did you want something, Mrs. Partridge?" I asked.

She put her hand to her lips. "Hmm," she said.

Phoebe snatched the envelope and ripped it open. She read the message aloud: "Don't judge a man until you've walked two moons in his moccasins."

Mrs. Partridge turned to go. "Bye-bye," she said.

"Mrs. Partridge," Phoebe called. "We've already had this one."

"I beg your pardon?" Mrs. Partridge said.

"It was you, wasn't it?" Phoebe said. "You've been creeping around leaving these things, haven't you?"

"Did you like them?" Mrs. Partridge said. As she stood there in the middle of the sidewalk, with her head tilted up at us, and that quizzical look on her face, she looked like a mischievous child. "Margaret reads them to me from the paper each day, and when there's a nice one, I ask her to copy it down. I'm sorry I gave you that one about the moccasins already. My noggin forgot."

"But why did you bring them *here*?" Phoebe said.

"I thought they would be grandiful surprises for you—like fortune cookies, only I didn't have any cookies to put them in. Did you like them anyway?"

Phoebe looked at me for a long minute. Then she went down the steps and said, "Mrs. Partridge, when was it you met my brother?"

"You said you didn't have a brother," Mrs. Partridge said.

"I know, but you said you met him. When was that?"

She tapped her head. "Noggin, remember. Let's see. Some time ago. A week? Two weeks? He came to my house by mistake. He let me feel his face. That's why I thought he was your brother. He has a similar face. Isn't that peculible?"

Phoebe said, "No more peculible than most things lately." As Mrs. Partridge tottered back to her house, Phoebe said, "It's a peculible world, Sal." She walked across the grass and spit into the street. She said, "Come on, try it." I spit into the street. "What do you think?" Phoebe said. We spit again.

It might sound disgusting, but to tell the truth, we got a great deal of pleasure from those spits. I doubt if I ever could explain why that was, but for some reason it seemed the perfect thing to do, and when Phoebe turned around and went into the house, I knew that was the right thing for her to do too.

With the courage of that spit in me, I went to see Margaret Cadaver, and we had a long talk, and that's when I found out how she met my father. It was painful to talk with her, and I even cried in front of her, but afterward I understood why my father liked to be with her.

Ben was sitting on my front steps when I got home. He said, "I brought you something. It's out back." He led me around the side of the house and there, strutting across that little patch of grass, was a chicken.

I was never in my life so happy to see a chicken.

Ben said, "I named it, but you can change the name if you want."

When I asked him what its name was, he leaned forward, and I leaned forward and another kiss happened, a spectacular kiss, a perfect kiss, and Ben said, "Its name is Blackberry."

"Oh," Gram said, "is that the end of the Peeby story?"

"Yes," I said. That wasn't quite true, I suppose, as I could have told more. I could have told about Phoebe getting adjusted to having a brother, and to her "new" mother, and all of that, but that part was still going on, even as we traveled through the mountains. It was a whole different story.

"I liked that story about Peeby, and I'm glad it wasn't too awfully sad."

Gram closed her eyes and for the next hour as Gramps drove toward Coeur d'Alene, he and I listened to her rattly breathing. I watched her lying there so still, so calm. "Gramps," I whispered. "She looks a little gray, doesn't she?"

"Yes she does, chickabiddy, yes she does." He stepped on the gas and we raced toward Coeur d'Alene.

41
THE OVERLOOK

AT COEUR D'ALENE, WE WENT STRAIGHT TO THE hospital. Gramps had tried to wake Gram when he saw the lake. "Gooseberry?" Gramps said. She slumped sideways on the seat. "Gooseberry?"

The doctors said Gram had had a stroke. Gramps insisted on being with her while she underwent tests, though an intern had tried to dissuade him. "She's unconscious," the intern said. "She won't know whether you're here or not."

"Sonny, I've been by her side for fifty-one years, except for three days when she left me for the egg man. I'm holding on to her hand, see? If you want me to let go, you'll have to chop my hand off."

They let him stay with her. While I was waiting in the lobby, a man came in with an old beagle. The receptionist told him he would have to leave the dog outside. "By herself?" the man said.

I said, "I'll watch her. I had a dog just like her once." I took the old beagle outside, and when I sat down on the grass, the beagle put her head in my lap and murmured in that special way dogs have. Gramps calls it a dog's purr.

I wondered if Gram's snake bite had anything to do with her stroke, and if Gramps felt guilty for whizzing off the highway and stopping at that river. If we hadn't gone to that river, Gram would never have been bitten by that snake. And then I started thinking about my mother's stillborn baby and maybe if I hadn't climbed that tree and if my mother hadn't carried me, maybe the baby would have lived and my mother never would have gone away, and everything would still be as it used to be.

But as I sat there thinking these things, it occurred to me that a person couldn't stay all locked up in the house like Phoebe and her mother had tried to do at first. A person had to go out and do things and see things, and I wondered, for the first time, if this had something to do with Gram and Gramps taking me on this trip.

The beagle in my lap was just like our Moody Blue. I rubbed her head and prayed for Gram. I thought about Moody Blue's litter of puppies. For the first week, Moody Blue wouldn't let anyone come anywhere near those puppies. She licked them clean and nuzzled them. They squealed and pawed their way up to her with their eyes still sealed.

Gradually, Moody Blue let us touch the puppies, but she kept her sharp eyes on us, and if we tried to take a puppy out of her sight, she growled. Within a few weeks, the puppies were stumbling away from her, and Moody Blue spent her days herding them back, but when they were about six weeks old, Moody Blue started ignoring them. She snapped at them and pushed them away. I told my mother that Moody Blue was being terrible. "She hates her puppies."

"It's not terrible," my mother said. "It's normal. She's weaning them from her."

"Does she have to do that? Why can't they stay with her?"

"It isn't good for her or for them. They have to become independent. What if something happened to Moody Blue? They wouldn't know how to survive without her."

While I prayed for Gram outside the hospital, I wondered if my mother's trip to Idaho was like Moody Blue's behavior. Maybe part of it was for my mother and part of it was for me.

When the beagle's owner returned, I went back inside. It was after midnight when a nurse told me I could see Gram. She was lying, still and gray, on the bed. A little dribble was coming out of one side of her mouth. Gramps was leaning over her, whispering in her ear. A nurse said, "I don't think she can hear you."

"Of course she can hear me," Gramps said. "She'll always be able to hear me."

Gram's eyes were closed. Wires were attached to her chest and to a monitor, and a tube was taped to her hand. I wanted to hold her and wake her up. Gramps said, "We're gonna be here a while, chickabiddy." He reached in his pocket and pulled out his car keys. "Here, in case you need anything from the car." He handed me a crumpled wad of money. "In case you need it."

"I don't want to leave Gram," I said.

"Heck," he said. "She doesn't want you sitting around this old hospital. You just whisper in her ear if you want to tell her anything, and then you go do what you have to do. We're not going anywhere, your grandmother and I. We'll be right here." He winked at me. "You be careful, chickabiddy."

I leaned over and whispered in Gram's ear and

then I left. In the car, I studied the map, leaned back in the seat, and closed my eyes. Gramps knew what I was going to do.

The key was cold in my hand. I studied the map again. One curvy road ran direct from Coeur d'Alene to Lewiston. I started the car, backed it up, drove around the parking lot, stopped, and turned off the engine. I counted the money in my pocket and looked at the map once more.

In the course of a lifetime, there were some things that mattered.

Although I was terrified when I drove out of the parking lot, once I was on the highway, I felt better. I drove slowly, and I knew how to do it. I prayed to every passing tree, and there were a thumping lot of trees along the way.

It was a narrow, winding road, without traffic. It took me four hours to drive the hundred miles from Coeur d'Alene to the top of Lewiston Hill—which, to me, was more of a mountain than a hill. I pulled into the overlook at the top. In the valley far below was Lewiston, with the Snake River winding through it. Between me and Lewiston was the treacherous road with its hairpin turns that twisted back and forth down the mountain.

I peered over the rail, looking for the bus that I

knew was still somewhere down there on the side of the mountain, but I couldn't see it. "I can do this," I said to myself over and over. "I can do this."

I eased the car back onto the road. At the first curve, my heart started thumping. My palms were sweating and slippery on the wheel. I crept along with my foot on the brake, but the road doubled back so sharply and plunged so steeply that even with my foot on the brake, the car was going faster than I wanted it to. When I came out of that curve, I was in the outside lane, the one nearest to the side of the cliff. It was a sharp drop down, with only a thin cable strung between occasional posts to mark the edge of the road.

Back and forth across the hill the road snaked. For a half mile, I was on the inside against the hill and felt safer, and then I came to one of those awful curves, and for the next half mile I was on the outside, and the dark slide of the hillside stretched down, down, down. Back and forth I went: a half mile safe, a curve, a half mile edging the side of the cliff.

Halfway down was another overlook, a thin extra lane marked off less as an opportunity to gaze at the scenery, I thought, than to allow drivers a chance to stop and gather their wits. I wondered how many people had abandoned their cars at this point and walked the remaining miles down. As I stood looking over the side, another car pulled into the overlook. A man got out and stood near me, smoking a cigarette. "Where are the others?" he asked.

"What others?"

"Whoever's with you. Whoever's driving."

"Oh," I said. "Around—"

"Taking a pee, eh?" he said, referring, I gathered, to whoever was supposedly with me. "A helluva road to be driving at night, isn't it? I do it every night. I work up in Pullman and live down there—" He pointed to the lights of Lewiston and the black river. "You been here before?" he said.

"No."

"See that?" He indicated a spot somewhere below.

I peered into the darkness. Then I saw the severed treetops and the rough path cut through the brush. At the end of this path I could see something shiny and metallic reflecting the moonlight. It was the one thing I had been looking for.

"A bus went off the road here—a year or more ago," he said. "Skidded right there, coming out of that last turn, and went sliding into this here overlook and on through the railing and rolled over and over into those trees. A helluva thing. When I came home that night, rescuers were still hacking their way through the brush to get to it. Only one person survived, ya know?"

I knew.

42
THE BUS AND THE WILLOW

WHEN THE MAN DROVE OFF, I CRAWLED BENEATH the railing and made my way down the hill toward the bus. In the east the sky was smoky gray, and I was glad for the approaching dawn. In the year and a half since the trail was hacked out, the brush had begun to grow back. Wet with dew, straggly branches slapped and scratched at my legs and hid uneven ground so that several times I tripped, tumbling and sliding downward.

The bus lay on its side like an old sick horse, its broken headlights staring out mournfully into the surrounding trees. Most of the huge rubber tires were punctured and grotesquely twisted on their axles. I climbed up onto the bus's side, hoping to make my way down to an open window, but there were two enormous gashes torn into the side, and the jagged metal was peeled back like a sardine tin. Through a smashed window behind the driver's seat, I saw a jumbled mess of twisted seats and chunks of foam rubber. Everything was dusted over with fuzzy, green mold.

I had imagined that I would drop through a window and walk down the aisle, but there was no space inside to move. I had wanted to scour every inch of the bus, looking for something—anything—that might be familiar.

By now the sky was pale pink, and it was easier to find the uphill trail, but harder going as it was a steep incline. By the time I reached the top, I was muddy and scratched from head to toe. It wasn't until I had crawled beneath the railing that I noticed the car parked behind Gramps's red Chevrolet.

It was the sheriff. He was talking on his radio when he saw me, and he motioned for his deputy to get out. The deputy said, "We were just about to come down there after you. We saw you up on top of the bus. You kids ought to know better. What were you doing down there at this time of day, anyway?"

Before I could answer, the sheriff climbed out of his car. He settled his hat on his head and shifted his holster. "Where are the others?" he said.

"There aren't any others," I said.

"Who brought you up here?"

"I brought myself."

"Whose car is this?"

"My grandfather's."

"And where is he?" The sheriff glanced to left and right, as if Gramps might be hiding in the bushes.

"He's in Coeur d'Alene."

The sheriff said, "Pardon?"

So I told him about Gram and about how Gramps had to stay with her and about how I had driven from Coeur d'Alene *very carefully*.

The sheriff said, "Now let me get this straight," and he repeated everything I said, ending with, "and you're telling me that you drove from Coeur d'Alene to this spot on this hill all by yourself?"

"Very carefully," I said. "My gramps taught me how to drive, and he taught me to drive very carefully."

The sheriff said to the deputy, "I am afraid to ask this young lady exactly how old she is. Why don't you ask her?"

The deputy said, "How old are you?" I told him. The sheriff gave me a stern look and said, "I don't suppose you would mind telling me exactly what was so all-fired important that you couldn't wait for someone with a legitimate driver's license to bring you to the fair city of Lewiston?"

And so I told him all the rest. When I had finished, he returned to his car and talked into his radio some more. Then he told me to get in his car and he told the deputy to follow in Gramps's car. I thought the sheriff was probably going to put me in jail, and it wasn't the thought of jail that bothered me so much. It was knowing that I was this close and might not be able to do what I had come to do, and it was knowing that I needed to get back to Gram.

He did not take me to jail, however. He drove across the bridge into Lewiston and on through the city and up a hill. He drove into Longwood, stopped at the caretaker's house, and went inside. Behind us was the deputy in Gramps's car. The caretaker came out and pointed off to the right, and the sheriff got back in the car and drove off in that direction.

It was a pleasant place. The Snake River curved behind this section, and tall, full-leaved trees grew here and there across the lawn. The sheriff parked the car and led me up a path toward the river, and there, on a little hill overlooking the river and the valley, was my mother's grave.

On the tombstone, beneath her name and the dates of her birth and death, was an engraving of a maple tree, and it was only then, when I saw the stone and her name—Chanhassen "Sugar" Pickford Hiddle—and the engraving of the tree, that I knew, by myself and for myself, that she was not coming back. I asked if I could sit there for a little while, because I wanted to memorize the place. I wanted to memorize the grass and the trees, the smells and the sounds.

In the midst of the still morning, with only the sound of the river gurgling by, I heard a bird. It was singing a birdsong, a true, sweet birdsong. I looked all around and then up into the willow that leaned toward the river. The birdsong came from the top of the willow and I did not want to look too closely, because I wanted it to be the tree that was singing.

I kissed the willow. "Happy birthday," I said.

In the sheriff's car, I said, "She isn't actually gone at all. She's singing in the trees."

"Whatever you say, Miss Salamanca Hiddle."

"You can take me to jail now."

43
OUR GOOSEBERRY

INSTEAD OF TAKING ME TO JAIL, THE SHERIFF DROVE me to Coeur d'Alene, with the deputy following us in Gramps's car. The sheriff gave me a lengthy and severe lecture about driving without a license, and he made me promise that I would not drive again until I was sixteen.

"Not even on Gramps's farm?" I said.

He looked straight ahead at the road. "I suppose people are going to do whatever they want to on their own farms," he said, "as long as they have a lot of room to maneuver and as long as they are not endangering the lives of any other persons or animals. But I'm not saying you ought to. I'm not giving you permission or anything."

I asked him to tell me about the bus accident. When I asked him if he had been there that night and if he had seen anyone brought out of the bus, he said, "You don't want to know all that. A person shouldn't have to think about those things."

"Did you see my mother?"

"I saw a lot of people, Salamanca, and maybe I saw your mother and maybe I didn't, but I'm sorry to say that if I did see her, I didn't know it. I remember your father coming in to the station. I do remember that, but I wasn't with him when—I wasn't there when—"

"Did you see Mrs. Cadaver?" I said.

"How do you know about Mrs. Cadaver?" he said. "Of course I saw Mrs. Cadaver. Everyone saw Mrs. Cadaver. Nine hours after that bus rolled over, as all those stretchers were being carried up the hill, and everyone despairing—there was her hand coming up out of the window and everyone was shouting because there it was, a moving hand." He glanced at me. "I wish it had been your mother's hand."

"Mrs. Cadaver was sitting next to my mother," I said.

"Oh."

"They were strangers to each other when they got on that bus, but by the time they got off, six days later, they were friends. My mother told Mrs. Cadaver all about me and my father and our farm in Bybanks. She told Mrs. Cadaver about the fields and the blackberries and Moody Blue and the chickens and the singing tree. I think that if she told Mrs. Cadaver all that, then my mother must have been missing us, don't you think?"

"I'm sure of it," the sheriff said. "And how do you know all this?"

So I explained to him how Mrs. Cadaver had told me all this on the day Phoebe's mother returned. Mrs. Cadaver told me about how my father visited her in the hospital in Lewiston after he had buried my mother. He came to see the only survivor from the bus crash, and when he learned that Mrs. Cadaver had been sitting next to my mother, they started talking about her. They talked for six hours.

Mrs. Cadaver told me about her and my father writing to each other, and about how my father needed to get away from Bybanks for a while. I asked Mrs. Cadaver why my father hadn't told me how he had met her, and she said he had tried, but I didn't want to hear it, and he didn't want to upset me. He thought I might dislike Margaret because she had survived and my mother had not.

"Do you love him?" I had asked Mrs. Cadaver. "Are you going to marry him?"

"Goodness!" she said. "It's a little early for that. He's holding on to me because I was with your mother and held her hand in her last moments.

271

Your father isn't ready to love anyone else yet. Your mother was one of a kind."

That's true. She was.

And even though Mrs. Cadaver had told me all this and had told me how she had been with my mother in her last minutes, I still did not believe that my mother was actually dead. I still thought that there might have been a mistake. I don't know what I had hoped to find in Lewiston. Maybe I expected that I would see her walking through a field and I would call to her and she would say, "Oh Salamanca, my left arm," and "Oh Salamanca, take me home."

I slept for the last fifty miles into Coeur d'Alene and when I awoke, I was sitting in the sheriff's car outside the hospital entrance. The sheriff was coming out of the hospital. He handed me an envelope and slid in beside me on the seat.

In the envelope was a note from Gramps giving the name of the motel he was staying at. Beneath that he had written, "I am sorry to say that our gooseberry died at three o'clock this morning."

Gramps was sitting on the side of the bed in the motel, talking on the telephone. When he saw me and the sheriff at the door, he put the phone down and hugged me to him. The sheriff told Gramps how sorry he was and that he didn't think it was the

time or place to give anybody a lecture about un-
derage granddaughters driving down a mountain-
side in the middle of the night. He handed
Gramps his car key and asked Gramps if he
needed help making any arrangements.

Gramps said he had taken care of most things.
Gram's body was being flown back to Bybanks,
where my father would meet the plane. Gramps
and I were going to finish what had to be done in
Coeur d'Alene and leave the next morning.

After the sheriff and his deputy left, I noticed
Gram's and Gramps's open suitcase. Inside were
Gram's things, all mixed in with Gramps's clothes. I
picked up her baby powder and smelled it. On the
desk was a crumpled letter. When Gramps saw me
look at it, he said, "I wrote her a letter last night.
It's a love letter."

Gramps lay down on the bed and stared up at
the ceiling. "Chickabiddy," he said, "I miss my
gooseberry." He put one arm over his eyes. His
other hand patted the empty space beside him.
"This ain't—" he said. "This ain't—"

"It's okay," I said. I sat down on the other side
of the bed and held his hand. "This ain't your marriage bed."

About five minutes later, Gramps cleared his
throat and said, "But it will have to do."

44
BYBANKS

WE'RE BACK IN BYBANKS NOW. MY FATHER AND I are living on our farm again, and Gramps is living with us. Gram is buried in the aspen grove where she and Gramps were married. We miss our goose-berry every single day.

Lately, I've been wondering if there might be something hidden behind the fireplace, because just as the fireplace was behind the plaster wall and my mother's story was behind Phoebe's, I think there was a third story behind Phoebe's and my mother's, and that was about Gram and Gramps.

On the day after Gram was buried, her friend Gloria—the one Gram thought was so much like Phoebe, and the one who had a hankering for Gramps—came to visit Gramps. They sat on our porch while Gramps talked about Gram for four hours straight. Gloria asked if we had any aspirin. She had a grand headache. We haven't seen her since.

I wrote to Tom Fleet, the boy who helped Gram when the snake took a snack out of her leg. I told him that Gram made it back to Bybanks, but unfortunately she came in a coffin. I described the aspen grove where she was buried and told him about the river nearby. He wrote back, saying that he was sorry about Gram and maybe he would come and visit that aspen grove someday. Then he asked, "Is your riverbank private property?"

Gramps is giving me more driving lessons in the pickup truck. We practice over on Gramps's old farm, where the new owner lets us clonk around on the dirt roads. With us rides Gramps's new beagle puppy, which he named Huzza Huzza. Gramps pets the puppy and smokes his pipe as I drive, and we both play the moccasin game. It's a game we made up on our way back from Idaho. We take turns pretending we are walking in someone else's moccasins.

"If I were walking in Peeby's moccasins, I would be jealous of a new brother dropping out of the sky."

"If I were in Gram's moccasins right this minute, I would want to cool my feet in that river over there."

"If I were walking in Ben's moccasins, I would

miss Salamanca Hiddle."

On and on we go. We walk in everybody's moccasins, and we have discovered some interesting things that way. One day I realized that our whole trip out to Lewiston had been a gift from Gram and Gramps to me. They were giving me a chance to walk in my mother's moccasins—to see what she had seen and feel what she might have felt on her last trip.

I also realized that there were good reasons why my father didn't take me to Idaho when he got the news of her death. He was too grief-stricken, and he was trying to spare me. Only later did he understand that I had to go and see for myself. He was right about one thing, though: we didn't need to bring her body back because she *is* in the trees, the barn, the fields. Gramps is different. He needs Gram right here. He needs to walk out to that aspen grove to see his gooseberry.

One afternoon, after we had been talking about Prometheus stealing fire from the sun to give to man, and about Pandora opening up the forbidden box with all the evils of the world in it, Gramps said that those myths evolved because people needed a way to explain where fire came from and why there was evil in the world. That made me think of Phoebe and the lunatic, and I said, "If I were walking in Phoebe's moccasins, I would have to believe in a lunatic and an axe-wielding Mrs. Cadaver to explain my mother's disappearance."

Phoebe and her family helped me, I think. They helped me to think about and understand my own mother. Phoebe's tales were like my fishing in the air: for a while I needed to believe that my mother was not dead and that she would come back.

I still fish in the air sometimes.

It seems to me that we can't explain all the truly awful things in the world like war and murder and brain tumors, and we can't fix these things, so we look at the frightening things that are closer to us and we magnify them until they burst open. Inside is something that we can manage, something that isn't as awful as it had at first seemed. It is a relief to discover that although there might be axe murderers and kidnappers in the world, most people seem a lot like us: sometimes afraid and sometimes brave, sometimes cruel and sometimes kind.

I decided that bravery is looking Pandora's box full in the eye as best you can, and then turning to the other box, the one with the smoothbeautiful folds inside: Momma kissing trees, my Gram saying, "Huzza, huzza," Gramps and his marriage bed.

My mother's postcards and her hair are still beneath the floorboards in my room. I reread all the postcards when I came home. Gram and Gramps and I had been to every place my mother had. There are the Black Hills, Mt. Rushmore, the Badlands—the only card that is still hard for me to read is the one from Coeur d'Alene, the one that I received two days after she died.

When I drive Gramps around in his truck, I also tell him all the stories my mother told me. His favorite is a Navaho one about Estsanatlehi. She's a woman who never dies. She grows from baby to mother to old woman and then turns into a baby again, and on and on she goes, living a thousand, thousand lives. Gramps likes this, and so do I.

I still climb the sugar maple tree, and I have heard the singing tree sing. The sugar maple tree is my thinking place. Yesterday in the sugar maple, I realized that I was jealous of three things.

The first jealousy is a foolish one. I am jealous of whoever Ben wrote about in his journal, because it was not me.

The second jealousy is this: I am jealous that my mother had wanted more children. Wasn't I enough? When I walk in her moccasins, though, I say, "If I were my mother, I might want more children—not because I don't love my Salamanca, but because I love her so much. I want more of these." Maybe that is a fish in the air and maybe it isn't, but it is what I want to believe.

The last jealousy is not foolish, nor is it one that will go away just yet. I am still jealous that Phoebe's mother came back and mine did not.

I miss my mother.

Ben and Phoebe write to me all the time. Ben sent me a valentine in the middle of October that said,

> *Roses are red,*
> *Dirt is brown,*
> *Please be my valentine,*
> *Or else I'll frown.*

There was a P.S. added: *I've never written poetry before.*

I sent a valentine back that said:

> *Dry is the desert,*
> *Wet is the rain,*
> *Your love for me*
> *Is not in vain.*

I added a P.S. that said, *I've never written any poetry either.*

Ben and Phoebe and Mrs. Cadaver and Mrs. Partridge are all coming to visit next month. There is a chance that Mr. Birkway might come as well, but Phoebe hopes not, as she does not think she could stand to be in a car for that long with a teacher. My father and I have been scrubbing the house for their visit. I can't wait to show Phoebe and Ben the swimming hole and the fields, the hayloft and the trees, and the cows and the chickens. Blackberry, the chicken that Ben gave me, is queen of the coop, and I'll show Ben her, too. I am hoping, also, for some blackberry kisses.

But for now, Gramps has his beagle, and I have a chicken and a singing tree, and that's the way it is.

Huzza, huzza.

((